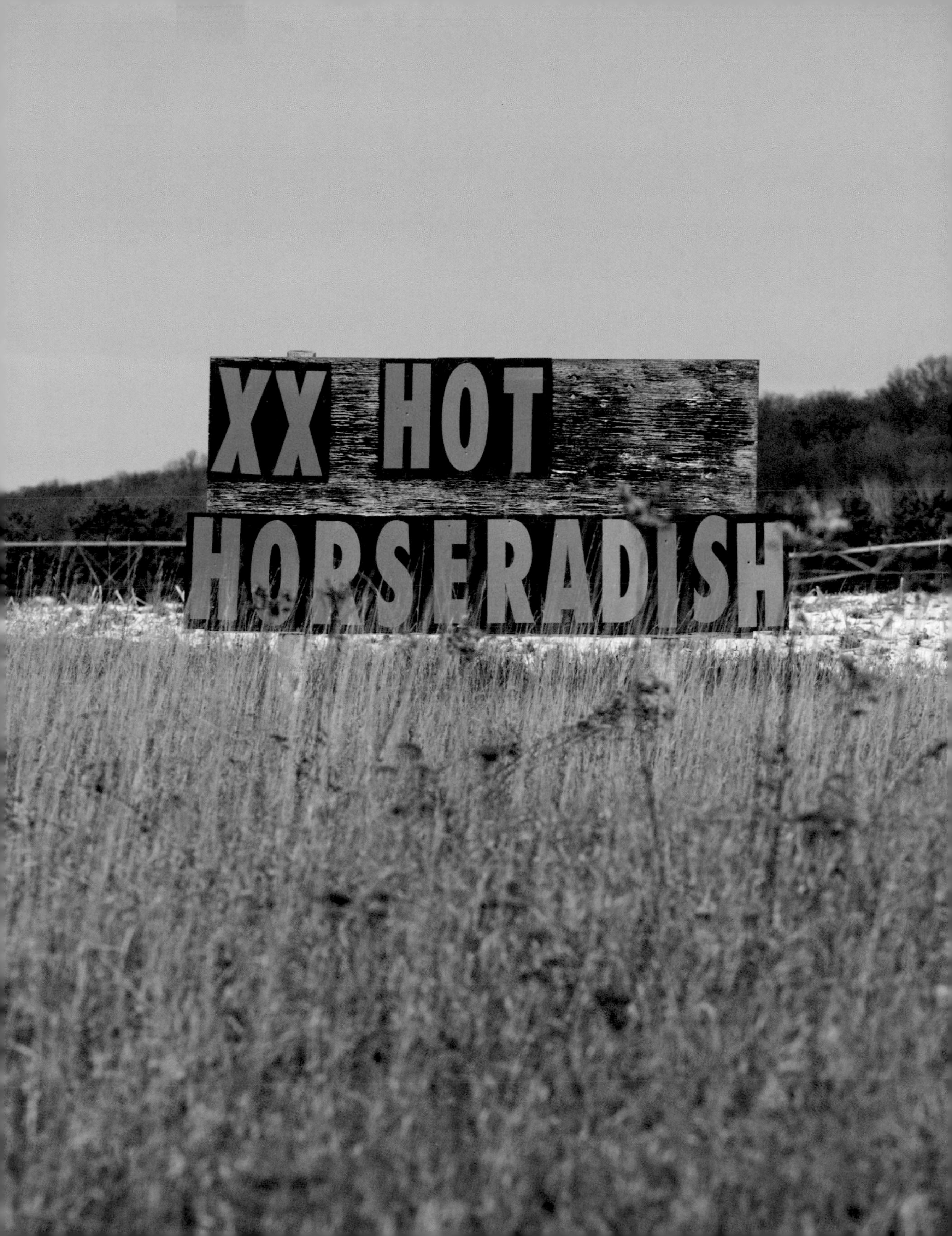
XX HOT
HORSERADISH

· THE NEW ·

MIDWESTERN TABLE

AMY THIELEN

200 HEARTLAND RECIPES

CLARKSON POTTER/PUBLISHERS
NEW YORK

Published in the United States by Clarkson Potter/Publishers,
an imprint of the Crown Publishing Group, a division of
Random House, Inc., New York.
www.crownpublishing.com
www.clarksonpotter.com

CLARKSON POTTER is a trademark and POTTER with colophon
is a registered trademark of Random House, Inc.

Library of Congress Cataloging-in-Publication Data
Thielen, Amy.
    The new Midwestern table/Amy Thielen.
        pages   cm
    1. Cooking, American—Midwestern style.   I. Title.
    TX715.2.M53T49   2013
    641.5977—dc23   2012047058

ISBN 978-0-307-95487-9
eISBN 978-0-307-95488-6

Printed in China

Book, jacket, and case design by Marysarah Quinn
Book, jacket, and case illustrations by Amber Fletschock
Jacket and case photography by Jennifer May

10 9 8 7 6 5 4 3 2 1

First Edition

TO

AARON AND HANK

And to the women who stirred the pots:
my mother, Karen Dion,

my own grandmothers, Adeline (Hesch) Dion
and Margaret (Le Blanc) Thielen,

and the two I picked up, Irene (Niebrugge) Dierking
and Margaret (Tjernagel) Annexstad

CONTENTS

INTRODUCTION

Returning to this remote spot in the upper Midwest, to the forest at the edge of the plains, I realize that the immensity and flatness of this landscape are part of its charm, its severe weather a main character in the greater drama. The views are long, the winters cold, the summers hot, and the harvests are small, potent, and brief.

Nearly anywhere you want to go here involves a drive, so that's what we do, black triangular pines lining the road like a corrugated edge, guarding our passage. Driving past houses whose lights shine in the dark, the hanging fixtures glowing hearth-like over the kitchen tables, I wonder, as I have since early childhood, *what's cooking inside those kitchens?* What are the flavors that make their lives different from mine?

If Midwestern cooking has been hard to pin down, I think it's because our best food has always been a celebration of this large, dynamic, plain-spoken place. Like the food, the vast interior of this country may seem ordinary to outsiders looking in, but it feels privately epic to those of us who live here. Film director Alexander Payne nails this sentiment when he writes that his home state, Nebraska, is "at once the middle of nowhere and the center of the universe."

Even though the region is dotted with great restaurants, you can't judge Midwestern cuisine entirely on its public face; as is the case with other rural foodways, our most iconic dishes get passed hand-to-hand around a kitchen table. The roots of our cooking remain behind closed doors, where the old ways of preparing food—gardening, preserving, fishing, hunting, and otherwise plucking good things from the woods or the fields—are not only still alive, but enjoying a transformative, active present tense.

Born and raised in the rural Midwest, I had an understanding of the region's food culture that deepened when, at age twenty-two, I moved with my boyfriend, Aaron, to his rustic nonelectric cabin on eighty acres near the unincorporated community of Two Inlets, twenty miles from my hometown in northern Minnesota.

A freshly minted English major, I cooked three days a week at a German-American diner on Park Rapids' Main Street, working the early breakfast shift, which on Sunday mornings was the hellstorm of brunch—schnitzels frying next to pancakes sitting next to spitting onions on the greasy griddle—and on weekdays a pretty mellow business of feeding the regulars. With each ding of the bell I sent basted eggs, smoked pork chops, and hash browns to the boisterous group of coffee klatchers in the corner booth; a single order of white toast to the elderly twin sisters who sat side-by-side, chain-smoking; a lunchtime "chef salad—no eggs" to my dad; and at 2:30 each afternoon, for Ron (a regular who

seemed to be serving a parched life sentence), I put up three eggs poached hard and burnt rye, dry.

The rest of my time was spent at our house out in the woods, where the long distance from any power line dictated days spent performing the rituals of simple living—wood-hauling, water-pumping, vegetable gardening, berry-picking, and, of course, cooking.

After putting a kettle of water on my 1940s propane-fired Roper stove to boil for dishes, I would set up shop at the dining room table, an oil lamp burning patiently in front of me. The blush from the flame illuminated stacks of cookbooks, everything from ring-bound community collections to obscure classics. Obsessed with my new chores, I often called my grandma Dion for a refresher on making her famous white bread, to find out the desired temperature for fermenting my crock of sauerkraut, or how finely to grind the poppy seeds—which, by the way, is "until they're as fine as snuff."

Our neighbors, descendants of the area's original homesteading families, didn't hold back on advice or memories, either. Electricity was late to canvas this far-flung community, so still-good metal buckets were freely slung in our direction; spare parts for our grain mill were dug out from the backs of sheds; outhouse jokes—oldies but goodies—were joyfully discharged on us. When we visited our friend Marie Kueber, she freely gave me her jelly recipe and my choice of the jeweled rows of jars setting up on her counter, but laughed heartily when I asked her to share her fruit-picking spot.

After three summers of nonelectric living (without power we couldn't stay past freeze-up), Aaron and I decided to move to New York City, instead of Minneapolis, for the winter. I signed up for culinary school and within nine months was working at David Bouley's Danube in Tribeca. Newly opened and recently given four stars from the *New York Times*, Danube was staffed with Austrian chefs (all veterans of three-star Michelin kitchens in Europe) and a strong brigade of New York City line cooks, and it was packed. I went straight from shelling garden peas on my porch to deveining foie gras. And back again, because I was still shelling peas, but now also blanching, peeling, splitting each one in half, and cooking them in truffle butter. I felt a weird kinship with these Austrians, who were frying noodles in browned butter and making pork sauce like my mom did. At Danube I saw how the European peasant food tradition has always influenced haute cuisine, and how simple rural dishes—such as those I grew up with—could be threaded into fine dining. One of the Austrian sous chefs drove it home, telling me that "good cooking is potatoes and onions."

Thus began a serious culinary tour of duty. I worked for David Bouley for two more years, then at Daniel Boulud's db Bistro Moderne, and on the opening teams for both Jean-Georges Vongerichten's 66 and Shea Gallante's Cru. In all, I spent the next seven years cooking on the line in Manhattan fine-dining kitchens. It was a highly focused yet hazy time during which I saw the contemporary food world at very close range.

A year after our son was born, Aaron and I moved back to that cabin in northern Minnesota. We traded in our secondhand solar panels and car battery for a connection to the grid, and "got power," as they say around here. Along with the fruit trees and the Norway pine plantation, my interest in Midwestern food had only thickened. I knew it to be a food culture that resisted easy definition, but at least I was in the right place, finally back home near the headwaters of the Mississippi, the spot on the map that

novelist David Treuer, from nearby Leech Lake reservation, calls "the heart of the heartland, and so a pretty good place to take its pulse."

Even though the cooking of the Midwest tends to avoid the national spotlight, our regional cooks have been directing the course of American cuisine for a long time: Betty Crocker cookbooks were created in a Minneapolis, Minnesota test kitchen by home economics graduates, most of them from Midwestern universities (and the brand lives on at General Mills). *The Joy of Cooking*, that seminal American text, was curated by Irma Rombauer, from

Ohio. Over the years, so many dishes that originated in the Midwest have been flung into the world and reclaimed by everybody as just "American."

And we're fine with that, really we are. In this book you'll encounter dishes whose Midwestern-ness may seem generous—Classic Beef Pot Roast with Pistachio Salt, for instance, or Artichoke Fondue Dip—and then some so deeply vernacular their regionality cannot be disputed: Nebraskan Runzas (yeasted meat pies), Booya (community stew), Cracker-Crust Pizza, Finnish Kalomojakka (creamy fish stew), Rullapølse (pressed beef and pork terrine), Upper Peninsula (U.P.) Pasties, Classic Duck in Wild Rice, and Rømmegrøt (Norwegian cream pudding), to name a few. But even the icons of American cooking can taste different here. When Midwesterners make fried chicken, for example, we usually bake it in the oven until crisp and serve it as part of a trilogy, with whipped potatoes and a golden gravy fashioned from the pan-stickings.

Michigander Jim Harrison, in *The Raw and the Cooked*, says about American food: "it is humorous to note that since we have no consistent tradition we are doomed to freedom"—a statement that may ring most true across the Great Plains. The willingness of this region's people to embrace new foods in order to become a community of Americans is palpable here. When settlers were homesteading each rectangular 160-acre plot, they planted the seeds of their native countries in their gardens—paprika peppers for Hungarians, paste tomatoes for Italians—but a generation or two later, many of them were willing to shuck off cultural identifiers and embrace a common mean: few spices, few herbs, just fine raw materials, and maybe a can of cream of mushroom soup or two.

That said, among all kinds of Americans, latent hungers for old-fashioned flavors have survived industrial food. And now, in an era of unprecedented foodie curiosity, those who hid their weakness for their strong ethnic tastes are now free to bring this stuff out of the closet—which may explain why pickled fish, fresh horseradish, hot mustard, cured meats, fermented vegetables, strong cheeses, and the like are all enjoying a resurgence.

Yet preferences continue to shift. The current wave of immigrants, notably from Mexico, East Africa, Central America, and Asia, is influencing Midwestern foodways just as strongly as the Scandinavians, Germans, Italians, Irish, Slovaks, and many others did a few generations earlier. (The tacquerías in small towns throughout Nebraska are a magnificent case in point, the Hmong food markets in St. Paul, Minnesota, another.) In rural areas like mine, there's also influence from the nearby native tribes, cultures whose cuisine was, and is, reflective of the food that thrives here. A survey of Two Inlets Township's early homesteaders reveals a diet not dissimilar to the local Ojibwe one, high in freshwater fish, wild rice, wild game, and berries, in addition to the crops and animals they raised.

Everyone who has lived here may have dropped their own seeds in the ground and been partial to the seasonings of their homeland. But they've also pulled up the same fish, hunted the same game, and harvested the same mushrooms, fruits, roots, and tree syrups. Like stakes driven into the ground of this vast food culture, these ingredients start to define what this place tastes like. Between what people have brought and what grows naturally in the Midwest, the food of this region has gradually developed into a voluminous cuisine of its own. As is always true with food, it's a story better communicated through tasting than telling.

The Midwest is home to a great tradition of American country cooking—food that's rustic, gutsy, and simple. From meals sampled at friends' and relatives' tables across the region, it's plain that generosity co-exists with thrift, culminating in spreads laden with a profusion of un-fancy, one-stroke dishes. The composition of a traditional plate generally goes like this: meat, starch, two vegetables, and bread, followed by dessert. Baking is important to us, and through our holiday recipes flow family traditions, taste memories, and inherited skills.

By and large, we're seasonal cooks—not just because it's currently fashionable, but because in-season ingredients are less expensive, taste better, and in our staunchly four-season climate are truly fleeting: When we come across wild berries, ducks, asparagus, pecans, or cherished morel mushrooms, we snap them up. A lot of the best Midwestern food involves a very American intimacy with the wilderness, some hunting and gathering, a principle that counts even if some of the gathering occurs in your backyard, either from bushes you planted or the "volunteers" that have invaded: wild blackberries, black currants, or grapes.

Taking advantage of seasonal outputs leads to a wonderful thing that I'll call "synchronized cooking," when cooks in all the kitchens around me, in farmhouses and in split-levels, seem to be making the same thing at the same time: rhubarb pie in the springtime, squash bread in the fall, and game stew at hunting time. Along the same lines, most people do some sort of stocking up, whether it's as simple as freezing whole heirloom tomatoes or topping off a jam pot of wild berries with a spot of rum. With winters this long, keeping some proof of summer in your pantry becomes essential.

A certain economy marks our cooking, and thrift isn't the only reason. Historically, the pristine ingredients we have around here just don't require much doctoring. The habit of cooking garden vegetables in rich milk may sound ordinary, but on the plate the farmhouse classic Milk Cabbage is unforgettable. It's the same story for Rosemary Brown Butter Chicken Breasts, a dish that demands a devotional attentiveness from the cook and top-deck perfection from its three main ingredients—farm-raised chicken breast, salted butter, and rosemary—to reach its higher calling.

Praiseworthy Midwestern restaurants—some in cities, some boldly outside their boundaries—are no longer what writer (and Kansas City native) Calvin Trillin called "La Maison de la Casa House" (hash-houses for bland continental food), but instead places where you'll find black walnuts from down the road and flawless trout from a nearby lake. In every state in the region I've found salumi and liverwurst and rillettes and aged ham made from local heritage breed hogs—all of it fresher than imported European charcuterie, and better for it. It's easy to locate bakeries making miches, dark ryes, long-fermented levains, and other breads in the European tradition alongside shiny loaves of farmhouse American white, so light and towering they could be my grandmother's. In Wisconsin, I've tasted soulful cheeses made from animals that had efficiently sheared the wet, green surrounding hills, and in nearly any small-town co-op I can pick up a glass jar of thick local cream, its top firmly clotted shut.

In general, the breakfasts are stellar: I can't shake the memory of a plate of homemade pork sausage and a couple of blistered, puffed eggs that had been fried in its grease (just as my mother used to do) in Brookings, South Dakota. I discovered sugar-sparkled morning buns in Madison, Wisconsin, and was rewarded nearly everywhere with perfect hardtop hashbrowns. I've sampled excellent fried catfish all across the southern Midwest, and found the local fish, from the diners in Michigan's Upper Peninsula to the fish shacks on the North Shore of Lake Superior, to be spanking fresh and as pearly and sweet as the cold waters from which it was pulled. In Madison, Wisconsin, I found what must be the country's best summer sausage,

tangy and tender; in Omaha I ate glazed pig's head one night and whiskey steaks the next, and in a small-box pupuseria in Grand Island, downed two cheese-filled corn cakes one rainy morning. Stretching the definition of "restaurant," I had lunch in a dusty gas station in Interior, South Dakota, where the Tater Tot hotdish was worth a drive, and bread service meant opening the full bag of sliced white at your table. (I only wished I could have returned for Friday's prime rib.) And recently, in Kansas City, I sampled exceptional, regionally inspired dishes that were not the renowned barbecue. Although as anyone in her right mind should, I drove out of that town with a burnt ends sandwich on my lap.

Some chefs in the Midwest's finest restaurants spoke of the debt they owed to the high standards set by their home-cooking parents, grandparents, and mentors—and I agree. While a handful of recipes in this book have been borrowed from restaurant chefs I've met over the years—all adjusted to work well in the home kitchen—the rest of them are either original recipes that come from my own experiments with the local bounty—for example, freshwater fish or my own garden produce—or reengineered classics. I picked my favorites among the iconic dishes—roping up *all* of them would be a noble project, but beyond the scope of this book—and I gave them the only kind of update that I could see my grandma Dion approving: a solid tweaking to fit modern tastes and then a step back, leaving them flush with all of their original attention to detail.

Speaking of the collective larder, these recipes hew to Midwestern practicality and don't require a world's bazaar of pantry ingredients. To keep things accessible to everyone, both urban and rural, I decided to stick to my own small-town limits: if I couldn't find an ingredient at either of my local grocery stores, and it couldn't be found in the garden, the yard, or the surrounding woods, it didn't go in the book. Subsequently, everything here can be made with a trip to a basic American grocery store or a stop at a vegetable farm stand. For example, you won't find veal, pancetta, or harissa. Yeah, I love them, but we don't have those things here. Endive? That would be a special order.

But it's the paradox of rural places that our access to high-quality ingredients is both enviable and frustrating. We're hitched to the seasons, like it or not. For example, I may have a pastured Amish pig in my deep freezer, but come January I won't be able to buy a fresh cob of corn within a 50-mile radius. (And yet all of the stores carry fresh kohlrabi all winter long, thanks to the northern European immigrant tradition.) So while some of the rarer imported ingredients didn't make the cut, the spoils of hunting, gardening, and foraging did. I make use of the chokecherries and wild cranberries that grow wild along the driveway and the creek, and the smoked freshwater fish so prevalent here, and I use a lot of venison because it's common for home cooks across much of the country to stock it themselves or know someone who does. (And lamb is always a good substitute for venison.) The sourcing is rural in spirit, but it's something that urban-dwellers should be able to pull off without a hitch.

The fact is, without the atmosphere—the daily drive past corn fields and pine plantations, felted green pastures dotted with cattle, and others scraped down to the nub, beautiful lakes and even prettier sloughs—this wouldn't have been the same book. The endless road pointed the way and led me on through countless cultural influences, many state lines, through city and countryside, meals of pure discovery and those ridden with teachable moments, haute cuisine, deer camp cooking, soup potlucks, and butter and lard, the fats of our land.

In the end, I found out that it wasn't necessary for me to restrict the big, raucous universe of Midwestern food to the Midwest proper, because the same natural, easy spirit of American cooking spills out beyond state boundaries. Nearly every dish I considered spoke to a more universal rural temperament, a grounded, dirt-bound yearning. Whether the food was fancy or garage-party casual, I sensed a common purity and pride in the way that Midwestern cooks approached their local ingredients. The proudest cooks across this broad region—professionals and home cooks alike—share a common nostalgia for the ingredients that remind them of the terrain and tenor of their Midwestern childhood. Everyone's most personal dishes contain transporting local flavors, and no matter the trigger—whether it is maple syrup, wild rice, rutabagas, long-braised beef, potato buns, or even frozen green beans—this is food that has the power to summon memories of a shared experience.

In fact, the local spirit in which I, my family, and my neighbors cook doesn't belong just to the Midwest. The recipes in this book resemble those that many Americans make and enjoy: hearty meat dishes, freshwater fish, dips, bar cookies, garden vegetables, and seasonal fruit pies . . . So it's my hunch that readers will find something that pulls a chord here. And it's my hope that some of the more iconic Midwestern flavors inspire an unexpected tenderness for this place, whether you already know it and love it or not.

FOOD & DRINKS

Dips and communal platters define our kind of entertaining. By and large, we Midwesterners don't mind eating outside in lawn chairs, our plates on our laps, our drinks at our feet. It follows that fussy, individual plated starters don't hold much special allure.

With that in mind, most of these recipes have an easy spirit. With the exception of a couple of skewered meats and a filled bun, they're served family-style and are meant for sharing. Fried Onion Dip, Iced Kohlrabi with Spiced Salt, Corn Fritters with Green Chile Buttermilk Dip: This is party food that encourages people to browse around the central table, to stretch out and settle into the evening.

More than any other chapter in this book, this one ropes together many of the iconic flavors of Midwestern cooking: the smoked freshwater fish, the horseradish, the bacon, the aged cheddar . . . I've tweaked many of these classics to fit contemporary tastes, giving spreadable pub cheese, smoked oyster dip, and sweet-and-sour meatballs a thorough makeover. Other recipes, such as the Steakhouse Deviled Eggs, served warm with a crumb topping of bacon and crisp nori, originate from a memory or a mood, and seem more modern. But even the stodgiest of appetizers can be resurrected. Braunschweiger was long a private indulgence for me, but making it at home seemed beyond my reach—until one day I just gave it a try. Homemade Braunschweiger is easier to make than one might think, and the first bite of the smooth pâté feels monumental, sentimental, and blessedly rich. (And rest assured, it will supply a snack table for days.)

But I hope that even these versions of the classics will inspire customization, for I really feel that a favored appetizer belongs to its host—that it should be, as I remember my mother and her friends saying as they hashed out the potluck over the phone, "the dip you do." After a few runs, a chosen favorite begins to pick up personal influence, and finding that perfect appetizer is a process not unlike a middle-school kid working out his or her signature, the carefully composed scribble that sets the tone for everything yet to come.

SMOKED WHITEFISH BRANDADE

Smoked Lake Superior whitefish is the perfect fish for a lap-lunch.

All around the perimeter of Lake Superior, fish shacks selling freshly smoked Lake Superior catch dot the roadside, and when you stop to ogle the display, smoked whitefish is the one to pick if you're planning to eat it while driving: Smoked lake trout is almost too greasy for the car; small smoked ciscoes have too many small bones, but smoked whitefish offers both good flavor and pickability. They grow nice and fat in Lake Superior, and their bones are easy to find and lift out.

When we get home I like to make smoked whitefish brandade, a variation on salt cod brandade, the classic Provençal specialty.

This thick, smoky pâté tastes good eaten straight off the spoon, but I like to douse it with Parmesan cheese and set it under the broiler until the peaks blacken so that I can serve the warm, garlicky puree slathered generously on grilled bread.

MAKES 3 CUPS

Combine the milk, garlic cloves, salt, and potato in a 2-quart saucepan. Wrap the bay leaves and thyme in a 4-inch square of cheesecloth, tie up the corners, and add it to the milk. Bring the milk to a simmer over medium heat. Cover, reduce the heat to medium-low, and simmer until the potatoes are very tender, about 15 minutes. Remove the pan from the heat, add the smoked whitefish, and let steep for 5 minutes. Strain the mixture, reserving the milk and the solids separately. Discard the herb sachet.

Put the solids in the bowl of a food processor (or in a large mortar, if you want to do it by hand) and process, adding some of the cooking liquid back in until you have a thick puree—you will use about ½ cup—and stopping to scrape down the sides, because the mixture will be thick. Add the olive oil and process until combined. Add ¾ cup of the Parmesan cheese and season with pepper.

Preheat the broiler.

Turn the mixture out into a shallow ovenproof dish and garnish it with a swirl of olive oil and the remaining ½ cup Parmesan cheese. Broil until the peaks turn dark brown, about 10 minutes. Serve hot.

1½ cups whole milk

7 cloves garlic

½ teaspoon fine sea salt

1 medium (5 ounces) Yukon Gold potato, peeled and cut into ¼-inch-thick slices

3 dried bay leaves

1 sprig fresh thyme

5 ounces (1 cup) boneless smoked whitefish fillet, picked through for bones

¼ cup extra-virgin olive oil, plus more for garnish

1¼ cups (3 ounces) freshly grated Parmesan cheese

Freshly ground black pepper

NOTES: *Feasting while driving works best if you have someone riding shotgun who can spread out the white butcher paper into a lap-napkin, pick out the bones, and top your crackers with fish.*

You can substitute smoked trout—lake trout or rainbow trout—for the whitefish. It's a little richer.

FRESH CHEESE BALL
with Ground Cherry Chutney

RICOTTA CHEESE BALL

1 quart whole milk (preferably not ultra-pasteurized)

4 to 5 teaspoons distilled white vinegar

1 teaspoon fine sea salt

GROUND CHERRY CHUTNEY

1½ tablespoons olive oil

⅓ cup minced red or yellow onion

2 teaspoons minced fresh ginger

¼ teaspoon fine sea salt

¼ teaspoon freshly ground black pepper

½ teaspoon curry powder

1 tablespoon fresh lime juice, plus more to taste

1 teaspoon sugar

1 cup (6 ounces) husked ground cherries

Dash of cayenne pepper

Crackers or bread, for serving

NOTES: *For years I made my fresh ricotta by acidifying the milk with buttermilk, but after trying this recipe developed by Jennifer Christman Kelly of the Underground Food Collective in Madison, I started using vinegar to curdle the milk. I think it makes a creamier curd and is more foolproof.*

The best local milk producer sells her milk only by the gallon, so if I'm faced with a quart or more nearing its expiration date, I'll often turn it into a fresh cheese ball.

Making the cheese ball is almost too easy; the fun comes in dressing this pale ball of cloud-soft ricotta. Sometimes I fry sage leaves in butter until they crisp and then pour it all over the top, but lately I've been making this ground cherry chutney, which takes inspiration from one of the Midwest's most enduring combinations, the chutney–cream cheese ball. It's a well-circulated recipe, and dead simple—just Major Grey chutney spooned over cream cheese—but this winning combination tastes so much better when it's made with warm curried fruit, fresh lime, and cheese so fresh it's still dripping.

Ground cherries are an old-fashioned garden fruit; in the last couple of decades they seem to have fallen to semi-rare status, although in the late summer you see them in farmer's markets. They have a few aliases: cape gooseberries in some markets, pineapple tomatillos in the seed catalogs. A little smaller than typical green tomatillos, these small seedless fruits grow inside translucent paper lanterns, as tomatillos do, and they do in fact taste like a cross between a tomato and a pineapple. Traditionally, they were made into jam or grown for children's summer snack. It's true: Kids love to peel back their papery skins and pop them into their mouths.

But don't let a lack of ground cherries stop you: this quick chutney is also delicious when made with cherry tomatoes. (And for a super-quick appetizer don't hesitate to spoon the curried chutney over a block of cream cheese or Neufchâtel.)

SERVES 8 TO 10

To make the cheese ball, pour the milk into a heavy-bottomed nonreactive saucepan and set it over medium heat. Clip a candy thermometer to the side of the pan and heat, stirring often to prevent scorching on the bottom, until the milk reaches 180°F. (Without a thermometer, this is the seething, steaming period just before the boil.)

Remove from the heat, add 4 teaspoons of the vinegar, and stir gently. You will notice white, fluffy curds separating from the whey, which will turn yellowish and transparent. If this doesn't happen, add another teaspoon of vinegar and stir again. Sprinkle the salt over the curds and whey. Let sit at room temperature for 15 minutes to give the curds time to gather softly together.

Cut a 4-foot length of cheesecloth, open it up, and fold it into a square three layers thick. Lay the cheesecloth in a fine-mesh strainer set over a bowl, and gently pour the curds into it, scraping the pan to get every bit.

Gather up the corners of the cheesecloth and twist the cheese into a teardrop shape; squeeze gently to remove any excess whey. Set the cheese in a small bowl or a teacup to firm up. As it cools to room temperature, the cheese will hold the rounded shape of the cup.

For the ground cherry chutney, heat a small skillet over medium-low heat. Add the olive oil and the onion, ginger, salt, and pepper, and cook until the onion softens, about 5 minutes. Add the curry powder, lime juice, sugar, and ground cherries. Cover the pan and cook until the ground cherries begin to exude liquid, 5 to 10 minutes, depending on their age and freshness.

Uncover and cook until the sauce clings to the ground cherries, another 2 to 3 minutes. Season with cayenne pepper to taste.

To serve, unmold the cheese ball onto a small platter and cover it with the chutney. Serve at room temperature with crackers. (If you want to make this a day ahead, refrigerate the cheese and the chutney separately, and let them return to room temperature before serving together.)

Ground cherries are easy to grow, but a bit trickier to harvest. As the pods ripen from green to gold, they fall to the ground, which puts them in the jurisdiction of squirrels and gophers, who like them too. So when they begin turning yellow I gently shake the plants to release any ripe ones and then gather them up. (To give whatever I'm making a bump of acidity, I pick some of the green-gold ones, too.) I drop them into an uncovered bowl or jar, where they keep well in their husks at room temperature—sometimes 2 weeks or even longer.

You can save the whey that drips from the cheese and use it to replace the liquid in homemade bread or add it to soup as a stock.

OLD-FASHIONED POUNDED CHEESE
with Walnuts *and* Port Syrup

½ cup port wine

1 tablespoon (packed) light brown sugar

7 ounces aged cheddar cheese (3 years old or more), at room temperature

6 tablespoons (¾ stick) salted butter, cool but not cold

1 teaspoon Dijon mustard

¼ teaspoon freshly ground black pepper

Pinch of cayenne pepper

⅓ cup walnut halves, toasted

Aged Cheddar

For the uninitiated, a stop at a Wisconsin cheese-tasting room provides an education in basic aged cheddars. Young cheddars are firm and rich. As years go by the acidity mounts, the flavor develops a twang, the texture turns creamy, and the shoulders of the wedge grow rounder, like old marble. A cheddar with more than three years of age on it (and you'll commonly see six, nine, or even ten years) will be as soft as a chunk of milk chocolate, and intense. After leaving a roadside cheese store, you can suck on a single small cube of aged cheddar like a lozenge, the flavor trailing out for miles.

Pounded cheese can be found in books of early American cookery from all areas of this country, but when made with aged Wisconsin cheddar, it's really a treat.

This recipe is basically a deconstructed cheese ball: You simply whip softened chunks of potent aged cheddar with butter until silky smooth, top with broken toasted walnuts, and drizzle with port syrup. Not much more difficult than unwrapping a square of cheddar, the success of this simple spread depends on the quality of the cheese you use—the older and more velvety it is, the more distinctive the spread will be.

The old recipes for pounded cheese call for beating the cheese in a bowl with a wooden spoon until soft, but I use a food processor because it results in a super-luscious whipped texture. Before beginning, make sure that the cheese is at room temperature and the butter a touch colder. It should have the consistency of putty, not rock-hard but firmer than mayonnaise—what a French chef would call *beurre pommade.*

This can be served with bread, but I think it's actually best with crackers.

MAKES 1½ CUPS

To make the port syrup, combine the port and brown sugar in a small saucepan over medium-high heat. Simmer gently until reduced to a light syrup (it will start to throw bigger bubbles and should be the consistency of maple syrup), about 3 minutes. Let cool to room temperature.

Break the cheddar cheese into chunks and drop them into a food processor. Process until pureed. Add the butter, mustard, black pepper, and cayenne and process, stopping often to scrape down the sides, until whipped and smooth.

Transfer the cheese to a shallow dish, break up the walnut halves and drop them on top, and drizzle with the port syrup.

NOTE: *The pounded cheese can be made a few hours ahead and kept at room temperature. Or it can be made the day before and kept in the refrigerator; just be sure to bring it back to room temperature before garnishing with the port syrup and nuts.*

Bleu Mont Dairy

Aged cheddars are fit for either eating or cooking, but many cheeses being made in Wisconsin, including Willi Lehner's award-winning Bleu Mont Dairy bandaged cheddars, are too perfect to bring near heat or to otherwise distress.

The day I visited, I found Willi shirtless and barefoot, on a tractor, plowing up a small field to plant garlic. After the tour of his modern wind-and-solar-powered underground cheese cave, loaded with wheels of cheddars sewn into their cloth suits in various states of mold-ripening, we sat at his kidney-shaped wooden kitchen island, each drinking a beer from the nearby New Glarus Brewing Company, lukewarm and fresh from my trunk. And Willi Lehner, maker of some the best cheeses in Wisconsin—really, in the country—did not want to talk about *terroir*, the idea that a specific terrain flavors the foods that come from it.

I felt the need to ask. Most of the best cheesemakers in Wisconsin work in the same Driftless region, one of the few spots in the upper Midwest that the glaciers didn't scrape down to the core. It's a land of almost cinematic beauty: green-carpeted swells, rocky cliffs, puffs of fog in the hollows, farm animals that lift their heavy eyes from grazing as you pass, as if on cue. Even the road ahead is picturesque in the Driftless; from a distance it looks like ribbon wrapping around the hills, streaming over the land, making the ancient hills seem new.

What was it about the Driftless region that produces so many great cheeses?

Willi didn't hesitate: "I don't want to get too hung up on that. *Terroir* is a word that can be abused."

He walked over to the wooden counter and whacked into a huge slab of cheese, golden and almost translucent, like a hunk of yellow quartz. Its edges fell off like cedar shakes, and even from a distance you could see its aged, granular temperament. He laid the board in front of me, providing a better answer to my question: "Four year, raw milk."

Although Willi grew up in the area watching his dad, a Swiss immigrant, make cheese, it wasn't until after some visits to European cheesemakers that he began making bandaged cheddar—the gauze-wrapped, old-school aged cheese for which he's probably best known. In particular, his visit to a group of Welsh women cheesemakers, who harness the local microflora to make some of the best bandaged cheddars in the world, made a lasting impression on him. Years later, his aged wheels all wear blue coats of shearling fur and the inner paste tastes grassy, pungent, and sweet. The mold cure contributes a dirty beetroot earthiness, well balanced by a round butterscotch caramel bubbling up from the milk. Influenced by its *terroir* or not, I would say it doesn't taste like any other cheese in America.

There aren't any cows milling around Willi's place; he buys his milk from local dairies, often from other cheesemakers, and only when the cows are feeding on summer grass. But there's a huge vegetable garden and groves of fruit trees, and inside the house, a fieldstone fireplace tattooed with a colorful mosaic of beach glass. A cozy house, but he and his partner, Kitas McKnight, clearly spend some time outside on the high swell behind the house, where a pair of Adirondack chairs point toward the Blue Mountains, in lookout mode. The cave down the hill, with its forward-thinking windmill and the native grasses sprouting from its top, is probably the best talisman of their place, a monument to a bunch of things at once—to old ways and to hippie progress, and to the timeless, transformative powers of mold.

FRIED ONION DIP

4 tablespoons (½ stick) salted
  butter

1 medium sweet onion, cut into
  ½-inch-thick rings

Fine sea salt and freshly ground
  black pepper

3 cloves garlic, roughly
  chopped

1 teaspoon honey

¼ cup dry vermouth or dry
  white wine

¼ cup (2 ounces) cream cheese,
  at room temperature

¾ cup sour cream

1 tablespoon finely chopped
  fresh chives, plus more for
  garnish

Dash of cayenne pepper

NOTE: *Serve this dip with kettle
chips or country bread.*

One night before a big move, because all of the cooking tools had already been packed away, I was forced to open a bag of ruffled potato chips, pop a tub of French onion dip, and call it an appetizer. We sat with our friends in the candlelight, among the ghosts of all the much classier nibbles I had served at the same table over the years, drinking beer, dipping chips . . . sometimes twice. That's when I discovered that double-dipping is the informal "you," a language used among friends.

Installed once again in my home kitchen, and with the tobacco-brown fried onions you get on a bar burger as my noble inspiration, I decided to work up this homemade version of that classic dip. Using a quick clarified butter in which to fry the onions makes all the difference, and the splash of vermouth adds mysterious depth.

MAKES 1½ CUPS

First, clarify the butter so that you can fry the onions at high heat and put a very dark, almost burnt crust on them: Heat the butter in a small skillet over medium-high heat until it foams and browns. Remove from the heat and let it sit a minute. Tilt the skillet and carefully spoon off the foam, saving it in a small bowl. Pour the clear butter into another bowl, and pour the dark dregs at the bottom of the skillet into the bowl with the foam. Add the clear butter to a larger heavy skillet.

Heat the skillet over medium-high heat. Add the sliced onion, ¾ teaspoon salt, and ¼ teaspoon pepper. Fry the onions, flipping them now and then, until they're dark on the edges, even black and crispy in spots, about 10 minutes. Add the garlic and honey and cook for 1 more minute. Add the vermouth, bring to a simmer, and cook until the liquid thickens, about 4 minutes. Remove from the heat and let cool.

Put the cream cheese and sour cream in a mixing bowl and mix with a rubber spatula until smooth. Finely chop the fried onions on a cutting board and add them, along with their pan juices, to the cream cheese mixture. Stir in the chopped chives. Season to taste with salt and cayenne pepper.

Transfer to a small bowl and garnish with more chives.

(This can be made ahead of time and refrigerated.)

ICED KOHLRABI
with Spiced Salt

I prefer my kohlrabi raw, preferably iced, served alongside a dish of salt. I grew up eating raw chilled kohlrabi before meals, but I first saw it "on ice" at Bologna Days, the weekly festival in my parents' hometown, where it is accompanied by endless baskets of fresh hot ring bologna, soft white bread, and snowy white horseradish. After a few minutes in crushed ice, kohlrabi grows crisper, adopting a texture that is more fall apple than turnip, and almost as sweet.

Since then, I've heard this method of serving kohlrabi attributed to the Bavarians and to the Polish people as well—but who wouldn't want to claim it? It's incredibly refreshing, and always the sleeper hit of a party spread.

SERVES 6 TO 8

Make the spiced salt: Stir together the salt, pepper, coriander, fennel, and cayenne, and pour into a small ramekin or dip bowl.

Lop the tops and bottoms from each of the kohlrabi. Generously pare the skin and cut the kohlrabi crosswise into ¼-inch-thick rounds.

Right before serving, put the ice cubes in a heavy plastic bag, seal the top, and crush the ice with a rolling pin until reduced to chunks the size of dimes. Pour about 1 cup crushed ice onto a large round platter (a chip-and-dip platter would work, too) and start arranging the kohlrabi slices around the edge of the dish in a layered corona, about three layers high, sprinkling more ice between the layers of kohlrabi. Sprinkle the top layer with a good amount of crushed ice.

Wiggle the ramekin of spiced salt into the center of the kohlrabi and serve, with guests dragging out a piece of kohlrabi and dipping its tip into the spiced salt before eating.

2 teaspoons fine sea salt

1 teaspoon freshly ground black pepper

1 teaspoon ground coriander

½ teaspoon ground fennel

Shake of cayenne pepper

2 pounds (4 or 5) kohlrabi

4 cups ice cubes

NOTE: *Buy fresh kohlrabi with smooth latex-textured feelers, and pare them thickly with a knife, because sometimes a thin layer of woodiness lurks beneath the skin. If growing your own, be sure to pull them before the heat of high summer descends, before they get tough.*

STEAKHOUSE DEVILED EGGS

6 large eggs

1 teaspoon baking soda, optional

6 tablespoons mayonnaise

1 teaspoon Worcestershire sauce

2 teaspoons fresh lemon juice

Fine sea salt and freshly ground black pepper

3 slices thick-cut bacon

⅔ cup fresh bread crumbs

1 sheet nori (dried seaweed)

NOTE: *If the eggs you're using are super-fresh (as farm-fresh eggs sometimes are), add 1 teaspoon baking soda to the cooking water. The alkalinity of the soda makes them easier to peel. (This, courtesy of food scientist Harold McGee.)*

These deviled eggs, with their particular blend of Worcestershire sauce, bacon, lemon, and crisp, iridescent nori, take vintage inspiration from the brazen metallic '80s period of the American steakhouse. (Think wrought iron, Neil Diamond, teriyaki, and votive candles in red glass.) It was a popular place in time throughout the nation, but one that I think the Midwest, with its love of glitz and aged beef, still holds close to its heart.

I really love these eggs best warm, when the lemony egg yolk cream fairly gushes. I played with getting rid of the scattered, somewhat messy bacon-and-nori bread-crumb topping and setting the eggs on wide croutons instead, but they were topple-happy. The only way it worked was to face-plant the egg on the toast and then . . . oh, just forget it. Embrace the crumbs. Serve with plenty of napkins. And if you're making these eggs for people who you worry might not take to the nori, rest assured that mixing dried seaweed with bacon is a very good way to make its introduction.

MAKES 12 DEVILED EGG HALVES

Put the eggs in a saucepan and cover with water by 2 inches. If you're using farm-fresh eggs, add 1 teaspoon baking soda to the water (see Note). Set the pan over high heat and bring the water to a boil. Reduce the heat and simmer for 2 minutes. Then remove the pan from the heat and let the eggs sit in the water for exactly 10 minutes.

Pour off the hot water and cover the eggs with fresh cold water. Crack the eggs gently and return them to the cold water. When cool enough to handle, peel the eggs underwater.

Slice each egg in half lengthwise and drop the cooked yolks into a medium mixing bowl. (Refrigerate the whites if making ahead.)

With a rubber spatula or a wide wooden spoon, paddle the yolks until smooth. Add the mayonnaise, Worcestershire sauce, lemon juice, ¼ teaspoon pepper, and a pinch of salt, and stir until light and fluffy. Transfer the yolk mixture to a clean quart-size plastic bag. (Refrigerate if making ahead.)

Cut each bacon slice into thirds and cook in a small skillet set over medium heat until lightly crisp. Remove the bacon from the skillet, reserving 2 tablespoons of the fat, and finely mince. Add the bread crumbs to the pan and cook over medium heat, stirring and seasoning with a pinch each of salt and pepper, until they turn golden and crisp, about 5 minutes. Combine the crumbs with the bacon.

Holding the nori sheet with tongs, toast it over an open flame (or if you have an electric stove, over a burner set on high) until it shines and becomes brittle, about 30 seconds. With scissors, cut the sheet into a thick stack and then into tiny pieces, as small as the bacon. Add ⅓ cup chopped nori to the bacon mixture.

When you're ready to serve the eggs, preheat the oven to 325°F.

Arrange the egg white halves on an oven-safe platter. Push the filling to the bottom of its bag and snip a ½-inch opening in one of the bottom corners. Squeeze the yolk filling into the egg whites.

Warm the eggs in the oven until the yolk mixture turns soft and luscious, about 5 minutes. Cover the eggs with a dense smattering of the bacon-nori crumbs, and serve.

CRACKER-CRUST PIZZA

PIZZA DOUGH

¾ cup cool water

¼ cup canola oil

1 teaspoon fine sea salt

1 teaspoon sugar

2 cups plus 2 tablespoons all-purpose flour, plus more as needed

NOTES: *Be sure to buy quality canned tomatoes for the sauce; they are the undersung hero of a stellar pizza. The grocery store in my hometown recently started stocking canned San Marzano tomatoes—to my joy. They're about a dollar more, but so much sweeter and more tender.*

Ideally you want to use a pizza peel and pizza stone, but I've had good luck making these pizzas on a heavy cookie sheet. Preheat the cookie sheet in the oven, as if it were a pizza stone, and then assemble the pizzas directly on the hot pan.

In other parts of the country, if you say "pizza" and "Midwest" in the same sentence, Chicago's deep-dish pizza will come to mind. It can be excellent, but deep dish is not the pizza that I grew up with.

Almost everywhere else in the Midwest, from St. Louis to Fargo, the pizza—like the Plains landscape—is dramatically flat. Without exception it arrives cut into squares, so that when you look down on it you might as well be looking from the window of a plane flying over a checkerboard of farm fields. The grid divides the pepperoni slices as if they were split by fencerows, and there's not a hill or a dough bubble in sight.

For years I struggled to reproduce the thin, crispy, almost crackery crust at home—to middling success. Finally, after cycling through all the possible permutations of flour, water, and heat, I realized that the only thing left to try to reduce the dough's tendency toward oven-springing was to take away the yeast altogether. It worked. And without the yeast, the dough comes together in about two minutes, though it's still best to give it a rest before portioning and rolling.

I've noticed that some Midwestern pizzerias roll out their dough between two sheets of parchment paper, and that's a good way to go at home too. Just lift off the top sheet and use the bottom one to transfer the crust to the baking sheet, leaving the parchment beneath the crust. At the ideal temperature for baking this style of pizza (around 500°F, a bit lower than the 800° to 900°F that New York and Neapolitan styles require), the parchment will turn a harmless dark-toast color but won't burn.

As for toppings, play away. Sausage is always welcome, and in true Midwestern style it is dropped raw onto the crust in mounds; the reddish liquid gold that flows onto the cheese as the sausage cooks is integral to the bliss of cracker-crust pizza.

The crust turns out even crisper when spread with a light topping of fresh cheese and slivers of smoked ham, making for a Swiss Tarte Flambée (page 36), a pale white pizza that tastes so right in the depths of the Midwestern winter.

MAKES THREE 12-INCH PIZZAS

For the pizza dough, pour the water, oil, salt, and sugar into a large bowl. Add 1 cup of the flour and whisk until smooth. Switching to a wooden spoon, gradually add the remaining flour, stirring until the dough comes together. Turn the dough out onto a clean surface and knead until it is smooth and supple, about 5 minutes. Divide the dough into three equal pieces, shape each one into a rough disk, cover with a cloth, and let rest on a board for at least 30 minutes (and up to 3 hours) before rolling.

To make the tomato sauce, heat a wide saucepan over medium heat and add the butter, onion, and ½ teaspoon of the salt. Sauté until the onion is very tender, about 10 minutes. Add the garlic and cook for another minute. Pour the tomatoes into a bowl and crush them with your hands. Add the tomatoes and ¼ cup water to the pan. Add the basil sprig, rosemary, sugar, remaining ½ teaspoon salt, and a few turns of pepper, and simmer until the sauce thickens and is no longer watery, about 20 minutes. Discard the basil.

Set a pizza stone on a rack on the bottom third of the oven and preheat the oven as high as it will go, or 500°F.

Roll one portion of the dough between two pieces of parchment paper into a round (more or less) about 12 inches in diameter. Peel off the top layer of parchment. Fold over the edges of the crust and pinch the edge into a small roll, as you would crimp a pie.

Brush the dough lightly with olive oil, and then spread on top one-third each of the tomato sauce, the sausage, and the basil. Top with one-third of the mozzarella cheese.

Slip a pizza peel beneath the paper and transfer the pizza to the pizza stone in the oven. Bake until browned on top and lightly charred at the edges, 15 to 18 minutes. Transfer the pizza to a cutting board, swiping the paper out from underneath the pizza. Cut the pizza into small squares and serve immediately. Repeat the process with the rest of the dough and the toppings.

SAUCE

2 tablespoons salted butter

½ large onion, diced

1 teaspoon fine sea salt

3 cloves garlic, minced

1 28-ounce can whole plum tomatoes, preferably San Marzano

1 large sprig fresh basil

1 tablespoon minced fresh rosemary, or 2 teaspoons dried, crushed

1 teaspoon sugar

Freshly ground black pepper

TOPPINGS

¼ cup extra-virgin olive oil, for brushing

8 ounces sweet Italian sausage, store-bought or homemade (see page 34)

1 cup fresh basil leaves

1 pound fresh mozzarella, shredded (3 cups)

HOMEMADE ITALIAN SAUSAGE

1 pound ground pork

1½ teaspoons fennel seeds

1½ teaspoons freshly ground
black pepper

1 tablespoon minced fresh sage

2 teaspoons sweet paprika

1¼ teaspoons fine sea salt

⅛ teaspoon cayenne pepper

I always stock plain ground pork in my freezer, and it's easy to turn it into bulk sausage. Here's a recipe for sweet Italian sausage; feel free to add more cayenne if you like it spicy.

MAKES 1 POUND

Put the pork in a bowl. Crush the fennel seeds in a mortar and pestle, or in a spice-devoted coffee grinder, until finely ground. Add the fennel to the ground pork, along with the pepper, sage, paprika, salt, and cayenne. Gently mix together, using your hands.

Midwestern Pizza

The upper Midwest is populated with pizza places named after not-so-famous men: Keith's Pizza, Sammy's Pizza, the old Gary's Pizza in my hometown. But my favorite Midwestern pizza emerges from the ovens at Dave's Pizza in Bemidji, Minnesota, a small college town about two hours south of the Canadian border.

Friday nights at Dave's are always charmed. The place gives you a good reception: You walk in, past the guys making pizza, past an oversize carved-wood pizza chef with a checkered neckerchief and a bulbous nose, and into the chamber-like dining room, its dim lights casting a red glow onto the carpeted walls and the twisted wrought iron dividing the booths.

The pizza—especially my standing order: extra-thin with sausage, spinach, and fresh garlic—dominates the cracker-crust genre. It is sturdy but delicate, crispy but tender, and topped with a few fresh toppings and a perfect quilt of cheese. Accompanied by a vial of cheap Chablis and some classic rock from the neon jukebox, the experience is pure, vintage Midwestern.

TARTE FLAMBÉE

¼ cup extra-virgin olive oil, for brushing, plus more for garnish

2 cups whole-milk ricotta cheese

½ cup heavy cream

1½ cups freshly grated Parmesan cheese

Fine sea salt and freshly ground black pepper

Cracker-crust pizza dough (page 32)

8 ounces meaty bacon, cut into matchsticks

½ large sweet onion, halved and sliced into very thin arcs

A few years ago on a trip to Switzerland, I sat down in a courtyard bar and ordered a *tarte flambée*. When it came to the table I realized that this pizza, this *tarte*, was a lot like my favorite extra-thin pie at Dave's Pizza in Bemidji, but with different toppings: a pool of heavy cheese-like cream, slivers of onion, twigs of ham, and a shower of good Parmesan. Clearly they had baked it in a raging-hot oven; the edges and the underside sported black blisters and the cream on top wore the telltale brown caps of blistering heat.

No one in Switzerland thought to help me out by cutting my pizza into saltine-size squares as they did at home, so I had to tear the fiery thing into hand-size pieces myself. I ate the ragged scraps of hot, floppy pizza, thought of home and of guys like the mysterious Dave from Dave's Pizza, and wondered if he knew how well his pizza measured up against that of the old country . . . and then I ordered another one. Delicate like my home slice, they were going down easily.

MAKES THREE 12-INCH *TARTES*

Set a pizza stone on a rack on the bottom third of the oven and preheat the oven as high as it will go, or 500°F.

To make the cream topping, combine the ricotta cheese, cream, ½ cup of the Parmesan cheese, ½ teaspoon salt, and ¼ teaspoon pepper in a bowl and mix until smooth.

Roll one portion of the dough between two pieces of parchment paper into a round (more or less) about 12 inches in diameter. Peel off the top layer of parchment. Fold over and pinch the edge of the crust into a small roll, as you would crimp a pie. Brush the dough lightly with olive oil and top it with one-third each of the cheese mixture, bacon, onion, and remaining 1 cup Parmesan cheese. Garnish with black pepper and a drizzle of extra-virgin olive oil before baking.

Slip a pizza peel beneath the paper and transfer the pizza to the pizza stone in the oven. Bake until browned on top and lightly charred at the edges, 15 to 18 minutes. Transfer the pizza to a cutting board, swiping the paper out from underneath it. Cut the pizza into small squares and serve immediately. Repeat the process with the rest of the dough and toppings.

GREEN PEA PESTO DIP

An army-drab hue is the enemy of pesto—and it's not just an aesthetic bummer. When the mixture loses its manic green color, its sharp basil flavor plummets, too.

The addition of a handful of sweet peas stabilizes the basil and also stretches a small amount of potent pesto into a larger swath of sea-green dip, the perfect accompaniment to toasted bread, crackers, or a platter of raw summer vegetables.

There is just one week in early July—when the basil is blooming and the shell peas in my garden fill out their pods—that I don't make this with frozen peas. At all other times a bag of petite peas works fine. If you like a sharper flavor, substitute pecorino for the Parmesan cheese.

MAKES 2 CUPS

Measure the frozen peas into a mesh sieve and run warm water over them until the ice melts. Drain well.

In the bowl of a food processor, combine the garlic and basil and process until finely chopped. Add the peas, ricotta, pistachios, salt, and pepper, and process again until coarsely ground. Add the olive oil and all but 1 or 2 tablespoons of the Parmesan cheese, and pulse until just combined.

Transfer the dip to a serving bowl. Roughly chop the extra pistachios and scatter them, along with the remaining Parmesan cheese, on top of the dip.

FAVA BEAN PESTO DIP: It's fiddly to shell and skin them, but this dip can also be made with the same measure of fava beans: Drop the shelled beans into a pot of salted boiling water and blanch for just 30 seconds to soften their skins. Chill them in ice water, drain, and slip them from their skins before processing with the other ingredients.

- 1 cup frozen petite green peas
- 1 clove garlic
- 1 cup (lightly packed) fresh basil leaves
- ½ cup whole-milk ricotta cheese
- ¼ cup shelled salted pistachios, plus a handful for garnish
- ½ teaspoon fine sea salt
- ¼ teaspoon freshly ground black pepper
- 6 tablespoons extra-virgin olive oil
- 1¼ cups (2½ ounces) freshly grated Parmesan cheese

NOTE: *Like basil pesto, pea pesto makes an excellent pasta sauce. Simply mix the remaining pesto with a ladleful (¼ cup or so) of the pasta cooking water. Stir, seasoning with salt, pepper, and a fresh dusting of Parmesan cheese, until the pea sauce clings to the pasta. To dress it up you can also add tiny cubes of summer sausage or salami.*

HOMEMADE BRAUNSCHWEIGER

Something about the seesawing summer temperatures in the upper Midwest—the sticky days that plunge into refrigerated nights—causes a craving for a little braunschweiger. The soft, smoky pâté is best consumed on a cracker, preferably when gazing at a windswept lake while wearing flip-flops and a hooded sweatshirt.

Finding good braunschweiger isn't difficult; lots of small meat markets across the Midwest still make it in-house. (Nueske's—a meat market in Wisconsin with a national profile—makes a particularly good version of this spreadable liver sausage, buttery and licked with wood smoke.)

So why should you spend a couple of hours making your own?

Because when it is made with good pork, heavy cream, sweet spices, and just enough liver for people to know that you're serious, braunschweiger is a luxury. It is to the Midwest what foie gras terrine is to France: an occasional indulgence, a regional tradition, and the perfect thing to celebrate life's minor triumphs.

SERVES 20

Combine the salt and pepper in a small dish.

Cut the pork and the slab bacon into 1-inch cubes and put them in a wide-bottomed 2-quart pot. (The pot should be large enough for the meat to fit almost in one layer, although a little double-up is okay.) Add water to just cover and ¾ teaspoon of the salt-and-pepper mixture, and bring to a simmer. Cover, reduce the heat, and cook at a slow-bubbling simmer until the meat is very tender when poked with a fork, about 3 hours.

Uncover and drain, reserving ¾ cup of the mixed juices and fat. Press plastic wrap on the surface of the meat and chill in the refrigerator.

Meanwhile, prepare the liver: Rinse the liver, blot it dry on paper towels, and cut it into 1-inch cubes. Heat a 10-inch cast-iron skillet over medium-high heat, and when it's hot season the meat with a bit of the salt-and-pepper mixture. (I always like to cook liver in cast iron—iron on iron—but any heavy-bottomed pan will work.) Add the canola oil to the skillet and when the oil is hot, add the liver. Sear the liver on all sides until browned

RECIPE CONTINUES

1½ teaspoons fine sea salt, or more if needed

1½ teaspoons freshly ground black pepper, or more if needed

1½ pounds fatty pork (either marbled pork butt or half pork butt, half fresh pork belly)

8 ounces slab bacon

8 ounces fresh pork liver

2 teaspoons canola oil

2 tablespoons salted butter, plus more for the pan

1 large onion, diced

4 cloves garlic, sliced

6 tablespoons dry sherry

½ cup heavy cream

1 teaspoon grated nutmeg

2 teaspoons dried marjoram

½ teaspoon ground allspice

Pinch of cayenne pepper

⅓ cup shelled salted pistachios

Dijon mustard, for serving

NOTE: *This recipe stakes its success on the freshness of the liver, which tastes sweet when brand new but grows slightly more bitter with each passing day. If you don't have access to a fresh liver, place a special order with your butcher. Fresh-frozen pork liver works fine.*

NOTE: *Leftovers are coveted for a singular purpose (not counting the following Braunschweiger Mousse and braunschweiger-smeared break-fast toast, which I privately adore): the Vietnamese* banh mi *sandwich. Any* banh mi *worth the name contains a swipe of liver to cushion the grilled meat, carrot and daikon pickles, spicy sauce, and cilantro, and leftover braunschweiger fits the bill perfectly.*

and crusty on the surface but still pink inside, about 5 minutes. Transfer the seared liver to a wide bowl. Add the butter and diced onion to the skillet. Season with a bit more of the salt-and-pepper mixture and cook over medium heat until the onion is sweet, golden, and tender, about 20 minutes. Add the garlic slices and cook for a few minutes longer, until softened.

Add the sherry and simmer until it is reduced and clings saucily to the onions. Add the cream and simmer until thickened, about 3 minutes. Pour the onion mixture over the liver in the bowl and chill in the refrigerator until very cold.

Preheat the oven to 325°F.

Fit a grinder with a fine blade (I use the grinder attachment for my stand mixer).

Alternately, feed the chilled cooked meat and liver mixtures through the grinder. Then grind the entire mixture again, this time into the bowl of a stand mixer or a heavy mixing bowl.

Add the remaining salt-and-pepper mixture and the nutmeg, marjoram, allspice, and cayenne pepper. Drizzle in half of the reserved rich cooking juices. Whip with the paddle attachment (or a hand mixer) until these final seasonings have been completely incorporated. Add the rest of the cooking juices and whip until fluffy. Fry a small amount of the pâté in a small pan to taste for seasoning, and add more salt and pepper if desired.

Scoop the mixture into a lightly buttered glass or metal 9 × 4-inch loaf pan. Smooth the top and press the pistachios into the surface. Set the loaf pan in a larger baking pan, and pour hot water into it to reach halfway up the sides of the loaf pan, making a water bath. Bake until the internal temperature reaches 150°F, about 50 minutes. Remove from the oven and cool to room temperature. Then unmold the loaf, wrap it in plastic wrap, and chill it deeply.

To serve, cut the braunschweiger into thick slabs and serve with Dijon mustard on the side.

BRAUNSCHWEIGER MOUSSE

A mousse-like spread of braunschweiger and cream cheese is traditional Midwestern fare, and tubs of this mixture are sold at meat markets across the region, my family's Thielen Meats of Pierz included. I've found that I like the extra refinement that mascarpone cheese gives to this spread. I always take the time to rub this through my finest-mesh sieve to give the mousse—especially the melting edges resting on the hot grilled bread—a gleaming, posh finish.

MAKES 1¾ CUPS

In a medium bowl, mix together the braunschweiger and butter, and paddle with a rubber spatula until very smooth and well combined. Add the mascarpone and mix well. Using the rubber spatula, push the mousse mixture through a fine-mesh sieve into a bowl.

To serve, transfer the mixture to a serving bowl and garnish with a drizzle of aged balsamic vinegar and a sprinkling of cracked black pepper. Serve with crackers or grilled slices of bread.

¾ cup braunschweiger, good-quality purchased or homemade (page 39)

2 tablespoons salted butter, at room temperature

¾ cup mascarpone cheese

Aged balsamic vinegar or saba (reduced grape must), for drizzling

Freshly cracked black pepper

Grilled bread or crackers, for serving

NOTE: *You can make the mousse ahead and store it in the refrigerator with a square of plastic wrap pressed to its surface for up to 5 days.*

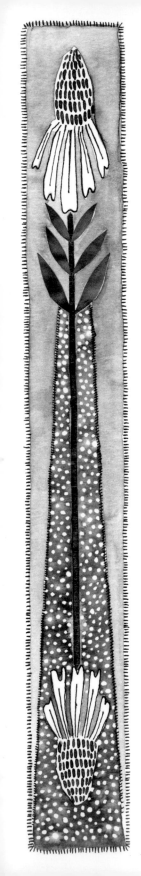

Baumgartner's, Monroe, Wisconsin

At Baumgartner's in Monroe, Wisconsin, deep in cheese country, you want to walk past the cheese counter into the back room and sit at a communal table. The menu is posted on the walls, somewhere amid the visual chaos: maps of Switzerland and bossy vintage signs compete for your attention with the mural behind the bar, an enormous painting in which beer stein armies do battle with wine bottle armies. The steins are armed with javelins but the wine bottles have one better: a terrifying catapult loaded with Limburger cheese.

Even the ceiling vibrates—a dark swarm of crumpled dollar bills hovers above. I remember seeing similar dollar-bill-covered ceilings in the bars in Pierz, my parents' hometown, and at Baumgartner's my curiosity falls prey to the same old trick. "How do you get those to stick up there?" I ask. The waiter gives me a crooked smile. "Takes a dollar bill to find out." (Shoot, not again!)

Soon enough you understand that the menu is the only soothing thing in the room. It limits its focus to cold cheese or cold meat sandwiches, which you can order with or without a bowl of chili or the soup of the day. Stripped to its snack-table basics, this menu puts the upper Midwest's cold-cuts-and-cheese culture on a pedestal.

Going on my third day in cheese country, I ordered the second-best thing on the menu, a braunschweiger sandwich. The plush pink braunschweiger came between two slices of downy rye bread, with arcs of raw onion sticking out the sides. A swipe of hot mustard drove it all home—though I will say that the cheese proximity induced an urge to try some. I couldn't help but steal a few bites from my kid's cold cheddar on soft white, which was simple but not slapdash, the sturdy yellow rectangles like spacers between two quilts of fleecy white bread. Somehow in this crazy place it was made with love, kindling fond memories of all the cheese sandwiches of my childhood.

ARTICHOKE FONDUE DIP

Let's be honest with ourselves: "artichoke dip" is a misnomer. It's really more like a cheese dip. I think of it as a Swiss fondue laid out flat on a plate, the artichokes just tangy bumps in the road.

I'll never forget the first time I tried an upscale version, at the Loring Bar in Minneapolis in the early 1990s. I can't remember which was more thrilling as I sat in the dim bohemian light, my underage attendance or the fancy artichoke dip. It arrived bubbling in a shallow crock as hot as a sauna rock, and while the brined artichokes were familiar, the dip was creamier than I remembered and the cheese emitted a wondrous, expensive funk.

Because this dip is really all about the cheese, the very best variety to use is BellaVitano, a nutty, creamy aged cheese produced in Wisconsin by Sartori. It tastes like the spawn of Parmesan and aged cheddar, combining a dense and silky mouthfeel with a telltale acidic snap.

Even better, BellaVitano is in wide release around the Midwest— I buy it at my hometown grocery store, but if you can't find it, use any Parmesan cheese.

MAKES 2 CUPS

Preheat the oven to 325°F.

Drain the artichoke hearts and give each one a gentle squeeze to release any excess brine. Chop the artichokes roughly.

In a medium bowl combine the artichoke hearts, cream, both cheeses, wine, parsley, ¼ teaspoon salt, ½ teaspoon pepper, and the cornstarch. Stir until combined. If you are using frozen edamame beans, rinse them in a fine-mesh sieve under running water to remove any ice particles. Shake off the excess water and add the edamame to the artichoke mixture.

Pour the mixture into a 9-inch pie plate (or shallow baking dish) and bake until the dip begins to brown at the edges, 35 to 40 minutes. Serve immediately, with baguette slices or crackers.

1 14-ounce can small brined artichoke hearts

½ cup heavy cream

1 cup shredded Parmesan cheese

1 cup shredded aged Gouda cheese

3 tablespoons dry white wine, such as Sauvignon Blanc

2 tablespoons chopped fresh parsley

Fine sea salt and freshly ground black pepper

2 teaspoons cornstarch

½ cup shelled edamame beans, fresh or frozen (optional)

1 baguette, sliced, or mild crackers, for serving

NOTE: *As I've found that my addition of edamame beans to this dip is polarizing (I was dressed down for it at Thanksgiving by one of my relatives), it is now optional.*

SPICY BEEF TARTARE

2 tablespoons extra-virgin
olive oil

3 cloves garlic, minced

1 tablespoon ketchup

1 teaspoon Worcestershire
sauce

8 ounces beef tenderloin or
strip steak, trimmed

1 tablespoon mayonnaise

3 tablespoons diced shallots

2 tablespoons chopped capers
or sour pickle

1 tablespoon minced fresh basil

Fine sea salt and freshly ground
black pepper

⅛ teaspoon minced hot chile
pepper, such as serrano, or
more to taste

Coarse salt, such as Maldon or
fleur de sel, for garnish

Lemon wedges, for garnish

Good-quality kettle potato
chips, for serving

NOTE: *For tartare always use
fresh, never-frozen beef. It has the
best flavor and color.*

If you unwrap a particularly nice roast of beef, as I did after a recent trip to South Dakota, and if it's purplish-red and as stunning as a cut of sushi-grade bluefin tuna, heed the call to chop the ends into a small appetizer tartare to smear on a potato chip.

I like tartare in the French style, with a few strong seasonings and a dab of mayonnaise to bind it all together. For the seasoning paste, I make a quick reduction of garlic and regular ketchup, a two-minute operation that cooks the garlic and caramelizes the ketchup to rid it of its processed tang. If I'm making this for a crowd of strangers, I'll tone down the chile, but for myself I usually multiply it because I think that beef tartare sings when it has some heat.

SERVES 6

Heat a small saucepan over medium heat, and add 1 tablespoon of the extra-virgin olive oil and the garlic. Cook, stirring, until the garlic softens, about 30 seconds. Add the ketchup and cook, stirring, until it reduces and begins to stick to the bottom of the pan, 1 to 2 minutes. Add 1 tablespoon water and the Worcestershire sauce to the pan, stir, and remove from the heat. Pour the sauce into a bowl and chill in the refrigerator.

For the tartare, cut the beef into thin strips, and then crosswise into the smallest possible pieces. When you've diced up all of the beef, roughly chop the pile with your knife until the pieces are reduced a little further. You don't want to mash it but you do want it finely chopped. Place the beef in a bowl and chill, topped with a piece of parchment pressed to the surface of the beef to prevent discoloration.

Right before serving, add the reserved ketchup reduction and the mayonnaise, shallots, capers, basil, remaining 1 tablespoon olive oil, ¼ teaspoon fine salt, ¼ teaspoon pepper, and the chile to the minced beef and stir until combined.

To serve this individually, divide the beef tartare among 6 plates and serve with coarse salt sprinkled on top and lemon wedges for garnish. Usually I serve it as a casual communal appetizer: I mold the tartare in the center of a pretty, shallow dish, scatter some salt on top, garnish it with lemon wedges, and serve the chips on the side.

SWEET-AND-SOUR POTLUCK MEATBALLS

Small sweet-and-sour crockpot meatballs bobbing in vaguely Asian sauces anchor many social events here in the Midwest—and every version, even the overly sweetened and the least loved, is delicious.

My meatballs of late take heavy influence from the day I spent cooking with Mai Ly, an excellent Hmong cook who lives in suburban St. Paul. The potted kaffir lime tree growing next to her front door was a portent of the incredible dishes to come out of her kitchen that day. In particular, her extravagant use of fresh chopped cilantro, one of the most fragrant hallmarks of Hmong cooking, changed my sweet-and-sour meatballs forever.

I'll always have a soft spot for the sweet tomato sauce that my mom's meatballs swam in, but I have to admit that a dash of fresh lime juice and a bit of fish sauce deepen the flavor even further.

MAKES 45 MINI-MEATBALLS

Preheat the oven to 375°F.

In a large bowl combine the pork, peanuts, bread crumbs, egg, cilantro, scallions, carrots, 1 tablespoon of the soy sauce, 1 teaspoon salt, and ½ teaspoon black pepper. Mix quickly with your hands to incorporate. Using about 1 rounded tablespoon of meat mixture for each, roll 45 small meatballs, lining them up on a baking sheet with a little room between them. Bake the meatballs until the tops turn golden, 15 minutes.

Pour the whole tomatoes and their juices into a food processor and process until smooth. In a wide-bottomed nonreactive skillet, heat the canola oil over medium-high heat. Add the ginger and cook until fragrant, about 2 minutes. Add the tomato sauce, ¾ cup water, the brown sugar, chile sauce, remaining 2 tablespoons soy sauce, and the fish sauce. Simmer, stirring often, and scraping the sides, until the sauce has reduced by about half, 5 to 10 minutes. Turn off the heat, add the lime juice, and season with salt.

Add the meatballs to the sauce and cook, stirring often, over medium-high heat until the meatballs are glazed with the sauce, 10 to 15 minutes. (At this point you can keep the meatballs warm in a crockpot.)

Serve on toothpicks.

- 1½ pounds ground pork
- ½ cup fresh bread crumbs or panko
- 1 large egg
- 1 cup finely minced cilantro (including stems)
- 4 scallions, white and green parts, minced
- 2 medium (¾ cup) carrots, finely grated
- 3 tablespoons soy sauce
- Fine sea salt and freshly ground black pepper
- 1 tablespoon canola oil
- 2 tablespoons grated peeled fresh ginger
- 1 (28-ounce) can whole plum tomatoes (2½ cups crushed), with juice
- ¼ cup packed dark brown sugar
- 1½ teaspoons hot chile sauce, such as Sriracha, or more to taste
- 1 tablespoon fish sauce
- 3 tablespoons fresh lime juice

NOTE: *As far as I know, you can't buy fresh, soft bread crumbs in a grocery store. After a loaf of bread goes stale, I tear what remains into chunks, process it to large flakes in my food processor, pour the crumbs into a plastic bag, and freeze them. Country loaves or ciabatta make the craggiest crumbs, the lightest meatballs, and the crispiest toppings.*

FRIED OYSTERS
with Egg Salad

3 large eggs

¼ cup mayonnaise

2 teaspoons fresh lemon juice

2 tablespoons extra-virgin
  olive oil

Fine sea salt and freshly ground
  black pepper

2 tablespoons (lightly packed)
  finely grated, peeled
  fresh horseradish root, or
  1½ tablespoons good-quality
  prepared

1 tablespoon minced red radish

1 tablespoon minced capers,
  plus 2 tablespoons whole
  capers

Cayenne pepper

2 dozen oysters, shucked, shells
  reserved

Crushed ice or rock salt, for
  serving

¾ cup cake flour, plus more for
  breading the capers

1 tablespoon fine cornmeal

¼ teaspoon baking powder

Canola oil, for frying

As promised, nearly every ingredient in this book can be found either at my local small-town grocery store or in the gardens, woods, and lakes of the rural Midwest; these fried oysters are one exception to that rule.

Nonetheless, oysters at holiday time are a Midwestern tradition and I am not alone in seeking them out to kick off a big fancy dinner. When they're perfectly fresh I prefer my oysters on the half shell, neat. But the truth is, if I serve them that way, most of my relatives will eat only one or two and I'll be left holding the bag—literally, the full bag. (True story.) Among oyster-eating home cooks in outlying areas in the middle of the country, it's more common to cook them.

Small oysters rolled in tender flour crumbs and fried until crisp are more like it. I didn't think that fried oysters needed much embellishment until I sat at the bar at Girl & the Goat in Chicago and tried chef Stephanie Izard's fried oysters topped with egg salad. No spackle-thick deli egg salad, this was softly flowing, truly upmarket stuff, made with flaky, neon-yolked farm eggs, fresh horseradish, minced radishes, and a flood of homemade mayonnaise. A single crispy fried caper balanced on top of the oyster, its perfect briny sidekick.

While sitting on my black barstool looking at the wrought-iron boiler plates above the bar at Girl & the Goat, I remembered a day when my husband's family came to visit us when we lived in Brooklyn. When faced with the daily puzzler—where should we eat for lunch?—my mother-in-law's face suddenly lit to 90 watts and she said, "Let's go home and eat egg salad!" Standing in the middle of a Brooklyn block amid at least half a dozen great restaurants, the aroma of freshly fired naan bread in the air, her farm-girl craving was incongruous . . . but catching. So we stopped by the farmer's market for eggs and went home to make egg salad.

I take the lesson as this: Egg salad can Midwesternize anything, even New York City, and even oysters.

This is my version of Chef Izard's recipe. Because it requires such a small amount of mayonnaise, I think it's okay to use store-bought mayo in place of the (likely) homemade of the original, but I recommend the freshly grated horseradish because there's just no substitute for its sweetness.

SERVES 8 TO 12

On the Annexstad farm, Norseland, Minnesota, circa 1930

First, make the egg salad: Put 2 of the eggs in a small saucepan and add water to cover by an inch (see Note, page 30). Bring to a gentle boil, cook for 2 minutes, and then remove the pan from the heat; let it sit for 10 minutes. Drain, crack the eggshells, and cover again with cold water. When cool enough to handle, peel the eggs underwater and finely chop.

Combine the mayonnaise, lemon juice, and olive oil in a medium bowl and whisk until smooth. Add ⅛ teaspoon salt, ¼ teaspoon pepper, and the horseradish, radish, minced capers, and chopped eggs. Mix together. Add a pinch or two of cayenne pepper, to taste.

RECIPE CONTINUES

Next, shuck the oysters: They sell impenetrable oyster-shucking gloves, but I generally just tuck the oyster, flatter side on top and hinge side facing outward, into the pocket of a thick folded towel, and secure it with one hand. With the other hand, stick an oyster knife (or a sturdy paring knife) into the crease on either side of the hinge until it just barely penetrates the shell. Twist the knife, popping the shell open. Gently scrape the oyster flesh from the shells and push the oyster onto a plate, reserving the oyster liquor in a small bowl. Under running water, rub off the plug of flesh from the bottom shell with your thumb. Dry the bottom shells and set them on a serving platter lined with a thick layer of crushed ice or rock salt (to stabilize the shells).

Prepare three small bowls for breading the oysters: one with ¼ cup of the cake flour; the second with the remaining egg, whisked with a touch of oyster liquor to lighten; and the third with the breading mixture: the remaining ½ cup cake flour, the cornmeal, the baking powder, and ¼ teaspoon salt whisked together.

Heat 2 inches of canola oil to 375°F in a deep saucepan.

To bread the oysters, drop them, a few at a time, into the flour, then the egg, and then the breading mixture. (I use a fork to fish them out of the egg.) Drop them onto a breading-dusted plate.

Drain the whole capers, dust them with flour in a sieve, tossing to coat, and then fry them in the hot oil until they float, about 1 minute. Drain on paper towels.

Fry the oysters in three batches, turning them with a metal spider or a fork, until golden brown, about 3 minutes. Drain on paper towels.

To serve, spoon ½ teaspoon of the egg salad mixture into each oyster shell, top with a fried oyster, garnish with another ½ teaspoon egg salad, and finish with a single fried caper.

Oysters in the Midwest

In big cities across the Midwest today, you can buy oysters on the half shell. But fresh oysters have a prominent place in Midwestern food history and were also an important part of the holiday table during the nineteenth and early twentieth centuries.

Their popularity swelled because at the time, compared to other proteins, oysters were cheap—relatively much cheaper than they are now. So they made their way from the East Coast oyster beds to the Middle West via the railroads, shipped either in the shell and packed in large iced barrels, or shelled and packed in iced tubs.

As early as the late 1800s, fresh oysters were served in Chicago's finest restaurants, including the famed Rector's. *Buckeye Cookery and Practical Housekeeping* (a book of reader-recipes from the heartland first published in 1877) states, "Oysters are the best known of shell-fish . . . and they are not more expensive than meats." Around the turn of the century a fish importer in Minneapolis named "Fish Jones" stressed in advertisements the abundant amount of fresh oysters he was bringing to the city. Even here, just west of the Mississippi, diners enjoyed sparkling fresh raw Atlantic oysters on the half shell.

According to the cookbooks of the time, fresh oysters were also popular pickled, scalloped, stewed, and fried. Canned oysters, steamed and sealed in heat-processed cans, were shipped in quantity to the Midwest, too. Among rural farm families of all stripes who didn't have access to the cities and the fresh oysters, the tradition of making oyster stew from canned oysters for their holiday supper continued for many generations.

To that end, Sara Woster, descended from a South Dakota ranch family, shares her family's recipe for Christmas oyster stew. Like my own great-grandma's recipe, it's a one-liner: "The oyster stew recipe, if you are interested in how a ranch family in central South Dakota in the 1950s would cook a seafood stew, consists of many tins of canned oysters, a sh**load of cream and butter and some pepper. There you go."

RUMAKI SPIEDINI
with Curried Mustard Vinaigrette

1½ tablespoons yellow mustard seeds

2 teaspoons Dijon mustard

½ cup plus 1 teaspoon light honey

½ clove garlic, finely grated

3 tablespoons fresh lemon juice

¼ cup plus 1 tablespoon red wine vinegar

Fine sea salt and freshly ground black pepper

¼ teaspoon curry powder

¼ cup plus 2 tablespoons extra-virgin olive oil

Freshly cracked black pepper

1 1-inch-thick slab of bacon, cut into 16 cubes

½ large Vidalia onion, cut into 8 chunks

4 large chicken livers, trimmed and halved

8 Medjool dates, pitted

This dish marries rumaki (bacon-wrapped chicken livers), the "it" hors d'oeuvre of my mother's era, with spiedini, an Italian kebab of skewered meat and various sweetmeats grilled over a hot fire.

Here I sauté the bacon cubes to precook them a bit, thread them onto a skewer with fresh chicken livers, sweet onions, and plump Medjool dates, and grill the entire kebab. After each element has picked up some char, I brush the skewer with a little sweet-and-sour honey-vinegar syrup and serve it with a dot of curry-accented mustard vinaigrette.

If you are using wooden skewers, soak them in water to cover for at least 20 minutes to prevent burning.

SERVES 4 TO 8

For the mustard vinaigrette, pour the mustard seeds into a spice-devoted coffee grinder and grind to a medium-fine powder. Transfer to a medium bowl. Add the Dijon mustard, 1 teaspoon of the honey, the garlic, lemon juice, 1 tablespoon of the vinegar, ¼ teaspoon salt, and the curry powder. Stir to combine. Whisk in ¼ cup of the olive oil. Add freshly cracked black pepper to taste.

In a skillet over medium heat, cook the pieces of bacon until browned on all sides. Set the cubes aside and pour out the excess bacon fat. (Save it for Bacon Soufflé Eggs, page 369.) Add the remaining ½ cup honey and ¼ cup vinegar to the pan and bring to a boil. Reduce the heat to low and simmer until the mixture feels sticky when pinched between your thumb and forefinger, about 5 minutes. Add another ¼ teaspoon salt and about 15 turns of black pepper.

Put the onion chunks, chicken livers, and dates in separate small bowls, and divide the remaining 2 tablespoons olive oil among them. Season the contents of each bowl generously with salt and pepper, and toss to combine. Toss the livers with 2 tablespoons of the mustard vinaigrette.

Preheat a grill or grill pan over high heat.

Thread each of 8 skewers with a date, 2 pieces of bacon, 1 chunk of onion, and a piece of the liver. Reduce the grill's heat

to medium-high and cook the skewers until the onions darken at the edges, the date slumps and softens, the liver feels firm to the touch, and everything is lightly charred, about 5 minutes per side. Paint each skewer thickly with the honey-vinegar syrup as it comes off the grill.

To serve, spoon a dot of mustard vinaigrette on each plate and lay a skewer across it.

POKER BUNS

6 tablespoons warm water (110°F, the temperature of a lukewarm bath)

1½ teaspoons active dry yeast

1½ tablespoons plus a pinch of sugar

1 large egg

1 large egg yolk

1¾ cups plus 2 tablespoons bread flour

12 tablespoons (1½ sticks) salted butter, melted, plus 6 tablespoons (¾ stick), at room temperature

1 teaspoon fine sea salt

1½ cups (5 ounces) grated Gruyère cheese

½ cup finely diced ham

½ cup finely diced brined sour pickle, such as Bubbies

Freshly ground black pepper

Truffled Poker Buns

If you're one of those people who is hoarding a small vial of truffle something-or-other (probably received as a gift) and you need to find basic recipes for its inclusion, this one is ridiculously good: Add 2 teaspoons black truffle paste or 1 teaspoon either white or black truffle oil to the ham-and-cheese mixture before filling the buns.

I found an entry for poker buns in a book of Wisconsin cooking from the early eighties, and the image sparked by those two words—*poker* and *bun*—resonated with me. I remember my mother piling buns (usually filled with double-smoked ham and butter) into pyramids in preparation for her card parties. The gaming alternated between bridge, blackjack, and poker, but the food remained the same: bowls of nuts, small sandwiches, Chex mix, bars for dessert—nothing too wet or sticky for the card table.

I don't deviate much from the original poker bun filling recipe except to swap out the Swiss for Gruyère and to make sure that the ham is decent and the pickles fermented instead of made with vinegar . . . but that's just personal preference.

I usually make my own butter-rich dough for this (the same easy recipe I use for Runzas, page 174), but you can use small store-bought "dollar buns" as well. Either way, split the buns, spread both sides with the ham-cheese-pickle filling, and bake them just long enough to make the cheese run. Sandwich them back together and serve immediately.

MAKES 12 BUNS

For the dough, combine the water, yeast, and pinch of sugar in a large mixing bowl and let sit until foamy, about 10 minutes. Add the egg and egg yolk, and whisk to combine. Add 1 cup of the bread flour and beat with a wooden spoon until good and thready, about 3 minutes. (This is important, as it develops the gluten.) Add the melted butter, the 1½ tablespoons sugar, the remaining flour, and the salt, using your hands if necessary to incorporate all the flour. The dough will be a little sticky. Leave it to rest and hydrate for 15 minutes, then turn it out onto the counter and knead for 3 minutes to develop the gluten. Let rise in a bowl, covered with a cloth, for 1 hour at room temperature. Punch it down and then chill it for 1 to 2 hours in the refrigerator, or as long as overnight.

Remove the dough from the refrigerator and divide it into quarters, then divide each quarter into thirds, which gives you 12 pieces. Roll each piece of dough into a ball and set them on a lightly greased baking sheet. Cover loosely and let double in size, about 1 hour.

Preheat the oven to 375°F.

Bake the buns until golden brown on top, 12 to 15 minutes. (You can also bake the buns ahead of time and store them in the freezer once they've cooled. To finish, thaw them slightly before splitting, filling, and baking.)

Remove the buns from the oven and raise the temperature to 400°F.

For the filling, combine the Gruyère, ham, pickles, remaining 6 tablespoons butter, and black pepper to taste. Mix until well combined.

Split the buns crosswise and spread the filling over the cut sides. Place the bun pairs on a baking sheet with the filling facing up, and bake until the filling has melted, 8 to 10 minutes.

Remove from the oven, sandwich the buns back together, and serve while warm.

SMOKED LAKE TROUT
Baked *in* Cream

8 ounces smoked lake trout
    fillet

½ cup heavy cream

Juice of ½ lemon

Freshly ground black pepper

Cayenne pepper

NOTE: *If smoked lake trout is
unavailable, substitute any other
thick, white-fleshed smoked fillet,
such as whitefish.*

Whenever I return from Russ Kendall's Smokehouse in Knife River, Minnesota, with a chunk of smoked lake trout (to my mind, the best to be found on Lake Superior's north shore), it's nice to open the fish like a book, lift out the spine and javelin rib bones, and bake the parchment-colored fillet in a shallow pond of cream.

I found this recipe in an old and battered book of Midwestern frontier food and was immediately struck by its purity and simplicity. In the oven the cream swells into a mushroom cloud over the fish and finally settles into a smoky, silky sauce. (And if the smoked fish you bring home tastes too salty alone, the cream bath will mellow it out.) Once sprinkled with lemon juice, black pepper, and cayenne and ushered onto a piece of bread, this fish tastes like a virtual melt of the upper Midwest: campfire, fine dairy, and lake all at once.

Like many of the dishes in this chapter, this one makes as much sense as a singleton dinner (accompanied by a green salad or a pan of cooked vegetables) as it does a warm starter (with bread and crackers) to kick off a party.

SERVES 6

Preheat the oven to 350°F.

Remove and discard any large bones and membranes from the top of the fish and nestle it into a close-fitting baking dish. Pour the cream over the fish.

Bake for 30 to 35 minutes, basting the fish with the cream twice: after 10 and after 20 minutes. Leave the fish untouched for the last 10 to 15 minutes of cooking; the cream will puff over the fish and begin to brown.

Season the fish with a squirt of lemon, many turns of pepper, and a light dusting of cayenne, and serve immediately.

SOUTH DAKOTA LAMB CHISLIC

1 teaspoon cumin seeds

Drop of canola oil, plus at least
2 cups for frying

1 pound boneless lamb,
shoulder or loin, cut into
1½-inch (two-bite) cubes

2 cloves garlic, minced

1 tablespoon minced fresh
thyme

1 tablespoon red wine vinegar

Fine sea salt and freshly ground
black pepper

½ teaspoon sweet paprika

½ teaspoon garlic powder

NOTE: *Instead of deep-frying, you
can also thread the marinated lamb
on skewers (leave lots of space) and
grill them quickly over a hot fire.*

Oil-Drop Mince
Here's a weird trick taught to me
by Mario Lohninger, one of the
first chefs I worked for: To grind
a small amount of fresh whole
spice—cumin or caraway or
fennel seeds, for example—don't
get out the spice grinder. Just
pile it on your cutting board,
cover it with a few drops of oil,
and mince until you have a fine
sludge. The oil will keep the
seeds from flying off the board,
you won't have to pull out a
machine, and you'll have the
vibrant, stronger flavor of the
whole spice.

Chislic—an appetizer of marinated, deep-fried cubes of lamb—was
brought to the southeastern corner of South Dakota by German-
Russian immigrants. Its name may be a corruption of *shashlik*, the highly
spiced, vinegary lamb kebab from the southern provinces of Russia,
but eating deep-fried chunks of meat as a precursor to a meat-centered
dinner strikes me as a particularly Midwestern thing to do.

Taverns in the region commonly deep-fry the lamb until it is
shingled and crisp on the outside and juicy-pink on the inside, and
serve it with hot sauce and a few packs of saltines. Emily Elsen, a
southeastern South Dakota native and proprietor of the Brooklyn pie
shop Four & Twenty Blackbirds, remembers her childhood friends
making chislic at home with cubes of venison.

No matter the protein, when fried hard and sprinkled with a
Lawry's-like blend of paprika, garlic powder, and salt, chislic is
uncommonly good. Serve with your favorite hot sauce or with my
version of chef David Bouley's ginger ketchup sauce (page 114), and
keep track of how many you eat by stacking the toothpicks, because it's
all too easy to spoil your dinner.

SERVES 6

Put the cumin seeds on a cutting board, add a drop of canola oil
to cover, and chop fine, to a paste. Add the cumin to a medium
bowl along with the meat, garlic, thyme, vinegar, ¼ teaspoon
salt, and ½ teaspoon pepper. Cover and refrigerate for at least
4 hours, and as long as 12.

For the spice dust, stir together ½ teaspoon salt, ½ teaspoon
pepper, the paprika, and the garlic powder.

Pour at least 2 inches of oil into a heavy pot, attach a candy
thermometer to its side, and heat until the oil reaches 375°F, or
until a drop of water dances when dropped on the surface.

Working in batches, drain the meat from the marinade and
drop the cubes into the oil, giving them some space to fry. Fry
quickly, until the corners turn dark brown but the insides remain
juicy pink, about 2 minutes.

Remove the lamb from the oil, drain on paper towels, and
dust with the paprika mixture. Serve on toothpicks.

RYE CRACKERS
with Smoked Oyster Dip

Oddly enough it was from Wylie Dufresne, chef of wd-50, one of the most cutting-edge restaurants in New York City, that I picked up this provisional little cracker. After working for him at a private party and plating numerous slices of cured duck breast on his delicate rye crackers, I asked him about the dough—expecting him to describe a process that somehow wed the properties of moist rye and Danish pastry.

But he told me that he simply ran a piece of sliced Jewish rye bread through a hand-cranked pasta machine until it became a thin noodle, then brushed it with fat and baked it until crisp. The resulting cracker was as buttery as a crouton, but fragile, as light as veneer.

For the holidays I usually top these crackers with smoked oyster dip, in homage to my family's Christmas Eve smoked-oysters tradition, the tin top simply rolled back to reveal their black pearl bellies. Lately I've taken to mixing the oysters with sour cream, pecorino cheese, and diced summer sausage, but you can just serve them straight up if you like, toothpick to tin to cracker.

SERVES 8

Preheat the oven to 375°F.

Drain the smoked oysters.

In a medium bowl, combine the cream cheese and sour cream, and paddle with a rubber spatula until smooth. Add the oysters, lemon juice, soy sauce, summer sausage, pecorino, ½ teaspoon pepper, and the parsley, and stir to combine.

For the crackers, use a rolling pin (or a pasta machine) to flatten each slice of bread until it's as thin as a sheet of lasagna— basically, as thin as it can be rolled without breaking. Stack the slices and trim the edges, forming a rectangle. Slice the rectangle in half to make 16 long rectangular crackers.

Using a pastry brush, paint one side of each bread cracker with a layer of soft butter. Flip the cracker onto a baking sheet, and brush the other side with butter. Bake for 10 minutes, turn the crackers over, and bake until crisp, about another 10 minutes. Cut the clove of garlic in half and lightly rub the surface of each warm cracker with the cut side.

Serve the warm, garlicky crackers with the smoked oyster dip.

1 13-ounce tin smoked oysters

¼ cup (2 ounces) cream cheese, at room temperature

½ cup sour cream

2 teaspoons fresh lemon juice

1 teaspoon soy sauce

⅓ cup finely diced summer sausage or cured salami

½ cup finely grated pecorino cheese

Freshly ground black pepper

1 tablespoon minced fresh parsley

8 slices rye bread

4 tablespoons (½ stick) salted butter, at room temperature

1 clove garlic

NOTES: *You can thread the bread through a pasta machine, but I usually thin mine out with a rolling pin because truth be told, I often make these when I realize that the guests are on their way and I can't find any crackers for the dip.*

You may want to rinse the oysters quickly under warm water to rid them of the sometimes inferior oil in which they're packed—unless it's extra-virgin olive oil, in which case simply drain them.

ROASTED SWEET PEPPERS *with* Sour Orange Vinaigrette *and* Goat Cheese

This appetizer's finest moment came a few summers ago when I served it as a precursor to the evening's main course, an enormous wood-fire grilled paella studded with smoked pork sausage and local crayfish, cooked in an oversize steel campfire pan. As the paella cooked over the open fire, I stewed the roasted, peeled peppers in a cast-iron pan of garlicky olive oil on the other side of the grill until they were limp and sweet, then bathed them in a tart orange vinaigrette and sprinkled them with locally made goat cheese. We ate the smoky pepper salad over grilled bread while sitting in lawn chairs, waiting for the paella to finish cooking.

But the flavors in this small dish are big enough to carry a meal. If you wanted to add a side of grilled shellfish or chicken and a loaf of bread, you'd have one.

SERVES 8

Turn on two gas-fired stovetop burners (or fire up the grill) and roast the peppers directly on the flames, turning them often with tongs, until fully blackened. Transfer the peppers to a bowl, cover tightly with plastic wrap, and let steam until cool enough to touch.

Rub off the black skins, cut out the stems, remove the seeds, and rip the peppers in half. Cut the pepper flesh into strips and then on the diagonal into 1-inch-wide diamonds.

Heat 2 tablespoons of the olive oil in a large skillet over medium heat. Add the garlic and cook, stirring, until it turns light golden brown. Add the peppers, season with ¼ teaspoon salt, a few cranks of pepper, and a pinch of sugar, and cook over medium-low heat, stirring occasionally, until the peppers soften and sweeten, about 15 minutes.

Meanwhile, for the sour orange vinaigrette, whisk together the remaining 1 tablespoon olive oil, ½ teaspoon salt, black pepper to taste, the red pepper flakes, and the orange and lemon juices.

Lay the cooked peppers out on a platter, drizzle with the sour orange vinaigrette, and top with the crumbled cheese. Serve warm or at room temperature, with grilled bread.

3 red bell peppers

3 tablespoons extra-virgin olive oil

4 cloves garlic, thinly sliced

Fine sea salt and freshly ground black pepper

Pinch of sugar

Pinch of red pepper flakes

2 tablespoons fresh orange or tangerine juice

2 tablespoons fresh lemon juice

2 ounces (½ cup) goat cheese or feta cheese, crumbled

Baguette or country bread, sliced and toasted on a hot grill, for serving

NOTE: *Alone, sour orange vinaigrette likes to be boosted with another tablespoon or two of olive oil and tossed with bitter greens (such as arugula, endive, or escarole).*

CORN FRITTERS *with* Green Chile Buttermilk Dip

2 tablespoons extra-virgin olive oil

2 medium-hot green banana or Italian frying peppers (or 1 large poblano)

Fine sea salt and freshly ground black pepper

½ clove garlic

½ cup buttermilk

¼ cup sour cream

1 teaspoon sugar

10 fresh basil leaves

1 teaspoon fresh lemon juice

1 tablespoon canola oil, plus 4 cups for frying

3 to 4 ears of corn

1 cup all-purpose flour

1 tablespoon baking powder

2 large egg whites

⅔ cup light beer

2 teaspoons chopped fresh tarragon

1 teaspoon grated lemon zest

NOTE: *Italian frying peppers and poblano peppers have a similar grassy half-spiciness, and if banana peppers aren't available, these are sometimes easier to find. If they're mild, add a few shakes of cayenne to ratchet up the heat.*

These corn fritters are light and crusty, but in truth I make them so that I have something to dunk into the addictive green chile buttermilk dip.

The main ingredient in this concoction is one that most people around here seem to grow themselves—a medium-hot pepper, such as Hungarian hot wax or banana. When I began gardening fifteen years ago, I saw that these peppers grew easily and seemed essential to a proper kitchen garden. They were a little foreign to me, but eventually I found things to do with them; and now, years later, I consider them indispensible to my summer cooking. (And there you have a classic example of a vegetable's survival instinct. Some of them just worm their way into your life.)

SERVES 8

For the buttermilk dip, heat the olive oil and the frying peppers in a small skillet over medium-low heat, seasoning them with ¼ teaspoon salt. Cook the peppers slowly, turning them often, until they are tender at the stem, about 15 minutes.

Pinch out the pepper stems and most of the seeds, and put the peppers in a blender. Add the olive oil from the skillet and the garlic, buttermilk, sour cream, sugar, basil, lemon juice, and ½ teaspoon salt. Process until smooth. Pour into a bowl for serving. (This sauce can be made a few hours ahead and kept refrigerated.)

For the fritters, heat the 4 cups oil to 370°F.

While the oil is heating, shuck the corn, cut the kernels shallowly off the cobs, and then scrape the rest of the pulp with the back of the knife. Measure out 2 cups of kernels and pulp.

In a medium bowl, sift together the flour, baking powder, and 1 teaspoon salt. In a large bowl, whisk together the egg whites, beer, remaining tablespoon of canola oil, tarragon, lemon zest, and reserved corn. Add the flour mixture and whisk quickly to combine. (Don't overmix—a few lumps are okay.)

Working in batches, drop the fritter mixture by the teaspoonful into the hot oil. Cook until dark golden brown, about 3 minutes. Drain well on paper towels and serve with the buttermilk dip.

BEET-PICKLED EGGS
with Hot Mustard Dust

1 medium beet

1⅓ cups apple cider vinegar

¼ cup sugar

1 teaspoon black peppercorns

5 small dried red chiles

1 3-inch cinnamon stick

1 teaspoon coriander seeds

Fine sea salt and freshly ground black pepper

12 eggs, preferably farm-fresh

2 tablespoons yellow mustard seeds

1 egg yolk

1 tablespoon fresh lemon juice

1 cup canola oil

¼ cup extra-virgin olive oil

1½ tablespoons honey

1 teaspoon Dijon mustard

NOTE: *The mayonnaise makes 1½ cups, about double what you need for this recipe, but it's difficult to make a smaller batch in a food processor. Besides, I find that the leftover honey-mustard mayonnaise makes an amazing addition to potato salad or egg salad. If you don't want to make homemade mayonnaise, however, you can always doctor store-bought—see Note on page 93.*

I've sat on barstools and eaten good pickled eggs and I've sat on barstools and eaten bad ones, and I've found that the condition of the barstool you're sitting on is a pretty good indicator of the quality of the eggs. Not to be a total snob, but if the seat is cracked or the stuffing is leaking out, you're probably going to want to ask for hot sauce.

At home I can make my eggs just the way I like them: I use farm-fresh eggs, a low-concentration vinegar pickling solution, plenty of whole spices, and a sliced beet to turn them hot-magenta-pink. Distinguished with a cap of homemade honey-mustard mayonnaise and a sprinkling of fresh sweet-hot mustard dust (made by quickly pulverizing some yellow mustard seeds), these racy-pink eggs are here to remind us of a good night at the bar, whether raucous or bittersweet or swinging in between.

MAKES 12 PICKLED EGGS

Wash the beet, trim the ends, and slice it into ½-inch-thick rounds. Pour 3 cups water into a saucepan and add the beets, vinegar, sugar, peppercorns, chiles, cinnamon stick, coriander seeds, and ¾ teaspoon salt. Bring to a simmer and cook for 10 minutes. Then remove from the heat and let cool to room temperature. Pour the pickling liquid into a large storage container and chill it in the refrigerator.

Set the eggs in a 2-quart saucepan and add enough water to cover by 1 inch (see Note, page 30). Bring the water to a gentle simmer, boil for 1 minute, remove from the heat, and leave the eggs in the water for 8 minutes. Drain the eggs, crack the shells against the side of the pan, and cover them with fresh cold water. Peel the eggs underwater and add them to the cold pickling liquid. Let steep in the pickling liquid in the refrigerator overnight or up to 7 days.

For the mayonnaise, pulverize the yellow mustard seeds in a spice-devoted coffee grinder until fine but not powdered. In a food processor, combine the egg yolk, lemon juice, and 1 tablespoon water, and buzz to combine. With the machine running, add the canola oil drop by drop until an emulsion forms; then add the rest of the canola oil and the olive oil in a very thin stream. Season with 4 teaspoons of the ground mustard seeds, the honey, the Dijon mustard, and salt and pepper to taste.

To serve the pickled eggs, blot them dry on paper towels, cut each one in half, and set on a platter (a deviled egg platter if you have one). Drop a small spoonful of honey-mustard mayonnaise over the yolk of each egg, and sprinkle generously with the remaining hot mustard dust.

HERRING SALAD
with Horseradish *and* Apple

6 tablespoons sour cream

¼ cup old-fashioned prepared horseradish, homemade (page 224) or store-bought

½ teaspoon freshly ground black pepper

1 teaspoon finely grated lemon zest

2 teaspoons minced fresh parsley

1 pound pickled herring in wine sauce

1 small sweet apple, such as Honeycrisp

1 medium shallot, thinly sliced and separated into rings

NOTES: *For this, you want to use herring in wine sauce, floating in a lightly sweetened brine of sugar and white wine, or homemade pickled herring (page 294).*

And if you cut the herring into small-enough pieces, you can load this mixture onto a cracker.

When my mother comes to visit, she arrives dragging a cooler the size of a small dresser down the footpath. Inside we have the requisite sausage, bacon, liver sausage, and ribeyes from the family meat market in Pierz, vegetables from the St. Paul farmer's market, and (I know it's in there somewhere) a tub of pickled herring.

After we've set the white wine to chill and unwrapped the steaks to let them breathe, the next move is always the same: We start hunting for the herring. Something about settling into a weekend of cooking and eating and stoking the campfire always makes my mouth run for the stuff.

This chopped salad with horseradish and apple is a traditional part of Sunday smorgasbord brunches around here, especially among those of northern European heritage, although I generally make it as part of a predinner assemblage of cold cuts, cheeses, and pickles. Pickled herring and apple have a natural affinity, and this mixture is motivated by plenty of horseradish, lemon, and freshly ground black pepper.

SERVES 8 TO 10

In a medium bowl, whisk together the sour cream, horseradish, pepper, lemon zest, and parsley.

Drain the pickled herring (discarding the onion). Cut the herring into ½-inch dice and add to the sour cream mixture.

Peel the apple and cut it into ½-inch dice. Add the apples and the shallots to the herring. Toss everything together and serve chilled.

DRINKS

It's always nice to be able to hand a guest a glass of something unexpected, whether it's a fancy cocktail or a fruit sangria or something as simple as well water muddled with garden cucumbers (which is incredibly refreshing).

Rhubarb Tarragon Sangria unites two of spring's early birds in a way that seems to force summer, and the resulting drink is a staggeringly beautiful shade of pink. The Blackberry Rioja Sangria was born the year that a friend, originally from Barcelona, came to visit in late July at the height of blackberry season; we all loved the low-down, brambly quality that the dark fruit gave to the earthy wine. Muskmelon-Ginger Cooler has come to rescue me on the most sweltering days of summer. (On those really sticky days, it's not just a drink, but almost a snack.) Finally, the herb soda is a house standard, as it works with any bouquet of herbs you find found. I especially love it when made with the incredibly floral, unripe buds of coriander (cilantro) that has gone to seed. As everyone who grows coriander knows, it doesn't hold too long; after it sprints to seed, what else do you do with those tiny green buds?

RHUBARB TARRAGON SANGRIA

SERVES 8

¼ cup sugar

2 cups thickly sliced fresh rhubarb

5 sprigs fresh tarragon

1 750-ml bottle white wine, chilled

1 750-ml bottle rosé wine, chilled

Juice of 1 lime

Combine 1 cup water, the sugar, and the rhubarb in a saucepan, and bring to a boil. Cook, standing by, until the rhubarb is just starting to get tender, 30 seconds to 1 minute. Remove from the heat and let steep until cool. Pour the rhubarb and its syrup into a large pitcher, and add the tarragon. Chill until very cold.

Add the white wine, rosé wine, and the lime juice to the cold syrup. Pour the sangria over ice cubes in a wine glass, or for a party, add ice cubes to the pitcher just before serving.

BLACKBERRY RIOJA SANGRIA

SERVES 8

1 pint fresh blackberries

⅓ cup dry sherry

5 tablespoons sugar

⅓ cup fresh orange juice

2 750-ml bottles inexpensive Rioja wine, chilled

Mix the blackberries, sherry, and sugar in a small bowl and leave to macerate in the refrigerator for at least 30 minutes or as long as overnight.

Pour the blackberry mixture into a pitcher, and add the orange juice and wine. Pour over ice cubes in a wine glass, or for a party, add ice cubes to the pitcher just before serving.

HERB SODAS

1 cup sugar

1½ cups fresh herbs, such as Thai basil, regular basil, cilantro, parsley, tarragon, mint, rosemary, or celery leaves, in any combination

⅓ cup fresh lemon juice

2 quarts sparkling water

Lemon or lime wedges, for serving

NOTE: *If you'd like to make a single drink, pour about ¼ cup (2 ounces) of the syrup into a glass and top it with sparkling water to taste.*

Combine the sugar and 1 cup water in a medium saucepan and bring to a boil. Cook, stirring, until the sugar dissolves, about 3 minutes. Add the herbs to the pan—as many as you can fit. Remove from the heat and let the herbs steep until the syrup has cooled to room temperature.

Pour the entire mixture, herbs and all, into a container. Add the lemon juice, and chill thoroughly.

Strain out the herbs and transfer the syrup to a large pitcher. Add the sparkling water and serve over ice, with a wedge of lemon or lime.

MUSKMELON-GINGER COOLER

⅓ cup sugar

1 ripe muskmelon

6 tablespoons chopped fresh ginger (from a 5-inch piece of ginger)

6 tablespoons fresh lime juice

Lime wedges, for garnish

Combine the sugar and ⅓ cup water in a small saucepan and bring to a simmer. Stir to dissolve the sugar, and remove from the heat.

Cut the muskmelon in half and scrape the melon, beginning with the seed material, into a blender. (The seeds will be strained out later.) Scrape as much as you can from the melon shell before discarding it. Add the sugar syrup, ginger, and lime juice, and blend on high speed until well mixed.

Strain the mixture through a fine-mesh sieve into a pitcher, pushing on the pulp with the back of a small ladle to extract as much juice as possible. Add 1 cup water to the melon juice and chill thoroughly. Serve over ice, garnished with a wedge of lime.

BLOODY MARY
with Pickle Juice

Whenever I've spent time at the horseshoe bar at the Two Inlets Country Store, I've been coaxed to try what they call a "Poor-Man's Bloody Mary," or half spicy V8 and half .32 (low-alcohol) beer. It's really more like a Mexican *michelada*, and I've bitten a few times, but I must say that while it tastes good there, I've never been compelled to try it at home.

I prefer a more proper Bloody Mary, and by that I mean something that reads like a spicy meat-and-cheese platter in a glass. Commonly, the good ones are made with fermented pickle juice and fresh horseradish. And a smoked beef stick. Or a skewer of grilled cherry tomatoes. And since having the excellent Bloody Mary served at Longman & Eagle in Chicago, I'm persuaded that a Bloody Mary really needs a soft chunk of aged cheddar cheese as well.

In my experience, the Bloody Mary is not a drink limited to brunch. Many people drink them for happy hour as well, especially in the summer, when snacking and meat-and-cheese table grazing is most common.

MAKES ONE 8-OUNCE COCKTAIL

To garnish the rim of each glass, rub the edge with the cut side of the lime half and upturn the glass into a saucer of the celery salt.

Combine the tomato juice, pickle juice, vodka, lime juice, horseradish, hot sauce, and a good pinch of the celery salt in the bottom of a pint glass, and stir to combine. Add ice to fill.

With a short skewer, impale the top of the pickle, the beef stick and the cheddar cube, and set the skewer across the glass so that the pickle and beef stick are submerged in the drink and the cheddar hangs over the surface of the drink. Serve immediately.

CELERY SALT

MAKES 5 TEASPOONS

Mix the celery seed, salt, and black pepper together.

---

1 tablespoon fresh lime juice, chilled, plus ½ lime

Celery Salt (recipe follows)

⅔ cup seasoned tomato juice, such as V8

¼ cup fermented pickle juice, taken from pickles such as Bubbies or homemade dills (page 280), chilled

3 tablespoons vodka, chilled

2 teaspoons (lightly packed) freshly grated horseradish or good-quality store-bought horseradish

Dashes of hot sauce, such as Tabasco, to taste

Fermented pickle spear, for serving

Beef stick, for serving

Small cube of aged cheddar, for serving

NOTE: *In place of the pickle juice, you can use the juice from pickled dilly beans, garlic, or any other kind of pickled vegetable.*

2 teaspoons celery seeds

2 teaspoons fine sea salt

1 teaspoon freshly ground black pepper

In this chapter, soup commingles with salad according to the famous question always posed to you by the small-town supper club server: "And what would you like with your entree—soup or salad?" After living elsewhere, when I moved back to my hometown I was freshly reminded that many meals benefit from being jump-started by one or the other.

From the pot of perpetual stew that snowed-in Midwesterners reinforce and reboil on their woodstoves each morning to the elegant purees made to kick off a gathering of the gourmet club, soup has reins on those who live a good portion of their year in the cold.

The most common soups in this region skirt the extremes of both of the above examples—neither too rough nor too fey—but they usually have in common big flavors and rugged good looks, as well as a reputation for being a generally welcoming pot. Here you'll find my versions of a few icons plucked from the wide, rotating wheel of regional soups, among them an elegant Iced Cucumber Soup with Grilled Honey Eggplant, Corn Soup with Maple-Lacquered Bacon, and the upper Midwest's favorite, creamy Wild Rice and Smoked Chicken Soup. Minneapolis chef Steven Brown's Best-Ever Beer Cheese Soup virtually mainlines aged cheddar yet manages to taste different from the standard—a real achievement for a soup that prides itself on staying the same—and is brilliant in every way, including its blazing orange color.

As for the salads, only one in this chapter references the era of Midwestern cooking when most salads were stacked, jellied, and otherwise pressed into shape. And who would guess: that one comes from a Minneapolis-raised New York chef who cooks Spanish food—proving how universally comforting a layered salad can be when made with homemade mayonnaise, imported tuna packed in extra-virgin olive oil, and care.

The green salads represent the mood year-round, including the summer season's Country Cream Dressing with Garden Greens and Grilled Mushroom Salad with Toasted Almonds, as well as the sturdier ones that stand up better to winter, such as the Smoked Sardine Caesar with Salami and Pan Croutons.

All of this brings us back to the original question: Soup or salad? For everyday eating, sometimes the answer is "both." Soup consumed on the heels of salad, or vice versa, makes a stellar meal.

ICED CUCUMBER SOUP
with Grilled Honey Eggplant

The genesis of this refreshing sipping soup, based loosely on Spanish *ajo blanco* (white garlic gazpacho), is a pretty good sketch of the ripening garden. The first time I made it, I was just using up the buttermilk left over from a batch of homemade butter. Then it must have been mid-July when I threw a couple of cucumbers into the blender because suddenly they were everywhere (and so needy) and their grassy flavor bonded naturally with the almonds and the green-gold olive oil.

The third time I made the soup I decided to replace the traditional soaked almonds with silky-smooth tahini, because my blender wasn't processing the nuts finely enough to remove the chalkiness; tahini adds a similar nuttiness. And because I was staring at a bunch of ripe eggplants, I topped the soup with a spoonful of grilled eggplant mixed with honey and paprika. Not only does the lush eggplant complement the light milkiness of the soup, it sends up beautiful plumes of paprika-red smoke and spice from the bottom of the bowl.

SERVES 8

Place the bread in a bowl, cover it with cold water, and let sit until fully hydrated, about 30 minutes. Squeeze out the excess water.

Scrub the cucumbers, trim the ends, and cut into thirds. In a blender, combine the cucumbers, garlic, tahini, buttermilk, rosemary, and bread, and process on high speed until smooth. Add the vinegar, 1½ teaspoons salt, and ¾ teaspoon pepper. With the blender running, add ½ cup of the extra-virgin olive oil. Pour into a large pitcher and chill thoroughly in the refrigerator before serving, at least 2 hours.

To make the grilled honey eggplant, preheat a grill or a stovetop grill pan over medium-high heat. Cut the eggplant diagonally into ½-inch-thick slices. Rub both sides of the eggplant slices with canola oil, and salt and pepper, and grill until both sides turn dark brown and the insides have collapsed and lost their cottony texture, about 10 minutes. (It may seem like overcooking, but it will taste divine.) Dice the eggplant into small cubes and mix with the honey, paprika, and remaining 2 tablespoons olive oil.

To serve, pour the chilled gazpacho into small cups and add a dollop of grilled eggplant to each.

3 cups torn chunks of day-old country bread

5 small (13 ounces) cucumbers, or 1 hothouse cucumber

1 large clove garlic

¼ cup tahini

3 cups buttermilk

1 sprig fresh rosemary, leaves only

1 tablespoon sherry vinegar

Fine sea salt and freshly ground black pepper

½ cup plus 2 tablespoons extra-virgin olive oil

1 large Asian eggplant, or ½ large globe eggplant

Canola oil

1½ tablespoons honey

¾ teaspoon sweet paprika

NOTES: *For this soup it's important to use a bread with an open structure and a stiff crust, such as ciabatta—anything that can be squeezed like a sponge after soaking. Also, use your best olive oil.*

If you'd like to use the buttermilk left over from making homemade butter, that recipe is on page 276.

CORN SOUP
with Maple-Lacquered Bacon

12 ears sweet corn, shucked

Fine sea salt and freshly ground
   black pepper

4 slices thick-cut bacon, diced

1 cup diced sweet onion

3 tablespoons salted butter

3 cloves garlic, minced

3 sprigs fresh thyme, minced

½ cup heavy cream

Extra-virgin olive oil, for
   garnish

6 to 8 pieces Maple-Lacquered
   Bacon (page 380)

Chopped scallion, for garnish

NOTES: *To make this vegetarian,
just omit all the bacon. The corn
stock carries the soup without it.*

*In old books of prairie cooking,
sweet corn soups are known as
"green corn soups," green corn being
the name they gave to fresh eating
corn, as opposed to dried field corn.*

Due to our geography and benevolent summer weather, our region
is blessed with a sweet corn harvest that begins in southern Indiana
around the Fourth of July and rolls northward throughout the summer.
Here at the source of the Mississippi, sweet corn generally ripens
during the first or second week of August. The tender kernels of the
first week's harvest are perfectly suited to eating on the cob, slathered
with butter and progressing to stronger-flavored toppings as the week
goes on. By the second week the corn flavor has deepened and the
kernel casings have thickened, which makes it ready for recipes like
Scalloped Corn (page 221) and this golden pureed soup.

The soup's brightness comes from the corn cob stock made from
the scraped cobs, a trick I picked up from working in restaurant
kitchens. After just thirty minutes of simmering, you'll have a stock
that tastes like a sun-scalded field, honey, and milk.

SERVES 6 TO 8

Cut the kernels off the corncobs, and reserve the kernels and
cobs separately. Break the cobs in half.

Make the corn stock: Put the cobs in a pot, add enough cold
water to cover, and season with salt to taste. Heat to simmering
and cook for 1 hour, or until the stock has a strong corn flavor.
Strain and reserve the stock.

Heat a large stockpot over medium heat, add the diced
bacon, and cook until it is shrunken but not crisp, about 5 minutes. Remove the bacon with a slotted spoon and set aside. Add
the onion and the butter to the bacon fat in the pot. Season with
¼ teaspoon each of salt, pepper, and cook until the onions are
very soft but light-colored, about 15 minutes. Add the garlic and
cook for another minute. Add the corn kernels and the thyme,
and season with ½ teaspoon each of salt and pepper. Cook until
the corn has turned bright yellow and no longer tastes raw,
about 10 minutes.

Add 6 cups of the corn stock, the cream, and the reserved
bacon, and cook for 15 minutes. Process the soup, in a few
batches, in a blender until finely pureed, and then push it
through a fine-mesh sieve into a clean saucepan. The soup

should have the pouring consistency of heavy cream. If it is too thick, whisk in some additional corn stock. Keep the soup warm.

Garnish each bowl of soup with a drizzle of olive oil and a piece of maple-lacquered bacon balanced across the bowl.

SMOKY SAUERKRAUT SOUP

A wide line divides the good sauerkraut from the bad. Raw salt-brined sauerkraut (whether homemade or not) is light and tingly, spirited, alive . . . truly the champagne of cabbage. It has none of that dankness of cooked commercial kraut. (And if you want to make your own, the recipe is simple; see page 288.)

In and around Two Inlets, a community founded largely by German immigrants, the stuff needs no lauding. Come early fall, fresh kraut makes the small-talk circuit, and we all register who's just punching down their cabbage and who's already checking their crocks.

A few weeks later, the topic turns to usage. This soup—with its creamy paprika-fired broth, sausage, roasted peppers, and lots of carbonated kraut—is strong enough to both satisfy the fermentation fiends and convert the uninitiated.

When faced with a surplus I drop off the leftovers with my neighbor Marie, who loves sauerkraut soup as much as I do. In fact, we persuaded her to scoop her soup in stop-motion for the photograph here, and the synchronicity of the table and her ring was just pure serendipity.

SERVES 6 TO 8

Heat a stockpot over medium heat. Add the bacon and cook, stirring, until it browns at the edges, about 5 minutes. Remove the bacon from the pot with a slotted spoon and reserve; pour out all but 2 tablespoons of the bacon fat in the pot.

Add the butter, onions, ¼ teaspoon salt, and ½ teaspoon pepper to the pot. Cook over medium-high heat, stirring often, until the onions soften and turn light golden brown, about 20 minutes. Add the garlic and diced roasted peppers, and cook for another 5 minutes. Add the flour and paprika, and stir to incorporate. Immediately add the sauerkraut, chicken stock, and thyme, and bring the soup to a simmer. Cook at a gentle simmer for 30 minutes.

Add the smoked sausage and simmer the soup gently for 20 minutes. Return the bacon to the pot.

Off the heat, whisk the sour cream into the soup. Taste the soup for seasoning, and add the vinegar until the soup has the desired piquancy. Depending on the saltiness of the sauerkraut and the chicken stock you used, add more salt and pepper.

- 10 slices (10 ounces) thick-cut bacon, cut into ½-inch pieces
- 2 tablespoons salted butter
- 2 large Vidalia onions, diced
- Fine sea salt and freshly ground black pepper
- 3 cloves garlic, minced
- 3 red or yellow bell peppers, roasted, peeled, and diced
- 2 tablespoons all-purpose flour
- 2 tablespoons sweet paprika
- 3 cups sauerkraut with juice, store-bought or homemade (page 288)
- 6 cups chicken stock, low-sodium store-bought or homemade (page 299)
- 1 tablespoon minced fresh thyme
- 1 pound (about 4 links) smoked pork sausage, cut into large dice
- ¾ cup sour cream
- 1 to 2 teaspoons apple cider vinegar, to taste

NOTES: *The Austrian chefs I worked for taught me the vinegar trick: In cooked sauerkraut dishes, a few drops of vinegar added at the end revive the sauerkraut's original bite.*

This soup is best made with homemade sauerkraut or Bubbies Sauerkraut (a salt-brined kraut that tastes just like homemade).

Natural Wild Rice

Real wild rice—natural wild rice—isn't black and shiny. The kind that grows wild on the creeks and lakes around me in northern Minnesota has a hue that ranges from light ash to dark maple.

In fact, the jet-black wild rice found in many grocery stores isn't wild at all, but cultivated. A strain of wild rice grown in man-made paddies, it is sometimes sprayed with fertilizers and pesticides to control worms, harvested with combines, and then parched (toasted) mechanically, without the benefit of the traditional wood fire.

Back in 1998 my husband, Aaron, and I wandered into a steam parching plant in Saskatchewan, Canada, stood in the moist cloud that surrounded the shiny black paddy rice as it came off the line, and chatted with the owner about all aspects of his process. That's when I learned that there's zero fragrance involved in a paddy rice operation—and not much romance, either.

Hand-gathered wood-parched wild rice is another story. In just twenty minutes it cooks into a mass of bent-elbowed curls, light and redolent of wood smoke. One of our few native grains, wild rice grows naturally in lakes and streams in the upper Midwest. My Ojibwe neighbors have been harvesting it here for ages, and in their culture wild rice is not only a traditional food but a ceremonial one as well. When you see how perfectly nature needs to collaborate with the rice for it to grow to harvestable size (compliant water levels and weather conditions and such) and then you look out over a thick stand in a good year, the dense stalks almost choking out the creek, the real value of wild rice—beyond filling a belly—starts to set in.

My house near the headwaters of the Mississippi sits on a hill over Indian Creek, a high-concentration wild rice bed even for this area, arguably the epicenter of American wild rice production. Rice has grown in this waterway that winds around my house for as long as anyone can remember. Midsummer, each plant looks like a thin blade of grass poking up out of the water, but by August they have all grown tall, forming thick stands that leave just a thin channel of clear water through the center of the creek. The rice (here the "wild" is often dropped and it's known simply as "rice") usually ripens around the first week of September, after the last burst of heat but before the rainstorms of autumn arrive.

Aaron and his father, Maurice, harvest it in our canoe. Aaron stands in the back and leans on a long duck-billed paddle (traction against the mucky creek bottom) to propel them through the rice. My father-in-law sits in front of him, a knocker (like a short pool cue) in each hand. He uses one to bend the rice over the plastic-lined canoe, and the other to knock in the loose, ripe rice heads. What doesn't make its way into the canoe shatters into the water, thickening the growth for the next year.

When it's really ripe they will bring in a canoe-load—150 pounds or so—in a few hours. And when they've accumulated 300 pounds of freshly gathered "green" rice, we bring it to our parcher. To be edible, and to loosen the rice kernel from its husk, it must be parched until solid.

At contemporary traditional rice camps, Ojibwe tribal members still parch their rice the old way: in cast-iron pots over the fire. They pour the rice into a deep buckskin-lined hole, outfit a willing child with high moccasins, and have him or her stomp on the toasted rice to loosen the husks. The loose chaff is then winnowed away by tossing the rice from shallow baskets high into the breeze.

Many parchers now have a shed full of homemade welded equipment to thrash and winnow the roasted rice. Some fire their barrels with gas, but the best ones have kept the most elemental part of the process, which is the fire.

We've always brought our rice to Lewy DeWandeler, on the edge of the Ponsford prairie, and now we hand our rice over to his son, Richard. Skilled parchers, Lewy and his family are known far and wide for producing delicate grains of rice with a heavy halo of woodsmoke. The DeWandeler operation parches hundreds of thousands of pounds of rice

each year, some of it for companies and some for individuals, some who belong to the tribe and others who apply for permits to harvest rice on nontribal land, as we do.

I remember the first year we came to the parching shed. We lugged in the burlap bags of green rice and Lewy immediately poured them into his large steel barrel parcher, matte black from its years of twirling over the fire. He set it in motion and fed the angry fire another ten-foot log of popple (the local vernacular for "poplar") from the pile just outside.

The air in the shed was impregnated with the smell of burning tree bark and toasting grain, not unlike the steamy aroma of a dark loaf of bread baking. Lewy, rolling around in an old office chair, kept half a mind on the parching as we talked, flipping a switch to speed the barrel with the pointy end of his cane while telling me how he could look at a batch of finished rice and predict—generally—which body of water it came from. "Mitchell Dam rice is short, fat, like coffee beans," he said. "And then there's a lake up north of [Highway] 200, where the rice is blond colored, pretty near transparent." He told me that the lighter the finished (parched) rice, the less time it takes to cook.

Rice like this pops at the bite and has a hard-to-place amphibian grace. I've come to think that it tastes like the extremes of this northern place—the wet, the dry, the cold, the hot—all coming together. You can see this polarity clearly when you stand behind the shed and watch the barrel turn: there's something powerfully conflicted in the way the silver plumes of smoke come off the hot rice and flounce out into the cold fall air.

WILD RICE
and Smoked Chicken Soup

In the upper Midwest, where wild rice grows naturally, you will find countless menu boards with the name of this soup written boldly. Should you find yourself in a crusty gas-stop café, it's a safe order because most versions, even the bad ones, are homemade.

This one has fresh brown mushrooms and smoked chicken—just enough to smolder in the background—and a creamy complexion. Although the smoky pop of the rice itself outshines all its adornments. For a soup whose power rests on a grain, it's full of umami (the "meaty" sixth basic taste) and supplies comfort in an elemental way.

SERVES 8 TO 10

Put the wild rice in a fine-mesh sieve and rinse under running water until the water runs clear. Transfer it to a medium bowl and add water to cover. Skim off any black bits or floating kernels. Pour the rice back into the sieve to drain.

Combine the drained rice, 1½ cups water, and a hearty pinch of salt in a small saucepan and bring to a simmer. Cover tightly, reduce the heat to low, and steam for 20 to 25 minutes, until the liquid is absorbed and the rice kernels have curled into a C shape. (If there's excess liquid in the pot, strain if off.) You should have about 2 cups cooked rice.

Meanwhile, heat a large stockpot over medium heat and add the butter, onion, celery, ½ teaspoon salt, and ½ teaspoon pepper. Cook until the onions are tender and sweet, about 10 minutes. Add the mushrooms, leek, and garlic and cook until the mushrooms have exuded their liquid and it has evaporated, about 5 minutes. Add the flour and cook, stirring until it's completely incorporated. Add the sherry and bring to a boil.

Add the stock, 2 cups water, the cream, and the bay leaves. Bring to a simmer, add the chicken, and cook at a bare simmer for 30 minutes to meld the flavors.

Add the cooked wild rice and cook for 5 minutes longer. Remove the bay leaves, and serve.

¾ cup natural wild rice

Fine sea salt and freshly ground black pepper

6 tablespoons (¾ stick) salted butter

1 large Vidalia onion, diced

3 stalks celery, diced

8 ounces brown cremini mushrooms, diced

1 medium leek, white and light green parts diced (1½ cups)

4 cloves garlic, minced

½ cup dry sherry

¼ cup all-purpose flour

6 cups chicken stock, low-sodium store-bought or homemade (page 299)

¾ cup heavy cream

2 dried bay leaves

2 cups coarsely chopped smoked chicken

NOTES: *I can find smoked chicken in my local grocery store, but it might require a trip to a meat market. If it can't be found, leftover roast chicken is a good substitute.*

During parching, the broken rice (called mizzon*) is divided from the whole rice and reserved for making soup.*

CREAM OF HOMEGROWN CELERY SOUP
with Crabmeat

8 tablespoons (1 stick) salted butter

4 cups chopped celery (from 1 head), inner yellow leaves saved for serving

1 kohlrabi (or turnip), peeled and diced (about 1¼ cups)

1 medium leek, limp outer leaves and top discarded, white and light green parts chopped (about 1¾ cups)

⅛ teaspoon celery seeds

Fine sea salt and freshly ground black pepper

5 tablespoons jasmine rice

4 cups chicken stock, low-sodium store-bought or homemade (page 299) or whey left over from making ricotta (see page 22), or more if needed

3 dried bay leaves

½ cup heavy cream, plus more for serving

¾ cup roughly chopped fresh parsley

1 cup chopped cooked lump crabmeat, cleaned

NOTE: *Lacking your own failed garden celery experiment, you can make this soup with store-bought, of course, or even better, with farmer's market celery or Chinese celery from an Asian market.*

Like Red Delicious apples and grungy russet potatoes, store-bought celery pales in flavor compared to the homegrown. Unfortunately, celery has never grown very well in my own garden, and every fall I vow to give it up. Then I tug on a wimpy outside shoot and suck on it, and its powerful, almost minty green flavor restores my hope that it will do better next summer.

Smooth cream of celery soup is a good vehicle for garden celery because its physical condition—spindly or robust—doesn't matter; it's all about the flavor. Following the script for a classic bisque, I sauté a lot of celery along with a few handfuls of seasonal green vegetables—leeks and kohlrabi—and then add a handful of rice. Once pureed, the swollen rice makes for a velvety texture with minimal use of cream.

This soup's shining moment came last winter, when in an extravagant mood I bought two enormous king crab legs at the grocery store, picked the legs clean of their meat, warmed the crabmeat in butter, and divided it among the warm soup bowls. The grassy garden met the sweet meat from cold waters in the most elegant but natural way.

SERVES 6 TO 8

Heat 6 tablespoons of the butter in a wide pot over medium heat, and add the celery, kohlrabi, leek, and celery seeds. Season with 1 teaspoon salt and ½ teaspoon pepper. Cook until the vegetables soften and look pearly, about 10 minutes. Add the rice, stock, 2 cups water, and the bay leaves. Bring to a simmer and cook until the vegetables are fully tender, about 20 minutes. Add the cream and parsley, and stir to combine. Taste for salt and add more if necessary. Remove the bay leaves.

Puree the soup in two or three batches in a blender (holding a thick towel over the lid to prevent overflow), and then push the puree through a fine-mesh sieve into a clean saucepan. It should have the consistency of heavy cream; if it's too thick, add a little more stock. Keep the soup warm.

Heat the remaining 2 tablespoons butter in a medium skillet over medium heat, and add the crabmeat. Cook gently, until just warmed through, about 3 minutes. Divide the crabmeat and hot soup among soup bowls. Garnish each bowl with a little swirl of cream and the reserved chopped celery leaves.

BEST-EVER BEER CHEESE SOUP

Scoring a table at Steven Brown's newest restaurant, Tilia, feels exactly like walking into a slamming Minneapolis house party: the interior is full of dark embossed wooden trim and built-in alcoves, low ceilings with shiny cream-colored paint, tight corners, shadowy old mirrors, and people and plates of food you're hoping to get to know.

With a mop of silver hair, the loose-hinged gait of an ex-rocker, and a flowing imagination tempered with Plains-state discipline, Steven Brown is widely considered among the best chefs in the Midwest. So when I dropped into Tilia for a lunch with my four-year-old and ordered the beer cheese soup, my expectations were high—I knew it wouldn't come with the traditional popcorn garnish—but still, the bowl of glowing orange liquid that appeared shocked me into the present.

Thankfully thinner than any beer cheese soup I'd had before, this was also bolder, with a mysterious brightness, an inspired gleam of spicy mustard oil in the foreground and a lingering charge of aged cheddar flavor trailing behind it. By the bottom of the bowl, I knew that this recipe needed to be clipped and filed. In fact, I have an urge to laminate it—I love it that much.

SERVES 6

In a large stockpot, melt the butter over medium heat. Add the carrots, peppers, and ½ teaspoon salt and cook, stirring, until the vegetables are soft, about 5 minutes. Add the flour and cook, stirring, until well incorporated, about 5 minutes more.

Add the stock, beer, and half-and-half and cook, whisking often, at a very slow simmer over medium-low heat for 15 minutes.

Add the cheese to the soup by the handful, whisking each batch until smooth. Add the Worcestershire sauce, hot sauce, ½ teaspoon pepper, the nutmeg, mustard, and lemon juice, and stir to combine.

Puree the soup, in batches, in a blender (holding a thick towel over the lid to prevent overflow) until very smooth.

Just before serving, reheat the soup until steaming and taste for seasoning, adding salt as necessary. Ladle it into bowls and garnish each bowl with a swirl of mustard oil and a sprinkle of fresh thyme.

8 tablespoons (1 stick) salted butter

1½ large carrots, diced (about ¾ cup)

¾ cup small-diced piquillo peppers, or ½ large red bell pepper, diced

Fine sea salt and freshly ground black pepper

¾ cup all-purpose flour

4 cups chicken stock, low-sodium store-bought or homemade (page 299)

1 12-ounce bottle of beer, preferably a mildly flavored blond or pale ale

1½ cups half-and-half

12 ounces aged white cheddar cheese, grated

½ tablespoon Worcestershire sauce

Dash of hot sauce

⅛ teaspoon grated nutmeg

2 tablespoons Dijon mustard

2 tablespoons fresh lemon juice

Mustard oil, for serving

Fresh thyme leaves, for garnish

NOTE: *Mustard oil can be found in the Indian foods section of large supermarkets.*

DOUBLE CHICKEN SOUP
with Rolled Noodles

1 pound (4 or 5) bone-in
   chicken thighs, or whatever
   dark chicken parts are decent
   and affordable

1 small onion, halved

3 large carrots: 1 halved,
   2 diced

5 stalks celery: 2 halved,
   3 diced

½ large leek, white and
   light-green parts trimmed
   and diced, tops reserved for
   stock

1 head of garlic, halved
   crosswise

Fine sea salt and freshly ground
   black pepper

4 dried bay leaves

1 teaspoon black peppercorns

12 allspice berries

3 sprigs fresh thyme

Clump of fresh parsley

1 egg

½ cup plus 2 tablespoons
   all-purpose flour, plus more
   for kneading and rolling

1 4-pound chicken

⅛ teaspoon grated nutmeg

I use boxed stock regularly, but when I'm looking for a potent, old-fashioned chicken soup—one with a broth that's powerful enough to cure ailments—I go all-natural.

However, I really don't want to spend an entire day making a rich double chicken broth, and I don't have instant access to an old hen, the traditional foundation of a good chicken noodle soup. Recently, I figured out a solution: If I simmer dark meat chicken pieces, vegetables, garlic, and whole spices for 45 minutes, then submerge an entire chicken into the liquid and poach it slowly, I quickly get a strong, golden broth, a remedy in a bowl.

Once you have the elixir, there's nothing better than setting some chewy, old-fashioned homemade noodles to swim in it. Even though most people have stopped rolling out noodles by hand, it's really no more difficult than rolling out a pie crust. (Although if you'd like to save time on that front, egg noodles are a good substitute.)

SERVES 8 TO 10

Rinse the chicken thighs, place them in a large stockpot, and cover with 12 cups water. Bring to a boil and skim off all the gray foam and rising sludge from the surface of the pot. Add the onion, the carrot halves, the celery halves, the green leek tops, the garlic, 1¼ teaspoons salt, and the bay leaves, peppercorns, allspice, thyme, and parsley. Bring to a simmer, partially cover, and cook at a slow-bubbling simmer for 45 minutes.

While the broth cooks, make the noodles: In a large bowl, whisk together the egg, 2 teaspoons water, and ¼ teaspoon salt. Add the flour and stir with a wooden spoon until fully combined. The dough will be firm and somewhat tacky to the touch. Turn it out onto a floured surface and knead, adding more flour if needed, until smooth, about 5 minutes. Let the dough rest, covered with a clean towel, for 15 minutes.

Dust your counter sparingly with flour and rub a little on your rolling pin. Roll the dough into a large round, stopping every few passes to lift the dough and make sure it isn't sticking too much to the counter, until it is evenly very thin and about 14 inches in diameter. Lift the dough and throw a little flour beneath it and over the top, cover with a clean towel, and leave it to dry out for about 30 minutes.

Rinse the whole chicken and add it the pot of broth (and the neck, too, if it comes with one). Burrow the chicken down into the pot, and with tongs or a long fork, dig up some chicken thighs and large vegetables to lay on top of the chicken to submerge it. Poach at a slow simmer until cooked through and tender, about 40 minutes. Remove the pot from the heat and set it aside for at least 10 minutes to allow the meat to rest and reabsorb the broth.

Strain the contents of the pot through a colander to catch the large pieces, and then strain the broth through a fine-mesh sieve back into the large, clean pot. Skim well to remove any excess fat from the surface of the broth, and return the liquid to a slow simmer. Add the diced celery, diced carrots, and diced leek, and simmer until the vegetables are tender, about 10 minutes.

Bring a medium pot of water to a boil for the noodles.

Pick the meat from the whole chicken (discarding the skin and bones), cut it into bite-size pieces, and add 4 cups of the meat to the soup. (Reserve the rest, along with the extra thigh meat, for making chicken salad. See Notes.)

Dust the top of the dough with flour, roll it into a tight cylinder, and slice it thinly, separating the coils of dough with your fingers and tossing them with flour.

Add some salt and the noodles to the boiling water and poach until they are al dente, 1 to 2 minutes. Drain the noodles and add them to the soup. Taste the soup, add the nutmeg, season with salt and pepper if necessary, and serve.

NOTES: *You will find yourself with some extra chicken meat on your hands, but thankfully this slow-poached meat makes excellent chicken salad. To make the mayonnaise base stand out against the tub of pure-flavored chicken soup in my refrigerator, I nearly always spike it with curry, diced fruit, toasted almonds, cilantro, and a generous squirt of lime.*

My grandma Dion always cut her noodles filament-thin, but they're delicious any which way you slice them.

The recipe for the noodles (halved here) was apparently universally known among cooks and is easy to memorize: 2 eggs, half an eggshell full of water, and a cup of flour. The salt is assumed.

Booya

We parked on the tree-lined street across from the stretched-out flag proclaiming "St. Agnes's Booya here!" and marched up the hill to the park shelter, joining a string of people who were carrying containers for taking home leftover stew, many holding empty Crock-Pots at belly height, the cords dragging behind them.

This year about 350 gallons of Booya were made in the three cartoonishly large cast-iron kettles lined up beneath the pavilion's screened windows. We could have attended any one of the events held in St. Paul during Booya season in October—some people swear by the North Dale Club's Booya, the Roseville Firefighters', or their brother's union's—but we decided to hit the largest of them, the one with the loudest signs.

It's widely believed that the tradition of booya—the long-cooked minestrone-like mixture of beef, chicken, and vegetables—came from French Canadians who settled in Wisconsin and Minnesota ("booya" being a perfect corruption of the French *bouillon*), but Dick Wiggins, stewmaster of the St. Agnes event, thinks it began as a Bohemian, or Hungarian, thing. "There were lots of Hungarian families up and down 7th Street [a main drag in St. Paul]," he said, "and they kept geese in their front yards. The little ones had goose sh** in between their toes. And I tell you, those guys made the best booya."

Like a lot of community food traditions of dubious or contested provenance, the truth has been so larded with jokes and stories as to become nearly untraceable. Start to poke your stick into the meaning of booya and it quickly becomes obvious that the recipes are as reliable as sleep-talk and not nearly as crucial as the sheer quantity of it—and that in addition to stirring, the stewmasters also have a responsibility to feed the fire of mysterious lore surrounding the event. That's what keeps the spirit of the booya alive.

Dick Wiggins begins his preparations the night before the event, with a large quantity of bone-in beef. (Back in the day, it was always oxtail, but as that has become more expensive, most booya-makers now use beef shin. You could also use short ribs.) Any booya worth the name must also include dark-meat chicken, lots of vegetables (rutabaga, carrots, potatoes, onions, corn, green beans), and some chopped tomatoes added early in the game. Herbs and spices are strictly dealer's choice, although most I've tasted reveal a hint of sweet mysterious spice in the plume—either cinnamon or allspice or clove—and like Dick Wiggins's, most include a fair amount of paprika.

Like devoted barbecue masters, Dick and his team moonlight with their concoction, and sometime during the night the stew lost the original definition of its many distinct parts. Originally bred of chicken and beef, after a day of cooking it tasted like their exotic rebel offspring.

The booya line was magnificent, curling back on itself like a chain necklace. Once my eyes became adjusted to the dim light of the park shelter, I could see on the other side of the pavilion another crooked line, this one discharging people holding *pupusas* and roasted corn and bowls of soup, which, upon closer inspection, weren't booya at all, but pozole. It turns out that a large faction of St. Agnes parishioners hail from South and Central America, and they had made their own massive brew. My husband, Aaron, fueled by memories of our favorite *pupuseria* in Grand Island, Nebraska, promptly defected to that line.

We sat at a concrete picnic table and ate our booya, and then we all fought forks over the treats from the other line, especially the excellent pozole, a self-assured potage of smoky chicken, pork, and floating hominy. Given the same overnight start, the stew was just as well knit, and just as bold-flavored and outlandish, as the booya.

When the St. Paul police department marching band started up, banging their beats through the park, so did we, and as rose we felt the full effects of having eaten not one, but two, community stews.

Booya-Pozole
COMMUNITY STEW

4 tablespoons (½ stick) salted butter

½ large sweet onion, diced

1 large carrot, diced

2 stalks celery, diced

½ large red bell pepper, diced

1 jalapeño, minced

Fine sea salt and freshly ground black pepper

4 cloves garlic, minced

1 cup crushed fresh or canned plum tomatoes

2 chicken legs (1½ pounds)

1 pound pork butt steaks

1 tablespoon minced fresh thyme

1 tablespoon sweet paprika

1 3-inch cinnamon stick

4 cups chicken stock, low-sodium store-bought or homemade (page 299)

3 dried bay leaves

1 15.5-ounce can white hominy, drained and rinsed

2 ears fresh sweet corn, kernels cut off the cobs

Chopped fresh cilantro, for serving

It's an extra step, but grilling the chicken and pork before adding them to the stew contributes precious smoky flavor and really makes this hybridized South American–French-Canadian/Hungarian booya sing. This recipe is made for doubling, and in the spirit of booya, feel free to improvise.

SERVES 8 TO 10

Heat a large stockpot over medium heat and add the butter. When it melts, add the onion, carrot, celery, bell pepper, jalapeño, and ½ teaspoon each salt and pepper. Cook, stirring, until the vegetables are soft and sweet, about 20 minutes. Add the minced garlic and crushed tomatoes, and cook until thick and jammy, about 10 minutes.

Meanwhile, preheat a grill or a stovetop grill pan over medium-high heat. Blot dry the chicken legs and the pork, and season with salt and pepper. Grill until everything is well marked on both sides and partially cooked through, about 10 minutes. Cut the pork into 1-inch cubes.

Add the thyme, paprika, cinnamon stick, 1 teaspoon salt, and 1 teaspoon pepper to the stockpot. Add both meats, the stock, 4 cups water, and the bay leaves. Bring to a simmer and cook, partially covered, stirring once in a while, until the pork is very tender when poked with a fork, about 1½ hours.

Remove the chicken legs, pick the meat from the bones, chop it into large pieces, and return it to the soup. Add the hominy and simmer the soup for another 30 minutes to 1 hour, or until everything is really tender and the meat is falling apart. (Mash the pork against the side of the pot to break it up, and don't worry if the chicken looks so tender that it's almost dissolving: that's typical of booya.) Add the corn and cook for 5 more minutes. Remove the bay leaves and cinnamon stick. Taste to check the seasoning, add more salt if needed, and serve, garnished with the chopped cilantro.

(Booya tastes even better if given an overnight rest in the refrigerator before serving, and it can be made ahead and stored in the refrigerator for up to 1 week.)

BEAR *and* PORTER STEW
with Fall Spices

A few years ago, seven hunters were dispersed on our acreage on deer firearms opener. I took on the duties of camp cook, and it was with a hopeful spring in my slipper that I stirred the soup pot that chilly morning, daydreaming of brandied deer liver pâté and of plunging my hands into a ruby tub of venison merguez. Around 11:00 a.m., the hunters filed in for lunch. As they silently shucked off safety orange bibs and pried off boots, I realized that I hadn't heard a single shot. It would be the most vicious shutout in history.

So it turned out to be a good thing that John had brought the bear leg. When he heaved it onto the counter the night before, I had smiled a sweet thanks but secretly hoped I wouldn't have to cook it.

I regarded the dark claret–colored meat on my cutting board with a suspicious eye, but I quickly came around to it when it was in the stewpot. After a few hours of gentle simmering, the bear was melting at the bite yet still succulent. And it tasted deep, with a flavor that can be described as falling somewhere between beef and pork, but maybe with a tumbler of port wine on the side—not unlike wild boar.

And now I can say: If young and reared on berries and finished on Twizzlers (the classic bear bait), bear makes a really great stew, especially when it wallows in a rich brew of porter—fall's stoutest beer—exotic spices, and dried fruit.

SERVES 6 TO 8

Heat the butter in a large stockpot over medium-high heat. Add the onions and cook until browned on the edges, about 5 minutes. Reduce the heat to medium and cook until the onions are soft and golden brown, about 25 minutes.

Add the ginger, diced tomatoes, and 1 teaspoon of the salt, and cook, stirring, until you have a soft sludge, about 10 minutes. Add the cardamom, coriander, cumin, and paprika, stir to incorporate, and then add the porter, chicken stock, and bay leaves.

Add the meat to the pot. Bring the stew to a simmer and skim the foam from the surface. Add the remaining ½ teaspoon salt and the pepper.

Reduce the heat and simmer the stew slowly, partially covered, until the meat is very tender, about 3½ hours. Add the raisins, remove the bay leaves, and serve, garnished with the toasted almonds.

4 tablespoons salted butter

5 cups large-diced sweet onion (2 large vidalias)

2 tablespoons minced fresh ginger

2 cups peeled, diced fresh tomatoes

1½ teaspoons fine sea salt

½ teaspoon ground cardamom

2 teaspoons ground coriander

1 teaspoon ground cumin

2 teaspoons sweet paprika

1 12-ounce bottle porter beer

4 cups chicken stock, low-sodium store-bought or homemade (page 299)

4 dried bay leaves

3 pounds boneless shoulder bear roast or beef chuck roast, cut into 2-inch cubes

1 teaspoon freshly ground black pepper

½ cup golden raisins

Toasted slivered almonds, for serving

NOTES: *If bear cannot be found, a bison or beef chuck roast is a good substitute.*

This is great served alone, with crusty bread, but also wonderful over wide pappardelle noodles.

SMOKED SARDINE CAESAR
with Salumi *and* Pan Croutons

3 cloves garlic: 1 finely grated, 2 smashed

2 small smoked sardines (kippers)

½ cup mayonnaise

3 tablespoons fresh lemon juice

Fine sea salt and freshly ground black pepper

5 tablespoons extra-virgin olive oil

1½ cups grated Parmesan cheese

3 tablespoons salted butter

1 teaspoon sweet paprika

1½ cups torn chunks of ciabatta bread

12 cups torn romaine lettuce (from about 1 head)

3 ounces *salumi* (cured Italian salami), cut into wide matchsticks

2 tablespoons chopped fresh mint

This is not only a winter salad for grocery-store days but also an unapologetic vehicle for the excellent Italian-influenced *salumi* being made from our homegrown Midwestern hogs. In a crosscut slice of well-made salami (which can now be found in any number of urban gastronomic hot spots across the region), the colors don't fade together. Instead, the pattern of gleaming white fat pops against the dark burgundy night of the cured meat—making its case, I imagine, for what starry heights a well-ranged pig, ancient technique, and a little controlled fermentation can achieve.

SERVES 8

For the dressing, combine the grated garlic and smoked sardines in a small bowl and mash to a rough paste with a fork. Add the mayonnaise, lemon juice, ¼ teaspoon salt, ½ teaspoon pepper, 3 tablespoons of the olive oil, and ½ cup of the Parmesan cheese, and mix together. Thin the dressing with a tablespoon or so of water, until it has the consistency of thick cream.

For the croutons, heat a large heavy skillet over medium heat. Add the remaining 2 tablespoons olive oil to coat the bottom of the pan, and then add the smashed garlic cloves, butter, paprika, and bread. Season with salt and pepper and cook, stirring often, until the bread turns crisp throughout and darkens on the edges, about 5 minutes. Discard the garlic, and allow the croutons to cool.

To serve, place the lettuce in a bowl and season with a little salt and pepper. Add enough dressing to coat, and then add the *salumi*, remaining 1 cup Parmesan cheese, the croutons, and the mint, and toss.

SEVEN-LAYER RUSSIAN SALAD

As folksy, cheerful, and totable as it is, a stacked salad is the opposite of trendy; it's not something you make to match contemporary cravings, but rather something you *remake*, one foot anchored someplace else.

I sampled this one at Txikito, chefs Alex Raij and Eder Montero's restaurant in New York City, where the cuisine is a tribute to the Basque region, Eder's homeland. This traditional *ensalada rusa*, or Russian salad, came to Alex's mind because of the infamous one that Eder's Aunt Lourdes brings each year to the family Christmas in Bilbao, Spain—or then again, maybe because it resembled the Midwestern layered potato salads that her Jewish Argentinian mother made when she was growing up in Minneapolis. (She says that her mother gave most typical Midwestern dishes a warm Argentinian spin.)

But if you brought this salad to a potluck in the Midwest, no one would pin it for Russian or Basque. They'd say, "Seven-layer salad—thanks!," find a serving spoon for it, and drop it in an empty spot on the table.

Alex's version has layers of potatoes, carrots, beets, peas, and hard-cooked eggs, and—because we're talking about Spain—tuna packed in olive oil, each gently mixed with a flavorful homemade mayonnaise. It's the perfect salad to make ahead and tote to a potluck, and its dramatic good looks make it worth your search for the perfect serving bowl.

SERVES 8 TO 10

Preheat the oven to 350°F.

Slice ½ inch off the top of the head of garlic and put the head in the center of a piece of foil. Top with the tablespoon of olive oil, wrap up the sides of the foil to make a packet, and bake the garlic until soft and fragrant, about 30 minutes. When cool enough to handle, push the garlic cloves from their skin and mash with the side of a knife. Set aside.

Put the beets in a saucepan and add water to cover by a couple of inches. Generously salt the water and bring to a simmer over medium heat. Partially cover and simmer until the beets are tender, about 45 minutes, depending on their size. Drain, and when cool enough to handle, twist them one by one in a paper towel to rub off the skin.

RECIPE CONTINUES

---

1 head of garlic

¾ cup plus 1 tablespoon extra-virgin olive oil

2 medium (10 ounces) beets

Fine sea salt and freshly ground black pepper

2 small (8 ounces) Yukon Gold potatoes

2 large carrots, halved

8 large eggs

1½ cups frozen peas

1 large egg yolk

4 tablespoons red wine vinegar

2 teaspoons Dijon mustard

1 teaspoon honey

¾ cup canola oil

2 5-ounce cans tuna packed in olive oil

Sweet paprika, for garnish

Chopped fresh parsley, for garnish

NOTE: *Here's my recipe for mock homemade mayo, a time-saver: To 2 cups Kraft Homestyle or Hellmann's mayonnaise add 2 tablespoons fresh lemon juice, 6 tablespoons extra-virgin olive oil, and a hefty pinch each of salt and pepper.*

Fill another saucepan with water and add the potatoes. Season with salt, bring to a simmer over medium heat, and cook just until easily pierced, about 25 minutes. Lift out the potatoes with a slotted spoon. Add the carrots to the water and simmer until they're just tender, 5 to 7 minutes. Lift out.

Add the whole eggs to the water, and simmer for 3 minutes. Then remove the pan from the heat and let them sit in the water for 10 minutes. Drain, crack the eggshells, and cover again with cold water. Peel the eggs underwater.

Place the peas in a bowl and let thaw.

Meanwhile, make the mayonnaise: In a medium bowl combine the egg yolk, 1 tablespoon of the vinegar, the mustard, the honey, ¾ teaspoon salt, and ½ teaspoon pepper. Combine the canola oil and the remaining ¾ cup olive oil in a spouted measuring cup, and begin adding the oil drop by drop, whisking constantly, forming a smooth emulsion. When it gets thick, add 1 teaspoon water and continue whisking and dribbling in the oil until the mayonnaise is full and shiny. Add the mashed roasted garlic and whisk to combine.

To make the salad, drain off any excess oil from the tuna, put it in a small bowl, and add 3 tablespoons of the mayonnaise and a good pinch of black pepper. Arrange the tuna in the bottom of a glass bowl.

Peel the potatoes and cut them into very small dice. Dice the carrots the same size, and combine the two in a bowl. Add 6 tablespoons of the mayonnaise, 1 tablespoon of the vinegar, and plenty of salt and pepper to taste. Drop the carrot and potato mixture over the tuna.

Mix the peas with 3 tablespoons of the mayonnaise, and season with salt and pepper to taste. Drop the peas over the potato mixture.

Slice the beets thinly and lay them out on a plate. Season well with salt and pepper, and drizzle with the remaining 2 tablespoons vinegar. Arrange the beets in overlapping concentric layers over the peas.

Roughly chop the hard-boiled eggs, and mix them with 6 tablespoons of the mayonnaise and salt and pepper. Arrange the egg salad over the beets.

Thickly dust the top of the salad with sweet paprika, sprinkle with parsley, and serve right away (or refrigerate for up to 2 days).

KALE SALAD
with Fresh Ricotta *and* Black Walnuts

3 tablespoons minced shallots

2 tablespoons fresh lemon juice

1½ tablespoons sherry vinegar or white wine vinegar

5 tablespoons sunflower oil

Fine sea salt and freshly ground black pepper

6 cups thinly sliced kale (from about 2 bunches)

¾ cup broken black walnuts (or regular walnuts)

12 fresh sage leaves

¾ cup fresh ricotta (page 22)

NOTE: *For this salad Jonny always toasts the nuts in a pan on the stovetop because he tends to forget about the nuts toasting in the oven, as we all do, and you don't want to risk burning precious black walnuts.*

Salads of julienned raw kale have been circulating in recent years, and this one, from Jonny Hunter of the Underground Food Collective in Madison, Wisconsin, highlights one of the Midwest's hardest-won ingredients—black walnuts.

As nuts go, the black walnut is about as obdurate as they come. The trees grow in much of the Midwest, but the nuts are rare because their prickly black outer husks famously foil the nutcracker (although everyone says that running over them with a heavy truck will crack them). And once you crack the nut, they must be painstakingly hand-plucked from their shells, resulting in small priceless nuggets of sweet meat. In fantasy, shelling black walnuts is a sitting-by-the-woodstove-all-winter-long sort of occupation, like tatting or whittling.

In reality you can just buy them at the store, or at the farmer's market, already shelled—and you should do so when you see them, because they have an intoxicating apricot scent. Their warm fruitiness stands up well here to the kale, putting a decidedly Midwestern spin on an Italian-inflected salad.

Jonny says that this salad is best when made with young, tender kale and locally made cold-pressed sunflower oil, which has a milder, nuttier flavor than olive oil.

SERVES 4 TO 6

For the vinaigrette, mix together the shallots, lemon juice, vinegar, 3 tablespoons of the sunflower oil, and ½ teaspoon each of salt and pepper in a small bowl.

Put the kale in a large bowl and toss with the vinaigrette.

Combine the walnuts and the remaining 2 tablespoons sunflower oil in a small skillet set over low heat. Season with a pinch each of salt and pepper and cook, stirring often, until the nuts turn a shade darker and smell fragrant, 5 to 7 minutes. Scoop the nuts from the oil and add the sage leaves to the skillet.

Cook, gently stirring, until the leaves turn crisp, about 3 minutes. Remove the sage leaves, saving them for garnish, and add the oil in the skillet to the kale salad.

To serve, arrange the kale salad on a shallow platter. Drop dollops of ricotta cheese over the kale, and scatter the toasted black walnuts and crisp sage leaves over the salad.

FIRE-*and*-ICEBERG SALAD

At my child's preschool they sometimes serve miniature piles of torn iceberg lettuce tossed with French dressing. I can understand why: The crunch is fun and the dressing candy-sweet.

When made at home, where you can control the sugar and add some heat and smoked paprika, French dressing is a more interesting concoction. I like it spicy, because I find that a little chile fire goes a long way toward igniting the cold crisp heart of the iceberg. Ripped radicchio—raging pink—adds color and maturity.

SERVES 6 TO 8

For the dressing, combine the garlic, tomato paste, both paprikas, honey, vinegar, and lemon juice in a small bowl, and stir to combine. Whisk in 6 tablespoons of the olive oil. Season with the cayenne, ¼ teaspoon salt, and ⅛ teaspoon pepper. Pour the dressing into a small pitcher for serving at the table.

To toast the walnuts, combine them with the remaining 1 tablespoon olive oil and the tablespoon of butter in a small skillet set over medium-low heat. Season with salt and pepper. Cook, tossing regularly, until the walnuts are fragrant and have turned golden brown, about 5 minutes. Let the nuts cool.

Tear the iceberg lettuce and the radicchio into bite-size pieces, and combine in a large salad bowl. Add the celery and the walnuts (cooking fat and all), and toss to combine. Sprinkle the blue cheese over the top and serve immediately, passing the dressing alongside.

½ clove garlic, finely grated

1 teaspoon tomato paste

1 teaspoon sweet paprika

½ teaspoon smoked paprika

1 tablespoon honey

2 tablespoons red or white wine vinegar

1 tablespoon fresh lemon juice

7 tablespoons extra-virgin olive oil

⅛ teaspoon cayenne pepper, or to taste

Fine sea salt and freshly ground black pepper

½ cup (2 ounces) walnut halves or pieces

1 tablespoon salted butter

½ large head (1 pound) iceberg lettuce, outer leaves removed

1 small head (7 ounces) radicchio

1 light green celery heart, thinly sliced

4 ounces blue cheese, crumbled

NOTE: *For perfect crispness, let each person drizzle the dressing over his or her own salad. Tossing the iceberg with the dressing before it reaches the table causes the lettuce to wilt.*

GRILLED MUSHROOM SALAD
with Toasted Almonds

7 ounces shiitake mushrooms

1 clove garlic, finely grated

7 tablespoons extra-virgin
olive oil

Fine sea salt and freshly ground
black pepper

2 teaspoons sweet paprika

½ cup slivered or sliced
almonds

1 tablespoon salted butter

2 tablespoons fresh lemon juice

Pinch of sugar

10 cups mesclun greens

NOTE: *You can make the marinated grilled mushrooms well ahead
of time. In the summer, grill the
mushrooms outside. In the winter, I
char them on a stovetop grill pan or,
in a pinch, in a hot cast-iron pan.*

The alchemy of these paprika-and-lemon-marinated shiitakes sizzling on metal makes them a close vegetarian second to great barbecue. Smoky and tart, they're definitely a force, especially when paired with pan-fried almonds and baby garden greens.

To add extra savoriness, the nuts here are given a sort of butter-obsessed Midwestern finish: I add a bit of butter to the oil and nuts in my small cast-iron pan, cooking until the butter foams up into a canopy, under which the nuts slowly turn golden and crisp. Then I pour the lukewarm nuts, butter, and oil onto the salad. You might think that the butter would stiffen upon contact with the cold greens, but it doesn't. Somehow it rounds out the entire venture.

SERVES 6 TO 8

Trim off and discard the mushroom stems. Wipe the caps with a damp cloth. Combine the garlic, 3 tablespoons of the olive oil, ¼ teaspoon salt, and 1 teaspoon of the paprika in a medium bowl. Add the mushroom caps, toss, and marinate for at least 20 minutes, and as long as a couple of hours.

To toast the almonds, combine them with 1 tablespoon of the olive oil, the butter, ⅛ teaspoon salt, and ¼ teaspoon pepper in a small pan. Cook over medium-low heat, stirring, until the almonds turn golden brown and crisp, about 5 minutes.

Preheat a grill or a cast-iron grill pan over medium-high heat. Grill the mushrooms, starting gill-side down, until cooked through and well marked on both sides, about 7 minutes in all.

Drop the mushrooms back into the marinating bowl to catch any juices. Then transfer them to a cutting board, chop roughly, and return to the bowl. Add the lemon juice, sugar, remaining 1 teaspoon paprika, salt and pepper to taste, and the remaining 3 tablespoons olive oil.

Just before serving, pile the greens into a serving bowl, and season them lightly with salt and pepper. Scatter the almonds over all, and toss with the mushroom and enough of the dressing to lightly coat.

COUNTRY CREAM DRESSING
with Garden Greens

¼ cup sour cream

1 teaspoon sugar

½ tablespoon apple cider vinegar

1 tablespoon fresh lemon juice

1 teaspoon minced fresh tarragon or chives

Fine sea salt and freshly ground black pepper

10 cups mesclun or mixed garden greens

1½ cups cherry tomatoes, halved

1 small garden onion or shallot, thinly sliced

⅓ cup (lightly packed) torn fresh basil

When my grandmother talked about the summer salads they ate on the farm when she was young, I could assume two things: The greens were leafy, soft, and freshly pulled from the garden, and the dressing was made with cream or, possibly, homemade soured cream. In central Minnesota in the 1940s, olive oil was an ingredient on the fringe, but dairy they had in abundance.

This dressing is a rural classic, and begins with a dollop of sour cream, to which you can add or subtract flavorings at will. Light and luscious at the same time, this is a dressing to celebrate tender summer lettuces. I like to add fresh herbs, garden cherry tomatoes, and thin slivers of fresh onion to the mix.

SERVES 6

For the dressing, stir together the sour cream, sugar, vinegar, lemon juice, tarragon, and ¼ teaspoon each of salt and pepper.

Just before serving, put the greens in a large bowl and season lightly with salt and pepper. Toss with enough dressing to lightly coat. Then add the tomatoes, onion, and basil, and toss again.

The seven Hesch sisters, Buckman, Minnesota

GREENS *with* Birch-Mushroom Dressing, Fried Pecans, *and* Pickled Shallots

I made this salad the day my friends Marsha and Chuck gave me some of their foraged and dried candy cap mushrooms in trade for a bag of my own wood-parched wild rice. I stowed the candy caps in a lidded quart jar in the pantry, but somehow their strong woodsy-sweet scent—like the smoking end of a cinnamon stick—managed to escape into the air.

It was early spring and we were boiling birch sap outside to make syrup, and in the course of the day the two scent trails converged in the kitchen. When dinnertime rolled around, I made this birch-mushroom dressing, a concoction that taught me it takes just a few dried mushrooms to return sweet tree syrup (either birch or maple) to its forest roots.

SERVES 6 TO 8

For the pickled shallots, peel them and thinly slice them crosswise. Rinse in a fine-mesh sieve and shake dry. In a small bowl combine the shallots, ½ teaspoon salt, ¼ teaspoon pepper, ¼ cup of the sugar, and the lime juice. Let sit for at least 30 minutes and as long as a day.

Pour boiling water over the dried mushrooms in a small bowl, and then cool, squeeze them, and chop finely.

For the pecans, lightly coat a plate with butter, and set it aside. Heat a small skillet over medium heat and sprinkle the bottom evenly with the remaining 2 tablespoons sugar. Cook until the sugar melts and turns amber brown, about 1 minute. Add the butter and the pecans, and quickly stir together until the nuts are coated with caramel. Pour the pecans onto the plate, spread them out with a spoon, and don't touch them until they are cool. Carefully wash out the hot skillet.

For the dressing, heat the small skillet over medium heat. Add 2 tablespoons of the olive oil, the garlic, and the mushrooms, and cook until the garlic sizzles and cooks through, about 1 minute. Add the sherry and pour into a bowl. Add the lemon juice, sherry vinegar, birch or maple syrup, ¼ teaspoon each of salt and pepper, and the remaining 1 tablespoon olive oil.

In a large bowl, toss the salad greens with a bit of salt and pepper, and enough of the mushroom-maple dressing to lightly coat. Add the strained pickled shallots and pecorino, and serve.

2 small shallots

Fine sea salt and freshly ground black pepper

¼ cup plus 2 tablespoons sugar

⅓ cup fresh lime juice

About 2 cups boiling water

Small handful (⅛ ounce) dried mushrooms

1 tablespoon salted butter, plus more for the plate

½ cup pecans

3 tablespoons extra-virgin olive oil

1 clove garlic, minced

1 tablespoon dry sherry

1 tablespoon fresh lemon juice

1 tablespoon sherry vinegar

2 teaspoons birch syrup (page 274) or maple syrup

10 cups (about 5 ounces) mixed greens

1 cup freshly grated pecorino cheese

NOTES: *If you don't have candy caps on hand (understandable), substitute dried morels or dried porcini mushrooms.*

This recipe calls for cooking the dressing, which the dried mushrooms need, and though it may look fussy, cooking a few things in a small hot pan gives any salad a lively jolt.

LAKE
FISH

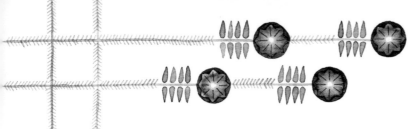

Freshwater fish-eating is something of an underground pleasure in the Midwest. The best fish caught in our lakes and rivers isn't sold in stores.

There are exceptions to that, of course. Here in Minnesota some commercial fishing comes out of the Great Lakes, the Red Lake Band of Ojibwe sell freshly caught walleye and perch, and of course there are fish farms. But when it comes to lake fish, the story throughout the region is fairly similar: limited commercial fishing, lots of recreational fishing, and lots of fresh eating. And so the story of the fish we eat follows that script, making for a table tradition that begins with a flopping fish, and feels all the more elemental and celebratory for it.

In fact, the only way you would know that people eat a lot of fish around here is to talk to them. Throw out an opinion, something controversial like "northern pike is better eating than walleye" (knowing full well that walleye is revered, and northerns cursed for their Y-shaped bone structure), and watch the opinions fly. That's when you learn who likes to eat bass (only fresh, though, not frozen), who makes pickled northern, who traps crayfish, who actually eats eelpout. And you'll hear just about everyone say that a bucket of bluegills is the best treat you could ever have.

For flavor, lake fish has a delicacy unmatched by ocean fish; those in the sole family come the closest. Very much in step with the prevailing flavors of Midwestern food, our cold water–raised lake creatures have a subtle, clean taste—even our lake crayfish taste more pristine and less funky than their southern counterparts. All of them—the trout, the walleye, and the lake herring—are best appreciated with monkish reverence: poached, fried, or grilled, with butter and/or lemon. And honestly, that's usually how most people eat them here.

I pay that tradition my respects with a few recipes: Lake Trout with Kitchen Butter Sauce, Cracker-Crusted Panfish (because junky butter crackers and panko make a peerless crust) and Butter-Basted Walleye with Thyme and Garlic. The others are for special dinners on the occasion of a large harvest.

FRIED SMELT
with Sour Pickle Sauce

In spring in northern regions across the United States, you can't throw a rock without hitting a smelt fry. Around here, local churches and service organizations—Legions, Eagles Clubs, Shriners, and the like—get their fish from the rivers surrounding Lake Superior and fry them up by the thousands. To local crowds caught between two angling seasons (after ice fishing but before lake fishing opens up), the smelt fry is easily the hottest address in town.

Even though they're small, smelt aren't buttery like sardines or lake herring; they're flaky and as soft as the first day of spring, with silver skins that twinkle under the overhead fluorescent lights of the hall.

At home I like to wrap the smelt in a light cornmeal jacket, fry them in butter, and serve them with a tartar sauce that leans hard on the pickle.

SERVES 4 TO 6

For the sauce, finely chop the pickles and put them in a bowl. Add the brine, mayonnaise, dill, ¼ teaspoon salt, and the cayenne.

Rinse the smelt and blot them dry. In a wide shallow bowl, whisk together the eggs and cream. In another wide shallow bowl, combine the cornmeal, cake flour, 2 teaspoons salt, and ½ teaspoon pepper.

Heat a large cast-iron pan over medium-high heat.

While the pan is heating, bread the smelt: Dip a handful of fish into the egg mixture, let any excess drain off, and then drop them into the flour mixture. Shake the bowl to coat them evenly, and then toss the breaded smelt onto a platter. Repeat until you have a good pile.

Add a thin layer of canola oil and a thick pat of butter to the pan. When it's hot, add the smelt. Fry until brown and crispy on each side, about 3 minutes. Serve, hot from the pan, with the pickle sauce. Repeat with the remaining fish.

3 small brined fermented pickles, such as Bubbies or homemade (page 280)

3 tablespoons pickle brine (from the pickle jar)

1 cup mayonnaise

3 tablespoons chopped fresh dill

Fine sea salt and freshly ground black pepper

¼ teaspoon cayenne pepper, or to taste

1 pound smelt, cleaned and gutted

2 large eggs

¼ cup heavy cream

½ cup fine yellow cornmeal

½ cup cake flour

Canola oil, for frying

Butter, for frying

LAKE TROUT
with Kitchen Butter Sauce

11 tablespoons salted butter, cold, cut into pats

3 cloves garlic, smashed

2 sprigs fresh thyme

¼ cup heavy cream

Fine sea salt and freshly ground black pepper

2 teaspoons sherry vinegar or wine vinegar

1½ tablespoons sliced fresh chives

1 teaspoon minced fresh tarragon

2½ pounds lake trout, filleted and cut into 6 pieces

Flour, preferably Wondra, for dusting the fish

Canola oil, for sautéing

NOTES: *If lake trout is unavailable, substitute rainbow trout or brook trout or arctic char.*

Wondra flour is found in most grocery stores labeled as "gravy flour."

Any kitchen with a French backbone makes *beurre monté,* or emulsified butter. A cousin to beurre blanc (but even simpler), it's typically used by the vat as a medium for heating up shelled lobster and shrimp, and by the teaspoonful for adding gloss to sautéed vegetables. It's so basic to professional cooks that it barely registers as a recipe at all.

I never thought to make it at home, either—until the day I brought home an entire lake trout from Dockside Fish Market in Grand Marais, Minnesota, a fish that just called out for a hot pan and a simple butter sauce.

Lake trout has the same warm tint, succulent flesh, and nearly scaleless skin as the other fish in its family: arctic char and brook trout. But no matter how fresh it is or how neatly you fillet it, lake trout always has a raggedy, roughshod look to it. To stay neat, it needs its skin. Which works, because its skin is fine-pored and crisps to brittleness.

To ensure crunchy skin, let the fillets ride out on the skin side in a cast-iron pan for what seems like almost too long before flipping them. Cook the flesh side ever so briefly before setting the fish face-down in the warm platter of vinegar-spiked herbed butter sauce, crisped skin pointing into the air.

This meal, nearly perfect on its own, turns a corner if you serve it with boiled fresh potatoes.

SERVES 6

Preheat the oven to 200°F.

For the kitchen butter sauce, add 1 tablespoon of the butter to a small saucepan set over medium heat. Add the garlic and thyme, and cook, stirring, until fragrant, about 3 minutes. Add the cream and bring to a simmer, cooking until it thickens and reduces, 2 to 3 minutes. Gradually add the rest of the cold butter, whisking to incorporate one pat before adding the next, until the entire sauce is smooth and thick. Season to taste with salt and pepper. Discard the garlic and thyme, and then whisk in the vinegar, chives, and tarragon. Keep the sauce warm on a diffuser, or set over low heat; don't let it come to a boil or it will break.

Warm a platter for the fish in the oven.

Heat two large heavy-bottomed skillets over high heat. Lay the fish out on a baking sheet and blot both sides dry. Season both sides of the fish with salt and pepper, and dust the skin side with flour. Add a film of canola oil to the skillets, and when they're hot, add the fish, skin-side down. Cook over medium-high heat until the skin crisps and browns completely, 5 to 7 minutes. As the opaque evidence of doneness creeps up the fillet, the fish will look about two-thirds done, but the top will still be raw. Flip the fish, remove the skillets from the heat, and let the fish sit on the flesh side just a minute.

Pour the warm butter sauce onto the warm platter. Arrange the fish skin-side up on the butter sauce, and serve immediately.

HERRING
with La Quercia Prosciutto

Petite and rich, lake herring (aka cisco) shares a skin-deep resemblance, but no real relation, to Atlantic herring. This member of the *Salmonidae* family, which also includes trout, salmon, and whitefish, once teemed in all of the Great Lakes. It decreased in numbers during the twentieth century but in the last decade has rebounded in Lake Huron and Lake Superior.

Lake herring have dense, buttery flesh, delicate but also hefty enough to balance a tangy prosciutto wrapping. Conveniently, they also tend to hit the shore in single-serving size.

This is a good campfire recipe, the kind of thing that tastes even better when eaten on the lakeshore, pinched off in chunks with your fingers.

SERVES 2 TO 4

Preheat a grill to medium-high heat.

Rinse the fish and blot dry. Season the fish with salt and pepper on both sides, and stuff the cavities with a couple of lemon slices and 2 sprigs of thyme each.

Lay 2 basil leaves over each fish, and then wrap the prosciutto tightly around the fish in overlapping slices. Rub the entire fish, including the prosciutto, with a thin layer of olive oil.

When the grill is hot (you can't hold your hand above it for more than 5 seconds), wipe the grate with an oil-dipped towel and deposit the fish on it, prettiest side down. Grill the herring until the doneness creeps up the sides and the underside is lightly charred, about 5 minutes. Flip them over and cook until the underside is lightly charred and the center of the fish tests juicy and hot when poked with a long, thin fork, about 5 minutes. (If the outside has cooked at a greater rate than the inside, continue cooking over lower heat.)

Remove the herring to a plate and serve with the lemon quarters.

2 medium (1 to 1½ pounds total) lake herring, scaled and gutted

Fine sea salt and freshly ground black pepper

2 small lemons: 1 halved and cut into thick half-moons, 1 quartered

4 sprigs fresh thyme

4 large fresh basil leaves

6 large slices prosciutto, preferably La Quercia Americano

Extra-virgin olive oil

Herring Roe

In the late fall at Dockside Fish Market in Grand Marais, Shele and Harley Toftey harvest and sell herring roe. Last year I got a ringside seat to watch Harley roll the plump orange sacks out of a school of freshly caught lake herring.

They clean and salt the petite eggs to make a herring caviar, which they call Lake Superior Gold. It is indeed golden, with a warm sunrise tint and the same pristine, clean flavor possessed by all of the fish that exit the frigid waters of Lake Superior. Most fans of herring caviar simply spoon the tiny, crunchy eggs onto crackers—but you can also dollop them on hot, crispy potato pancakes (page 252).

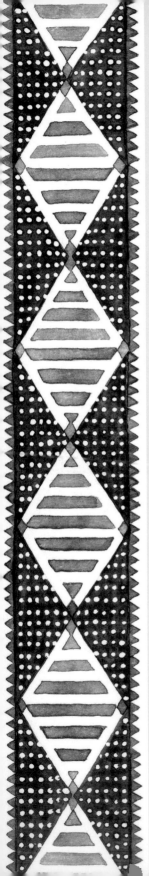

Parma, Iowa

The delicacy of the herring recipe (page 111) is pegged equally on the tender herring and the fine prosciutto, both of which can be obtained in the Midwest. La Quercia in Norwalk, Iowa, turns out world-class Italian-style cured ham from well-raised Midwestern hogs.

When I stopped at the nearby Cheese Shop in Des Moines, Iowa—a veritable hub for the best Midwestern raw materials—I had the chance to try La Quercia's top-flight prosciuttos from heritage breeds: the woodsy Berkshire; the delectably smoky speck; the buttery dark, cherry-red Tamworth, sliced from a chunk as round as a football; and then finally, for what you might call dessert, some silken sheaves of lardo (cured pork backfat) thrown to melt on hot toast and gold-plated with good olive oil.

Having fallen in love with the famed local prosciutto when they lived in Parma, Italy, La Quercia's owners, Herb and Kathy Eckhouse, began researching and testing with the finest of Iowa's heritage-breed hogs raised on small farms. Years later, they continue to personally salt the approximately 40,000 legs of cured ham that La Quercia makes each year, so as to control—via intuition and experience—just how much seasoning the finished product receives.

How right it feels to say that some of the finest prosciutto in America is being produced in the middle of a farm field in central Iowa, in the largest pig-producing state in the Union. This might have sounded unlikely ten years ago during the "Other White Meat" era, but now it's clear that Herb and Kathy Eckhouse were pretty wise to squint at their Iowa landscape and see the potential in its horizon.

CRACKER-CRUSTED PANFISH
with Two Sauces

When you're catching it, fish is the only thing you want to eat for breakfast.

As children, my brothers and cousins and I caught lots of panfish off the end of our dock in the morning. When we had a full stringer of perch and bluegills, we'd clean them in the old screened fish-cleaning house that sat on the hill behind the cabin. We scraped off the scales with kitchen forks (flicking fish eyes at each other from their tips) and filleted the small fish with paring knives, using a hose to wash them clean. Our mothers dredged the fillets in egg and crushed butter crackers and fried them up for our late breakfast. All in all, the fish was maybe an hour from lake to plate, and we ate them with our hands, some of us dipping them into ketchup, some of us eating them plain, the shell of the crust breaking to release the juice from those thin fillets into our mouths.

These days I like to serve fried fish with a couple of sauces: a quick and very surprising sauce (which I took away from Chef David Bouley's kitchen) made of brown butter, caramelized ketchup, and freshly squeezed ginger juice; and a peanut sauce made of crushed peanuts, orange juice, and minced cilantro.

If fresh fish isn't available, the same breading and sauces are also good with shrimp.

SERVES 4

Combine the cracker crumbs and panko in a pie plate, and season with a hefty pinch each of salt and pepper. In a small bowl, whisk together the eggs and milk.

If the fillets are large, cut them in half.

Mix together ½ teaspoon each of salt and pepper in a small bowl, and season both sides of the fish fillets with the mixture.

Pour canola oil into a large cast-iron skillet set over medium-high heat until it is ¼ inch deep. Heat until a pinch of bread crumbs sizzles in the oil.

While the oil heats, bread the fish: Working with 2 or 3 pieces at a time, dip the fish fillets in the egg mixture, hold them up to drain off the excess, and then drop them into the cracker meal mixture. Shake the pie plate of crumbs to coat the fish, reach

RECIPE CONTINUES

1 cup very fine crumbs from butter crackers, such as Ritz (from about 1 sleeve)

1 cup panko bread crumbs

Fine sea salt and freshly ground black pepper

2 large eggs

2 tablespoons milk

1½ pounds filleted panfish, such as bluegill, perch, or catfish (preferably skin removed)

Canola oil, for frying

Ginger Ketchup (page 114)

Spicy Peanut Vinaigrette (page 115)

NOTE: *Crush the crackers to a fine meal in a food processor or by putting them in a plastic bag and running over them with a rolling pin.*

beneath each piece to flip it over in the crumbs, and press the crumbs firmly onto the fish to make sure that each piece has a significant crumb cover. Lay the pieces on a plate and repeat with the remaining fish fillets.

Gently drop the breaded fish into the hot oil, and keeping careful watch, metal spatula in hand, fry at a steady sizzle until the fish is nut-brown on both sides, 3 to 4 minutes.

Briefly blot the fish on a paper towel–lined plate before serving with one, or both, of the dipping sauces on the side.

GINGER KETCHUP

3 tablespoons salted butter

4 cloves garlic, smashed

2 large sprigs fresh basil

½ cup ketchup

2 tablespoons fresh lime juice

3 tablespoons fresh ginger juice (see Note)

¼ teaspoon fine sea salt

¼ teaspoon freshly ground black pepper

Cayenne pepper, to taste

This is also wonderful on hamburgers and pork burgers, with crab cakes, or alongside anything you think might benefit from an ersatz ketchup sauce.

MAKES ¾ CUP

Get all of the ingredients for this sauce ready before you begin to cook, because it moves fast.

Heat a medium skillet over medium-high heat, and add the butter and garlic cloves. Cook, stirring often, until the butter turns nut-brown, about 2 minutes. Quickly add the basil and ketchup. Cook, simmering, until the ketchup thickens and turns a shade rustier, 1 to 2 minutes. Remove from the heat and whisk in the lime juice, ginger juice, salt, and pepper. Season to taste with cayenne, and remove the basil sprigs and garlic.

Serve warm or at room temperature. (You can make this sauce up to a few hours before serving.)

NOTE: *Fresh ginger juice, made from squeezing a pile of grated fresh ginger, has an inimitable spicy bite and fragrance, and it's not difficult to make: fresh ginger holds more juice than it looks. To extract the juice, lay a small square of cheesecloth (or even a thick paper towel) over a bowl. Grate a large knob of peeled ginger onto the cheesecloth. Gather up the corners of the cloth, twist, and squeeze the ginger juice into the bowl. A 4-inch-long knob of ginger usually yields 3 to 4 tablespoons juice.*

SPICY PEANUT VINAIGRETTE

MAKES ⅔ CUP

Pour the peanuts into a plastic bag and pound them to fine crumbs with a rolling pin. In a bowl, mix together the peanuts, garlic, red pepper flakes, dill, cilantro, vinegar, orange juice, olive oil, and salt and pepper to taste. (You can make this up to a day ahead of time; store it in the refrigerator.)

⅓ cup roasted, salted peanuts

1 clove garlic, finely grated

½ teaspoon red pepper flakes, or to taste

1 tablespoon minced fresh dill

2 tablespoons minced fresh cilantro (include plenty of the stems)

1½ tablespoons white wine vinegar or rice vinegar

¼ cup freshly squeezed orange juice

3 tablespoons extra-virgin olive oil

Fine sea salt and freshly ground black pepper

Midwestern Crayfish

Midwestern waters are literally crawling with large, lovely crayfish, and honestly, most people ignore them—it's the children who know how plentiful they really are. I can testify that over the course of a childhood spent belly-crawling in shallow lake waters, I teased, taunted, and made frenemies of hundreds of them. I no more thought of eating them than I did the minnows that nibbled at my toes.

But the crayfish that scuttle around in many bodies of water across the middle and eastern United States, in watery holes all along the Mississippi and points east, are some of the the meatiest crayfish in the country. Here near the headwaters of the Mississippi they thrive, and you can find teeming schools of these natural burrowers living in permanent spring-fed water bodies.

In fact, the local Department of Natural Resources (DNR) consider the crayfish to be an invasive species. Native to the Ohio River basin, the rusties hitched a ride here as bait and quickly put down roots. They're more aggressive than our native crayfish, and larger. In fact, their claws are large enough to hold chunks of meat worth the effort of shelling. To the DNR their presence threatens the habitat of the precious walleye, the king of the sport-fishing industry.

Over the years, some Midwesterners saw the obvious solution: we should be eating them. I spoke to Gary Florczak, a trapper who spent twenty-four years selling freshwater crayfish from Minnesota and Wisconsin to domestic and international markets, and he said that he and his friends thought our rocky-bottomed crayfish were the best they'd ever had, but that it had been a rough road selling crayfish to northerners. (In my area, they're mostly sold as bait, at bait prices—around $2 a pound.)

Our genus of crayfish differs slightly from southern crayfish. Professor Jay Huner, director of the Crawfish Research Center at the University of Louisiana and widely thought of as the expert on crayfish habitat, told me that our northern crayfish, the ones who move around in cold, rocky lakes rather than burrow in southern swamps, don't store the same volume of funky, flavorful yellow lipids in their heads—the main draw for many southern crayfish eaters. However, I'd say that among the Midwestern-ers who have come to my crayfish boils, about 95 percent have refused to suck on the head, so maybe it's okay: what Louisiana crayfish lovers might call bland, we call clean. I'd say our taste in crayfish heads is in step with our collective taste for mild, nonfishy fish.

Gary quickly learned that there was a lot more business to be done shipping them to Scandinavia and to the southern United States, places where crayfish eating was already well established. During the boom, he made a few good runs. One summer they drove a U-Haul (usually carrying 7,000 or 8,000 pounds of crayfish) down to the Galveston-Houston area of Texas once a week, and he told me in detail about one of those drives.

"We sold the crayfish to a guy who called himself the Crawfish King. By the time we got to Louisiana it was tipping a hundred degrees, and thinking how the crayfish must be roasting in the back of the truck, we laughed and said to each other, 'One more day and we'll be chucking these guys over the side into the ditch.'

"When we met the Crawfish King, the first thing he said was, 'You guys are out of your minds, bringing these crawdads all this way.' We followed him through the worst rush-hour Houston traffic, and when we got to this restaurant we opened the back of the truck. Not knowing at this point if they'd be alive or dead and stinking, we pulled the first tray and they were all snapping; there were only three dead out of five hundred. Tremendous odds. The guy bought the whole truck. We got ten thousand dollars, turned in the U-Haul, partied for three days in Houston, and then bought a flight back home."

MIDWESTERN CRAYFISH BOIL
with Spicy Mayo

1 large Vidalia onion, halved crosswise

½ cup salt (regular iodized or fine sea salt)

½ cup sugar

1 head garlic, halfed crosswise

1 orange, halved

4 lemons: 1 halved, 3 quartered

3 tablespoons coriander seeds

15 small dried hot red chiles

2 tablespoons black peppercorns

12 dried bay leaves

1½ pounds (about 15) new red potatoes

2 pounds andouille sausage

10 pounds live freshwater crayfish

5 ears corn, snapped into thirds

6 heads flowering crown dill

Spicy Mayonnaise (recipe follows)

NOTE: *As with all big-event cookery, your setup is part of your recipe. I conduct the crayfish boil in a huge, thin pot that I bought at the local farm and fleet store, the kind used for deep-frying turkeys. While you could in theory boil the crayfish in your kitchen, an outdoor gas burner is pretty essential to the project as well, and I use a wok burner purchased at an Asian cooking supply store.*

Nothing celebrates a place like a local crayfish boil. It has become a regular summer event at my house, and couldn't be easier to stage: We spread the wealth from the boiling pot out onto a butcher-paper-lined door propped on sawhorses, weight down the paper with bowls of spicy mayo for dipping, set a couple of buckets underneath for discarded shells, and let the nibblers rush the stage.

Crown dill, the flowered-out head of the dill plant, adds great fragrance and a Nordic note to the pot, and conveniently tends to bloom during the apex of the Midwestern crayfish harvest: late June through early August. Be sure to cut the spicy andouille sausage into chunks so that everyone gets a piece of it with their pile of crayfish, corn, and potatoes.

SERVES A PARTY OF 20

For extra flavor, blacken the face of the onion: Line the bottom of a cast-iron skillet with a layer of aluminum foil. Turn the heat to medium and lay the onion halves, cut-side down, on the foil. Cook until the undersides turn black, about 25 minutes. Let cool before peeling off the foil.

Fill a large (4- to 5-gallon) pot with 12 quarts of water and bring to a boil. Add the salt, sugar, blackened onion, garlic, orange, lemon halves, coriander seeds, dried chiles, peppercorns, bay leaves, and potatoes. Simmer until the potatoes are almost tender, about 20 minutes.

Add the andouille sausage and cook for about 10 minutes.

Add the crayfish, corn, and dill, and cover the pot. When the water returns to a boil, cook for exactly 5 minutes. (Test a crayfish for doneness by breaking back the skinny pincer claw; the meat should be firm throughout but not stiff.)

With a large strainer, lift everything from the pot onto a picnic table covered with butcher paper or newspaper. Serve immediately, with the lemon quarters and spicy mayonnaise.

SPICY MAYONNAISE

MAKES ABOUT 2⅓ CUPS

In a medium bowl, mix together the mayonnaise, chile sauce, pepper, lemon juice, and olive oil. Divide between two smaller bowls for the crayfish boil, and set one at each end of the picnic table. (This can be made a day ahead and stored in the refrigerator.)

2 cups mayonnaise

1½ tablespoons spicy chile sauce, such as Sriracha

½ teaspoon freshly ground black pepper

3 tablespoons fresh lemon juice

2 tablespoons extra-virgin olive oil

NORTHERN PIKE CAKES

2 tablespoons salted butter

1 bunch scallions, white and green parts, trimmed and thinly sliced

2 tablespoons minced fresh ginger

1 pound (about 2 large) skinless northern pike fillets

1 large egg

1 large egg yolk

2 teaspoons soy sauce

2 teaspoons dark sesame oil

Fine sea salt and freshly ground black pepper

½ cup heavy cream

2 tablespoons minced fresh cilantro, including stems

2 cups panko bread crumbs

Canola oil, for frying

NOTES: *You'll need a food processor to make these cakes, which have a fish mousse base in addition to chunks of roughly chopped fish.*

I won't dive into how to fillet a northern here, but I can quickly say that you want to remove the fillets on either side of the backbone in curved swoops, keeping close to the central Y-shaped backbone. A quick Internet search yields dozens of wonderful homemade videos that illustrate the process in elaborate detail.

Of lake fish, northern pike are the pawns: plentiful, sacrificial, and somewhat taken for granted. They're known for their Y-shaped bone structure, which is difficult to navigate, and for their habit of growing small thin bones in random places.

For all that, they're still my favorite local fish. Juicier than walleyes and firmer than perch, northerns have an elegant white marble sheen that resembles the revered John Dory from saltier waters.

The vexing bone structure is the reason that many people pickle their northerns (see Home-Pickled Fish, page 294). And the odd stray bone, along with the pile of scraps yielded from filleting mistakes, also often leads me to make fish cakes from our northern pike spoils.

This Asian-inflected version of mine has always received a good reception—and most of these ingredients are pantry staples. These cakes are great alone, with a lemon wedge, or with a bowl of Spicy Mayonnaise (page 119). And there's nothing better than fish cakes for breakfast; a liquid-set fried egg on top is probably the best sauce of all.

MAKES 12 FISH CAKES; SERVES 4 TO 6

Heat the butter in a small skillet over medium heat, and add the scallions and ginger. Cook, stirring, until tender, about 2 minutes, and then transfer to a large bowl to cool.

Roughly dice the fish, put it in the bowl of a food processor, and pulse to chop it into pea-size pieces. Scoop out one-third of the chopped fish (about ¾ cup) and add it to the bowl containing the scallion mixture.

To the remaining fish in the processor add the egg, egg yolk, soy sauce, sesame oil, ½ teaspoon salt, and ¼ teaspoon pepper. Process until smooth, scraping down the sides of the bowl as needed. With the processor running, add the cream in a stream. Process until the mixture thickens into a mousse-like texture, 1 to 2 minutes.

Transfer the mixture to the bowl containing the fish and scallions, add the cilantro, and mix well. Refrigerate for at least 20 minutes and up to 12 hours before forming into cakes.

Put the panko in a pie plate and season with 1 teaspoon salt and ½ teaspoon pepper.

With a serving spoon, scoop up about 3 tablespoons of the fish cake mixture and drop it onto the panko. Repeat twice more, making 3 cakes at a time. Digging underneath each fish cake, flip it over and gently form it into a hockey puck shape. The mixture is soft but it will take direction, and the cakes don't need to be perfect. Repeat until you have used all the fish cake mixture.

Heat a large heavy skillet over medium-high heat and add canola oil to a depth of ½ inch. When the oil sizzles on contact with the edge of a fish cake, add as many fish cakes as will comfortably fit in the skillet and fry until dark golden brown on both sides, about 4 minutes. If it goes faster than that, reduce the heat.

Blot the hot cakes on a paper towel–lined plate and serve immediately.

KALAMOJAKKA

6 slices (6 ounces) thick-cut
  bacon, cut into 1-inch-thick
  pieces

3 tablespoons salted butter

2 medium Yukon Gold
  potatoes, diced (1½ cups)

1 large leek, diced (1½ cups)

4 stalks celery, diced (1 cup)

Fine sea salt and freshly ground
  black pepper

1½ tablespoons all-purpose
  flour

¼ cup dry vermouth or
  white wine

3 cups whole milk

1 pound skinless, boneless
  walleye, perch, or northern
  pike fillets

1 tablespoon minced fresh dill

1 tablespoon minced fresh
  chives

Most good stews have a story. For details on this one I turned to an expert in Scandinavian cooking, cookbook author and teacher Beatrice Ojakangas from Duluth, Minnesota. Growing up in a Finnish-speaking family in Floodwood, Minnesota, on the Finnish-Italian-Slovak-settled Iron Range, she knows a thing or two about *mojakka* (a beef stew) and its cousin *kalamojakka* (a fish stew). Both seem to have been invented by Finnish Americans as a way to give leftovers some buzz.

"The fish version is pronounced kala-MOY-yacka," she said. "And actually, if you go to Finland and mention either one of them, they don't know what you're talking about. It gets people going in all directions."

The name may have originated in the Finnish-settled towns of northern Minnesota, but according to Beatrice, the recipe for a simple fish stew has a true old-country precedent called *keiito*, a farmhouse dish traditionally made from rich milk, fish, and butter—maybe a few potatoes, nothing fancy—and eaten with rye bread (see page 365 for a rye bread recipe).

My version pulls in bacon and dry vermouth, but it doesn't take long to put together, and the milky broth nicely supports the pearly freshwater fish.

SERVES 4 TO 6

Heat a 3-quart saucepan over medium heat and add the bacon. Cook until lightly browned, about 5 minutes. Transfer the bacon to a dish and discard all but 2 tablespoons of the bacon fat in the pan. Add the butter to the pan, and then the potatoes, leek, and celery. Season with ½ teaspoon salt and ¼ teaspoon pepper. Cook until the vegetables begin to soften at the edges, 5 to 7 minutes, reducing the heat if necessary to avoid browning.

Add the flour and stir until it's incorporated into the buttery vegetables. Add 1 cup water and the vermouth, and raise the heat to medium-high. Cook, stirring constantly, until the liquid thickens into a smooth slurry, about 5 minutes. Add the milk and bring the soup back to a simmer, stirring until it is smooth and thick. Add ¾ teaspoon salt and ¼ teaspoon pepper, and cook at a bare simmer until the vegetables are tender, about 10 minutes.

Cut the walleye into roughly 1-inch pieces. Add the bacon and walleye to the stew, simmer gently for 2 minutes, and remove from the heat. Let the soup sit for 2 minutes, or until the fish is opaque at the center but still juicy. Add the minced dill and chives, and serve immediately.

BUTTER-BASTED WALLEYE
with Thyme *and* Garlic

Here in walleye country, where most of the fresh catch is automatically crusted and dropped in a vat of hot oil, pan-roasting is a clever way to fry fish without *frying* fish. There's no breading involved, but the deeply browned finish has its own addictive quality.

You heat the pan, dust the fillets with flour, fry one side to a dark caramel, flip, and then baste the fish with cascading spoonfuls of hot browning butter and the scraggly twigs of herbs and chunks of garlic caught up in its tide. I like to save the excess golden cooking butter to sop an accompanying side of rice or potatoes or (best yet) cooked winter squash.

I give amounts here for two fillets, enough to serve two and to fit in one large pan. To make this for four, six, or more people, multiply the ingredients accordingly, and fry the fish in two pans to save time.

SERVES 2

Heat a large skillet (one that can accommodate both fish fillets with space to spare) over high heat.

Sprinkle both sides of the fish with salt and pepper, and dust the prettier side (that which was closest to the bone) with a thin layer of flour.

Add the canola oil to the hot skillet, and then add the fish, flour-side down. Press the fish gently into the pan with a flat spatula, and cook over high (but not raging) heat until the underside turns dark golden brown and doneness creeps two-thirds of the way up the sides of the fish, about 2 minutes.

Add the garlic and thyme to the skillet, and flip the fish. Add the butter and immediately begin basting the fish with a large serving spoon, tilting the pan slightly and spooning the hot foaming butter over the fillets until the inside of the fish begins to flake, the exterior has turned evenly golden, and the butter has browned, 1 to 2 minutes. Transfer the fish to plates and serve immediately.

2 (6- to 8-ounce each) boneless, skinless walleye fillets

Fine sea salt and freshly ground black pepper

Wondra or all-purpose flour, for dusting

1 tablespoon canola oil

4 cloves garlic, smashed

3 sprigs fresh thyme

4 tablespoons (½ stick) salted butter, at room temperature

NOTES: *At first glance, it seems like a lot of butter for basting, but keep in mind that it's topical and just a flavor conduit. As it washes over the fish it carries with it the flavors of the garlic, the herbs, and the brown crusty roasting residue left in the pan. And when the fish heads to the plate, the brown butter can either stay in the pan or not, as you wish.*

The key to pan-roasting any fish is to cook it two-thirds of the way through on the first side before flipping it over. This ensures a crisp-edged golden brown surface and a moist interior.

FRIDAY-NIGHT FISH FRY

4 cups canola oil

2 cups Wondra flour (see Note, page 108), plus ½ cup for dredging

1½ teaspoons baking powder

¼ teaspoon baking soda

1 tablespoon cornstarch

Fine sea salt and freshly ground black pepper

1 egg

1 egg white

¾ cup wheat beer

1 cup whole milk

½ tablespoon finely chopped fresh chives

Grated zest of ½ orange

2 pounds boneless, skinless freshwater fish fillets (such as lake perch or whitefish), cut into 4- to 6-inch lengths

NOTE: *Most firm white-fleshed fish are good for frying, and if you don't have access to freshwater fish, saltwater fish work as well. Cod is probably the best choice.*

Friday-night fish fries are one of the unifying characteristics of the Midwest, and their ubiquity dispels the myth that we are landlocked.

From Sioux Falls to Cleveland and all points in between, some restaurants and bars fry fresh local fish on Fridays; but in the weeks preceding Catholic Lent, these ritual affairs are a madhouse. Meat may be banned, but beer isn't, and whether you're eating fish because of Catholic edict or not, by and large the atmosphere at any fish fry is charged and convivial.

Michael Symon, well-known chef and Ohio native, serves a perfectly light fried fish on Friday nights at B-Spot, his string of burger joints in Ohio. (B-Spot is also worth a pilgrimage for its fried bologna sandwiches.) He shared his recipe, which uses low-gluten Wondra flour to give his fish an almost impossibly delicate yet still crusty surface. As for the fish, he serves lake perch, walleye, or whitefish, all of which arrive wearing crisp amber balloons, the fish inside still running juice.

SERVES 6 TO 8

Pour the oil into a deep heavy-bottomed pot (at least 3 quarts in capacity) so that it reaches about halfway up the sides. Heat the oil over medium-high heat until a flick of flour sizzles on the surface or the oil measures 370° to 375°F on a deep-frying thermometer.

While the oil is heating, prepare the batter: Whisk together 2 cups of the flour, the baking powder, baking soda, cornstarch, and 1 teaspoon salt in a medium bowl. Whisk the egg, egg white, beer, milk, chives, and orange zest in a larger bowl. Pour the flour mixture into the liquid mixture, and mix swiftly with a whisk.

Put the remaining ½ cup flour into a small bowl.

Dip and fry the fish in batches: Season both sides of the fish with salt, dip into the flour, shake the excess off well, and then dip into the batter, covering it completely. Let the excess batter drip off, and then drop the fillet into the hot oil. Cook, adjusting the heat to maintain the temperature, until the underside turns dark golden brown, about 2 minutes. Turn the fish over and cook until the entire crust is dark amber brown and the fish is cooked inside, about 4 minutes. Lift out with a large slotted spoon, drain on paper towels, and serve each batch as it is ready.

Really Fresh Fish

I filleted plenty of fish in restaurant kitchens, but that really didn't prepare me for the fish that I clean now in Two Inlets—which nearly always arrive at my kitchen door alive.

And I'm not alone; most people who enjoy eating freshwater fish in the Midwest rely on their own fresh catch. For those who lack experience with really fresh fish, I'll share what I've learned over the years.

It's most humane to process them right after you bring them into the boat. For the very best tasting fish, you want to slice deeply right behind their eyes and let them bleed out in cold water: either string them up and drop them into the lake, or drop them into a cooler or a large bowl of ice water.

Once they've chilled, you can gut them and scale them. Some anglers I know around here don't scale their fish first, but it's a lot easier on your knife if you do, and it makes for much cleaner-looking fillets. (Those in the trout family—rainbow, brook, char, and lake trout—have such small scales that they don't need to be removed.) Use a fish-scaling tool, such as those sold at outdoor sports stores, or in a pinch, a fork.

The directions for filleting each fish are slightly different, but in general, you want to slice along either side of the backbone, keeping your knife as close as possible to the rib bones, and cleanly take off each fillet.

To remove the skin, lay the fillet skin-side down on a cutting board, and make a small angled cut into the tip of the tail end. With your non-dominant hand, grip the bit of loose tail skin (a paper towel helps here) and then begin swinging it back and forth, at the same time pressing the knife forward, blade held at a 45-degree angle pointing toward the board. In other words, you don't want to move your knife, you want to move the skin.

Lay the fillets out flat in one layer on a parchment- or waxed paper–lined baking sheet, and cover tightly if not using right away. Fresh fish fillets last 2 days if kept in a very cold refrigerator.

EELPOUT, or BURBOT, Almondine

½ teaspoon smoked paprika

¼ teaspoon hot paprika or ground chipotle pepper

1 teaspoon sweet paprika

½ teaspoon garlic powder

4 4-ounce skinless, boneless burbot fillets (or substitute catfish or monkfish)

Fine sea salt and freshly ground black pepper

Canola oil, for frying

4 wide strips of lemon zest

2 medium shallots, quartered

4 tablespoons salted butter

⅓ cup sliced almonds

NOTE: *To fillet a burbot, you'll want to remove the skin (it doesn't have any scales). You can cut the skin behind the head and yank, or if you're doing this in any quantity, it might be easier to remove the skin as you'd remove the skin from an actual eel: by securing the head with a clamp or a screw and tugging the skin forcefully from the top to the tail. (My young son absolutely loves watching this crazy operation.)*

To visitors, the annual International Eelpout Festival in Walker, Minnesota, is a shock. Taking place in February on the shores of expansive Leech Lake, this ice-fishing festival is ostensibly a contest to determine who can catch the largest, the smallest, or the most numerous of the spawning eelpout—but in truth, it's more like an ambitious frat village on ice.

Here, late-winter northerners assemble to burn off their cabin fever by drinking, skiing on couches pulled behind snowmobiles, "polar bearing" into the enormous hole cut into the lake ice, and otherwise jigging and honking and letting loose in the bright below-zero air. Mukluks and fur hats are de rigueur.

The eelpout, a silly-looking fish, is a fitting mascot for these shenanigans. In fact, the fish that comes to Walker Bay to spawn in late February is not even an eelpout, but in fact its freshwater lookalike, the burbot. (Technicalities are not what this festival is about.) A freshwater cod, sometimes called ling cod, the burbot has whiskers like a catfish, a long tail that tends to spiral up your arm, and an enormous belly housing a huge liver. It's found in many cold, deep freshwater lakes circumnavigating the 40th parallel around the world, and is revered as a table fish in France. The subtext of the eelpout/burbot festival, generally overshadowed by the festivities, is that the fish itself is tender and sweet and makes excellent eating. The short stalked fibers make for an excessively juicy fish that takes well to hot, dry cooking treatments, and not so much to deep-frying.

Anglers in the know call this fish "poor man's lobster" and advocate boiling it briefly in a brown sugar brine and serving it with drawn butter—which is great, but I like to dust it with some spices and roll it in hot buttered almonds and shallots. This is a cooler, rustier version of sole almondine, and the accompanying lemony butter-fried shallots are not to be missed.

SERVES 2 TO 4

Combine the three paprikas and the garlic powder in a small bowl. Season the fish with salt and pepper, and then sprinkle evenly, but sparingly, with the paprika mixture, and rub it in.

Heat a large, heavy skillet over medium-high heat, and add enough oil to coat the bottom of the skillet. When the skillet is hot, add the fish and sear on one side until dark, about 3 minutes. Add the lemon zest and shallots to the skillet. Flip the fish, add the butter and almonds, and cook, basting the fish with a large spoon, until the almonds brown and the fish tests tender in the center when poked with a fork or toothpick, about 2 minutes. Pick out the lemon zest and discard.

Transfer the fish, along with the shallots, almonds, and some of the butter, to plates and serve right away.

WILD RICE–CRUSTED STURGEON

½ cup wood-parched wild rice

½ cup panko bread crumbs

Fine sea salt and freshly ground black pepper

2 large eggs

1 cup all-purpose flour

6 tablespoons (¾ stick) salted butter

4 5-ounce portions fresh sturgeon

Lemon wedges, for serving

NOTES: *At his restaurant, Gavin Kaysen serves the crispy sturgeon in a pool of gingery carrot broth, surrounded by spring vegetables, but at home it can be garnished with a lemon wedge and left at that.*

Be sure to fry the fish in the specified clarified butter and not to move it until the underside turns deep brown; you want to maintain the crust's seal.

Halibut is a good substitute for sturgeon, but make sure any fish you use is fresh, not frozen—frozen fish can make for a less-crispy crust.

The old black-and-white photograph of the angler standing next to a man-size hanging sturgeon is the Great Lakes equivalent of the one of the guy standing next to the swordfish on the coast of Florida. These freshwater fish can be monsters.

The extremely slow-growing and late-maturing sturgeon are distinguished by their elongated bodies, hard exterior "scutes" instead of scales, and a mythic reputation as a prehistoric creature. The hunch that sturgeon are taxonomically different from most other freshwater fish is confirmed when you open them up: the orange fat runs in waves throughout the ivory flesh, as if it were intramuscular fat in a piece of meat. This fattiness makes sturgeon a prime candidate for hot-smoking, the treatment that many anglers in the upper Midwest give their sturgeon if they're lucky enough to catch a keeper. (Because they're so late to reproduce, the slot limit is narrow: legal fish must measure between forty-five and fifty inches in length.)

Sturgeon's rarity gives it luxury status even in fine-dining kitchens, where it's considered by many chefs to be the most decadent of freshwater fish.

Gavin Kaysen, executive chef at Café Boulud in New York City and a Minnesota native, counts sturgeon among his favorite freshwater fish. When it comes into his kitchen, he likes to give it a crust that reminds him of the upper Midwest: an earthy mixture of toasted wild rice and panko bread crumbs, the very same breading he sends with his dad on his fishing trips. The thin crust, as brittle as birch bark, breaks in sheets to reveal the clean, neutral juices of the fish.

SERVES 4

Put the rice in a small skillet and toast over medium heat, tossing, until fragrant, about 3 minutes. Pour out onto a plate. When the rice is cool, grind it into a fine dust in a clean coffee grinder. Transfer it to a shallow bowl or pie plate. Pulse the panko in the coffee grinder until fine, and mix it into the rice, along with ¼ teaspoon each of salt and pepper.

Prepare a breading station: Have the wild rice mixture ready, put the eggs in a second shallow bowl and lightly beat them, and put the flour in a third shallow bowl.

Heat a small skillet over medium-high heat and add the butter. When it melts, remove the skillet from the heat, scrape off the stiff froth from the top, and deposit it in a small bowl. Pour the clear golden butter into another bowl, and add the milky fluid at the bottom of the skillet to the bowl containing the froth. Reserve the clear butter for frying the fish, and the froth for another purpose (scrambled eggs, sautéed vegetables, rice, etc.).

Preheat the oven to 200°F.

Season the sturgeon on both sides with salt and pepper, and bread it: Roll it first in the flour, shake off the excess, then coat with the egg, let the excess drip off, and then coat thoroughly with the wild rice mixture, handling the fish carefully so that there are no holes in the breading.

Heat a large skillet over medium-high heat, and when it's hot, add the clarified butter. When a drop of water dances on the surface of the butter, add 2 pieces of fish and cook until deeply browned on the bottom, about 3 minutes. Flip carefully, and fry the other side until the crust is crisp and golden and a thin skewer held for a second in the middle of the fish feels hot when touched to your bottom lip. Remove the fish from the skillet, and keep it warm in the oven while you fry the rest. Serve with the lemon wedges on the side.

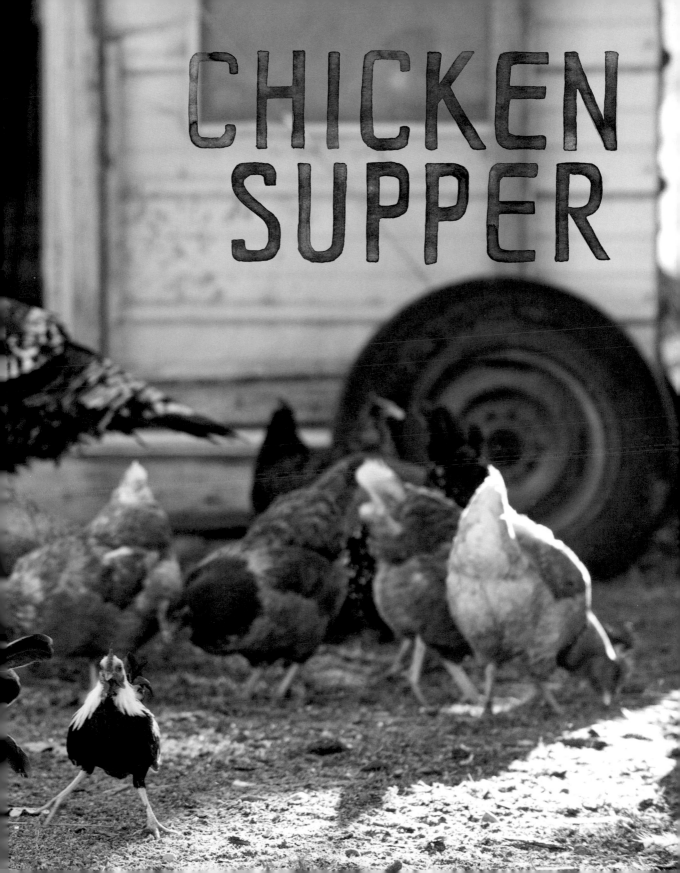

The name for this chapter comes from an entry found in an old spiral-bound community cookbook called "Chicken Supper," a recipe title I've never forgotten. A simple one-pan bake made with chicken, rice, and cheese, the utilitarian, plain-spoken name says so much about welcoming a family to the table.

Because they're so quick to mature, I feel that chickens really express the conditions of their raising. Eating local chicken has taught me valuable lessons about animal husbandry. For example, after trying chickens raised by different local farmers, I now know what I like: a bird raised outside on pasture, but on a short leash. Not too small and flabby, and not too big either.

Rosemary-Infused Brown Butter Chicken Breasts—pieces of white meat rolled around in sweet-smelling brown butter—was made one night from just such a chicken. The same goes for Midwestern Fried Chicken and Gravy, a twist on an American classic that broadens the focus from the rough-textured crust to the accompanying pond of gravy and potatoes.

For the times when one's preferred chicken isn't available, there are spices and crusts and glazes to dress up even the most common supermarket birds—Malt and Chile–Glazed Chicken, for example, or Upside-Down Spiced Roasted Chicken—for nights you're craving something with some punch and crispy skin.

Finally, I've included a duck dish in this chapter, only because everyone from the local pawn-shop owner to the retired guy having coffee in the grocery store has told me how he cooks his ducks embedded in wild rice. For wilderness types, Classic Duck in Wild Rice is the equivalent of chicken comfort.

BAKED CHICKEN
with Porcini Spice Rub

A basic spice-rubbed baked chicken recipe like this one is something that every working person—whether they work in the home or out—should have in their possession. For all the long-cooked and intricate meat dishes I put on our table, this dashed-off chicken baked on a foil-lined baking sheet is probably my family's favorite.

Basically any spice mixture rubbed on chicken destined for slow baking will taste fabulous, but this spiced porcini rub—an idea borrowed from Shea Gallante, chef at Ciano in New York City—sinks richly into the crevices and corners. After loving the Scandinavian baked chicken at The Old Fashioned in Madison, Wisconsin, I added sweeter spices—allspice and ginger—to the mix.

By the way, this dish turns out best when you're not continually opening the oven to poke at it. Baked chicken is not something over which you fret.

SERVES 4

1 4½-pound chicken, cut into 8 pieces (or 6 chicken legs)

1 tablespoon coriander seeds

1 teaspoon black peppercorns

15 allspice berries

2 teaspoons yellow mustard seeds

¼ ounce (1 handful) dried mushrooms, preferably porcini

1 teaspoon fine sea salt

2 teaspoons minced fresh sage

¾ teaspoon grated nutmeg

1 tablespoon canola oil

Rinse the chicken pieces, pat them dry with paper towels, and put them in a large bowl.

Combine the coriander seeds, peppercorns, allspice, and mustard seeds in a small pan set over medium heat, and toast until fragrant, about 2 minutes. Combine the spices with the dried porcini in a spice-devoted coffee grinder; pulverize until finely ground but not powdery. Pour into a small bowl and add ½ teaspoon salt, the sage, and the nutmeg.

Rub the chicken with the oil and the remaining ½ teaspoon salt, and coat generously but not completely with spice mix. Lay the chicken on a foil-lined rimmed baking sheet, and let it sit at room temperature for up to 20 minutes to absorb the flavors of the spice crust.

Meanwhile, preheat the oven to 375°F.

Bake the chicken until it begins to brown, about 25 minutes. Reduce the temperature to 350°F and continue to bake, until the chicken tests tender when poked with a thin fork and registers an internal temperature of 165°F when tested in the deepest part of the thigh, about 20 minutes. (The chicken breast pieces will be done after 35 minutes, so remove them and keep them warm while you continue baking the rest.) Serve immediately.

CHICKEN PAPRIKASH

- 1 4- to 4½-pound chicken

- 1 tablespoon canola oil

- Fine sea salt and freshly ground black pepper

- 2 tablespoons salted butter

- 2½ large (1½ pounds) sweet onions, diced

- 1 large (8 ounces) red bell pepper, diced

- 5 cloves garlic, sliced

- 1½ teaspoons tomato paste

- 1 tablespoon minced fresh rosemary, or 2 teaspoons dried rosemary, crushed

- 1 teaspoon dried marjoram

- 2 tablespoons sweet paprika

- ½ cup dry white wine

- 2 cups chicken stock, low-sodium store-bought or homemade (page 299)

- 1 teaspoon grated lemon zest

- 1 teaspoon sherry vinegar

- ⅓ cup sour cream

- 1 teaspoon fresh lemon juice

- Shot of sour pickle juice (optional), from a jar of fermented pickles

A good Eastern European brings along his fresh paprika when he heads to the country house, as I learned from Gabor Nemeth, my Hungarian-born neighbor here in Two Inlets. Last summer he showed me his stash of paprika; the red powder had an iron-y, fruity scent to it, the clinging evidence of the peppers from which it had so recently come.

Gabor corroborated the two important requirements of proper paprika-based stews that I learned from the Austrian chefs I once worked for: One, that you must use plenty of fresh paprika and toast it briefly in the hot oil, and two, that you must focus on creating a thick base of long-cooked onions.

For this chicken paprika, I lighten things up with some red bell peppers, white wine, lemon zest, and a swirl of sour cream added at the very end.

SERVES 4

Cut the chicken into 10 pieces, as for fried chicken (see page 151).

Heat a large, high-sided skillet over medium-high heat and add the oil. Season the chicken with ¼ teaspoon each of salt and pepper, and add it, skin-side down, to the hot pan (as many pieces as will fit comfortably). Cook until browned on both sides, about 4 minutes per side. Transfer the chicken to a bowl and brown the rest of it, taking care not to burn the bits on the bottom of the skillet.

Pour out all but 1 tablespoon of the cooking fat from the skillet. Add the butter, onions, and red bell pepper, and sprinkle with ½ teaspoon each of salt and pepper. Cook over medium heat, stirring, until the vegetables are soft and very tender, 20 minutes.

Add the garlic, tomato paste, rosemary, marjoram, and paprika, and cook another minute. Pour in the white wine and stir with a wooden spoon, working to release the stuck bits on the bottom of the skillet. Add the chicken stock, lemon zest, vinegar, and ¼ teaspoon each of salt and pepper. Nestle the dark-meat chicken pieces in the liquid and bring to a simmer. Reduce the heat slightly, partially cover to let some steam escape, and cook, turning the chicken once in a while, at a slow-bubbling simmer over medium-low heat for 40 minutes.

Add the white-meat pieces and any residual juices in the

bowl to the skillet, and cook, partially covered, at the same slow simmer until the white meat feels firm and the dark meat tests tender when poked with a slim fork, 25 to 30 minutes.

As the chicken cooks, make the sour cream sauce: Stir the sour cream and lemon juice together in a small bowl, and season to taste with salt and pepper.

Transfer the chicken pieces to a wide bowl or plate. With an immersion blender (or in a standing blender) process half of the pan sauce, to thicken the broth. Pour the sauce back into the skillet, return the chicken to the pan, taste for seasoning, and add the pickle juice, if using. Warm the chicken a minute in the sauce, and then serve it with the sour cream sauce to pass at the table.

Pan Smut

Because the deep flavor of this paprikash, like many braised dishes, depends upon the cook's skillful treatment of the stuck-on bits left in the pan from browning the chicken, I prefer to use a stainless steel pan (not a nonstick pan) here, one to which a bit of the chicken skin will stick when you're browning.

Creating and then maintaining the delicious pan stickings left on the bottom after you've fried meat or vegetables, and carrying that delicious caramelized residue throughout the dish, is arguably the most important task when making a stew or a braised dish. Yet sometimes I find it hard to write about the progression of the braise when there seems to be a lack of a single vocabulary word to describe this part, the foundation of so many stews, sauces, and other liquid delights.

The French have a word for it: the *fond*, or foundation—which is elegant and makes sense. The Austrian chefs I worked for adopted that, and called it the *fond* as well. My mom calls hers "the schnibbles." I remember my grandmother frying potatoes and saying, "Make sure to scrape up the schmutz on the bottom of the pan." And again, "Get all that pan schmutz when you're making gravy." As a kid I heard "smut" instead, and repeated it back to myself for years, though it took me a long time to get the joke. Now, just for kicks, and because there's no other word for it, I privately think of that delicious stuck-on crud, the pure flavor shellacked to the bottom of the pan, as the "pan smut."

Whatever it's called, you want to be sure to get it.

CLASSIC CHICKEN AND WILD RICE HOTDISH

Year-round in Minnesota, hotdishes (known as casseroles everywhere else) are both standard and redemptive fare, offered up for school lunches, sports potlucks, weekday dinners, friends who are grieving, neighbors who have a new baby. The ingredients are usually pretty homespun, but I have a hunch that the rhythm of the returning fork—the tempo of scooping that a hotdish requires—is a big source of the comfort.

Hotdishes grow more valuable—essential, even—in the winter. When the sky begins to darken at 3 o'clock and the arctic wind picks up and starts to blow mean, it's nice to make a bubbling hot dish. Around here, chicken–wild rice is the most famous of them all, and it's even better when made in an updated style, with delicate wood-parched wild rice and a simple fresh mushroom sauce in place of the traditional canned creamy-soup base.

My husband, Aaron, remembers returning home from outdoor hockey practice after school, walking from the black driveway toward the bright lights of the kitchen window just in time to see his mother pull a hotdish from the oven, its thick juices blowing big, blond, creamy bubbles as it made its journey to the trivet in the middle of the table. With his toes tingling from the nip of frostbite (like ice cubes on fire) and with the wet, sticky, thawing sensation that only hockey practice in subzero wind can create, he would shovel in the mixture of creamy chicken, fragile grains of wild rice, and crunchy cracker top before it had a chance to stop steaming.

SERVES 6 TO 8

Put the rice in a fine-mesh sieve and rinse it under cold running water, swishing the rice with your hand until the water runs clear. Transfer the rice to a medium bowl, and add water to cover. Pour off any black bits or floating kernels, pour the rice back into the sieve to drain, and then put it in a small saucepan. Add 1¼ cups water, a pinch of salt, and the bay leaf, and bring to a simmer. Cover the pan and reduce the heat to low. Steam for 25 minutes, or until the rice is tender and the water has evaporated. (If liquid remains after the rice is done, drain it in a sieve.)

Meanwhile, preheat the oven to 375°F.

½ cup natural wild rice

Fine sea salt and freshly ground black pepper

1 dried bay leaf

6 tablespoons (¾ stick) salted butter, plus more, at room temperature, for the baking dish

2 leeks, white and green parts, cut into small dice (2½ cups)

3 stalks celery, cut into small dice

3 tablespoons all-purpose flour

1½ cups whole milk

⅔ cup heavy cream

¾ cup chicken stock, low-sodium store-bought or homemade (page 299)

¾ teaspoon dried thyme leaves, or 1½ teaspoons fresh

¼ teaspoon grated nutmeg

2 cups roughly chopped cooked chicken meat

4 ounces aged Gouda or aged cheddar cheese, grated (1½ cups)

2 cups coarsely ground buttery crackers, such as Ritz or Club (about 2 sleeves)

2 tablespoons extra-virgin olive oil

RECIPE CONTINUES

NOTES: *If you have leftover gravy on hand, by all means use it in place of the chicken stock in this recipe.*

You can use a supermarket rotisserie chicken for the cooked chicken, but in that case, reduce the salt by ¼ teaspoon.

If you have cooked wild rice on hand, use 2 cups for this recipe.

While the rice cooks, heat the butter in a large, high-sided skillet over medium heat. Add the leeks and celery, and season with ¼ teaspoon each of salt and pepper. Cook until tender, about 10 minutes.

Add the flour to the vegetables and stir until well combined with the butter. Pour in the milk and bring to a simmer, whisking to prevent any lumps. Add the cream, chicken stock, thyme, nutmeg, and ½ teaspoon each of salt and pepper. Simmer over low heat until the floury taste dissipates, about 5 minutes. Add the cooked chicken, wild rice (minus the bay leaf), and half of the cheese, and heat until the cheese melts.

Put the crushed crackers in a heavy plastic bag and add ¼ teaspoon pepper and the olive oil. Shake to combine, and set aside.

Rub a 9 × 13-inch baking dish with a thin layer of soft butter. Pour the hotdish mixture into the dish and top with the remaining cheese. Bake for 25 minutes.

Pull the dish from the oven, sprinkle the cracker mixture evenly over the top, and bake until the crackers turn dark golden brown and the hotdish bubbles in the center, about 25 minutes. Serve immediately.

Upside-Down
SPICED ROASTED CHICKEN

Many cooks have an idiosyncratic method for getting juicy white meat, tender dark meat, and crispy skin out of a single roast chicken, and here's mine, the result of all of my quirks coming to bear on a single bird.

To protect the breast meat (which is prone to dryness), I rub the skin with spices, stuff butter beneath the breast skin, blitz it in the oven to melt it, flip the bird over, and roast it upside-down on a soft bed of butter-fed onions. I roast the chicken at a fairly high heat—425°F— which thoroughly bronzes the skin on the back of the bird and cooks the exposed legs all the way through to tenderness.

Of course when the bird is cooked upside-down you lose the chance to savor the brown skin that stretches over the breast meat. But after a year working in a Chinese restaurant (Jean-Georges Vongerichten's 66) cooking next to Chinese master chef (*si-fu*) Lam Lun on the wok line, and watching him chop up hundreds of crispy-skinned garlic chickens and reassemble each one on the platter in the shape of a turtle, I learned that the skin on the back of the chicken is thicker and, consequently, actually crispier than the breast skin.

SERVES 4 TO 6

Wash the chicken under cool running water and pat it dry with paper towels. Sprinkle 1 teaspoon salt evenly over and inside the chicken, and let it sit for 1 hour at room temperature (or up to 4 hours in the refrigerator).

Preheat the oven to 425°F.

Combine the peppercorns, fennel seeds, and bay leaves in a small skillet over medium-low heat. Toast until fragrant, about 3 minutes. Allow to cool slightly, and then grind the toasted spices in a spice-devoted coffee grinder until fine. Add the ginger, nutmeg, cayenne, and ½ teaspoon salt, and set the spice mix aside.

Blot the chicken to remove the excess moisture. Peel the onion, cut it crosswise into 5 thick rings, and lay them on the bottom of a roasting pan. Loosen the skin over the chicken's breasts. Insert the butter under the skin of the chicken breasts and push down to disperse it. Rub the chicken all over with the cut side of a lemon quarter, and then pat the spice mixture all over the chicken. Add the lemon quarters to the cavity of the

RECIPE CONTINUES

- 1 4-pound chicken
- Fine sea salt
- 1 tablespoon black peppercorns
- ½ teaspoon fennel seeds
- 5 dried bay leaves
- 1 teaspoon ground ginger
- ½ teaspoon grated nutmeg
- ¼ teaspoon cayenne pepper
- 1 large Vidalia onion
- 4 tablespoons (½ stick) salted butter, cut into pats, slightly softened
- 1 lemon, quartered

Granny-Style Chicken

My reckoning with a truly fresh chicken came the day that my favorite chicken grower offered a bird she'd processed a few hours earlier for me to cook that night, "granny-style," she said. It was a roast chicken of almost heart-breaking perfection. The skin turned so crusty in the heat that the crunch was audible, and upon close inspection the broken skin had layers, like a French pastry of chicken skin. The meat was fresh and tender, and the juice ran down in buttery rivers. It was nothing like the stiff old bird I had always imagined a day-of chicken would be; it was honestly revelatory.

chicken and set the bird breast-side up on top of the onions. If the legs are really flopping open, tie the ankles together with a bit of kitchen string; if you don't have any string, don't worry about it. Roast the chicken until the skin dries and the butter melts, about 20 minutes.

Remove the pan from the oven, and with a spatula in one hand and a fork in the other, flip the chicken so that the back faces upward. Roast the chicken until the skin is burnished golden brown and the thickest part of the thigh registers 170°F on an instant-read thermometer, 40 to 45 minutes.

Remove the pan from the oven. Transfer the chicken back-side up to a cutting board and the browned onions beneath it to a serving platter. Strain the pan juices into a bowl and skim off the fat. Pour ¼ cup water into the roasting pan, set it on a burner on high heat, and scrape up any stuck-on bits on the bottom with a rubber spatula. Return the defatted juices to the pan to make a thin, *jus*-like gravy.

To carve the chicken, slice on either side of the neck and remove the crispy skin from the back; set it on a plate. Flip the chicken over and remove the thighs: Slice the gaping skin between leg and breast and then push down on the leg to pop the joint. Follow your knife around to the joint on the back of the chicken, and then cut up and around it. (Ideally, you want to rope in the nugget of dark meat that lies in a little hollow at the base of the spine, which is known as the "oyster" because it's so plump and succulent.) With a diagonal cut, split the leg into drumstick and thigh, and lay both on the platter. Do the same with the other leg. Now cut off the wings, taking a little of the breast meat with them if you like (and I do), and lay them on the platter as well. Flip the bird over, and remove the soft skin covering the breast meat. Starting on the bottom of the breast, carve thin slices until you reach the cartilaginous breastbone, and repeat on the other side. Lay the white meat on the warm platter. Ladle the pan sauce over the breast meat. Quickly chop the back skin and lay it over the breast meat. Lay the wedges of softened lemon decoratively on the platter (for squeezing on the meat), and serve immediately.

SPRING CHICKEN POTPIE
with Bev's Crust

1¾ pounds (about 8) boneless, skinless chicken thighs

Fine sea salt and freshly ground black pepper

1 tablespoon canola oil

2 cups chicken stock, low-sodium store-bought or homemade (page 299)

¾ cup plus 2 tablespoons heavy cream

5 tablespoons salted butter

8 ounces button mushrooms, quartered

1 medium kohlrabi, cubed

1 large leek, white and light-green parts, diced

2 cloves garlic, minced

5 tablespoons all-purpose flour, plus extra for rolling the dough

1 14-ounce can small artichoke hearts, drained and quartered

1 teaspoon dried thyme leaves

3 tablespoons minced fresh parsley

Bev's Crust (page 159)

1 large egg yolk

Back in the day, making a pie—any kind—wasn't such a big deal, but these days setting a double-crust chicken potpie on the table is pretty much a declaration of love.

This traditional chicken pie seems destined for winter days, but it lightens up when you add a couple of springlike ingredients: artichokes (I like the tang of canned brined ones) and a few cubes of kohlrabi.

MAKES 1 DEEP-DISH 9-INCH PIE; SERVES 6

Rinse the chicken thighs, pat them dry with a paper towel, and set them on a cutting board. Season the chicken lightly with ½ teaspoon each of salt and pepper.

Heat a large, high-sided skillet over medium-high heat, and add the oil. Add the chicken, skin-side down, to the hot oil. Cook until browned on the underside, about 8 minutes, and then flip over. Pour in the stock and ¾ cup of the cream, and bring to a simmer. Cover the skillet and reduce the heat to maintain a simmer. Cook until the chicken tests tender when poked with a fork, about 30 minutes.

Transfer the chicken to a bowl and pour the liquid into another bowl. Chop the chicken meat and add to the liquid.

Clean and dry the skillet, set it over medium-high heat, and add the butter. When it has melted, add the mushrooms and season with ½ teaspoon each of salt and pepper. When the mushrooms have begun to shrink, add the kohlrabi, leek, and garlic, and cook, stirring often, until the vegetables have wilted, about 5 minutes. Add the flour and stir until no pockets of flour remain. Add the reserved chicken and liquid, and stir until incorporated. Reduce the heat to low and add the artichoke hearts, thyme, and parsley. Cook gently, stirring often, until the sauce loses its raw taste, about 5 minutes. Remove from the heat. (At this point you can cool and refrigerate the filling for up to 1 day.)

Preheat the oven to 375°F.

To roll out the dough, dust a worktop and rolling pin with flour. Roll out the dough disk a little less than ¼-inch thick, about 14 inches in diameter. Fold the dough in half, transfer it to a deep 9-inch pie plate, and unfold it. Press the dough into the corners, leaving the overhang for now. Roll out the second disk of dough.

Fill the pie with the chicken filling and top it with the second piece of dough. Trim the dough to a ½-inch overhang all around. Tuck the overhanging dough into a roll and crimp the edge, pressing down to hook some of the dough over the lip of the dish to hold the pie. Cut a hole in the center of the top crust and add some decorative slashes. Bake the pie for 40 minutes.

Remove the pie from the oven. Whisk together the egg yolk and remaining 2 tablespoons cream, and brush the pie crust lightly with the egg wash. Return it to the oven and bake until the crust is dark golden brown and the filling is bubbling in the center hole, about 20 minutes. Let the pie cool for 10 minutes before slicing it into wedges and serving.

Rosemary-Infused Brown Butter
CHICKEN BREASTS

2 8-ounce boneless, skinless chicken breast halves, preferably farm-raised

4 tablespoons (½ stick) salted butter

2 sprigs fresh rosemary

Fine sea salt and freshly ground black pepper

2 teaspoons minced fresh parsley

NOTE: *As the tenderloin pieces may be a bit smaller and cook more quickly than the others, when they're done, set them on top of a larger piece in the pan.*

I order roasting chickens each year from George and Mary's Best Darn Chickens 'Round, a farm in nearby Frazee. Mary rotates her chickens on pasture in movable coops, which puts them on fresh grass but still keeps them on a short leash. In other words, they exit the farm possessing both free-range flavor and coop tenderness.

Mary likes to process her chickens on the larger side, and they have what she calls "valentine breasts." Because of their maturity, such muscular chicken breasts need more coddling than smaller ones. But once you've slowly rolled a deeply flavored chicken breast in a buttery pan until no pinkness remains in the interior and the fibers remain one degree short of tightly knit —a doneness best described as barely blushing—all immature chicken breasts will seem dull in comparison. (Although if you apply this technique to commercial chicken breasts they will be as tender as custard.) One thing: Stand by the pan as you cook this. Moving chicken breast pieces slowly around in butter requires a kind of devotional attentiveness.

I originally published this recipe in an article about George and Mary's chickens for the *Minneapolis Star Tribune*. Because the lessons in this recipe inform all of the chicken breasts I cook at home, I think it bears repeating.

SERVES 2

Place each chicken breast on a cutting board so that its underside faces up. Generously lop off the flap of the tenderloin from both breasts, and then slice the breasts lengthwise, so that each breast half has been divided into 3 long, fairly equal pieces.

Heat a heavy-bottomed 12-inch skillet over medium heat, and add the butter. When it foams and then turns nut-brown, remove it from the heat and add the rosemary sprigs. Tilt the pan so that the butter foams up over the rosemary. Set aside to infuse for 5 minutes. Then remove and discard the rosemary sprigs.

Set the skillet back on the burner over medium-low heat. Season the chicken pieces generously with salt and pepper, and add them to the butter. Cook very slowly—over either medium-low or medium heat, whatever it takes to cause the butter to emit a whispered sizzle—moving and turning the pieces often, until all surfaces have turned white and the pieces all feel firm to the touch, 15 to 20 minutes. (Cut one open if you like: the inside should have just lost its pinkness but still be shiny with juice.) If the buttery juices begin to simmer, reduce the heat to low.

Add the parsley, and transfer the chicken to a warmed platter. Pour the pan juices over the chicken, and serve.

Malt *and* Chile–Glazed
CHICKEN

1¾ cups malt vinegar

⅓ cup (lightly packed) light
   brown sugar

¼ cup fine sea salt

4 sprigs fresh thyme

1 4- to 4½-pound chicken
   (or 6 chicken legs)

2 dried pasilla chiles, stemmed
   and seeded

2 teaspoons fennel seeds

1 teaspoon coriander seeds

2 teaspoons black peppercorns

2 dried bay leaves

1 3-inch cinnamon stick

½ teaspoon red pepper flakes

½ cup molasses

5 tablespoons honey

Canola oil, for rubbing the
   chicken

¼ cup pomegranate seeds, for
   garnish

NOTE: *Brined and glazed chicken
cooked in a wood-fired oven is hard
to replicate for most home cooks. I
keep the brining (which makes for
juicy chicken) but transplant the
cooking to a grill. After the initial
sear, you will need to cook the
chicken over indirect heat, basting
and turning, until the skin turns
chocolate brown and when the bird
is poked, juices run bronze out of the
pinholes.*

At the restaurant Avec in Chicago, all eyes are on the wood-fired
oven—and the steaming plates that issue from its fiery opening.

The spicy, malty sauce that Chef Koren Grieveson made there
marks a new standard for barbecued chicken. The malt vinegar and
molasses establish the sweet-tart ratio that typifies a good barbecue
sauce, but the pasilla pepper and sweet spices steer the glaze more
toward mole. In typical Midwestern vanguard fashion, Koren makes a
magical sauce out of a common stash of condiments, flinging basics in
exotic directions while keeping the backbone of the thing sensible.

SERVES 4

For the chicken brine, combine 2 cups water, ¼ cup of the malt
vinegar, and the brown sugar, salt, and thyme in a large saucepan. Bring to a boil, stirring until the salt and sugar dissolve.
Add 6 cups cold water, and pour the brine into a container large
enough to hold the chicken. When the brine is cold, submerge
the chicken in it and refrigerate for at least 4 hours and up to 24.

For the glaze, combine the pasilla chiles, fennel seeds, coriander seeds, peppercorns, bay leaves, cinnamon stick, red pepper
flakes, molasses, honey, and remaining 1½ cups malt vinegar
in a medium saucepan. Bring to a boil and cook, stirring, until
the glaze blows huge bubbles and reduces to the consistency of
maple syrup (a good thickness for basting), about 8 minutes.

Set up a grill for indirect grilling—one side heated to
medium-high, the other to low. (If using a charcoal grill, prepare
a bed of hot coals and then rake them to one side of the grill.)

Take the chicken from the brine. Cut it into 8 pieces, leaving the breast meat on the bone for moisture, and blot dry with
paper towels. Rub the skin lightly with oil.

Put the chicken skin-side down on the hot part of the grill.
Cook until both sides are marked and brown, about 5 minutes.
Paint both sides with glaze and move the chicken to the cooler,
more indirect part of the grill. Keep cooking, turning and glazing, until the juices in the thighs run clear and an instant-read
thermometer registers 160°F, about 30 minutes longer.

Transfer the chicken to a platter, garnish with the pomegranate seeds, and serve.

MIDWESTERN FRIED CHICKEN
and Gravy

Compared to Southern fried chicken, Midwestern-style fried chicken offers different joys. Both are a treat, of course, but when I recall the pan-fried chicken of my Midwestern youth, I remember the gravy being the star.

The recipe begins the way you might expect. You soak the chicken briefly in buttermilk and fry it until crisp in a shallow pool of fat (lard if you want to get authentic). But here's where it veers off: Then you bake the chicken until the meat begins to sag on the bone, giving you time to whip up a creamy liquid-gold gravy made from the sticky brown pan deposits. There's a natural progression here, but the baking of the chicken can sometimes wreak havoc on the crust: how do you keep the skin really, truly crisp?

When I was invited to a dinner party at an Amish house twenty miles down the road, I found the answer.

The chicken skin looked a lot like my mother's chicken—the color and texture of the rough side of cowhide. The crust crackled at the fork—a little more loudly than my mother's, or mine. Around the table, everyone was engaged in a sort of triangular communion with their fried chicken, mashed potatoes, and puddle of magnificent gravy. "Deborah," I asked our hostess, "how do you keep it so crisp?" Her reply: "Cracker meal. I use half cracker meal, half flour." I glossed a piece of milk bread with her marigold-yellow butter and her glassy strawberry jam, and finished the meal in the heavy, warm glow of kerosene lamplight and good conversation.

Later, as we pulled onto the blacktop, I whipped out my cell phone and called my mom with the news.

SERVES 4 TO 5

Put the chicken pieces in a large bowl, and add the buttermilk, 1 teaspoon salt, ½ teaspoon black pepper, the thyme, and 4 of the garlic cloves. Marinate for at least 1 hour at room temperature or, refrigerated, overnight.

Preheat the oven to 350°F, and set a baking sheet fitted with a rack on the middle shelf.

Meanwhile, prepare the chicken coating: Combine the 1½ cups flour, the ground crackers, 1¾ teaspoons salt, 1 teaspoon pepper, and the paprika in a large bowl. One at a time,

RECIPE CONTINUES

1 4- to 4½-pound chicken, cut into 10 pieces (see page 151)

1 cup buttermilk

Fine sea salt and freshly ground black pepper

2 teaspoons minced fresh thyme

7 cloves garlic, smashed

1½ cups plus 5 teaspoons all-purpose flour

1 cup finely ground buttery crackers, such as Ritz or Club (about 1 sleeve)

2 teaspoons sweet paprika

About 2 cups lard or canola oil, for frying

1 small bunch fresh sage

2½ cups chicken stock, low-sodium store-bought or homemade (page 299)

Mashed potatoes, for serving

Quick Homemade Stock

You can make stock from the backs, ribs, necks, and scraps left over from portioning a chicken—and a homemade stock makes the best gravy. Season the chicken parts with salt and pepper, and add to an oiled saucepan over medium heat. Brown the meat lightly on both sides. Pour off any excess oil, cover the meat with cold water, and season with a little salt. Add some onion tops or garlic skins, half of a carrot, celery tops, parsley stems—whatever herb or vegetable trimmings you have on hand. Simmer the stock for 30 to 40 minutes, and then strain it through a fine-mesh sieve, discarding the solids. Makes about 3½ cups.

take the chicken pieces from the buttermilk and dunk them in the flour dredge, pressing hard to make the coating adhere to every spot. Set aside on a plate.

In a large, high-sided cast-iron pan, add lard or oil to a depth of 1 inch. Heat over medium-high heat until a droplet of water sprinkled on the surface sizzles loudly.

Give the chicken pieces a fresh roll in the flour mixture if they've absorbed it, and add as many pieces of the dark meat (thighs, wings, and drumsticks) as will fit comfortably in the pan. Fry, turning as needed, until all sides turn dark golden brown, 10 to 12 minutes. Transfer the cooked chicken to the baking sheet in the oven. Continue frying the rest, saving the white breast meat until last, and being careful not to burn the residue forming at the bottom of the pan; that's your gravy base. When it is browned, add the chicken to the baking sheet. (Ideally the dark meat should bake in the oven for about 20 minutes and the light meat for about 10 minutes, until cooked through.)

Pour the fat in the pan into an empty saucepan (a safe place to let it cool down), and discard all but 2 tablespoons of the brown sludge at the bottom of the pan. (If any of it looks burnt, discard that as well.) Let the pan cool down for a minute. Then add the remaining 3 garlic cloves and the sage, and fry for 1 minute. Add the remaining 5 teaspoons flour and cook, stirring, until the mixture is smooth and light brown, about 2 minutes. Add the stock and whisk until smooth. Cook the gravy over low heat until it thickens softly, about 5 minutes.

Season the gravy with salt and pepper to taste, remove the garlic and sage, and pour it into a spouted pitcher to pass behind the hot chicken and the mashed potatoes.

Cutting a Chicken into Ten Pieces

Set the chicken on a cutting board, legs pointing toward you. Make an incision between a leg and the breast and open the leg to separate it from the body. Flip the chicken over, press down on the back, and find the thigh socket on the back of the chicken; cut around the joint. Try to rope in the nugget of meat in the small of the chicken's back (the "oyster"), just above the thigh joint. Slice downward toward the chicken's rear to free the leg. Repeat with the other side so that you have two chicken legs. Make a diagonal cut through the joint between the thigh and the drumstick on each leg, to make four pieces of dark meat.

Pull out the wings and cut generously around one wing joint, freeing the wing and including a bit of the breast meat with it; repeat with the other wing. Cut off both wing tips at the joint, and save them for stock.

Put the chicken into a shoulder stand on your board. Cut downward, through the ribs, separating the front from the back of the chicken, and bend the back until it is doubled over. Free the entire back from the breast. (Save the back and ribs for stock.) Lay the breast skin-side down. Trace a line down the center of the cartilage and press down on it to cut through the breast, separating it in half. Whack each breast half in half again, to make four pieces of white meat—or ten chicken pieces total.

CLASSIC DUCK
in Wild Rice

1 4½- to 5-pound farm-raised duck

1½ teaspoons ground aniseed or fennel seeds

1½ tablespoons dried thyme leaves

1 teaspoon freshly ground black pepper

Fine sea salt

½ cup dark beer

3 dried bay leaves

2 tablespoons salted butter

3 cups diced Vidalia onions (from 2 large onions)

1½ cups diced celery

1 pound brown cremini mushrooms, quartered

5 cloves garlic, minced

1¼ cups natural wild rice

NOTES: *I use a farm-raised duck here—because it's more readily available and I love its rich, dark meat—but to substitute its wild kin use two, and hold them back from the roasting pan until the second hour; add them when you add the rice. Wild ducks are smaller and leaner and require only half the time to bake.*

Duck baked in wild rice is one of those tidy "circle of life" sorts of dishes.

Wild mallards feed on the wild rice—a native, wild aquatic grass—that grows to fill Indian Creek, the wide, beaver-dammed, swollen waterway that meanders around our house. So if we're lucky enough to get a duck from our neighbors who hunt the creek, we can sit on our front porch and feast on the duck and *its* feast, the rice, at the same time.

Baking a bird in a nest of wild rice is a traditional Ojibwe method for preparing wild birds. It's also popular among hunters in the wild rice belt, which runs vertically from Saskatchewan, Canada, through Minnesota and Wisconsin. It turns out that steaming is an extremely kind way to cook a duck (whether wild or domestic), producing meat that caves at the touch of a spoon. Even the breast meat, historically dry when cooked alongside the legs, comes out tender and moist.

But make no mistake: As with a Spanish paella or a jambalaya, other dishes whose rice foundations catch and absorb the meat's juices, the savory bed of wild rice is the star of the show.

SERVES 4

Preheat the oven to 325°F.

Remove the neck and giblets from the duck, and reserve the neck and heart. Rinse the duck, and blot it dry. Cut the duck into 4 pieces: 2 breast halves, 2 legs. To do this, use strong kitchen shears or a large sharp knife to cut between the breast halves. Open up the duck. Cut alongside the left side of the backbone, through the ribs all the way to the end, and then do the same on the right side of the backbone; remove it. You should now have 2 identical sides of duck. Cutting diagonally, separate the breasts from the legs, to make 4 pieces total. (You can also ask your butcher to do this.)

Blot the duck again. Combine the ground aniseed, thyme, pepper, and ½ teaspoon salt in a small dish, and sprinkle the mixture sparingly on both sides of the duck pieces.

Heat a large, high-sided skillet over medium heat. When it is hot, add the duck legs, skin-side down. Brown the legs thoroughly on both sides, rendering as much fat as possible, taking care not to burn the bottom of the pan, about 10 minutes. Transfer the legs to a large roasting pan with a cover (I use my enamelware turkey roaster). Then, in turns, add the breasts, the the backbone, and the neck to the pan and brown each on both sides the same way; add them to the legs. Reserve the skillet, pouring out all of the fat (save it for frying potatoes).

Nestle the reserved neck and heart alongside the browned duck in the roasting pan. Pour in the beer and 1 cup water, add the bay leaves and ¾ teaspoon salt, and cover the pan tightly. Bake for 1 hour. (It's best not to check the duck as it cooks, because then it loses its trapped steam.)

Meanwhile, cook the vegetables in the duck-browning skillet: Add the butter, and set the skillet over medium heat. Add the onions, celery, and remaining spice mixture, and cook, stirring often, until tender, about 15 minutes. Add the mushrooms and garlic and cook, stirring, until the mushrooms have browned, the liquid has reduced, and you have a sludgy, highly flavorful base, 15 to 20 minutes.

Clean the rice by rinsing it in a fine-mesh sieve under cold running water, swishing the rice with your hand until the water runs clear. Transfer the rice to a medium bowl and add water to cover. Pour off any black bits or floating kernels, and pour the rice back into the sieve to drain.

Remove the duck pieces from the roasting pan. Add the mushroom mixture and the rice to the cooking juices, and mix to combine. Set the duck pieces on top of the rice, cover the pan tightly, and bake until the duck is fork-tender and the rice is cooked through, about 1 hour (check for tenderness after 45 minutes). Remove the bay leaves and serve immediately, directly from the pan.

Aniseed and fennel seeds are interchangeable here, but I prefer anise. It's a softer, less shrill version of fennel.

This recipe is calibrated to work with light-brown natural lake rice, so if you have another kind of wild rice, you may need to add another ½ cup or so of water and bake longer. If so, transfer the cooked duck to a dish, cover tightly to keep warm, and continue baking the rice until tender.

I have two words to describe how important meat is to me and my fellow Midwesterners: *meat raffle.*

On Friday nights at bars, service organizations, and "munis" (municipal liquor stores) in small towns and cities across the region, you'll find block-lettered evidence to support the suspicion that the real currency in the Midwest is meat.

A great joint of protein fuels holidays, hunting season, and special occasions. And in the winter, should you run into a meat raffle in progress, you'd discover just how high the stakes can go for a single pack of pork chops. Their worth isn't measured only in dollars raised for a local organization, either; that pack earns out its weight in entertainment value.

Most meat raffles resemble the comfortably no-frills Wolf Lake Muni raffle, which is nearest to my house and so the dearest to my heart. A guy digs out a white bundle of frozen meat from a large cooler, calls it out—"Country ribs! Going to number 178!"—and holds the ribs high in the air for the perusal of a couple dozen meat raffle participants. With the buzz of suspense in the air, people glance at their tickets and fish complimentary cocktail wieners from a Crock-Pot sitting on the bar. After a long pause, someone walks up to claim their loot, to spirited applause.

Here you'll find recipes to make the most out of your virtual winnings. From large crowd-feeding roasts (Classic Beef Pot Roast with Pistachio Salt, Black Maple-Glazed Pork Belly) to old-fashioned chops on a plate (Breaded Stuffed Pork Chops with Ham and Gruyère), to the meat-filled hand pies unique to the Midwest (Nebraskan Runzas and Upper Peninsula [U.P.] Pasties), these are the big proteins that feed the Midwestern soul.

TOURTIÈRE:
The French-Canadian Meat Pie

This hot pork pie is the traditional centerpiece of my mother's family's Christmas Eve dinner, as it is for many French-Canadians who emigrated to the United States.

Some contemporary *tourtière* recipes call for ground pork, but I've found that it doesn't really compare with the long-simmered chopped pork filling of my great-grandmother Bertha Dion's version, fragrant with her own combination of the French *quatre-épices,* the four basic pâté spices.

The recipe may have come from her grandmother, but we credit my mother with the idea of cooking the filling like a risotto: by slowly adding broth to the chopped pork you can really control the final moisture of the filling, and that careful suspension of juice and meat is what makes the pie.

The simmering pot of meat and spices might be the best reason to make *tourtière*: it fills the house with an intoxicating perfume.

MAKES ONE 9- OR 10-INCH PIE; SERVES 6 TO 8

Put the pork in a large pot and add water to cover. Bring to a simmer and skim off the foam. Add the peppercorns, bay leaves, ¾ teaspoon salt, and the onion half. Simmer very slowly, partially covered, for 3½ hours, or until the meat is tender in the center when pierced with a fork.

Transfer the pork to a platter, discard the bones, and cover with plastic wrap. Pass the liquid through a fine-mesh sieve into a medium saucepan, and with a ladle, skim the fat from the top and discard it.

Bring the liquid to a lively simmer and cook until it has reduced by half and tastes concentrated, about 20 minutes. You should be left with approximately 3 cups broth.

Meanwhile, melt the butter in a wide-bottomed saucepan. Add the diced onion and the garlic, season with ½ teaspoon each of salt and pepper, and cook slowly until golden and soft, about 20 minutes.

Roughly chop the reserved meat. Put the cloves, allspice, and ginger in the center of a square of cheesecloth, and tie up the corners to make a sachet.

- 1 3-pound bone-in Boston butt pork roast
- 1 teaspoon black peppercorns
- 3 dried bay leaves
- Fine sea salt and freshly ground black pepper
- ½ large onion, plus 1 large onion, finely diced (2 cups)
- 3 tablespoons salted butter
- 3 cloves garlic, minced
- 2 whole cloves
- 7 allspice berries
- 1 ½-inch piece of fresh ginger, smashed
- 2 sprigs fresh thyme, minced
- 6 fresh sage leaves, chopped fine, or 4 dried sage leaves
- 1 medium Yukon Gold potato, coarsely grated
- ½ teaspoon grated nutmeg
- Bev's Crust (page 159)

NOTE: *At the end of the twentieth century, many Québécois— including two wings of my family—moved to St. Paul, Minnesota, to work as laborers on the twin constructions of the state capitol and the cathedral. The area in which they settled was named—because of their predilection for* cuisses de grenouille*—"Frogtown."*

Measure 4½ cups meat (save any extra for piling on toast later) and add it to the onions, along with the sachet, thyme, sage, and enough of the reduced broth to cover. Cook the meat gently, simmering it over medium heat. As soon as the meat absorbs the broth, add more, cooking until the mixture has a loose saucy consistency, about 20 minutes total. Discard the sachet. Season with the nutmeg and salt and pepper to taste. Stir in the potato and transfer the mixture to a wide bowl to cool.

Preheat the oven to 375°F.

Dust a worktop and rolling pin with flour. Roll out one dough disk a little less than ¼-inch thick, about 14 inches in diameter. Fold the dough in half, transfer it to a deep 9- or 10-inch pie plate, and unfold it. Press the dough into the corners, leaving the overhang, and fill it with the pork mixture. Roll out the second disk of dough, and place it on top. Trim the overhanging dough to ½ inch, fold it under into a rope, and pinch the edge decoratively to seal. Cut a small hole in the center of the top crust and add a few radiating slash vents.

Bake the pie until the crust is deep golden brown and the juices are bubbling up through the center hole, 55 to 60 minutes. Allow it to cool for 10 minutes before serving. Refrigerate any remaining pie.

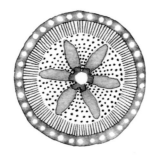

BEV'S CRUST

My cousin Bev Adams's crust (also used for the Tourtière, page 157) uses egg yolk and milk for the liquid binding. I have no idea where she got the recipe, but it makes a perfectly sealed yet delicate vessel for savory pies and is miraculously foolproof. I pass on this recipe to my most crust-frustrated friends, and they report back with the jubilation of winners.

MAKES ONE 9- OR 10-INCH DOUBLE PIE CRUST

- 2½ cups all-purpose flour
- 1 teaspoon fine sea salt
- 16 tablespoons (2 sticks) unsalted butter, cold
- 1 large egg yolk
- Generous ½ cup whole milk, or more if needed

In a large bowl, combine the flour and salt. With a pastry blender, cut the butter into the flour until the larger remaining chunks are the size of small peas.

Drop the egg yolk into a liquid measuring cup and add milk until you reach exactly ⅔ cup (you'll use about ½ cup plus 1 tablespoon). Whisk the egg yolk and milk with a fork until combined, and then add it to the flour mixture all at once. Mix the dough with a fork until you can gather most of it into a ball. It should be like packing a large snowball; if it seems any drier or more difficult than that, add another tablespoon of milk.

Divide the dough in half and pat each half into a 1-inch-thick disk. Wrap each disk in plastic wrap and chill in the refrigerator for at least 1 hour and as long as 2 days. (You can also freeze this dough up to six months.) Let it come to room temperature for 30 minutes before rolling it.

Pig's Head on a Platter at
The Boiler Room, Omaha

You've got to love a chef who, after running out of the whole roasted fish for two, doesn't hesitate to run half a roasted pig's head in its place, with garnishes that successfully bridge both: *gribiche* (caper and herb mayonnaise), French lentils, and a creamy Savoy cabbage slaw.

When it arrives, it's truth in advertising: really and honestly half a pig's head on a platter, glossed over with reduced meat juices. It's best not to stare but instead to get right in there, your eyes level with the tines of your fork, a vantage from which to best hunt for the most succulent nuggets—some of which will look familiar, most of which will be new discoveries. Each cheek, for instance, houses a wide, almost impossibly succulent runway of meat, a stripe of lean and fat woven together in a chunky knit: my new favorite spot on a hog. But that's not to overlook the tender tongue, or the sweet meat tucked beneath the scruff, or the small gems of meat on either side of the snout.

I can't think of a better restaurant in which to indulge in such a bacchanalian feast than The Boiler Room in Omaha. The subterranean space has an open kitchen in the lower level, anchored by a lumbering, bona fide boiler apparatus whose giant metal arms wrap around the bar and then reach upward through five floors of the old 1887 warehouse in the downtown Old Market district. (The Boiler Room's owners, Vera and Mark Mercer, have dramatic vision to spare; they're the restaurateurs and developers largely responsible for making the neighborhood look like the Marais in Paris.) The dining room is located on the floor above, lining the sunken kitchen like a bulwark. Taken in altogether, the soft lighting, preserved rust, thick tablecloths, and walls hung with Vera Mercer's vivid, oversize gastronomic still life photographs—for example, the head of a plucked pheasant resting on a wedge of ripe melon—the effect is something like stepping into a lavishly staged drama in a private supper club. So the pig head on the table actually brings you back down to earth, as does the rest of the menu, which is fresh and contemporary but, in general, not keen on whimsy.

The chef, Paul Kulik, is serious about the pig's head. He says that the impulse to put the dish on the menu arose naturally; he brings in two to six pigs at a time from local farms, each of them with a head, and when he grew tired of making headcheese, he began thinking of ways to present them whole. He's well aware that feasting on a pig's head is not only thrifty but gets people thinking about food and our primal connections to eating: "The fun comes in finding all of those super-delicious half-buried pockets of meat. And with a whole head you naturally have rich, marbled stuff sitting on top of the tongue, on top of the cheek, all of it self-basting in the oven."

Not only does a pig's head on a platter remind you where you are—close to the epicenter of pig production in America—but few dishes stir up the nether regions of one's appetite quite so dramatically.

CLASSIC BEEF POT ROAST
with Pistachio Salt

For years I cooked on a 1940s-era Roper stove, a stocky thing with four widely spaced burners and husky, white enameled shoulders.

For all its bulk, the stove had a tiny ovenbox, and on the open door was printed a chart titled "Roper Scientific Cooking Chart," whose recommendations were a bit at odds with today's kitchen wisdom. At the far left of the spectrum, under "Low Temperature Cookery, 275°F," were the words "beef roast, pork roast, veal and ham." Lately, possibly in reaction to our accelerated lifestyles, most pot-roasted beef recipes call for an oven temperature of 325°F. And yet from my professional cooking days I remember always setting the oven temperature for such covered-dish braises lower, to 285°F, a magic number that cooks the meat slowly without causing the liquid to boil and the meat to toughen.

So in equal emulation of both early-twentieth-century farm women and twenty-first-century professional chefs, I braise my pot roast at 285°F for almost five hours, during which time it obediently sinks into its own juices. At this temperature the pot roast takes about an hour longer than a higher-temperature braise, but the cooking time is largely hands-off, and it gives me plenty of time to stir together a quick pistachio salt topping. Modeled on the traditional Italian *gremolata*, it functions here as a finishing salt for the meat.

SERVES 8

Season the roast liberally with salt and pepper. Heat your largest high-sided skillet over high heat, add the oil, and then add the roast. Sear it quickly until dark brown on all sides, about 8 minutes. Set the roast aside, pour off and discard the excess fat from the skillet, and let the skillet cool a bit. Then add the butter, celery, carrots, turnips, ½ teaspoon salt, and ¾ teaspoon pepper. Cook over medium heat, tossing, until the vegetables begin to soften at the edges, about 5 minutes. Transfer them to a wide bowl and reserve.

Preheat the oven to 300°F.

Add the wine to the skillet, bring to a boil, and cook until slightly reduced, about 3 minutes. Add the beef stock, and bring to a simmer.

Arrange the onions in the bottom of a large covered roasting

RECIPE CONTINUES

---

1 4-pound beef chuck roast, the more marbled the better

Fine sea salt and freshly ground black pepper

1 tablespoon canola oil

2 tablespoons salted butter

3 stalks celery, cut into thirds

3 large carrots, quartered

2 medium turnips, quartered

¾ cup dry red wine

2 cups beef stock, low-sodium store-bought or homemade (see page 299)

2 large Vidalia onions, cut into eighths

11 cloves garlic: 10 whole, 1 minced

4 dried bay leaves

1 tablespoon minced fresh rosemary

1 tablespoon minced fresh thyme

1 cup cherry tomatoes

¼ cup shelled salted pistachios, chopped

¼ cup chopped fresh parsley

NOTE: *It's easy to peel a large quantity of garlic if you use the method I learned from New York's finest prep cooks: Split apart the garlic cloves, discarding all excess papery skin, and soak them in a bowl of water for at least 20 minutes. Then peel the garlic with a small knife (a small serrated one works really well). The cloves will pop right out of their skins.*

pan and set the beef on top of them. Scatter the whole garlic cloves, bay leaves, rosemary, and thyme over and around the roast. Pour the beef stock mixture over the meat and cover the pan tightly. Bake for 1 hour.

Reduce the oven temperature to 285°F, and continue to braise for 2 hours.

Uncover the pan, skim off the fat around the edges with a small ladle, and discard it. With two large forks, carefully turn the meat over and ladle some juice over the top. Add the reserved sautéed vegetables, arranging them around the perimeter of the meat. Cover the pan and braise for 1 more hour.

Skim the fat again with a small ladle, baste the top of the meat again, and then scatter the cherry tomatoes across the top, some dropping onto the meat, some onto the vegetables. Don't stir again. Braise, uncovered this time to allow the tomatoes to split and shrink and the top of the meat to brown, until the meat feels extremely tender at the touch of a fork, 30 minutes to 1 hour. Discard the bay leaves.

For the pistachio salt, combine the pistachios, parsley, minced garlic, and ¼ teaspoon each of salt and pepper in a small bowl.

Before serving, dust the pistachio salt evenly over the roast (reserve any extra for passing at the table). Serve the pot roast right from the pan, pulling apart the meat with two forks for most of it, and gently carving the marbled top end of the chuck into thick slices.

Black Maple-Glazed
PORK BELLY

There's a reason why bacon is manna, and it's not entirely on account of the twin powers of salt and smoke. Part of the due belongs to the belly itself, a naturally self-basting layer cake of fat, lean, and—my favorite—the in-between.

After a few fall pigs in a row, I've learned the wisdom of saving a bunch of fresh belly for roasting and glazing. Nothing could be more hands-off. The sweet-and-tangy glaze condenses at the fatty edges into irresistible black shellac, and after a few hours in the oven, the meat practically shreds itself. It's perfect served over something that can catch its juices, such as Wild Rice and Brown Rice Pilaf (page 235).

SERVES 6 TO 8

½ teaspoon sugar

Fine sea salt and freshly ground black pepper

3 pounds skinless fresh pork belly

6 cloves garlic, smashed

3 dried bay leaves

2 sprigs fresh rosemary

½ cup maple syrup

¼ cup balsamic vinegar

1 tablespoon soy sauce

1-inch piece of fresh ginger, smashed

Mix together the sugar, 1½ teaspoons salt, and 1 teaspoon pepper, and rub into both sides of the pork belly. Leave to cure, refrigerated, for 2 hours or as long as overnight.

Preheat the oven to 325°F.

Blot the moisture from the pork belly and set it, fat-side up, on a rack inside a large rectangular baking dish or a roasting pan. Scatter 4 of the garlic cloves, the bay leaves, and the rosemary sprigs around the pork belly, and pour in enough water to reach just below the rack. Cover the pan tightly with aluminum foil and bake until the center of the pork belly tests tender when poked with a thin fork, 3½ to 4 hours, depending on the thickness of the pork.

Raise the oven temperature to 425°F.

Combine the maple syrup, vinegar, soy sauce, ginger, remaining 2 garlic cloves, ¼ teaspoon salt, and ½ teaspoon pepper in a small saucepan and bring to a boil. Simmer until the mixture thickens and throws big bubbles, about 5 minutes.

Lift out the pork and pour out all but a thin layer of the liquid in the baking dish. Thickly paint both sides of the belly with glaze. Roast the pork belly for 10 minutes, apply more glaze, and roast for another 5 minutes. Reapply glaze and roast until the glaze sticks to the belly and turns dark and caramelized, about 5 minutes.

Transfer the pork belly to a cutting board, cut the belly crosswise into ½-inch-thick slices, and serve.

WILD BOAR SLOPPY JOES

Canola oil

2 pounds ground wild boar
(or 1 pound ground venison
or beef and 1 pound ground
pork)

Fine sea salt and freshly ground
black pepper

2 tablespoons salted butter

1 cup small-diced onion

¾ cup small-diced carrot

½ cup small-diced celery

⅓ cup minced garlic (from
1 head garlic)

5 tablespoons tomato paste

1½ cups (14-ounce can) crushed
plum tomatoes

1¼ cups dry red wine

2 cup beef stock, low-sodium
store-bought or homemade
(see page 299)

2 dried bay leaves

⅔ cup heavy cream

½ teaspoon red pepper flakes

2 teaspoons minced fresh thyme

2 teaspoons minced fresh
rosemary

2 shallots

Wondra flour

2 bunches (about 20 leaves)
fresh sage, leaves only

8 soft buns

Ground-meat sandwiches have had a hold on the Midwest for ages, starting with the nubbly loose-meat sandwich created at the Maid-Rite chain, which originated in Iowa in 1926, and including the ubiquitous sloppy joe. With nearly four decades of them under my belt, I can say with authority that even though they all look alike, some sloppy joes are better than others; the worst of them seem to be made via a blind grope in the condiment cupboard, coming out with some crazy combination of ketchup, mustard, and hot sauce.

Jared Wentworth's take on the sloppy joe at his restaurant, Longman & Eagle, in Chicago, adds class to the genre, using deep-red ground wild boar, diced vegetables, red wine, cream, and fresh herbs. He cooks the mixture for what seems an unreasonably long time, until the sauce and the meat become one savory, solid mass—earthy and highly tuned at the same time, not unlike a sandwich-ready Italian bolognese sauce. Piling the filling in a cottony egg bun, he gilds the meat with a killer tangle of crisp fried shallots and sage leaves.

Jared's recipe is reproduced faithfully here but for one detail. In the restaurant they let the meat bubble and perk on a slow part of the stove for six to eight hours, with intermittent stirring. That's not very practical at home, so I put the pot in the oven, where it slow-cooks to tenderness in nearly half the time. (The filling can also be made in a Crock-Pot on low heat.)

SERVES 6 TO 8

Preheat the oven to 325°F.

Heat a large, wide-bottomed ovenproof pan over medium-high heat. Add a thin film of canola oil to the pan, and then add the ground meat. Season with salt and pepper and cook, stirring, until browned, about 5 minutes. Transfer the meat to a bowl, leaving 2 tablespoons fat in the pan.

Add the butter, onion, carrot, celery, and ½ teaspoon each of salt and pepper to the pan. Sauté until the vegetables begin to soften, about 10 minutes. Add the garlic and cook for 1 minute. Stir in the tomato paste and cook until the bottom of the pan turns coppery, 2 minutes.

Pour in the tomatoes and cook until they start to soften, about 5 minutes. Add the wine, bring to a boil, and cook until reduced by half, about 10 minutes. Add the beef stock and bay leaves, and return the ground meat to the pan.

Put the pan in the oven and bake, uncovered, stirring once in a while, until the meat softens and the sauce thickens to a stew-like consistency and tastes rich, about 4 hours.

Add the cream, red pepper flakes, thyme, and rosemary, and bake for 20 minutes to incorporate. Remove the bay leaves.

Slice the shallots crosswise into thin rings. Heat 1 inch of canola oil in a medium saucepan until a sprinkle of flour sizzles on the surface, about 375°F. Toss the shallots in Wondra flour and fry them, in two batches, until crisp; drain on paper towels. Toss the sage leaves in the flour and fry until crisp. Season the shallots and sage with salt and pepper.

To serve, cut open the buns. Stuff them with the sloppy joe mixture, top each with a few fried shallots and sage leaves, and serve.

FANCY MEAT LOAF
with Bacon *and* Mushrooms

2 tablespoons extra-virgin
olive oil

2 tablespoons salted butter

1 large sweet onion, cut into
small dice (2 cups)

Fine sea salt and freshly ground
black pepper

3½ ounces shiitake mushrooms,
stemmed and chopped

5 cloves garlic, minced

3 tablespoons dry sherry or
dry white wine

½ cup whole milk

2 cups coarsely ground fresh
bread crumbs (from about
4 slices country bread)

1 pound ground beef chuck

1 pound ground pork

½ teaspoon grated nutmeg

¼ teaspoon ground allspice

2 tablespoons chopped fresh
thyme

1 tablespoon Worcestershire
sauce

2 large eggs

½ cup shelled salted pistachios

10 slices bacon

2 tablespoons (packed) light
brown sugar

With its whole pistachios and savory bits of herb and mushroom, what you have here is fancier than basic meat loaf yet more rustic (and easier to make) than a French pâté. An honorable, decadent thing when hot, it also tastes divine cold.

My meat loaves started tilting in an upscale direction once I discovered how much I enjoy a cold meat loaf sandwich the next day, whether open-face or between slices of soft white bread spread with a smear of Dijon or a dollop of chutney. And to tell the truth, part of the lure of cold meat loaf is the way the cool slices look: shiny on the surface, smooth, the fat and meat mottled together into an old-fashioned terrazzo pattern.

SERVES 6 TO 8

Preheat the oven to 375°F.

Heat a large skillet over medium heat. Add the olive oil, butter, and onion, season with ½ teaspoon each of salt and pepper, and cook until the onion is soft and light brown, about 10 minutes.

Add the mushrooms and garlic to the skillet and sauté until the mushroom juice exudes and then evaporates, about 5 minutes. Add the sherry and simmer for 1 minute to reduce slightly. Pour the mushroom mixture onto a wide plate to cool slightly.

In a bowl, add the milk to the bread crumbs and fluff with a fork.

In a large bowl, combine the beef, pork, nutmeg, allspice, thyme, Worcestershire sauce, eggs, pistachios, mushroom mixture, bread crumbs (including any milk left in the bowl), 1 teaspoon salt, and ½ teaspoon pepper. Mix quickly but thoroughly with your hands.

Transfer the mixture into a 9 × 13-inch baking dish, and form it into a squared-off log, 6 inches wide and 12 inches long, down the center of the length of the pan. Lay the bacon slices across the meat loaf, slightly overlapping. Rub the bacon with the brown sugar.

Bake until an instant-read thermometer inserted in the center reads 160°F, 50 to 55 minutes. Rest for 5 minutes before cutting the loaf into thick slices and serving.

SHERRY-GLAZED HAM
with Marjoram Salsa

1 9-pound double-smoked cooked ham (half of a whole ham)

¼ cup orange juice

¾ cup (lightly packed) light brown sugar

½ cup dry sherry

½ cup plus 1 tablespoon sherry vinegar or apple cider vinegar

5 whole cloves

1 whole star anise

1 teaspoon cracked black pepper

1 tablespoon sweet paprika

Juice of 1 lemon

2 cloves garlic

¼ teaspoon fine sea salt

2 tablespoons pine nuts

1 tablespoon chopped fresh marjoram (or oregano)

¼ cup chopped fresh parsley

2 tablespoons extra-virgin olive oil

Freshly ground black pepper

One sunny fall day a few years back, Uncle Merle left our place on his Harley to ride back to Lincoln, Nebraska, with plans to stop at the famous Tea Steak House in Tea, South Dakota, just outside of Sioux Falls. Behind his lion's mane of a beard, Merle is a tender-hearted guy with an appreciation for old guns, old whiskey, and serious cooking, and I was expecting a call from him reporting back on the steaks. But he told me that he'd ordered the ham dinner instead. The chunk of smoked ham on his plate had been as large as a roast, and with it arrived a vision: "It was like one of those women in the back had dug into that ham and pulled out a huge hunk of it to put on my plate. It was steaming hot. It was so good."

The green sauce passed with this platter of tangy sherry-glazed ham is what I'm calling marjoram salsa—a loose pesto enlivened with the piney, floral charge of marjoram, which is like a stronger oregano. Its outgoing character complements the smoky ham.

SERVES 8 TO 10

Preheat the oven to 325°F.

With a sharp knife, score the ham by cutting a ¼-inch-deep crosshatch pattern into its surface. Set the ham on a rack inside a large baking or roasting pan, and pour water to reach ½ inch up the sides of the pan. Cover tightly, with a cover or foil, and bake the ham until it tests hot at the center, about 2 hours. (To test it, poke a thin meat fork deep into the ham, leave it there for a second, and then press the tines to your lower lip, where you'll be able to feel its temperature.)

Remove the ham from the oven and raise the temperature to 425°F.

For the glaze, combine the orange juice, brown sugar, sherry, ½ cup vinegar, cloves, star anise, pepper, and paprika in a medium saucepan. Bring to a boil over high heat and cook, stirring, until the glaze reduces to a syrup, about 5 minutes. Add the lemon juice and stir to combine.

Uncover the ham, and pour off and reserve all but enough liquid to cover the bottom of the pan. Thinly brush the glaze over the surface and roast the ham in the oven for 10 minutes.

Continue to roast the ham, basting it twice more and using all of the glaze, until the surface is deeply caramelized, another 15 minutes.

For the herb salsa you can either mince everything to a paste on a cutting board or use a mortar and pestle. Either way, chop the garlic, add the salt, and smash it with the side of the knife until it starts to weep. Add the pine nuts and smash to a paste. Add the fresh marjoram and parsley, and chop or pound until fine. Scrape into a bowl. Add 2 tablespoons of the reserved ham cooking juice, the remaining 1 tablespoon vinegar, and the olive oil. Season with pepper to taste.

Slice the ham thinly and serve on a platter, passing the marjoram salsa at the table.

BARBECUED PORK
Butt Steaks

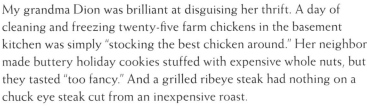

4 1-pound bone-in Boston butt pork steaks, each 1½ inches thick

Fine sea salt

4 teaspoons coriander seeds, or 1 tablespoon ground

1 tablespoon ground ginger

1 tablespoon sweet paprika

1½ teaspoons ground mustard

½ teaspoon cayenne pepper

6 tablespoons (packed) light brown sugar

⅓ cup ketchup

2 tablespoons fresh lime juice

2 tablespoons rice vinegar

My grandma Dion was brilliant at disguising her thrift. A day of cleaning and freezing twenty-five farm chickens in the basement kitchen was simply "stocking the best chicken around." Her neighbor made buttery holiday cookies stuffed with expensive whole nuts, but they tasted "too fancy." And a grilled ribeye steak had nothing on a chuck eye steak cut from an inexpensive roast.

In our family, the grilled pork butt steak is considered to be one of her best inventions. And she was not shy in telling the butcher how she liked it: two inches thick, cut across the bone, all in one piece. The pork butt is the most hardworking and well-larded cut on a hog, and most people slow-cook it, as for pulled pork. But my grandma instinctively knew that these steaks are almost as tender when cooked to medium pinkness as they are when cooked to fork-pulled shreds.

This snapped-together barbecue rub is distinguished by its insistent coriander seed. I know that most people probably stock preground coriander in their own pantries, but ever since I worked in a place that toasted all of its own coriander seeds before crushing them, I can't stop thinking about the intense, citrusy fragrance of the freshly ground.

SERVES 4 TO 6

Lay the pork steaks out on a baking sheet and rub them with 1 teaspoon salt.

Toast the whole coriander seeds in a small dry skillet over medium heat until fragrant and a shade darker, about 1 minute. Pour into a spice-devoted coffee grinder or a mortar, and process until fine.

In a large bowl, combine the coriander, ginger, paprika, mustard, cayenne, brown sugar, ketchup, lime juice, vinegar, and 1 teaspoon salt. Stir to combine. Rub half of the barbecue sauce on the pork steaks. Marinate for 30 minutes at room temperature, or as long as 12 hours refrigerated. Refrigerate the remaining sauce.

Set up a grill for indirect grilling: one side heated to high, the other to medium. Grill the steaks until darkly marked on the underside, 5 to 7 minutes. Flip the steaks and paint them with a thin layer of barbecue sauce. Cook until marked on the underside again, 5 to 7 minutes. Flip and paint the top again with sauce. Move the steaks to the medium-hot part of the grill and cook until the meat feels bouncy but firming up when poked and the internal temperature reads 145°F, 5 to 10 minutes.

Remove the steaks from the grill and let them rest for a few minutes. Serve whole, like a steak, or sliced on a platter.

NOTE: *The USDA has recently changed its tune on pork cookery. They've acknowledged that the color of the meat is not an accurate measure of doneness: after all, cured pork will always be pink, no matter how long it's cooked, and so will some of the darker cuts on a hog, such as the Boston butt. It's best to go by internal temperature. While they once dictated that pork was safe only when cooked until gray and dry (160°F), now they're admitting that pork is safe when cooked to a medium-rare 145°F plus a 3-minute rest time. It's a good thing, too, because these steaks taste best when cooked to exactly that temperature, when they're pale pink inside and still juicy.*

NEBRASKAN RUNZAS

DOUGH

¾ cup lukewarm water (approximately 110°F)

2½ teaspoons (1 .25-ounce packet) active dry yeast

Pinch plus 3 tablespoons sugar

4 large eggs: 3 for the dough, 1 for the egg wash

3¾ cups bread flour, plus more for the counter

12 tablespoons (1½ sticks) salted butter, softened, plus more for the bowl

2 teaspoons fine sea salt

FILLING

1 pound medium-lean ground beef

Fine sea salt and freshly ground black pepper

3 tablespoons salted butter

1 large Vidalia onion, diced

3 cloves garlic, minced

2 teaspoons minced fresh thyme, or 1½ teaspoons dried

1 teaspoon minced fresh rosemary, or 1½ teaspoons dried

1 tablespoon canola oil, plus more for the baking sheet

8 ounces baby spinach

It was at Aaron's grandparents house in Grand Island, Nebraska, that I first met the runza, the meat-filled bun popularized by German-Russian immigrants. We picked them up from The Runza Hut, a fast-food restaurant that serves only its namesake meat pies (which no one outside of Nebraska ever believes). Clearly, they were greasy versions of the real thing; but it was the way Grandma Irene analyzed hers that taught me what a runza should be.

"This is pretty much right," she said. "Just beef and onions. Some people add cabbage."

"Not cabbage," intoned Grandpa Clarence drily, dropping his runza onto its ruffled paper.

"Cabbage is common," said Irene, smiling. "Some people don't like it."

The shades were drawn against the searing September heat, and we sat at the Formica kitchen table amid the butterfly-wing fluttering of runza wrappers and the sound of the bawling wind outside. Sometimes in Nebraska the wind whines and complains through every tight space it can't freely blow.

"The crust is a little too sweet, but the beef is right," said Irene, picking at her runza. "I haven't made these in a while," she said, her dimples bottomless. "With the Runza Hut, I guess you don't have to," I said. She gave me a conspiratorial wink, because neither of us believed it.

When I got around to making them, I thought of Clarence and didn't add cabbage—but I did add spinach. The greens add softness to the filling and virtually melt into the beef. I don't think he'd even notice.

MAKES 8 LARGE RUNZAS; SERVES 8

For the dough, combine the water, yeast, and pinch of sugar in a large mixing bowl and let sit until foamy, about 10 minutes. Add 3 of the eggs and whisk to combine. Add half of the bread flour and beat with a wooden spoon until good and thready, about 3 minutes. Add the butter, remaining 3 tablespoons sugar, remaining flour, and the salt and mix well. The dough will be a little sticky. Leave to rest and hydrate for 15 minutes.

Knead the dough to develop the gluten, until it feels tight and smooth, about 5 minutes. Transfer the dough to a lightly buttered bowl, cover, and let rise for 1 hour at room temperature. Then chill for 1 to 2 hours in the refrigerator, until cold to the touch, or as long as overnight.

Remove the dough from the refrigerator and divide it into 8 even portions. Roll each one into a ball and leave on the counter, covered loosely, to warm up.

Meanwhile, make the filling: Heat a large skillet over medium-high heat, and when it's hot, add the beef. Season with ¾ teaspoon salt and ½ teaspoon pepper and cook, chopping to separate the beef, until lightly browned, about 5 minutes. Use a slotted spoon to transfer the beef to a bowl. Drain and discard all but a film of the fat from the skillet.

Add the butter to the skillet and when it has melted, add the onion. Cook over medium heat, stirring, until light golden brown, about 15 minutes. Add the garlic, thyme, and rosemary and cook for 3 minutes. Scrape the mixture into the bowl containing the beef.

Without cleaning the skillet, add the tablespoon of oil to it. Over high heat, sauté the spinach until wilted, about 1 minute, and cook until the excess liquid has evaporated. Chop the spinach, add it to the beef mixture, and set aside to cool.

Flatten a dough ball on a heavily floured surface, and roll it to form a 3 × 5-inch rectangle. Then make wrapping flaps from the four corners of the rectangle by rolling each corner out thinly, so that you have a thick rectangle with four thinner triangular wings at the corners. Spoon ½ cup of the filling onto the rectangle and wrap the flaps over it, pinching to close. Flip the bundle over in your hands, gently forming the runza into a fat football shape. Set the runza seam-side down on an oiled baking sheet. Repeat with the remaining dough balls and filling.

Preheat the oven to 375°F.

Let the runzas rise, uncovered, about an inch, about 45 minutes.

Mix together the remaining egg and 2 tablespoons water to make an egg wash, and brush it thinly over the tops of the runzas. Bake the runzas until dark golden brown, 25 minutes. Serve hot.

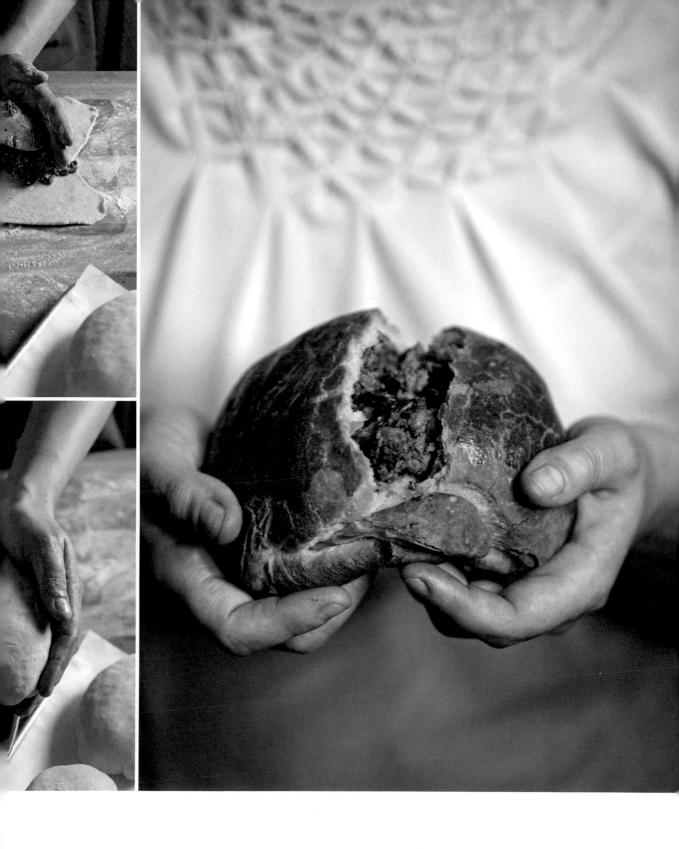

GRILLED SHORT RIB STEAKS
with Marinated Cherry Tomatoes

4 6-ounce boneless short ribs

2 teaspoons soy sauce

2 teaspoons balsamic vinegar

5 tablespoons extra-virgin olive oil

1 teaspoon minced fresh rosemary

Freshly ground black pepper

1 pint cherry tomatoes, halved

1 small clove garlic, grated

2 tablespoons fresh lemon juice

1 teaspoon sugar

¼ teaspoon red pepper flakes, or more to taste

Fine sea salt

¼ cup torn fresh basil leaves

Once you've fallen in love with Korean barbecue and its thinly sliced, caramelized, grilled short ribs wrapped up with kimchi in a leaf bundle, you look differently at the short rib, a cut that Western cooks usually braise low and slow.

One day a few summers ago, I tried grilling rectangular steaks cut from the boneless short rib—and was blown away. For value, I know of no better summer steak: this cut is as finely marbled as a map of rivers but as ruby-red and flavorful as the more common hanger steak. A scoop of marinated summer cherry tomatoes, shedding their tart juice, is just the thing to counter the steak's deep minerality.

If you can't get boneless short ribs from your butcher shop, you can sometimes find their next-door neighbor, the highly marbled cut on the chuck side of the short ribs, a patterned strip that sometimes gets roped into a large chuck roast and sometimes get ground for burgers.

SERVES 4

Marinate the steaks: Rub the steaks with the soy sauce, balsamic vinegar, and 1 tablespoon of the olive oil. Sprinkle with the rosemary and ½ teaspoon black pepper. Marinate at room temperature for at least 30 minutes.

Combine the cherry tomatoes, garlic, lemon juice, sugar, red pepper flakes, ¼ teaspoon salt, ⅛ teaspoon pepper, and the basil. Marinate at room temperature, stirring now and then, for at least 30 minutes. Then mix in the remaining 4 tablespoons olive oil.

Preheat a grill to medium-high heat.

Blot the steaks with paper towels and sprinkle both sides with salt. Grill, turning as needed, until you feel some resistance when you poke the steaks and they reach 128°F on an instant-read thermometer, about 10 minutes total. (I like these steaks cooked just slightly more than medium-rare.) Remove from the grill and let rest, flipping the steaks occasionally, for 5 minutes.

To serve, slice the steaks thinly across the grain and cover with the marinated tomatoes.

Deer Camp
KEFTA KEBABS

The lean garnet meats—lamb and venison, especially—seem most themselves when they're padded with a heady mix of sweet and savory spices, such as the one I first encountered in Claudia Roden's recipe for Moroccan lamb kefta in *The New Book of Middle Eastern Food.*

The shape of these spiced venison kebabs depends on the weather during hunting season: If it's temperate enough to grill outside, I'll make traditional *doner kebabs,* forming the meat around the skewers. But if it's cold and snowing, I'll just pat them into flat oval patties and fry them indoors in my heavy cast-iron pan. Either way, the Middle Eastern mood of this mixture lends an exotic edge to the freshly ground meat. Instead of venison, these kebabs are also wonderful made with either ground lamb or beef.

SERVES 6

If using wooden kebab skewers, soak them in water to cover.

Heat a large skillet over medium-high heat. Add the butter, oil, onion, and ½ teaspoon salt. Cook, stirring, until the onion starts to turn light brown, about 5 minutes. Reduce the heat to medium-low and cook slowly until the onion is tender, caramelized, coppery, and sweet, about 20 minutes. Transfer to a plate to cool.

In a large bowl combine the venison, pork, coriander, cumin, cinnamon, cayenne, 1 teaspoon salt, 1 teaspoon black pepper, and the cilantro, ginger, garlic, egg yolk, pine nuts, and cherries. Add the cooled cooked onion. Mix with your hands until well combined.

Divide the meat mixture into 6 balls and thread a skewer through the center of each one. To form a *doner kebab,* squeeze the meat mixture to an even thickness around the skewer and roll it between your hands until you've formed an 8-inch-long cylinder. Set the kebab on a platter and continue forming the rest. (If you are frying the kebabs in a pan, pat each portion into an approximately ½-inch-thick patty, roughly the width and length of your palm.)

Prepare a medium-hot grill. Grill the kebabs, rotating to cook all sides, until cooked through but still juicy inside, about 10 minutes. Serve immediately.

1 tablespoon salted butter

2 tablespoons extra-virgin olive oil

1 large Vidalia onion, diced

Fine sea salt and freshly ground black pepper

1½ pounds ground venison

8 ounces ground pork

2 teaspoons ground coriander

¾ teaspoon ground cumin

½ teaspoon ground cinnamon

⅛ teaspoon cayenne pepper

3 tablespoons minced fresh cilantro stems

2 teaspoons grated fresh ginger

2 cloves garlic, finely grated

1 large egg yolk

2 tablespoons pine nuts

3 tablespoons dried sour cherries, chopped

BUTCHER'S KRAUT

4 whole cloves

2 teaspoons black peppercorns

1 teaspoon caraway seeds

1½ tablespoons canola oil, plus
more for the caraway

2 pounds pork spareribs or
meaty country ribs

Fine sea salt and freshly ground
black pepper

⅓ pound slab bacon, cut into
1-inch-square chunks

2 tablespoons salted butter

2 medium onions, finely diced

1 tablespoon (packed) light
brown sugar

4 cloves garlic, chopped

1½ cups dry white wine

3 pounds sauerkraut, with
a little juice, preferably
homemade (page 288) or the
kind sold in a bag

3 cups chicken stock,
low-sodium store-bought or
homemade (page 299)

¾ teaspoon dried thyme leaves,
crushed

3 dried bay leaves

4 links (1 pound) smoked
country sausage

3 skin-on old-fashioned wieners

10 small tart crab apples

NOTE: *Serve this with buttered
boiled potatoes and spicy mustard.*

If you take a minute to procure good-quality sauerkraut and pork, this dish practically makes itself. Traditionally, it is made with a mixture of fresh and smoked pork—fresh spareribs, sausages, skin-on wieners, smoked pork chops, chunks of bacon or salt pork—buried in a sea of sauerkraut and its juice, white wine, and a few spices. The juices from the meats lend a butteriness to the sauerkraut while the tamed kraut maintains a thrilling electric tartness. Feel free to make your own substitutions and to scale up the quantities and cook this in a portable electric roaster to feed a crowd.

SERVES 8 TO 10

Preheat the oven to 325°F.

Put the cloves and peppercorns in the center of a square of cheesecloth, and tie up the corners to make a sachet. Pour the caraway onto a cutting board and cover with a little oil. Finely chop until it becomes a paste, and set aside.

Season the pork ribs with a light dusting of salt and pepper. Heat the 1½ tablespoons oil over high heat in a roasting pan or Dutch oven large enough to hold all of the ingredients. Brown the ribs on all sides, about 5 minutes and transfer to a plate.

Pour out the fat from the pan and discard it. Add the bacon and brown on all sides; set it aside with the ribs. Add the butter, onions, and brown sugar to the pan, season with salt and pepper, and cook for 20 minutes, or until the onions are soft. Add the garlic and cook for 1 minute. Pour in the wine and cook at a boil for 5 minutes, or until reduced a bit.

Add the ribs, bacon, sauerkraut, chicken stock, thyme, bay leaves, spice sachet, and caraway paste. Cover the pan with a parchment paper lid (see page 196) or partially cover with its own lid, and bake for 2 hours at a slow simmer. (Lower the oven temperature if the liquid is boiling.)

Add the sausages, wieners, and apples, snuggling them down into the kraut, and cook until all the meats are tender, 45 minutes to 1 hour. (You can keep this warm in a low oven for up to an hour before serving.)

Skim any pooling fat from the surface of the sauerkraut with a ladle, and discard the bay leaves before serving.

Sausages

When he started working for the Kozkas, their trade increased, for Fidelis had his father's talent for making sausage and he'd learned his father's secrets. . . . There is no ingredient too humble. Use the finest of everything. Even the grade of salt matters. The garlic must be perfectly fresh, never dried out. The meat of course, and the casings, the transparent guts of sheep. Clean. They must be exquisitely fresh as well. Fidelis, following his father's dictum when he made up his first batch of Swedish sausages for the Scandinavian trade, did not use just any potato in the filling, but sought the finest in the area. He triumphed.

—Louise Erdrich, *The Master Butchers Singing Club*

The Midwest is awash in excellent sausages, many of them descendants of the immigrant tradition. When they homesteaded the region, the Swedes brought their mild potato sausage, made for the holidays and gently poached to firmness; the Italians made sweet and hot fresh sausages, and of course a vast array of cured *salumi*; and the German and Slavic people arrived with the perfume of smoked sausage still on them and promptly began making their favorites, including the now iconic Midwestern bratwurst. More recently, people from Mexico have been popularizing fresh chorizo, and Southeast Asians (as evidenced at the Hmong markets in St. Paul) have been winning many converts to their spicy smoked pork sausages, nearly green with chopped herbs.

Because I grew up in a family of German-American butchers, in the shadow, often literally, of skeins of smoked pork sausage looped high above my head, that is the kind I know something about.

The story of my family's meat market resembles those told by many other families who peddle hand-cut and handmade meat in the Midwest. Some of them (notably Usinger's and Nueske's) have gone federally inspected and do an extensive mail-order business, and others loom large only in the minds of their loyal fan base.

My great-uncle Phil Thielen started Thielen Meats in 1922 in the back of his furniture store in downtown Pierz, Minnesota. His sausages were made in the Bohemian style, as were most of the sausages in the area—which is to say, more coarsely ground than your typical Berliner sausage, yet less heavily smoked than many Polish sausages. His smokehouse, busy churning out treats for seasonal visitors on their way to their cabins in the northern lake country, perfumed that end of town, and also all the couches and chairs for sale in the front of his store.

Out of an appreciation for the flavor of the original sausages, the market in Pierz (now run by my uncle Keith and my three cousins Matt, Andy, and Joe) continues to turn out the products of an earlier era, still made by hand and finished in one of their many fruitwood-fired smokehouses. They've expanded but never changed the process, which means that the long and gentle smoke bath shrinks the sausages, resulting in water loss (the thing that many contemporary meat producers want to avoid) and, yes, flavor magnification. This isn't a sausage that comes ready to eat; both the country and the longer garlic sausages require further cooking. They still make ring bologna (it comes out fresh every Thursday) and fruity, thick bacon (with a reassuringly dense, white cap of fat) and homemade dried beef and skin-on wieners, among other things, and whenever I stop by to restock my essential cache, I often walk out snacking on a wiener, cold from the case, still with the adamant snap and essential tang that I remember from my childhood.

When it comes to preparing all of these Midwestern sausages, there is some dissent among the ranks of local cooks. For fresh unsmoked bratwurst, some people parcook them in a stew of caramelized onions and beer before rolling them on a hot grill, although I usually skip that step and grill them over low heat, with a vulture's attention to make sure they don't split. Smoked sausages can also be grilled, but it's more traditional to steam them in a little water in a covered pan until firm throughout and then lift the lid and let the water boil off to glaze the sausages in their own rich juices.

That golden pan juice, by the way, is a traditional and precious liquid to the Bohemians. My grandma Dion spoke very highly of it, what she called "dip-dee." She literally foisted her taste memories from the old farmhouse on us grandkids, ordering us to dip our bread into the hot, gooey pan sludge.

At least I know she didn't make it up. When I was driving around Sioux Falls with Jim Woster talking about South Dakota beef, he told me how his Bohemian grandmother would reserve the rich sausage pan juices for the kids, and how there was nothing better than a smoky smear of that juice on a heel of homemade white bread.

Upper Peninsula (U.P.) PASTIES

1 pound ground beef chuck

8 ounces ground pork

1½ cups diced rutabaga

1 cup diced onion

1 cup diced carrots

¾ teaspoon fine sea salt

½ teaspoon freshly ground
black pepper

1½ teaspoons minced fresh
rosemary

¼ cup minced fresh parsley

2 tablespoons sour cream

Bev's Crust (page 159)

1 large egg

NOTES: *Parbaked pasties freeze
very well and are wonderful to have
on hand. Bake them for 30 minutes
and remove from the oven. When
they're cool, wrap each pasty individually in plastic wrap and freeze
in a plastic bag. To finish baking, unwrap the frozen pasty and
bake at 350°F until golden brown
outside and bubbling inside, about
40 minutes.*

*In the shops they're often served
with a teacup of gravy, but unless
you're making the pasty filling
with leftover roast beef—which is
wonderful, by the way—and you
have extra gravy on hand, it doesn't
make much sense.*

I've made countless drives between New York City and northern Minnesota, and without a doubt, the best road food will be found on the scenic, snaking northern route—the one that takes you through the Upper Peninsula (U.P.) of Michigan. In addition to the frequently delicious pies and fried fresh perch found in diners throughout the U.P., there are lots of roadside pasty ("pass-tie") shops, small buildings redolent with the aromas of the only glorious thing on the menu: a meat-and-vegetable-filled hand pie.

The lore goes that this savory pastry is Welsh, or Finnish, miner's food. For the working families who settled across this rugged, spectacular terrain, the half-moon-shaped pasty was a great thing to bring for lunch: filling yet delicate, and equally good hot, cold, or in between. Conveniently, they say, a pasty also fits perfectly into the front pocket of bib overalls.

I opt for a filling of ground beef and pork studded with small cubes of buttery rutabaga, a combination that is popular in contemporary pasty shops in the Upper Peninsula. It's excellent when accompanied by coleslaw and a pickle.

MAKES 6 LARGE PASTIES

Divide the pie dough into 6 equal disks. Chill them in the refrigerator, covered, for at least 30 minutes and as long as 2 days.

Preheat the oven to 375°F.

Combine the beef, pork, rutabaga, onion, and carrots in a large bowl. Add the salt, pepper, rosemary, parsley, and sour cream, and mix with your hands until well combined.

On a lightly floured surface, roll out each piece of dough until it is ³⁄₈-inch thick, about an 8-inch diameter. Divide the filling among the 6 rounds of dough, spooning it onto the lower half of each one. Flip the top half of the dough over the filling, making a half-moon shape. Lightly press to form the dough over the filling, and pinch the edges of the dough together to seal. Carefully transfer each half-moon pasty to a heavy baking sheet, leaving room between them.

Whisk together the egg and 2 tablespoons water, and lightly brush the egg wash over the pasties. Bake the pasties until golden brown, 45 minutes. Serve immediately.

GRIDDLE BURGER

The menu at Edzo's Burger Shop in Evanston, Illinois, illustrates the burger divide in the Midwest, maybe even in this country. It pits old-fashioned griddle burgers (thin burgers cooked on a flat griddle) against char burgers (fat, pink-centered burgers cooked on a grill).

My sister-in-law and I took the menu's obvious challenge and ordered one of each.

Maybe it's because we grew up with the thin pan-fried burgers, but we could not dispute the griddle burger's superiority, the way its running juices fused burger to bun. I love a great fat pink charburger, too, but as I love a steak: for its metallic, red-blooded appeal. The griddle burger is more like an artifact, a soft chunk that you turn in your hands to scrutinize for the next endearing spot to bite.

Old burger stands across the Midwest are almost always equipped with flat griddles, as was the case at Nick's Hamburger Shop in Brookings, South Dakota. The burgers there were small, misshapen, and fried in a floodplain of grease until crusty on the outside and moist within. The tiny puffed buns, freshly made, didn't disappoint, either.

In response to the spicy peanut butter burger that circulates on Midwestern brewpub menus, here's its mischievous cousin, a spicy bacon Gjetost cheeseburger. Gjetost, a brown cooked-whey goat cheese from Norway that you can find in grocery stores across the Scandinavian-settled Midwest, is a curious, addictive cheese that tastes kind of like an unsweetened nut butter.

SERVES 8

Divide the meat into 8 portions, pat each out thinly, to a roughly 7-inches diameter, and make a shallow divot in the center of each. Combine the salt, pepper, and ancho chile in a small dish and sprinkle both sides of the burgers with the mixture, using it all.

Preheat two large skillets over high heat. When hot, add the burgers and cook, at a controlled high, until the undersides are dark brown and doneness has crept halfway up the side of each burger, about 3 minutes. Flip the burgers, top with the cheese, cover the skillets tightly, and remove from the heat. Let cook until the cheese melts, about 2 minutes.

Slip the burgers between the toasted buns, garnish each one with pickles, bacon, and mayonnaise, and serve.

3 pounds good-quality ground beef

1½ teaspoons fine sea salt

1½ teaspoons freshly ground black pepper

1½ teaspoons ground ancho chile

4 ounces aged cheddar or Gjetost cheese, sliced

8 hamburger buns, split and toasted

Refrigerator Bread-and-Butter Pickles (page 283)

Cooked bacon

Spicy Mayonnaise (page 119)

NOTES: *The best burgers are made with freshly ground, not-too lean beef.*

Minneapolis is known for an inside-out cheeseburger called the "Jucy Lucy," two thin griddle burgers encasing a heart of molten yellow cheese. I suppose you could make them at home, patting hamburger around a lump of mixed grated cheddar and American cheese, but they're really best consumed at the source: either The 5-8 Club or Matt's Bar, both in South Minneapolis. For new-style Jucy Lucys, head to the Blue Door in St. Paul.

BARBECUED SPARERIBS
with Tomatoes *and* Lemon

1 tablespoon coriander seeds

1½ teaspoons cumin seeds

½ teaspoon celery seeds

2 teaspoons mustard seeds

2 teaspoons sweet paprika

¼ teaspoon cayenne pepper, or
more to taste

4 pounds pork spareribs or
meaty country ribs

Fine sea salt and freshly ground
black pepper

2 tablespoons canola oil

1 large Vidalia onion, diced

4 cloves garlic, sliced

2 tablespoons salted butter

3 pounds fresh plum tomatoes,
or 42 ounces canned

¼ cup ketchup

3 tablespoons apple cider
vinegar

⅓ cup (packed) light brown
sugar

1 tablespoon Worcestershire
sauce

1 cup chicken stock,
low-sodium store-bought or
homemade (page 299)

1½ lemons, preferably Meyer
lemons, scrubbed, thinly
sliced, and seeded

NOTE: *I use spareribs here because
I love their rich, dark meat, but
country ribs are actually more
traditional.*

In the famed barbecue villages of Kansas City and St. Louis, you will
find great slabs of spareribs slowly cooked with a calibrated mixture of
heat and smoke and brushed with a tangy, spicy barbecue sauce: mind-
blowing, life-changing, proper barbecue.

Driving north, you'll still find serious barbecue in Omaha, and
in fact throughout most of the Southern and Middle Midwest. It's
only in the northernmost reaches that the influence of long-coddled,
smoke-based barbecue starts to really thin—in Minnesota, North
Dakota, and Wisconsin. The northern style tends to move the
operation indoors and involves stewing pork ribs in the oven in a tangy
tomato-based sauce.

This recipe comes from my French-Canadian great-grandmother,
Bertha Dion, who ran a small roadside restaurant in the late 1920s near
her home in St. Paul, Minnesota, at the intersection of White Bear and
Gladstone roads. A pop-up shack designed to generate some quick
income, it was called The Chicken Bungalow, and she served only two
things: fried chicken and gravy, and these barbecued ribs baked with
thin slices of lemon on the top. The shack is long gone, but the recipe
lives. As the lemon slices cook and sink into the meat, their juices
contribute a welcome acidity, the rinds a hoppy bitterness.

SERVES 6 TO 8

Combine the coriander and cumin seeds in a small skillet and
toast over medium heat until fragrant, about 3 minutes. Pour
into a spice-devoted coffee grinder or a mortar, add the mustard
seeds and celery seeds, and grind until fine. Add the paprika and
cayenne, and set aside.

Heat a large, wide-bottomed pan or a roasting pan over
high heat. Blot the ribs dry, and season with 1 teaspoon salt and
½ teaspoon pepper. Add the oil to the pan and brown the ribs
in batches (for optimal caramelization, give them some space),
about 8 minutes per batch. Transfer the ribs to a bowl.

Discard the fat in the pan and add the onion and garlic, along
with the butter and a pinch of salt. Cook until the onion is soft
and tender, about 15 minutes.

If using fresh tomatoes, peel and chop them. If using canned,
pour them into a wide bowl and crush them by hand.

Add the ground spice mixture to the onion, cook for 30 seconds, and then add the tomatoes, ketchup, vinegar, brown sugar, Worcestershire sauce, and 1 teaspoon salt. Cook until the tomatoes start to soften, 10 minutes. Pour in the chicken stock and bring the mixture to a simmer. Submerge the ribs in the sauce. Partially cover the pot, or cover a roasting pan with a parchment-paper lid (see page 196), cut to fit. Bake in the oven for 2 hours.

Remove from the oven, skim off any excess fat pooling in the corners, and turn the ribs over. Lay the lemon slices on top of them, and bake until the ribs are meltingly tender, another 1½ to 2 hours. Serve directly from the pan.

RIBEYE
with Homemade Steak Sauce

3 ounces thick-cut bacon, diced
   (½ cup)

1 tablespoon salted butter, plus
   more for basting

1 cup finely diced onion

3 cloves garlic, smashed

Fine sea salt and freshly cracked
   black pepper

¼ cup tomato paste

3 tablespoons ketchup

1 tablespoon sweet paprika

⅓ cup dried sour cherries

½ cup dry vermouth

½ cup apple cider or juice

2 tablespoons apple cider
   vinegar

2 tablespoons light brown sugar

1 tablespoon Worcestershire
   sauce

10 dried juniper berries,
   cracked

3 dried bay leaves

2 teaspoons Asian fish sauce

Juice of ½ lime

2 1-pound bone-in ribeye steaks

Canola oil

For a long time I was of the mind that when faced with a perfect char-grilled ribeye steak, you brought nothing to the table but a fork and a big knife. But as my friend Chris Hand said as we worked our way through the bone-in cowboy-cut steaks that stretched out languorously over our plates, "This is amazing but, I hate to say it, a little monotonous toward the end. Pass me some of that homemade steak sauce."

I remember my dad collecting six-packs of bottled steak sauce from venerated steak houses across the Midwest (and beyond), and this concoction is based on my memories of those—which were surprisingly varied. In this brew, smoky bacon, sour cherries, and leathery juniper are in the driver's seat. It's a little less sweet than commercial sauces, and because it's homemade you can get away with adding the brightening splash of lime juice at the end.

Depending on appetite, one large ribeye will serve either one or two.

SERVES 2 TO 4

In a medium skillet, fry the bacon over medium heat until lightly crisp, about 3 minutes. Remove the bacon with a slotted spoon, and pour off all but 1 tablespoon of the fat from the pan.

Add the 1 tablespoon butter and the onion, garlic, ¼ teaspoon salt, and ½ teaspoon pepper to the pan. Sauté the onion, stirring often, until it turns coppery brown and tastes sweet, about 15 minutes.

Add the tomato paste and ketchup and cook, stirring constantly, until caramelized, about 5 minutes. Stir in the paprika, and then add ½ cup water, the cherries, vermouth, cider, vinegar, brown sugar, Worcestershire sauce, juniper berries, and bay leaves. Simmer until the sauce thickens and bubbles evenly, about 20 minutes. Let the mixture cool slightly.

Discard the bay leaves. Puree the mixture in a food processor, and then push it through a fine-mesh sieve into a bowl. Season with the fish sauce and lime juice, and add more salt if necessary. (You can store the sauce in the refrigerator, tightly covered, for up to 2 weeks, or in the freezer for 6 months.)

Preheat the oven to 375°F.

Heat two large (or one huge) cast-iron pans over high heat. Scrape the steaks with a butter knife to remove any bone grit, and season them liberally with salt and pepper. Pour a coating of oil into each pan, and then wipe it out with a paper towel so that just a thin film remains. Add the steaks to the hot pans. Cook steadily, reducing the heat to medium-high if they threaten to burn, until the steaks caramelize deeply on the bottom, 3 to 4 minutes. Flip the steaks and cook for 3 minutes. Transfer the pans to the oven and roast the steaks for 3 to 5 minutes more. Remove the pans from the oven, set the steaks on their sides, and test for doneness. The steaks are ready when they begin to feel firm when poked or reach 125°F on an instant-read thermometer.

Transfer the pans to the stovetop, off the heat. Add a large spoonful of butter to each pan, and using a large spoon, baste the steaks with the foaming melting butter. Transfer the steaks to a warm platter and let them rest for 5 minutes. Serve with the steak sauce.

BREADED STUFFED PORK CHOPS
with Ham *and* Gruyère

I don't know what's better, a breaded stuffed pork chop—the rough brown edges, the cheese slowly spilling out like lava—or the sight of someone standing at the stove frying one for you.

I have vivid memories of the breaded pork chops that my mother made, of the warm fragrance they gave to the house, of the tender, rosy meat . . . but mostly I remember the bone, which was blunt and covered in a delectable brown coat that just called out to be gnawed upon.

My rendition, with the pocket holding double-smoked ham and Gruyère cheese, is kind of like saltimbocca-meets-chicken-cordon-bleu-meets-home.

SERVES 4

Give the pork chops a quick cure for added flavor: Mix together 1 teaspoon salt and the sugar, and sprinkle this over both sides of the chops. Leave them to cure for 30 minutes at room temperature or up to 4 hours in the refrigerator.

Preheat the oven to 350°F.

Blot the pork chops dry and cut a pocket into the chops all the way to the bone, and as wide as you can without cutting through to the side, leaving a 2-inch-wide opening. Stuff each chop with 1 slice of ham and 1 slice of cheese, cut to fit the pocket.

Prepare three shallow bowls for breading the chops: fill one with the flour, one with the eggs, and one with the bread crumbs and panko. Season the bread crumbs with ½ teaspoon each of salt and pepper, and lightly beat the eggs.

Lay 1 sage leaf on each pork chop. Carefully coat one chop at a time with flour, shaking off any excess; dip it into the egg, covering the surface and letting the excess drip off; and then bury it in the bread crumbs, gently patting to make them adhere.

Heat two large skillets over medium-high heat and add enough oil to reach ½ inch up the sides. When hot, add the pork chops and cook until the bottom turns dark golden brown, 3 to 5 minutes. Flip and cook the other side to the same color. Transfer the chops to a baking sheet fitted with a rack, and bake until the chops feel firm when pressed and a bit of cheese is beginning to escape from the pockets, about 5 minutes. Serve hot.

4 (12- to 14-ounce) bone-in pork rib chops, each 1½ inches thick

Fine sea salt and freshly ground black pepper

1 teaspoon sugar

4 thin slices double-smoked ham

4 slices Gruyère cheese

1 cup all-purpose flour

3 large eggs

1½ cups plain dry bread crumbs

1½ cups panko

4 fresh sage leaves

Canola oil, for frying

NOTE: *It's always important with bone-in chops, or anything that might have been portioned with a saw, to be sure to scrape the surfaces of the pork chops with a butter knife to remove any bone grit.*

The Heartland to the North

In 1998 my husband, Aaron, and I embarked on a road trip into the midwestern heart of Canada, driving straight north from Minnesota into Saskatchewan. Our only plan was to indulge his natural urge to drive down the main streets of every little dot on the map, no matter how small, to see firsthand the outline of the town's ambitions and how it either met them or missed them. Just like around here, the communities that took our hearts were the ones that had fallen the farthest from their grand visions: lines of vacant town lots that you could trace along weedy fencerows, wonky sidewalks that ended in fields of weeds, and town squares that were empty but for a bandaged courthouse, its lonely bell tower piercing the wide northern sky.

Remarkably, these places were still alive, tenacious, vibrant. Somehow in this land of ghosts we met more people than we've ever met when traveling, and despite the lack of public places to eat, I gathered a packed notebook of recipes and ideas.

Rose and Eddie, for instance, were sitting in lawn chairs in front of their garage in an unincorporated town, just enjoying the big sky when we pulled up. ("Bluer here than anywhere!" boasted Eddie—and it kind of was.) Aaron pointed an elbow out his window and let loose the questions that were always percolating in him. What came next was a local history lesson of the town, then a tour of Rose's canning cupboard and a sampling of her excellent fruit leather. (The best was the color of port wine, made from a dusky miniature cold-hardy plum.) Before we knew it, we were sitting with them in a circle of lawn chairs in the driveway, next to Eddie's big rig, marveling at the same immense clouds above.

But we had a long way to go.

A few days later in Fisherton, we met Josie Davidow in the middle of a dirt road that stretched beyond her forever, the kind of road so straight that after thirty miles of it you itch for a curve just so that you can steer. She sat on an old field tractor, her blond waves escaping their bun (Jessica Lange–style), her grandson on the rubber seat behind her.

Within ten minutes she was giving us strangers a tour of her farm, which at one time had been the Fisherton town center. "Here," she said, "you can still see the gas station pump."

She then led us into a huge room, a cavernous farmhouse kitchen. It could have been a period room in a museum—the high walls papered in a faded pink-and-yellow floral, the corner bead crumbling—but it had serious presence. "It needs some fixing up," she said, sighing, though it was obvious that she cared more about preserving its mood than remodeling it.

Josie was talking to Aaron, saying, "You have to live in a place your whole life before you really know it" as she handed me the book I'd been staring at, a spiral-bound collection of Fisherton community recipes. On the first page of the meat chapter was a recipe for Peppered Pork Roast—her own. "Take it with you," she said.

I've since made it many times, and although I've updated it to use fresh black peppercorns in place of preground, this recipe reminds me of Josie and her place: not fancy, and not shy, either.

PEPPERED PORK ROAST

½ teaspoon sugar

Fine sea salt

1 3½-pound pork loin roast,
   fat cap left on

3 tablespoons black
  peppercorns

5 tablespoons salted butter

6 cloves garlic, finely grated

2 tablespoons chopped fresh
  thyme

3 tablespoons apple cider
  vinegar

2 tablespoons canola oil

There are hardly any pitfalls to roasting a pork loin, a uniformly lean cut; the only crucial thing is gauging its doneness. Cooked to the proper temperature, it will be evenly pearly from edge to edge but have just a blooming pinkness to it, and each cut slice will immediately bead up with moisture, hardly able to contain its juice.

SERVES 6 TO 8

Give the roast a quick cure for added flavor: Stir together the sugar and ½ teaspoon salt, rub the mixture all over the roast, and refrigerate it for 2 hours or as long as overnight.

Blot the roast dry. Crush the peppercorns with a mortar and pestle or in a spice-devoted coffee grinder to a medium-coarse texture. (Some will be finely ground, but you want the larger pieces to resemble cracked pepper.) Rub the pepper into the meat, saving what doesn't stick for the marinade.

Preheat the oven to 375°F.

Heat a small saucepan over medium-low heat, and add the butter and garlic. Cook until the butter bubbles; then add the thyme, vinegar, and any remaining black pepper, and remove from the heat.

Season the pork with 1 teaspoon salt. Heat an ovenproof skillet large enough to fit the pork roast over high heat, and add the oil. Brown the meat quickly on all sides.

Brush the meat generously with some of the butter mixture, put the skillet in the oven, and roast for 10 minutes. Then remove the skillet, roll the roast to another side, and baste it with more of the butter mixture. Roast the meat, removing it from the oven every 10 minutes or so to flip and mop, until an instant-read thermometer inserted in the center of the roast reads between 142° and 145°F, about 50 minutes total.

Remove the skillet from the oven, transfer the meat to a platter, and let it rest for 10 minutes, rolling the pork around to sop up its exuded juices. Slice thinly and serve.

DELUXE BAKED BEANS
with a Crumb Top

Baked beans have deep roots in this region, and in some communities for summer festivals they still cook them the old way: in heavy pots buried deep in the ground.

Most people have since modernized the method, but one thing stays the same: The flavor rests surely on the quality of the meats that flavor the beans. To that end, this one gets a nice assortment of smoked proteins: a chunk of homemade salt pork, some sausage, and a whole turkey leg. Overall, this pot of beans will taste less sweet than most others, and the crispy mantle of buttery bread crumbs—an idea borrowed from the famous French *cassoulet*—provides valuable contrast and crunch.

A memorable (and economical) dish to make for a crowd, this recipe is easily doubled.

SERVES 8 TO 10

Put the beans in a medium bowl and sift them through your fingers, discarding any rocks if you find them. Cover the beans generously with cold water and leave to hydrate for at least 6 hours or overnight.

Drain the beans, put them into a deep pot, and cover generously with water. Season with salt, bring to a simmer, and cook for 1 hour or until the beans are tender but not mushy. Drain the beans, reserving the cooking water.

Cut the salt pork into 2-inch cubes. Heat a deep, wide-bottomed ovenproof pot over medium heat, and when it's hot, add the salt pork. Cook until browned on all sides, about 8 minutes. Transfer the pork to a bowl, and then add the onions to the fat in the pot. Season with ½ teaspoon each of salt and pepper, and cook over medium heat, stirring often, until the onions turn very soft and light brown, about 25 minutes.

Meanwhile, preheat the oven to 300°F.

Pour the canned tomatoes into a bowl and crush them with your fingers.

Add the molasses, brown sugar, soy sauce, paprika, and cayenne to the pot and cook until the sugar dissolves, about 1 minute. Add the crushed tomatoes and cook, stirring, until

RECIPE CONTINUES

Ingredients

- 1 pound dried pinto beans
- Fine sea salt
- 1 12-ounce slab salt pork (page 298) or slab bacon
- 3 cups diced Vidalia onions (from 1½ large onions)
- Freshly ground black pepper
- 1 14-ounce can whole plum tomatoes
- 2 tablespoons molasses
- 2 tablespoons (packed) light brown sugar
- 1½ tablespoons soy sauce
- 1 tablespoon sweet paprika
- ¼ teaspoon cayenne pepper
- 1½ cups chicken stock, low-sodium store-bought or homemade (page 299)
- 2 teaspoons minced fresh rosemary, or 2 teaspoons dried
- 1 tablespoon minced fresh thyme, or 2 teaspoons dried
- 3 dried bay leaves
- 1 1-pound smoked turkey leg
- 3 links (12 ounces) smoked pork sausage
- ¼ cup extra-virgin olive oil
- 1 clove garlic, grated
- 2 cups fresh bread crumbs

they've reduced and begun to fall apart, about 10 minutes. Add the chicken stock, rosemary, thyme, bay leaves, ¼ teaspoon each of salt and pepper, and the drained beans. Pour in enough of the reserved bean cooking liquid to bring the liquid in the pot level with the beans, and stir to combine. Nestle the turkey leg and salt pork cubes into the beans.

Partially cover the pot (or cover it with a parchment-paper lid, see below), transfer it to the oven, and bake for 1½ hours.

Add the sausages and bake for 1 more hour.

Combine the olive oil and garlic in a medium bowl. Add the bread crumbs and a pinch each of salt and pepper, and toss to combine. Remove the lid from the beans, remove the bay leaves, and sprinkle the bread crumbs evenly over the top. Bake, uncovered, until the bread crumbs turn brown and crisp, about 45 minutes. Let rest for 10 minutes before serving straight from the pot.

How to Make a Paper Lid, and Why

Topping my baked dishes with a parchment-paper lid (or *cartouche*) is one of the few tics that I took away from the professional kitchen. (An addiction to super-clingy professional plastic wrap is another.) Here's why: A paper lid allows for about 20 percent evaporation (which concentrates the sauce, a good thing) yet it keeps the food beneath it moist. A tight-fitting cover doesn't allow any evaporation at all, and an uncovered surface gets dry pretty quickly.

These disposable lids, which look like paper manhole covers, really protect roasts and braises. Here's how to make one: Fold a square of cooking parchment into quarters and then begin folding to the point, as if you were making a paper airplane. Point the tip into the very center of the dish, find where the edge of the pot hits the paper, and cut there. Snip off the very tip of the paper triangle to make a small center hole, and then unfold the paper. Press the lid gently right onto the surface of the sauce. The parchment may darken in the heat of the oven, but it will still work fine and won't catch fire—just don't turn on a broiler above it.

Bologna Days

Anyone just glancing at the sign would think that this festival lasts a few days and is an annual event.

Actually, Bologna Days lasts two hours over lunch and has been occurring weekly in my parents' hometown since the 1960s. It's less a festival than it is a tradition designed to work hot ring bologna—eating into your life via regular weekly installments.

Spring, summer, winter, or fall, you can walk into Patrick's Bar & Grill in Pierz on Wednesdays and The Red Rooster in nearby Genola on Thursdays, and the ring bologna will come to you, ruddy and hot from the smoker, with all the necessary accoutrements: the stack of white bread, the stinging dish of snow-white horseradish, the golden light American beer.

According to the lore, the whole thing began back when Harold Meyer walked into the bar across from Meyer's Meats carrying a ring of freshly made bologna and said to the bartender, Red Schmidtbauer, "Here, taste this bologna and tell me if it has enough seasoning." From then on "taste-testing" the fresh-from-the-smoker bologna became a practice, and the next thing you know, it was a weekly ritual. When Meyer's closed, Thielen Meats of Pierz, my family's shop located just up the street, took its place.

It's more than a fifty-year-old running joke, though. There is actual good sense behind eating hot ring bologna when it's fresh. My cousin Joe admits that even his own bologna, as smoky and peppery as it is, is just bologna the next day. Day-old bologna is good cut into slabs, fried until gleaming, and made into a bologna sandwich, absolutely, but unlike fresh bologna, it's nothing to warrant a town-wide celebration.

My grandma Dion, who thrilled at festivals (the more insignificant the better) loved this one. She dropped the "days" altogether and just called it "going to Bologna." On Wednesdays at noon, you would often find her at Patrick's, sitting at her table marked with a "reserved" easel, leaning over to converse with friends or to stir up conversation with a stranger. Then, as now, the room was carpeted in red swirls, and lit with the flickering lights of neon bar signs hung salon-style on dark paneled walls, and the air was usually ringing with bursts of laughter and the porcelain sound of knocking dice.

I was just a little kid twirling around on my barstool when she first taught me how to properly eat a hot ring bologna sandwich. First you wedge a fingernail under the thin skin and peel back the casing in one papery piece, as if stripping off the back of a sticker. The casing is perfectly edible, but removing it reveals the hidden thrill in eating the sandwich. With the meat laid bare, the horseradish spread on thinly but weightily like a cotton blanket, the barge of pink bologna teetering precariously on the bread, you then give the whole thing a deft smashing, which causes the hot, smoky juices of the bologna to run through the bread until they reach its chewy brown edges. Now the focus rests, as it should, on the hot bologna itself. Only a few minutes old, it remains just as old-world as can be.

SIDES

Pete Kueber, a Two Inlets native who went on to live in many countries around the world, once told me, "Growing up here, we ate what was basically a Mediterranean diet—but with butter instead of olive oil." Recalling rutabagas stored under the bed and gardens full of three or four varieties of beans, he remembers their meals being just peppered with bits of meat, usually salted or smoked. "Obviously, we ate more meat in the fall, when the pigs were slaughtered."

My great-aunt Irene concurs, remembering that in rural Pierz in the 1930s, you couldn't even buy vegetables at the local store. "They might have sold a few onions, or potatoes, for emergencies. But everyone grew the rest in their gardens and canned it for winter."

In rural places today, even though the stores sell a wide range of produce, gardens and truck farms still abound. And most people grow something in their yards, at the bare minimum a clump of chives, some rhubarb, or a fruit tree or two. In the city, the farmer's markets make everyone who visits them feel flush with summer's windfall. During the growing season in the Midwest, getting your hands on peak vegetables has never been a problem; the question has always been, rather, what to do with them.

And that brings us to the real history of cooking vegetables in this region, which can border on piety. In other words, it's as simple as boiled, buttered, done. A spear of garden broccoli or a small magenta beet, boiled with care in salted water, shaken dry, and anointed with salted butter, is a thing of seasonal beauty.

But let's be honest: no one needs a string of recipes for buttered, boiled vegetables. So what follows are suggestions for ways to prepare vegetables after you've tired of eating each of them in their pure form.

Perhaps more than any other place in this book, here you'll see the paradox of living in a rural outpost: like the dramatic weather swings, vegetable availability follows a schedule of feast or famine. In the summer we're flooded with everything, much of it arriving all at once in July. In August we're busy preserving the surplus harvest for the winter (and you can find more of those recipes in the Projects chapter). And by October the killing frosts have arrived and it's a race against time to yank the freezing, slippery leeks from the stiffening ground. In the winter we recharge our creative batteries, working hard on making something interesting from pantry and grocery store shelves.

GRILLED ASPARAGUS
with One-Morel Dressing

Morel mushrooms may be legion across much of the Midwest, but I have finally come to admit that they just don't grow very well in our particular mix of woods. So this is a recipe for hopeful foragers like me who always seem to find just one token morel during the season. Usually it's a grand one, just impressive enough to goad me into looking for more.

You can substitute shiitakes if you don't have any morels at all, and of course add more morels if you find a good load.

SERVES 4 TO 6

Toast the hazelnuts: Pour them into a small pie plate, place it in a cold oven, and set the oven to 350°F. Bake until the nuts begin to smell fragrant, the papery skins have loosened, and the centers have turned light brown, about 25 minutes. Pour the nuts into a clean tea towel, gather up the ends, and knead the nuts in the towel to loosen the skins. Open the towel, roll the nuts to the side, put them in a bowl, and discard the skins. Remove the nuts from the bowl and chop roughly.

Cut the morel mushroom in half and swish it in a bowl of water to remove any dirt or insects. Dry on a towel. Chop roughly.

Preheat a grill or a grill pan over medium-high heat.

Heat a small saucepan over medium-low heat, and add 3 tablespoons of the olive oil and the mushroom. Cook very gently until the mushroom begins to sizzle and give off its fragrance, 2 minutes. Pour the contents of the pan into a small bowl and add the lemon zest, lemon juice, and chives. Season with ½ teaspoon salt and ¼ teaspoon pepper.

Rub the asparagus with the remaining 1 tablespoon olive oil, and sprinkle with salt and pepper. Grill the asparagus until charred on the outside and just tender inside, about 5 minutes. Transfer to a platter, spoon the mushroom dressing on top, and sprinkle with the chopped hazelnuts. Serve either warm or at room temperature.

¼ cup hazelnuts

1 extra-large morel mushroom, or 2 large shiitakes, stemmed

4 tablespoons extra-virgin olive oil

1 teaspoon grated lemon zest

1 tablespoon fresh lemon juice

1 tablespoon minced fresh chives or parsley

Fine sea salt and freshly ground black pepper

1½ pounds asparagus

A Couple of MILK-COOKED VEGETABLES:

BUTTERED MILK PEAS

My great-aunt Irene first told me of the farmhouse habit of cooking vegetables in milk, explaining that her mother sold their cream for extra money but poured lots of milk into her cooking. "And that, I think," she said, "is why we were such healthy girls."

A very scant amount of cornstarch mashed into the butter efficiently thickens these quick-cooked peas. I love them with chervil, a feathery herb that tastes like a milder tarragon or a licorice-y parsley. It grows easily in soft fluffy rows in the herb garden and goes well with most green things.

SERVES 4

Mix 1 tablespoon of the butter with the cornstarch, and set aside.

In a saucepan set over medium heat, melt the remaining 3 tablespoons butter. Add the garlic, and cook until the garlic begins to soften, 2 to 3 minutes. Add the peas and ¼ teaspoon each of salt and pepper, and cook until the peas turn bright green, about 1 minute. Add the half-and-half and cook until it bubbles in the center, about 30 seconds. Add the cornstarch mixture and cook, stirring, until the contents of the pan thicken and the peas lose their starchy, raw taste, 1 to 2 minutes.

Add the lemon zest and chervil. Taste for salt and pepper, and adjust if necessary. Serve immediately. You may want to remove the garlic cloves before serving, but I never do because some people like them.

- 4 tablespoons (½ stick) salted butter, at room temperature
- ¾ teaspoon cornstarch
- 3 cloves garlic, smashed
- 2½ cups shelled fresh peas (from 2 pounds in the pod)
- Fine sea salt and freshly ground black pepper
- ½ cup half-and-half or whole milk
- ½ teaspoon grated lemon zest
- 2 tablespoons chopped fresh chervil, or 1½ tablespoons chopped fresh parsley and ½ tablespoon chopped fresh tarragon

MILK CABBAGE

3 tablespoons salted butter

2 cloves garlic, minced

1 very small sprig fresh
rosemary

8 cups (packed) shredded
cabbage

¾ teaspoon salt

½ teaspoon freshly ground
black pepper

¾ cup whole milk

½ cup walnuts, toasted (see
below) and roughly chopped

Cold-Toasting Nuts

When I need to toast nuts in
the oven (skin-on hazelnuts, for
instance, or whole almonds) but
don't need the oven for baking
anything else, I give the nuts
a cold start, so as not to waste
time or propane: I put the nuts
in the oven, turn it to 350°F, and
then set a timer. Every oven will
heat at a different rate, so this is
not an exact science, but in my
oven pecans toast in 10 minutes,
almonds in 15, walnuts in 20, and
hazelnuts in 25 minutes. This
method is especially valuable
during the hot days of summer,
when you want to keep the heat-
throwing-appliance usage to a
minimum.

I was buying raspberry bushes at Brenda Bozovsky's nursery, a few
miles east of my place, when the talk rolled around to cabbage. She
must have had fifty of them in her garden, their bald heads exposed to
the sun. Originally from North Dakota, Brenda's mother gave a lot of
their garden vegetables a bath in milk, most notably the green ones:
the peas, the beans, and "oh, the milk cabbage . . . " she burst out. "That
is just the best!"

A farmhouse tradition modernized with a little rosemary and a few
toasted walnuts, this is excellent served next to steamed rice, mashed
potatoes, or any kind of starch capable of sopping up the creamy cruci-
ferous juice.

Shave the cabbage as you would for coleslaw—about the width of
two nickels. The cooking goes quickly, so be sure to stand nearby so
you can pull the pan from the heat the second the cabbage softens.

SERVES 6

Heat the butter in a large saucepan over medium heat, and add
the garlic. Cook until fragrant, about 1 minute. Add the rosemary,
cabbage, salt, and pepper and stir to mix. Pour in the milk, raise
the heat slightly, and bring the milk to a simmer. Then reduce
the heat to medium, cover the pan, and cook, stirring once, until
the cabbage is just tender—not crunchy any longer but not
mushy, either—4 to 7 minutes. Discard the rosemary sprig.

Transfer the cabbage to a shallow serving bowl (I like a shallow
oval dish for this one), top it with the toasted walnuts, and serve.

Hot Mustard
CUCUMBER SALAD

Here's a noncreamy type of cucumber salad for the summer season. It was influenced by the Japanese tradition of cold marinated vegetables and is best served in small amounts, well chilled. A small seeping mound of these spicy cucumbers sitting next to a steak hot off the grill epitomizes summer. (And in the winter, it's nice next to the Sherry-Glazed Ham, page 170.)

SERVES 4 TO 6

Trim the ends from the cucumbers. If the cucumbers are large, cut them in half lengthwise and scoop out the seeds with a spoon. If they are small, leave the seeds. With a mandoline (or by hand), slice the cucumbers ½ inch thick.

Put the cucumbers in a large colander or sieve, and toss with ½ teaspoon salt. Mix with your hands, and then leave to drain for at least 30 minutes and as long as 2 hours.

Make the dressing right in the serving bowl: Combine the ground mustard and the vinegar and stir to make a paste. Then add the brown sugar, olive oil, coriander, ¼ teaspoon salt, the pepper, and the nutmeg, and stir until smooth.

Blot the cucumbers with a clean cloth or paper towels to absorb any excess liquid. Add the cucumbers and scallions to the mustard dressing, and toss to combine. Chill for 30 minutes before serving.

1 pound cucumbers (about 5 small Kirby cucumbers or 1½ hothouse)

Fine sea salt

1 tablespoon ground mustard

2 tablespoons white wine vinegar

1½ tablespoons (packed) light brown sugar

1 tablespoon extra-virgin olive oil

¼ teaspoon ground coriander

¼ teaspoon freshly ground black pepper

Pinch of grated nutmeg

4 scallions, white and green parts, thinly sliced on the diagonal

NOTES: *The freshness of your ground mustard may matter here. Sometimes I even pulverize whole mustard seeds to a fine dust in a spice mill. If you do, beware the flavor— and also the heat!*

This sweet-hot dressing was inspired by one of my favorite local condiments, Uncle Pete's Hot Mustard. Now made by Pete's nephew, the mustard retains both its secret Polish formula and its bite. Chef J. D. Fratzke of the St. Paul steakhouse The Strip Club calls the stuff "Polish wasabi."

CREAMY CUCUMBERS
with Borage Flowers

Cucumbers can explode from a green burr with a yellow blossom to full-fledged harvest size in the space of a day, so it makes sense that they contain a great deal of water. While cucumbers do need to be lightly salted to get them to perspire that excess water, I don't like to squeeze them too hard, which can turn them limp and soggy. Instead, let the salted cucumbers drain in a wide colander, cover them with a clean towel, and blot completely dry.

This is a very classic, cooling cucumber salad. The combination of lemon and vinegar gives it some zip, and the borage flowers give it some color and another layer of flavor. They taste exactly like cucumbers—but they're blue! If you have easier access to growing chives, you can use their blossoms instead.

SERVES 6

Peel the cucumbers and trim off the ends. If the cucumbers are large, cut them in half lengthwise and scoop out the seeds with a spoon. If they are small, leave the seeds. With a mandoline (or by hand), slice the cucumbers ¼-inch thick, a little thicker than a poker chip. You should have about 4 cups.

Put the cucumbers in a large colander or sieve, and toss with ¾ teaspoon of the salt. Mix with your hands, and then leave to drain for at least 30 minutes and as long as 2 hours.

In a small bowl, whisk together the sour cream, sugar, garlic, vinegar, lemon juice, pepper, and the remaining ½ teaspoon salt until smooth.

Blot the cucumbers with a clean cloth or paper towels to absorb any excess liquid. Combine the cucumbers and onion with the sour cream dressing in a serving bowl, and mix well. (This can be made up to a day ahead and refrigerated.) Garnish with the borage flowers, if using.

NOTE: *I've added smoked salmon to this in the past, with great success.*

1½ pounds cucumbers (about 8 small Kirby cucumbers or 2 hothouse)

1¼ teaspoons fine sea salt

⅓ cup sour cream

1½ teaspoons sugar

½ clove garlic, grated

1 tablespoon apple cider vinegar

1 tablespoon fresh lemon juice

¼ teaspoon freshly ground black pepper

¼ Vidalia onion, thinly sliced

10 fresh borage flowers (optional)

SWISS CHARD
with Honey-Roasted Garlic

2 heads of garlic

2 teaspoons honey

1 teaspoon extra-virgin olive oil

3 tablespoons salted butter

2 tablespoons pine nuts

2 bunches (almost 2 pounds) Swiss chard, stripped of stems and cut into 1-inch pieces (10 cups)

Fine sea salt and freshly ground black pepper

I've all but given up on growing spinach in my garden because it just bolts to seed before I can get to the second picking. So I now grow a large patch of Swiss chard, which sprouts quickly into a leafy canopy and keeps us in greens from early July until the first snow. (And usually it hangs on for a week or two beyond that.) I find it just as delicious as spinach, and when it's in the pan, not nearly as likely to wilt down to nothing.

Conveniently, fresh garden garlic arrives at the market around the same time as the Swiss chard, so you can make a batch of honey-roasted garlic to add a soft sweetness to the greens; the cooked cloves slip out of their skins like summer butter from its paper wrapper.

Preheat the oven to 350°F.

Cut the top ½ inch off each head of garlic, exposing the cloves. Set the garlic in the center of a square of heavy aluminum foil. Pour 1 teaspoon of the honey and the olive oil over the garlic, replace the tops, and fold up the sides of the foil to make a package, crimping the top tight. Bake until very tender and golden, 30 minutes.

Transfer the baked garlic to a bowl, including all the juices in the foil pouch. When cool enough to handle, remove the garlic heads and pop out the garlic cloves by pushing up from the bottom. Add the remaining teaspoon honey and stir to combine.

Heat a very wide skillet over medium heat, and add the butter and pine nuts. When they begin to sizzle, add half of the Swiss chard. Cook, stirring, until the greens wilt, a minute or two. Add the remaining chard. Season with salt and pepper, and cook until most of the liquid has simmered off, another 2 to 3 minutes.

Add the honey-roasted garlic, mix very gently to combine, and serve.

COLESLAW
with Bread-and-Butter Pickles

Coleslaw made from just-picked summer cabbage redeems every tired, washed-out batch of slaw ever made. A fresh head looks and feels different, too. It will be heavy with rainwater, it will squeak like a block of hard Styrofoam when cut, and the shards, after being shredded, will stand up in the bowl like a tangle of wire.

For pep, and to distinguish this from the standard slaw, I add a cup of drained bread-and-butter pickles (because I usually have an open jar in the fridge) as well as a dusting of freshly ground mustard seeds for sweet, honeyed heat.

SERVES 8

Put the cabbage, carrots, and scallions in a large bowl. Add the salt and pepper, and toss with your hands until well mixed.

Whisk the mayonnaise, sour cream, vinegar, ground mustard seeds, lemon juice, and sugar together in a small bowl. Add the dressing and the bread-and-butter pickles to the shredded vegetables, and mix thoroughly. Serve immediately, or keep refrigerated for up to 1 day.

Steamed Cabbage

This is a private recipe: modest, but worth knowing. Piled alongside a sausage, steamed cabbage makes a really good, quick workday dinner, and there's something kind of virtuous in it, even if one splurges with the butter.

Cut half of a small cabbage into roughly 2-inch squares and toss them with salt, pepper, and a finely minced garlic clove. Arrange the cabbage in an extra-large steamer (I use two stacked bamboo steamers). Steam over high heat, tightly covered, for about 2 minutes past the moment the cabbage turns bright green, until the cabbage is just done. The only attention required here is in pulling the cabbage from the heat at the right moment. Too firm and it will taste boring; too soft and it will start to get that sulphurous flavor. But when taken from the heat at the moment that the cabbage collapses, its juices will run and taste buttery without being buttered—though by all means add a good lump of butter at this point and toss to combine. The same juicy inner-butter point of doneness can be achieved with steamed cauliflower as well.

10 cups shredded cabbage

1 cup coarsely shredded carrots (from 3 to 4 carrots)

3 scallions, white and green parts, thinly sliced

1 teaspoon fine sea salt

1 teaspoon freshly ground black pepper

½ cup mayonnaise

¼ cup sour cream or plain whole-milk yogurt

3 tablespoons apple cider vinegar

1 tablespoon freshly ground mustard seeds

2 tablespoons fresh lemon juice

2 teaspoons sugar

1 cup drained bread-and-butter pickles, store-bought or homemade (page 283)

NOTE: *You can, of course, make this coleslaw ahead of time and keep it in the refrigerator, but served freshly made, it's unbeatable.*

CRISPY CABBAGE
with Poppy Seeds

5 tablespoons salted butter

1 tablespoon minced fresh ginger

8 cups shredded cabbage

4 cloves garlic, sliced

1 tablespoon minced fresh thyme

2 teaspoons poppy seeds

1 tablespoon sesame seeds

½ teaspoon fine sea salt

¼ teaspoon freshly ground black pepper

NOTE: *First, make the ghee: Put the butter in a small pan, bring it to a simmer, and cook until it turns brown at the edges, 3 to 4 minutes. Let the butter sit for a minute. Then tilt the pan and carefully skim off the solidified top crust with a spoon, taking care to remove as much of this stiff white froth as possible. Put it in a small dish. Pour the clear golden butter into another small dish, and pour the darker brown dregs at the bottom of the pan into the dish containing the froth. This can be done well ahead of time, even a day or two before; ghee keeps well in the refrigerator.*

If I were tracking which side dish my family most often circles back for at the end of the meal, it would be this crispy, caramelized spiced cabbage. No matter how much I make, it always disappears at some point on its second trip around the table.

The trick to browning cabbage (or any dry vegetable), taught to me by an Indian instructor in cooking school, is to fry the vegetable in ghee, or clarified butter, over high heat. The ghee is the key. Making it is a simple cooking process that separates the milk solids and whey from the clear golden fat so that it can be heated to a high temperature like an oil, but still retain all the warm flavors of butter.

Anything benefits from being fried in this stuff, but the sweet nuttiness of the brassicas (cauliflower, Brussels sprouts, collard greens, cabbage, and their relatives) rises to the surface when they're cooked this way, without any added moisture. I think cabbage fried in ghee is the best, though cauliflower is a close second.

SERVES 4 TO 6

Ready your seasonings, because once the cooking starts, it will go fast.

Heat your very widest skillet over high heat. Seriously, it should be almost comically oversize for this amount of cabbage. If you have nothing larger than a regulation 10-incher, you should probably cook this in two batches to avoid steaming—instead of lightly charring—the cabbage.

When the skillet is hot, add the ghee and the ginger. The ginger should fry immediately. Dump in the cabbage and stir. Add the garlic, thyme, poppy seeds, sesame seeds, salt, and pepper. Spread the cabbage out evenly and continue to fry over very high heat, stirring every 45 seconds or so, giving the cabbage time to caramelize on the bottom. Watch that it doesn't actually burn, but let it get a little dark on the edges. Cook until the cabbage has lost its raw taste but before it goes completely limp, about 5 minutes. Add the reserved butter froth, stir to combine, turn out into a serving dish, and serve immediately.

Cooking Fat Allegiances

The foundation of a cuisine is its fat. In fact, in *The Food of France*, Waverly Root divided that country into four culinary regions according to their preferred cooking fat: butter in the north, duck and goose fat in the central region, olive oil along the Provençal coast, and a certain mixture of the three in the Pyrenees.

In America our allegiances are far more varied. If you zero in on fat you'll notice that every distinguished cook, whether professional or home-based, favors a certain special one, and the options are surprisingly wide-ranging.

For example, the first chef I worked for cooked most of his vegetables in garlic oil (made by slowly baking heads of garlic in vegetable oil), the second had a thing for duck fat, and the third sautéed in canola oil but finished dishes with beautiful extra-virgin olive oil.

My friend Bruce bastes his garden carrots with unrefined coconut oil until they soften and turn into soil-sprung candy corn. My mother bathes her vegetables in salted butter. Her mother loved butter too, and used the dense lightly salted butter available to her at the time from the Little Rock Creamery just down the road. But, with one foot in her mother's generation, she also poured bacon fat and sausage drippings into a clean coffee can until there was enough fat there to lubricate her cast-iron pan and all its contents, which was especially welcome when she was frying potatoes and onions.

Most of the Midwesterners I know cook with salted butter, with bacon fat or lard coming in a distant, historical second. I lean on my Midwestern roots and reach for the butter, too—but sometimes with a twist. Ghee, or clarified butter, is the fat in my coffee can. This is a fat that has all of the kaleidoscopic flavor of browned butter but the frying properties, and the higher smoking temperature, of an oil. With ghee, you can sear vegetables and get some browning on them without fear of burning the butter.

Many experts in Indian cooking describe ghee as simply heated clarified butter—and it is. But I follow the teaching of an Indian instructor from my cooking-school days who told us to brown the ghee lightly before separating it, which transforms an already amazing substance into liquid gold.

I enjoy making it. I like to watch the butter burnish at the edges, scrape the stiff mask of froth from the top, pour off the clear ghee, and then pour the milky residue at the very bottom into the bowl with the mottled froth. This small bowl of skimmed sediment—what I think of as the butter "lees," like the sludge at the bottom of a wine barrel—is beautifully dappled, foamy like beach spittle, and way too good to be discarded. Salty and delicious in its own indulgent way, the lees are not good for frying but add lots of brown, caramelized flavor to hot soups, scrambled eggs, vegetables, and even pancake batters. Madeleine Kamman, in *When French Women Cook*, writes about collecting the skim from clarified butter (what she calls the *gappe*) until she has a full cup to add to walnut bread.

My hero.

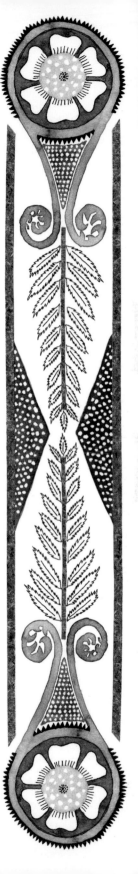

YOUNG GREEN BEANS
with Lemon-Vodka Cream

Brittle, fine-boned young beans like these do not need much embellishment, but they really shine when given a light creamy dressing. My progenitors probably enrobed the beans in a flour-daubed white sauce, but these days I lean toward a sauce of lemon cream, dill, and vodka—the very same one we used to anoint sautéed sturgeon when I worked in a high-end restaurant in Manhattan, although we added spoonfuls of caviar to it. Even without the glitzy roe, the vodka cream has a seductive Russian sensibility. (And if you omit the vodka, you have a nice lemony cream sauce.)

SERVES 4 TO 6

Bring a large pot of water to the boil, adding salt until it tastes like seawater. When it boils, add the beans and bring the water back to a boil as quickly as possible. Cook until they're just tender to the bite but still bright green, about 4 minutes. Drain the beans, shaking them to remove any excess water.

Meanwhile, in a skillet that is large enough to later accommodate the beans, heat the butter and garlic over medium heat. Once the garlic begins to sizzle, pour in the cream and bring to a boil. Cook rapidly, stirring the edges constantly with a spatula, until the cream has visibly thickened into a yellow cream, is throwing large bubbles, and can hold the trace of the spoon, about 3 minutes. Add the lemon zest, lemon juice, vodka, ¼ teaspoon salt, and the pepper.

Add the beans to the cream and toss to combine. Sprinkle with the dill, and transfer to a serving bowl. Toss again right before serving. This is good served either hot or lukewarm.

Fine sea salt

1 pound young green beans (haricots verts), trimmed

2 tablespoons salted butter

1 clove garlic, minced

⅔ cup heavy cream

½ teaspoon grated lemon zest

2 tablespoons fresh lemon juice

1½ tablespoons vodka or water

¼ teaspoon freshly ground black pepper

2 teaspoons minced fresh dill

GRILLED ROMANO BEANS
with Chive Pesto

1 small clove garlic

¼ cup minced fresh chives

¼ cup shelled salted pistachios

3 tablespoons olive oil

¼ cup freshly grated Pecorino Romano cheese

Fine sea salt and freshly ground black pepper

1¼ pounds Romano beans, trimmed and sliced diagonally into 1-inch pieces

Canola oil

No beans are more anticipated than the first fat, slightly furred Romano beans. I love to seek them out among the winding pole-bean vines, feeling around for something with a rabbit-ear shape that feels like thickly padded mullein.

This is a simple recipe because you don't want to upstage these exceptionally tender seasonal beans—the only kind of bean that's wide enough to stay on the grill. I cook the Romanos until they are lightly charred and tender, and then toss them with a quickly pounded summery gravel of pistachios, garlic, and chives.

SERVES 4 TO 6

Prepare a medium-hot fire in your grill.

Make the chive pesto in a food processor or by hand with a mortar and pestle: Process the garlic and chives together until combined. Then add the pistachios and pulse until coarsely ground. Add the olive oil, Pecorino, and ⅛ teaspoon each of salt and pepper, and process to incorporate.

Rub the beans with a light coat of oil, and season with salt and pepper. Grill until lightly charred on both sides and tender, about 3 minutes per side. Add the chive pesto to the hot beans in a bowl, toss to coat, and serve.

CAMPFIRE-BAKED BEETS
with Hazelnut-Sesame Salt

One night, staring into my campfire, I was entranced enough to want to test the heat properties of the hot coals.

I went to bed that night after burying three foil-wrapped bundles of beets under a thick bedding of smoking ash. The next morning they were still warm, and when I slipped them from their skins, the egg-shaped ruby beets were transformed: spoon-tender and as sweet as cake. All the starch had converted to sugar. And the dark char sores, formed where the beets had come too close to fire, were a smoky reward.

They were almost too rich on their own, so I pounded together a quick *gomasio*—a dry muddle of sesame and salt—and then added some toasted hazelnuts, finding a surprise affinity between the seed and the nut.

Even without the overnight detainment in the campfire, beets taste good when tossed with this fragrant dust, and on regular nights I often sprinkle it over roasted beets.

SERVES 6 TO 8

Wrap the beets in three or four foil packs, and then double-wrap the packs. Bury the packs in a healthy layer of lightly glowing (not pink-hot) campfire coals and leave them, untouched, for at least 6 hours or until morning.

Using a knife, mash the garlic to a paste on a cutting board. Put it into a bowl. Put the sesame seeds in a heavy plastic bag, pound until bruised, and add to the bowl. Pour the hazelnuts into the bag, pound until reduced to a coarse rubble, and add to the bowl. Stir in salt to taste, ¼ teaspoon pepper, the sugar, and the chives. (Alternatively, pour everything into a food processor or mortar and pestle and pulse or pound until coarsely ground.)

Pull the foil packages from the ash, unwrap the beets carefully, and rub off their skins. Rip the beets lengthwise into large bite-size chunks. In a bowl, toss the beets with the vinegar, olive oil, and a sprinkling each of salt and pepper. Pour into a shallow dish, sprinkle heavily with the hazelnut-sesame salt, and serve lukewarm or at room temperature.

2 pounds (about 5 medium) beets without tops

1 small clove garlic

1½ tablespoons sesame seeds

⅓ cup hazelnuts, toasted (see page 206)

Fine sea salt and freshly ground black pepper

Pinch of sugar

1 tablespoon minced fresh chives or chopped fresh parsley

2 tablespoons red wine vinegar

2 tablespoons extra-virgin olive oil

NOTE: *To roast the beets in the oven, rub them (unpeeled) with a little oil and put them in a 9 × 13-inch baking dish. Add ¼ cup water to the dish, cover with aluminum foil, pinching the sides tight, and bake in a 350°F oven for 2 hours, or until the beets are tender when poked with a fork. Hold the beets in a paper towel, rub off the skins, and proceed with the recipe.*

FRIED CORN

3 tablespoons salted butter

½ cup small-diced green poblano or medium-hot garden chile pepper

2 cloves garlic, minced

½ cup sliced sugar snap peas or diced zucchini

4 cups corn kernels (from 6 to 7 ears)

¼ teaspoon fine sea salt

¼ teaspoon freshly ground black pepper

¼ cup minced fresh basil

A pan of fried corn and garden vegetables reminds me of those early days of living in the cabin in Two Inlets. At the time, I took a lot of influence from a chef and cookbook author named Edna Lewis, from Freetown, Virginia. Her way with the country bounty, her generous spirit, and her skillful hand with doughs picked me up and swept me away in those days. So if she said that the corn turned nutty after ten minutes in the pan and to keep frying it, I did what she said. She taught me that cooking is about subtle differences—the way one person fries a pan of potatoes differs from the way another one fries it—and that these things are important distinctions and worthy of our attention.

And so, this is a dish whose success hangs more on technique than on recipe. You want to note your corn's ripeness; if it's young and sweet, it won't need to fry quite as long, but if it's mature and starchy, give it time for that starch to fully turn over into sweetness. Watch the bottom of the pan closely; scratch up the brown base with the round edge of your wooden spoon, then smack the spoon on the pan so that the base falls back into the corn.

SERVES 4 TO 6

Heat a wide, heavy skillet over medium-high heat. Add 2 table-spoons of the butter and the poblanos, and stir. Add the garlic, snap peas, corn, salt, and pepper. Cook, stirring often with a wide spoon to bring up the stuck-on bits, until the corn is tender and sweet, 10 to 15 minutes, depending on the corn's maturity. The corn should caramelize and brown in spots. Add the final tablespoon of butter and the basil, and serve.

SCALLOPED CORN

Traditional scalloped corn has a telltale dense but creamy texture that falls somewhere between a soufflé and a custard—a fullness that's usually contributed by a can of creamed corn.

In this casserole, the creaminess comes from freshly grated seasonal sweet corn, whose slushy texture rightly replicates the wonders of the canned. To give it something to pop in the teeth, I mix the grated corn with a few cut corn kernels. Fresh corn needs little boostering, but I've long been a fan of what happens when nutmeg and rosemary cross wires, as they do so naturally here.

SERVES 6 TO 8

8 ears sweet corn, shucked

5 large eggs

1 cup heavy cream

1 teaspoon minced fresh rosemary

½ teaspoon salt

¼ teaspoon freshly ground black pepper

¼ teaspoon grated nutmeg

Salted butter, for the dish

NOTE: *Grating corn can be messy, but if you stand the corn up in an oversize bowl and rub it against a large box grater, it stays under control.*

Preheat the oven to 400°F.

One at a time, stand 5 of the ears of corn in a large shallow bowl and grate them against a box grater, down to the cob. Stand the remaining 3 ears in the center of the bowl, and with a large knife, slice the kernels from the cobs. Add the eggs, cream, rosemary, salt, pepper, and nutmeg to the bowl and whisk well.

Rub a 2½- to 3-quart baking dish with butter, pour in the corn mixture, and bake until puffed, golden brown, and no longer jiggly in the center when shaken, 40 to 45 minutes.

Serve immediately.

TOMATO CARPACCIO
with Horseradish Ice

According to a quick survey of friends from Wisconsin, South Dakota, and Missouri, the regional platter of sliced fresh summer tomatoes is not traditionally garnished with olive oil, which is a habit I've picked up in recent years. In fact, our childhood memories are there to remind us of the truth, the thing that my practical dad (lover of both beef steaks and beefsteak tomatoes) and all his kinsfolk have always known: Sun, salt, and pepper, that's all a tomato needs.

That said, after you've eaten your fill of plain tomatoes, here's a garnish that doesn't obscure their purity. The horseradish ice looks fancy but is easy to prepare. And when you take the icy sweet horseradish granita and the warm juicy tomatoes in one bite, summer meets winter, sweetness meets heat, and the saline beads of moisture on the surface of the tomatoes are enough to make a drizzle of olive oil wholly unnecessary.

It nearly goes without saying, but this side dish is excellent with a steak.

SERVES 6 TO 8

1 cup whole milk

¼ cup grated fresh horseradish, (page 224), or 3 tablespoons good-quality prepared horseradish

1 teaspoon sugar

Fine sea salt

2 pounds mixed heirloom tomatoes, beefsteak and cherry

1 tablespoon fresh lemon juice

Freshly cracked black pepper

1 tablespoon chopped fresh parsley

Whisk together the milk, horseradish, sugar, and ⅜ teaspoon salt, and pour into a glass dish. Freeze for 1 hour, or until the milk at the sides of the dish begins to freeze.

With a fork, rake the frozen sides into the slushy center. Freeze for another 30 minutes. Rake it again, and then freeze until solid, another 30 to 60 minutes. Just before serving, rake it again to make fresh shards of horseradish ice.

Slice the tomatoes and lay them out on a platter. Drizzle the tomatoes with the lemon juice and sprinkle with a fine spray of salt, pepper, and the chopped parsley. Let sit until the tomatoes start to perspire from the salt, 15 minutes or so. Just before serving, top the tomatoes with raked clumps of horseradish ice. Rush to the table.

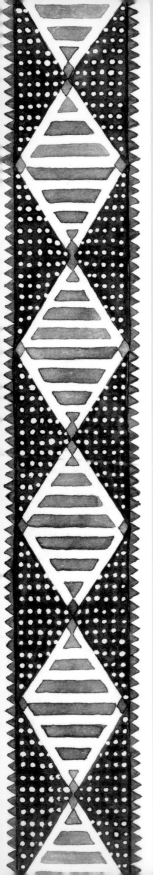

Fresh Horseradish

Horseradish is a sturdy perennial that can be harvested when it reaches full maturity in the fall, or overwintered and harvested when the ground thaws in the spring. I tend to harvest it in the fall, just because that's when I harvest everything else.

So does my friend and neighbor Katie, who throws an annual horse-radish party to coincide with the season. Guests sit around a table peeling fresh horseradish from a central bucket, drinking wine, and taking turns going outside to shred the peeled knobs in the food processor, adding a bit of sugar, salt, and vinegar to preserve its pale color and fresh bite.

That's right, outside. The aroma of freshly shredded horseradish pounds your nasal cavities with a teary, choking fire that makes the heat of chiles seem rational. Like wasabi or spicy ginger, it's a different kind of hot. Back in the day, someone who wanted to shred a bunch of horseradish would set up her crank grinder on an outside bench so as to do her business in the breeze, but these days it's easier to simply run an extension cord to a food processor set up on a picnic table, as Katie does.

A few days after the horseradish party, I was in the grocery store and ran into my neighbor Gwen, and she gave me the rundown on the differences between spring- and fall-harvested horseradish, and which she preferred.

"We always harvested it in months without an R in them—May, June, July, or August. Spring horseradish is drier and has a lot more bite. Frank's mother would grate it by hand and tears would just *stream* down her face. But see, that's the spring horseradish."

"I didn't think it could be any stronger," I said.

"Oh, it can be!" She winked. "Good if you like that sort of thing."

TOMATO *and* EGGPLANT COMPOTE

To put August's garden bounty to use, I often turn to a simple eggplant and tomato side dish made in a style borrowed from my Israeli friends Hagit and Uzi, who have brought their energetic cooking—and their collection of whole spices—with them to northern Minnesota. Think chunks of eggplant collapsing into marshmallow softness, whiffs of bay, cumin, and cinnamon—all of it smothered with grassy-green olive oil.

One day I was thinking of Hagit and how she teases me about what she sees as an American conservatism with spices—"They sell all these little tiny jars of spices here, but where are the big jars? I add a lot!"—and met her challenge by submerging an entire cinnamon stick into the eggplant, instead of just adding a pinch of the ground as usual. As I lifted the lid, the curling plumes of spice unfurled toward the rafters.

Heat half of the canola oil in a large skillet over medium-high heat. Add one-third of the eggplant and fry until dark brown on both sides, about 4 minutes. Transfer the eggplant to a paper towel–lined plate, blot it well, and cover with more paper towels. Repeat with the remaining eggplant, adding the rest of the canola oil as needed. Season the fried eggplant with a little salt.

Heat 2 tablespoons of the olive oil in the skillet and add the onion. Cook over medium-high heat until darkened around the edges, about 5 minutes. Add the garlic and cook for another 2 minutes.

Add the eggplant, tomatoes, cinnamon stick, bay leaves, honey, ½ teaspoon salt, pepper, and the remaining 2 tablespoons olive oil. Stir gently, turning the vegetables over to combine. Reduce the heat to low, cover the pan, and cook until the eggplant is soft and the mixture is liquidy, about 20 minutes. Uncover the pan, and don't stir, but shake the pan to shift things around. Continue to cook over medium-low heat until the thick liquid clings to the vegetables, about 15 minutes.

Squeeze the lemon juice into the pan and shake the pan softly to incorporate. Turn the vegetables out into a shallow bowl, remove the cinnamon stick and bay leaves, and serve warm or at room temperature.

⅓ cup canola oil, more or less

1 pound eggplant, preferably a small variety, cut into 1½-inch cubes

Fine sea salt

4 tablespoons extra-virgin olive oil

½ large onion

3 cloves garlic, thinly sliced

2 beefsteak tomatoes, peeled and cut into chunks

1 small cinnamon stick

2 dried bay leaves

1 teaspoon honey

Freshly ground black pepper

½ lemon

NOTES: *Real cinnamon bark— soft-stick cinnamon, not cinnamon oil–soaked sticks—can be found at Penzeys Spices, a store with locations across the United States, or online at www.penzeys.com.*

A good way to peel just one tomato: Stick a fork in the center of the tomato and hold it over a gas flame, rotating it until the skin pops.

GREEN *and* SHELL BEANS
with Almonds *and* Goat Cheese

1½ cups shell beans (from about 1 pound in the pod)

Fine sea salt

3 tablespoons extra-virgin olive oil

1 tablespoon salted butter

½ cup sliced or slivered almonds

Freshly ground black pepper

4 cloves garlic, sliced

12 ounces young green beans, trimmed

⅓ cup torn fresh basil leaves

½ teaspoon grated lemon zest

2 tablespoons fresh lemon juice

3 ounces fresh goat cheese, crumbled

At farmer's markets or large grocery stores, shell beans usually go by the name "fresh cranberry beans" and are sold in their pods. Totally different from dried beans, shell beans are the gardener's treat, the mature beans stolen from the bean pods before they dry out completely on the vine.

These beans cook quickly and have dissolving thin skins and a dense, fudgy interior—a final texture that splits the difference between vegetable and starch. When mixed with summer's skinny green beans, cheese, and nuts, they provide the heft to make an ideal lunch.

SERVES 6 TO 8

Put the shell beans in a saucepan, add enough water to cover by at least 2 inches, and salt the water. Bring to a simmer over medium heat, and cook until very tender, about 30 minutes. To keep them from drying out, let the cooked beans sit in the water until you are ready to assemble the salad.

Combine 2 tablespoons of the olive oil, the butter, and the almonds in a small saucepan and cook over medium-low heat until the almonds are toasted, about 5 minutes. Season with ¼ teaspoon salt and a little ground pepper, and remove from the heat. Stir in the garlic, which should sizzle in the hot fat, and set aside to cool.

In another pot, bring about 2 quarts water to a boil. Salt the water generously, add the green beans, quickly return to a boil, and cook until just tender, about 4 minutes. Drain well.

Combine the green beans and drained shell beans in a serving bowl, and add the almond mixture, basil, lemon zest, lemon juice, ¼ teaspoon salt, and remaining 1 tablespoon olive oil. Season with pepper, and toss to combine. Crumble the goat cheese over the beans and gently toss. Serve warm or at room temperature.

NOTES: *If the green beans are very mature (i.e., not skinny), simply slice them deeply on the diagonal before boiling.*

If fresh shell beans are unavailable, substitute drained canned cannellini beans.

GRILLED ZUCCHINI *with* Cherry Tomato–Ground Cherry Salsa

I know some gardeners who pick one zucchini and toss the second one over their shoulder, they have so many, but I'm more particular about mine. For years now I've grown one of two Italian varieties, Cocozelle or Tromboncino. Dark green with lime-green ridges, firmer and crisper than common hybrid zucchini, they're also slower growing. Last year I thought I'd try a standard over-yielding type so that I could experience the gardener's stereotypical green crush—and it worked, drowning me in them—but I missed the nutty firmness of my Italian stripers and went back to them.

Made with any variety of fresh zucchini, this dish is, to me, one of the treats of summer. In season I make it at least once a week because I crave the fruitiness that the ground cherries add to the cherry tomato salsa. If you don't have ground cherries (miniature tomatillos with a sweet-tart flavor that crosses lime with pineapple), just substitute additional cherry tomatoes. And if you're in the mood for something spicy, add a generous pinch of red pepper flakes to the mix.

SERVES 6

1½ cups cherry tomatoes, halved

⅓ cup husked ground cherries, halved

¼ teaspoon sugar

Fine sea salt and freshly ground black pepper

1 tablespoon fresh lemon juice

4 tablespoons extra-virgin olive oil

⅓ cup torn fresh basil leaves

2 pounds (3 medium) zucchini

About 2 ounces shaved Parmesan cheese, for serving

Put the cherry tomatoes and ground cherries in a small bowl. Add the sugar, ⅛ teaspoon salt, ⅛ teaspoon pepper, the lemon juice, 3 tablespoons of the olive oil, and the basil leaves. Toss until combined. Let the tomatoes and ground cherries macerate while you cook the zucchini—for up to a few hours if you like.

Preheat a grill or a cast-iron stovetop grill pan over medium-high heat.

Slice the zucchini ½ inch thick on a slight diagonal. Lay the slices out on a baking sheet, and rub both sides with the remaining 1 tablespoon olive oil, ½ teaspoon salt, and ¼ teaspoon pepper. Grill the zucchini quickly—turning each side an inch counterclockwise to get crosshatched grill marks—until both sides are browned, about 5 minutes. Arrange the grilled zucchini in one layer on a wide platter.

Scatter the marinated tomatoes and ground cherries over the zucchini. (This salad can be made up to 1 hour ahead of time. In fact, I think it gets better as it sits.) Just before serving, garnish the platter with curls of freshly shaved Parmesan cheese.

TURNIPS
with Their Greens *and* Bacon

1½ pounds (3 medium) turnips

6 ounces (about 6 thick-cut
    slices) bacon, sliced into
    1-inch pieces

2 tablespoons salted butter

Fine sea salt and freshly ground
    black pepper

3 cups (lightly packed) chopped
    washed turnip greens (or
    chop about ½ bunch collard
    greens)

2 tablespoons maple syrup

Turnips are easy to grow—especially the Hokkaido, or Japanese type, which mature in about forty days—quick to cook, tender, and naturally buttery. There's just a teensy shade of bitterness in their background, though, that seems to turn some people off. Too bad, because it's so easily remedied with a little bit of sweetener.

Here's a recipe for turnips cooked with their own greens (which are mild and fat, like collard greens), amended with a spoonful of maple syrup and flavored with lots of thick-cut smoky bacon. (The bacon plays a prominent enough role here to warrant breaking out the good stuff, which you can hardly walk through the Midwest without tripping over.)

SERVES 6 TO 8

Peel the turnips thickly (to remove the fibrous layer that sometimes lurks just beneath the peel) and cut them into roughly 1-inch cubes.

Heat a wide-bottomed sauté pan over medium heat, and add the bacon. Cook the bacon until it is crisp at the edges, about 5 minutes. Remove it from the pan, and pour out all but 1 tablespoon of the bacon fat. Add the butter and the turnips to the pan. Season the turnips with salt and pepper, and cook them over medium-low heat, covered, stirring often and taking care not to burn the bits on the bottom of the pan, until just tender, 10 to 15 minutes.

Uncover the pan, add the chopped greens and the bacon, and cook until the greens are tender at the stem and the turnips are glazed, about 3 minutes. Stir in the maple syrup, and serve.

BUTTERCUP SQUASH
with Ricotta *and* Fried Sage

This one gets a little gold star for Thanksgiving, mostly because of the extra-silky texture that the ricotta adds to the pureed squash (though it's also wonderful with pork chops any time of the year). You can whip the squash with the ricotta cheese and keep it warm until dinner; but once you dress it with the browned butter and sage, serve it immediately so that you can enjoy the crackling sage leaves.

SERVES 8

Preheat the oven to 350°F.

Cut the squash in half and scoop out the seeds and pulp. Season the squash cavities with salt and pepper. Lay the squash halves cut-side down on a heavy baking sheet, and bake until the squash is very tender when pierced with a knife at the deepest part, 45 minutes to 1 hour.

When the squash is done, combine the ricotta and 3 table-spoons of the butter in a food processor, and process until smooth. Measure 3 heaping cups of cooked squash, and add this to the processor. Season with salt, pepper, and the allspice, and process until smooth and whipped. Transfer the squash puree to a baking dish and keep warm.

Right before serving, heat the remaining 3 tablespoons butter and the sage leaves in a small skillet over medium heat. Cook, stirring now and then with a fork to submerge the sage leaves, until the butter turns a chestnut-brown color and the leaves turn crisp, about 3 minutes. Pour the sage brown butter over the warm squash puree and serve immediately, while the leaves are still brittle and crumbly.

1 small to medium buttercup squash

Fine sea salt and freshly ground black pepper

1 cup whole-milk ricotta cheese, at room temperature

6 tablespoons (¾ stick) salted butter, at room temperature

¼ teaspoon ground allspice

12 fresh sage leaves

NOTE: *Depending on how large your squash is, this recipe may leave you with some leftover mashed squash. When faced with an extra cup or so, I like to add it to pancake batter, stir it into my morning oatmeal, or spread a thin layer of it inside a grilled Gruyère sandwich.*

CHESTNUT, WILD RICE,
and Pistachio Dressing

For those who have never eaten freshly roasted chestnuts: Buy some, pour a glass of wine, etch an X into each chestnut, roast them in a 400°F oven until the skin curls backward from the X, and eat them one by one so as to fully appreciate their unusual texture, which seems to blend the dense, sweet cakiness of a kabocha squash with the scent of hazelnuts. Their stubbornness, clinging inside a tight casing and then a tough shell, makes eating chestnuts especially rewarding.

Between the rich chestnuts, the buttery grains of wild and basmati rices, and the crushed pistachios, this dish has the chops to be a main course, although I tend to serve it as a Thanksgiving side dish or alongside roasted pork.

SERVES 8

Put the wild rice in a fine-mesh sieve and rinse it under cold running water, swishing the rice with your hand until the water runs clear. Transfer the rice to a medium bowl and add water to cover. Pour off any black bits or floating kernels, and then pour the rice back into the sieve to drain.

Cook the rices separately: Combine the wild rice with ¼ teaspoon salt and 1 cup water in a small saucepan. Bring to a simmer, cover tightly, reduce the heat to low, and steam until the rice is tender and curling into a C shape, 20 to 25 minutes.

At the same time, combine the basmati rice, ½ teaspoon salt, and 1¾ cups water in another small saucepan. Bring to a simmer, cover tightly, reduce the heat to low, and steam until the rice is tender, 25 minutes.

Combine the rices in a large bowl and cover it tightly.

Cook the vegetable base: Heat the butter in a large skillet over medium heat. Add the celery and onion and cook, stirring often, until the vegetables are limp but still bright, about 10 minutes. Add the garlic and thyme, and cook for 5 minutes.

Pour the celery and onion over the rices, scraping the pan for the juices, and stir to combine. Add the pistachios, chestnuts, and parsley, and mix thoroughly. Serve hot.

½ cup natural wild rice

Fine sea salt

1 cup basmati rice

6 tablespoons (¾ stick) salted butter

2 cups diced celery (from 5 stalks)

2 cups diced yellow onion (from 1 large)

3 cloves garlic, minced

2 teaspoons minced fresh thyme

½ cup shelled salted pistachios, crushed

8 ounces cooked chestnuts, roughly chopped

2 tablespoons minced fresh parsley

NOTE: *If you're peeling any volume of chestnuts, I'd recommend another, less romantic method: Cut the X into the flat side of the chestnuts and then boil them until the skins soften and begin to peel back, about 5 minutes. Drain them, cover with a heavy towel, and peel them one by one. The boiling softens their skins, so it's more like shucking than peeling. In season, you can peel chestnuts, pile the sweet meat into plastic bags, and freeze for up to six months.*

RUTABAGA BAKE

2¼ pounds (1 extra-large or 2 medium) rutabaga

1 medium russet potato, peeled and cut into 2-inch cubes

Pinch plus 1 tablespoon sugar

3 tablespoons salted butter, melted, plus more at room temperature for the baking dish

1½ cups fresh rye bread crumbs (from 5 slices rye bread)

½ cup lightly toasted hazelnuts, skins rubbed off

3 large eggs

1 cup half-and-half or heavy cream

2 tablespoons Madeira wine

½ teaspoon grated nutmeg

¼ teaspoon freshly ground black pepper

Fine sea salt

Creamed Rutabagas

My mother makes a mean dish of creamed rutabagas to serve next to roasted pork, and the recipe is simple: Trim, boil, drain, and mash the rutabagas as directed at right, making sure not to whip them too smoothly. Add heavy cream and a lump of butter, season with salt and pepper, and mix. The volumes of butter and cream are a matter of personal taste, but knowing my mother, neither of them should be timid.

Ask anyone in this area who lived through the Depression what they think about rutabagas, if you dare. During times of hardship the stalwart roots did the heavy lifting, and many people of that generation were greatly overserved their rutabagas, parsnips, turnips, and beets.

Fodder vegetable or not, rutabagas have a sweet, buttery flavor, and they clean up well in this rutabaga soufflé, a traditional recipe popular among the Finnish immigrants in the Midwest. The deeply toasted nuts, grated nutmeg, and the wrinkled, billowy soufflé top do a lot to make a case for rutabaga's decadence. A perfect vegetarian main course, it's also a winning side that nestles up nicely next to just about everything.

SERVES 6 TO 8

Combine the rutabagas and potatoes in a 2-quart pot, add water to cover, and add the pinch of sugar. Bring the water to a simmer, cover the pot, and cook until the rutabaga and potato are both very soft when pierced with a fork, about 25 minutes. Drain and transfer to a large bowl.

Meanwhile, preheat the oven to 375°F. Butter just the bottom of a medium (2- to 2½-quart) baking dish.

Divide the rye bread crumbs evenly between two medium bowls. Roughly chop the hazelnuts and add them, along with the melted butter, to one of the bowls. Toss to combine.

Separate the eggs, and put the whites into a third bowl. Add the yolks to the bowl of plain crumbs along with the half-and-half, Madeira, nutmeg, pepper, and ¾ teaspoon salt. Mix to combine.

In the bowl of a standing mixer fitted with the whisk (or using a hand mixer), whip the egg whites and remaining 1 tablespoon sugar until soft peaks form; set aside. Separately, whip the rutabaga mixture until pureed.

Add the egg yolk mixture to the rutabaga mixture, and mix well. Gently fold in the whipped egg whites with a rubber spatula, mixing until just wisps of egg white remain. Pour the mixture into the buttered dish and top with the reserved hazelnut bread crumbs.

Bake until golden brown on top and set in the middle, 50 to 55 minutes.

PAN-ROASTED CAULIFLOWER
with Salt Pork *and* Capers

Blistered roasted brassicas—broccoli, cauliflower, Brussels sprouts, and cabbage—have been showing up on restaurant menus with increasing frequency, and for good reason. Cooking these kinds of vegetables at high heat unlocks their natural nutty sweetness.

I've found that giving cauliflower the same stovetop-to-oven one-two punch that I give a pork chop ensures a beautiful darkness every time and cauliflower that is tender, sweet, and never mushy. A bit of cured pork adds substance, and droplets of capers add a nice cutting acidity.

One thing: The pan-roasting technique is amenable to a small batch, but it's a bit more difficult to pull off in larger volume. If serving more than four people, double the batch and cook it in two pans.

SERVES 3 TO 4

Preheat the oven to 375°F.

Heat a heavy ovenproof 12-inch skillet (cast-iron is ideal) over medium heat and add the salt pork. Cook, stirring, until crisp on the edges, about 7 minutes. Remove the salt pork from the pan, leaving the fat behind.

If the salt pork fat does not cover the bottom of the skillet, add enough canola oil to just coat the bottom, and heat it over medium-high heat. Fry the cauliflower in batches—only as much as will fit in one snug layer at a time—until deeply browned on both sides, about 8 minutes. Season the cauliflower with pepper and a little salt (just a little because of the salt pork and the salty capers).

Return all of the cauliflower to the skillet, add the garlic, and transfer it to the oven. Roast, uncovered, for 5 minutes or until the cauliflower tests tender when poked with a fork.

Remove the skillet from the oven, and add the butter, sage, and salt pork. Stir until the butter foams and then subsides. Add the capers and parsley, stir to combine, and pour into a shallow serving dish or platter.

- 5 ounces salt pork (page 298) or pancetta, cut into small cubes (¾ cup)
- Canola oil, for the pan
- 7 cups medium cauliflower florets (from 1 small or ½ extra-large head cauliflower)
- Fine sea salt and freshly ground black pepper
- 3 cloves garlic, smashed
- 2 tablespoons salted butter
- 6 fresh sage leaves, sliced
- 3 tablespoons drained capers or chopped sour pickles
- 1 tablespoon chopped fresh parsley

BRAISED GREEN BEANS
with Onions *and* Vinegar

2 tablespoons extra-virgin
    olive oil

1 tablespoon salted butter

1 medium onion, halved and
    thinly sliced

¾ teaspoon fine sea salt

½ teaspoon freshly ground
    black pepper

1 teaspoon yellow mustard
    seeds

1½ pounds frozen green beans,
    thawed and halved crosswise

1½ tablespoons apple cider
    vinegar or white wine vinegar

NOTE: *To make this dish with fresh
green beans, simply boil them until
just tender (about 3 minutes). Add
them to the onions, and proceed from
there.*

For those who freeze summer green beans for winter consumption, as I do, here's your reward. This, my favorite bean dish, takes its inspiration from Italian cooking, a food culture in which a soft, well-cooked vegetable still can be a star—which is exactly the kind of love that frozen green beans require. When the beans thaw, the shrinking ice crystals take the beans' crispness and youth with them, and there's no getting that back. The beans' flavor remains, though, which is so much more valuable.

For this you want to caramelize a sliced onion until it turns into a candied mush, then add the beans and cook them until they're equally tender and rich. The dash of vinegar at the end has the miraculous effect of "sweetening" the beans. It's not necessarily the prettiest dish, but the flavors are huge.

SERVES 4 TO 6

Heat a large skillet over medium heat. Add the olive oil, butter, and onion. Season with the salt and pepper, and cook, stirring, until soft and caramelized, about 25 minutes.

Stir in the yellow mustard seeds, and then add the green beans. Cook until heated through, about 5 minutes. Add the vinegar and cook, stirring, until the beans are tender and sweet and have turned evenly olive green, about 5 more minutes. Serve immediately.

Wild Rice *and*
BROWN RICE PILAF

Mixed together, these two rices share an earthy nuttiness. It sounds unlikely, but this wild-and-brown-rice combination goes incredibly well with the rustic clay-pot whole-grain end of Asian cooking. When it's cold out, I like to serve this pilaf beneath a piece of maple-and-soy-glazed pork belly (page 165).

Real wild rice has a fragrance you don't want to obscure with chicken stock. The delicate aroma is best brought out by steaming the rice in plain water along with some strong aromatics such as thyme, bay leaf, garlic, and bacon. (It comes out: I believe bacon counts as an aromatic.)

SERVES 8

¾ cup natural wild rice

5 slices (5 ounces) thick-cut bacon, finely diced

1 cup finely diced onion

3 tablespoons salted butter

3 cloves garlic, minced

½ cup brown rice

2 sprigs fresh thyme

Fine sea salt and freshly ground black pepper

2 tablespoons sesame seeds, toasted

Put the wild rice in a fine-mesh sieve and rinse it under cold running water, swishing the rice with your hand until the water runs clear. Transfer the rice to a medium bowl and add water to cover. Pour off any black bits or floating kernels, and then pour the rice back into the sieve to drain.

Heat a medium saucepan over medium heat and add the bacon. Cook, stirring, until it's crisp at the edges, about 3 minutes. Remove the bacon with a slotted spoon, and add the onion and butter to the pan. Cook, stirring, until the onion is tender and light golden, about 8 minutes. Add the garlic and cook for 1 minute. Add the brown rice, 2½ cups water, the thyme, salt, pepper, and the reserved bacon. Bring to a simmer, cover tightly, and reduce the heat to the lowest setting. Steam, tightly covered, for 10 minutes.

Stir in the wild rice, replace the lid tightly, and continue to steam until the brown rice is tender to the bite and the wild rice has curled into a lowercase "c" shape, 30 to 35 minutes. Add the sesame seeds, stir, and serve.

SPAETZLE
with Brown Butter

Fine sea salt and freshly ground black pepper

3 large eggs

1 large egg yolk

½ cup whole milk

¼ teaspoon grated nutmeg, plus more for serving

3 cups plus 2 tablespoons all-purpose flour

6 tablespoons (¾ stick) salted butter

1 bunch scallions, white and green parts, sliced

When I was growing up, my mom made spaetzle about once a week, and I always thought that hers (chewy and buttery) were the best. Then, when I was working for Austrian chef Mario Lohninger in New York City, I learned to make a plusher and more delicate spaetzle, scented with nutmeg and browned on the bottom in a heavy pan like a hash. And that was pretty good. Then I went back to my mother's spaetzle recipe because I missed the rustic chewiness and the little brown butter scallions. Finally I combined the two recipes, making a softer but still sturdy spaetzle, scented with nutmeg and lightly fried in browned butter. For me, it remains—as it has since childhood—the king of starchy sides.

SERVES 6

Fill a large stockpot two-thirds full of water, salt it liberally, and start bringing it to a boil over high heat.

In a large bowl, whisk together the eggs and egg yolk. Add ½ cup water, the milk, ¾ teaspoon salt, ¼ teaspoon pepper, and the nutmeg. Whisk until smooth.

Set a fine-mesh sieve over the bowl. Sift in 1 cup of the flour and whisk to combine. Sift in another ½ cup and whisk until the batter is smooth.

Switch to a wooden spoon or a rubber spatula, and sift in the remaining 1½ cups plus 2 tablespoons flour, beating until the batter billows and forms elastic strands. You'll know it's right when after a good stir it huffs and expires and flops down, almost as if it were breathing. (You can make the batter a couple of hours ahead of time, covered and left at room temperature.)

Make the brown butter (and you can do this ahead of time as well): Heat a very wide bottomed pan over medium-high heat, add the butter, and cook until the froth on top deepens to an acorn-brown, about 4 minutes. Remove from the heat, and after giving it a minute or two to cool, add the sliced scallions.

Working quickly, pass the batter through a spaetzle maker or colander into the boiling water. Swish the water with a fork to break up any clumps. Bring the water back to a boil and cook the spaetzle for exactly 1 more minute. Drain the spaetzle well.

Set the pan of brown butter and scallions over medium-high heat and add the drained spaetzle, stirring to coat. Fry, stirring every 30 seconds or so, until the bottoms of the spaetzle turn light brown, about 8 minutes. Dust with a bit more grated nutmeg, and season with salt and pepper. Turn the spaetzle into a serving bowl, and serve hot.

NOTE: *Ideally, you want to use a spaetzle maker for this recipe, which looks like a sliding box on a flat grater. Of course, it's possible to push the batter through the holes of a colander held over the water, smashing it against the holes with a wide rubber spatula. I remember my mother doing this before she brought home a spaetzle maker, but it's a bit awkward and tough on one's wrists.*

CRISPY CHEESE CURD RISOTTO CAKE

10 tablespoons (1¼ sticks)
    salted butter

½ cup finely diced sweet onion

1 cup Carnaroli or Arborio rice

¾ teaspoon fine sea salt

¾ cup dry white wine

1¼ cups freshly grated
    Parmesan cheese

1 pound white cheese curds

About 1 cup rice flour

NOTES: *If you cannot locate rice flour for frying the risotto cakes (though it makes for an earth-shattering crispy crust), use a low-protein flour, such as Wondra or plain cake flour.*

Fresh cheese curds are a natural snack for a cheese-making region, a treat for those unafraid to filch a curd or two from the frothing vat of whey. In the cheese-rich state of Wisconsin, and also across the upper Midwest, they sell the salty, cold knobs in gas stations, and at fairs they call them "fried cheese curds," meaning that they've been dipped in beer batter, deep-fried, and handed to you while still in a volcanic state. A proper fried cheese curd should have the stretch and stick of rubber cement. A cold one should be so fresh that it lets out an audible squeak when you bite into it.

At Perennial Virant in Chicago, chef Paul Virant's Crispy Carnaroli Rice, stuffed with whole, melting cheese curds, threw us three girls from northern Minnesota for a loop. All childhood memories of Hubbard County Fair battered cheese curds vanished when this elegant slab of gooey risotto with the crispy edges arrived. Standing at the bar, we meant to share gracefully, but in truth we all fork-jousted our way through this dish, thin threads of cheese flying in front of us like a web.

Paul serves the dish as a starter garnished with a pitch-perfect circle of house-pickled green beans, but at home I make it as a meatless main course or as a side dish to accompany a protein.

MAKES 16 SMALL RECTANGLES; SERVES 8 TO 10

Melt 2 tablespoons of the butter in a large, high-sided skillet, and add the onion. Cook over medium heat until soft and sweet, about 10 minutes. Add the rice and salt and cook, stirring, until well coated in butter, 2 minutes. Pour in the white wine and cook, stirring, until it evaporates. Add ½ cup water and cook, stirring frequently, until it has been absorbed. Repeat, adding ½ cup water at a time, until the rice swells and becomes tender. This should take about 15 minutes and about 3½ cups water. The texture of the risotto should be softly flowing but not soupy.

Stir in the Parmesan cheese, and transfer the risotto to a wide bowl. When it is cool enough to touch, fold in the cheese curds.

Line an 8-inch-square baking dish with plastic wrap, leaving plenty of overhang on all sides. Pour the risotto into the dish, smooth the top, and cover with the overhanging plastic. Refrigerate until firm, about 3 hours, or as long as overnight.

Before serving, clarify the remaining 8 tablespoons butter: Heat the butter in a small skillet over medium heat until it foams and starts to turn dark blond on top, 2 to 3 minutes. Remove from the heat and let the butter sit for a few minutes. Then tilt the skillet toward you and gently spoon off the top layer of foam. Pour the clear golden butter into another bowl, and then pour the dark dregs at the bottom of the skillet into the bowl with the foam.

Unmold the risotto cake onto a cutting board. Cut it into eight 1-inch-wide slabs, and then cut each rectangle in half to make 16 pieces. Put the rice flour in a shallow dish. Dip the tops and bottoms of the risotto cakes into the flour, and transfer them to a platter or baking sheet.

Preheat the oven to 250°F.

Heat a large nonstick or cast-iron sauté pan over medium-high heat. Add enough clarified butter to lightly coat the bottom, and when it's hot, add as many risotto cakes as will fit in the pan. Fry until a dark golden brown crust forms on both sides and the cheese inside is melted, about 4 minutes. Keep the fried risotto cakes warm in the oven while you fry the rest of them. Serve immediately.

Potatoes

& Onions

*"I grow real vegetables in my garden. I've got half an acre of
potatoes and two hundred sets of onions."*
INGVALD ANNEXSTAD,
retired dairy farmer,
my husband's grandfather,
Norseland, Minnesota

If you believe, as I do, that inspiring dishes spring from moments of deprivation, and not from times of abundance, then the humble potato, sometimes the only thing left in a raided pantry, is the key to the very best of Midwestern cooking.

Hash browns, for instance, have deep roots here. They seem to be made best either in cast-iron pans over campfires or in small boxcar diners that sell cheap breakfasts to singles and lonesome travelers; those places (and I can think offhand of one in St. Paul, Minnesota, and one in Kansas City, Missouri) always show their mastery with the hash browns, achieving a proper crackle in the brown lid while maintaining the white, soft ticking of the interior.

At the other end of the spectrum, opposite the crisp browned edge, you have a tradition of simple boiled potatoes, truly fresh spuds that don't need much else. This habit of boiling, buttering, smashing, or otherwise decorating the potato mush to your liking was likely brought here by the Northern Europeans—for example, Scandinavians, Irish, and Germans who emigrated to the Midwest—although such no-nonsense eating is pretty universal, natural to the Plains character, and makes a fitting accompaniment to meat.

Among the potato recipes in this chapter, some are designed to fulfill that traditional promise, such as Whipped Potatoes with Horseradish and Creamy Yellow Potato Salad. But others, such as Bitter Greens with Potatoes and Salt Pork, or Potato Skins with Smoked Cheddar and Bacon, stand on their own very well.

GERMAN POTATO SALAD

A well-made German potato salad needs more than a simple mixing; it should be given a good muddling, a chance for the potatoes and bacon and vinaigrette to swap juices with one another. After all, nothing is worse than having three simple components in a bowl that sort of know each other but haven't officially met.

This is one of the best last-minute dinner solutions I know.

SERVES 6 TO 8

Put the potatoes in a saucepan and add enough water to cover generously. Salt the water, bring it to a soft boil over medium-high heat, and cook until the potatoes test just tender when poked with a fork, 15 to 20 minutes.

While the potatoes are simmering, cook the bacon: Heat a medium skillet over medium heat, add the bacon, and cook, stirring often, until it crisps at the edges but still feels pliable in the middle, 10 minutes. Remove it from the skillet, leaving at least 3 tablespoons bacon fat in the skillet. Add the butter, scallions, and garlic to the skillet, and sauté gently for 1 minute. Add the vinegar, 2 tablespoons water, the sugar, ¾ teaspoon salt, and the pepper.

Drain the potatoes, and when they are cool enough to handle, cut them into bite-size wedges, removing any clumps of skin that come off but leaving most of it on. Put the potatoes in a large serving bowl.

Pour the vinaigrette and the bacon over the warm potatoes, and mix well with a rubber spatula. Serve warm or at room temperature.

2½ pounds small potatoes, such as B-size reds, scrubbed but not peeled

Fine sea salt

9 ounces thick-cut bacon, cut into 1-inch pieces

2 tablespoons salted butter

1 bunch scallions, white and green parts, sliced

4 cloves garlic, minced

4 to 5 tablespoons apple cider vinegar, to taste

2 teaspoons sugar

¾ teaspoon freshly ground black pepper

WHIPPED POTATOES
with Horseradish

2 pounds (3 to 4) russet
  potatoes, quartered

Fine sea salt

¾ cup heavy cream

½ cup whole milk

¾ cup (lightly packed) grated
  fresh horseradish

1 teaspoon sugar

8 tablespoons (1 stick) salted
  butter, at room temperature

½ teaspoon freshly ground
  black pepper

Nothing holds gravy like a moat of properly whipped white potatoes. They're good plain, but even better with fresh horseradish.

When I was a kid it was my job on fried chicken nights to whip the potatoes, and my mother taught me to work them to a lofty meringue. When you lift out the beaters, the potato peak should be thick enough to stand upright, as light and as sturdy as a snowdrift.

Russets are the only kind of potato that can take this kind of beating without getting gluey. You can make this dish any time of year, but it's something to look forward to in the fall, when both the russets and the horseradish are fresh from the ground.

SERVES 6 TO 8

Put the potatoes in a saucepan and add enough water to cover generously. Salt the water, bring to a slow simmer over medium heat, and cook until the potatoes are tender when poked with a fork, 15 to 20 minutes.

Meanwhile, combine the cream, milk, horseradish, and sugar in a small saucepan and bring to a simmer. (The sugar brings out the flavor of the fresh horseradish.) Remove from the heat, cover, and let steep for at least 10 minutes.

Drain the potatoes, and push them through a ricer into a mixing bowl. Reheat the cream mixture if it has cooled. Begin whipping the potatoes—either in a stand mixer fitted with the whisk attachment or with a handheld mixer—adding the butter as you go. When the butter has melted, gradually add three-quarters of the hot cream mixture, whipping until the potatoes are soft and fluffy. Add ½ teaspoon salt and the pepper, and then any additional cream mixture as needed for the potatoes to achieve the texture of stiffly whipped cream. Serve immediately.

GLORIFIED HASH-BROWN CAKE
with Frying Peppers

The entire time we lived in New York City, my husband, Aaron, bemoaned the lack of hash browns. It's true: at the time, most breakfast places in Brooklyn served home fries, or sliced potatoes cooked with peppers and onions, sometimes tomatoes. Some of them were pretty tasty; all of them definitely lacked crunch. They might have called them home fries, but none of them felt like home. The importance of good hash browns had been drilled into us from birth, and we missed them: the dark brown flat-top, the flaky, buttery potato interior.

During my part-time summer job at the German diner on the main street of Park Rapids (where we made the hash browns from scratch with boiled russet potatoes), if someone asked for onions and green peppers fried into their hash browns we called them "glorified." So I do the same here.

Because the moisture from the peppers sometime threatens to compromise the crunchiness of the hash browns, I separate them and top one large hash-brown cake with a jumble of fried peppers. Cut this in wedges for serving. It goes with just about anything—obviously with steak—and also makes a dramatic vegetarian main course.

SERVES 6

Put the potatoes in a saucepan and add enough water to cover generously. Salt the water, bring it to a simmer over medium heat, cover partially, and cook until the potatoes are tender enough to stick a fork into but still on the firm side of done, about 20 minutes. Drain the potatoes and let cool. (You can boil the potatoes up to a day ahead of time and keep them in the refrigerator, if you like.)

While the potatoes are cooking, clarify the butter: Heat the butter in a small skillet over medium heat until it foams and starts to turn dark blond on top, 2 to 3 minutes. Remove from the heat and let the butter sit for a few minutes. Then tilt the skillet toward you and gently spoon off the layer of foam. Pour the clear golden butter into another bowl, and then pour the dark dregs at the bottom of the skillet into the bowl containing the foam. (For dregs uses, see page 215.)

2½ pounds (3 to 4) russet potatoes, scrubbed but not peeled

Fine sea salt

10 tablespoons (1¼ sticks) salted butter

½ teaspoon freshly ground black pepper

1 medium Vidalia onion, diced

8 ounces green frying peppers, such as Hungarian wax or baby poblano, whole if small, halved if large

NOTE: *To split up the process, you can boil and grate the potatoes and refrigerate them, loosely covered, for up to 8 hours before frying the hash-brown cake.*

RECIPE CONTINUES

Grate the potatoes coarsely, skins and all, onto a baking sheet, making sure to keep them loose and not to pack them down. Combine ½ teaspoon salt and the black pepper in a small bowl, sprinkle over the potatoes, along with the diced onion, and gently mix to combine.

Heat a 10-inch cast-iron skillet over medium-high heat, and add half of the clarified butter. Add all of the potatoes in an even layer, keeping them loose. Reduce the heat to medium and cook the potato cake until the bottom turns dark amber brown, about 15 minutes. (Peek on the sides: If it's browning too quickly, turn the heat down to medium-low.)

Put a large plate upside down over the skillet, and using two thick oven mitts, grab the sides of the skillet and turn it upside down, releasing the hash-brown cake onto the plate. Put the empty skillet back on the burner and add all but 1 tablespoon of the remaining clarified butter. Slide the potato cake back into the skillet. Cook until the underside turns dark amber brown, 10 to 15 minutes.

While the potato cake is cooking, fry the peppers: Heat a large sauté pan over medium heat and add the remaining tablespoon clarified butter. Add the peppers and ¼ teaspoon salt, and cook, flipping them often, until they blister and feel tender throughout, about 10 minutes.

To serve, lay the large plate upside down over the skillet, and using oven mitts, invert as before. (If the first side was prettier, invert the cake again onto another serving plate.) Top with a jumble of fried peppers. Cut into wedges and serve immediately.

A COUPLE OF NEW POTATO RECIPES

NEW POTATOES *with* GRILLED ONION BUTTER

This dish unites two pillars of Midwestern eating: potatoes and onions. However workaday these ingredients might be, when wholesome young potato meets the metallic flintiness of grilled butter-poached sweet onion, the duo makes my top-five food pairings of all time.

It's a split method, but easy. Set the potatoes to boil in salted water in the house and then head outside to grill the onions. After they've picked up some char, flip the onions into a cast-iron pan of brown butter and rosemary sitting on a more temperate part of the grill. (While you're at it, as the onions slowly melt into a buttery, tobacco-brown mess, throw a nice fat rib eye steak over the fire. With so much metal and char going on, you'll see the need: these potatoes pretty much beg for some red meat companionship.)

SERVES 4

Light a medium-hot fire in your grill.

Toss the onions with a little canola oil and salt and pepper, and grill over medium-high heat until charred and soft, about 10 minutes. On the same grill, heat a cast-iron pan. Add the butter to the pan and cook until it browns, about 3 minutes. Remove from the heat, add the rosemary, and give the pan a shake. The butter will foam hysterically. When it stops sizzling, flip the onions into the butter and cook over lower heat until they are very tender and the butter has taken on a pronounced oniony flavor, 8 to 10 minutes. Remove the rosemary sprigs, and keep the butter warm over low heat.

While the onions cook, start the potatoes: Put the potatoes in a saucepan and add enough water to cover generously. Salt the water, add the garlic and bay leaves, and bring to a slow simmer over medium heat. Cook until the potatoes test tender when poked with a fork, about 15 minutes, depending on size and freshness.

Drain the contents of the pan into a sieve set over a heavy bowl, filling the bowl with the hot water just to warm it. Throw out the water, drop the potatoes into the bowl, and discard the

RECIPE CONTINUES

12 ounces cipollini onions, halved crosswise

Canola oil

Freshly ground black pepper

8 tablespoons (1 stick) salted butter

3 sprigs fresh rosemary

1½ pounds fresh small potatoes

Fine sea salt

4 cloves garlic

2 dried bay leaves

NOTES: *In my garden I usually grow small sweet varieties of onions, such as cipollini or Red Torpedo, instead of the larger ones destined for storage. These small onions develop an even sweeter, almost sticky dark surface when grilled. Vidalias are a great substitute; just cut them into thick rings for grilling.*

When you're cleaning super-fresh potatoes, set aside the vegetable brush and just use your hands so as not to rub off their thin skins, because they're as fragile as eggs.

Unearthed Potatoes

Whether you use potatoes newly yanked from the garden or those found at the farmer's market, still cold from the earth, both New Potatoes with Grilled Onion Butter and New Potatoes with Herb Gravy are meant to highlight the shocking freshness of really new potatoes.

Any gardening expert will tell you to let new potatoes sit out in the air a couple of days to "cure" and harden their skins before storing, but to my mind the very best ones never even see the light of day; they go directly from the dirt to the sink to the pot. Once cooked, the flesh is sweet and moist, almost pudding-like, and the tissue-paper skins have none of the acidity that older or cured potato skins have.

Obviously it's a pretty small potato-window I'm rhapsodizing about here, and you can feel free to substitute any kind of small-ish new potato if you don't have freshly dug. As a rule, if they feel firm and cold in your hand, like stones, they will taste good. Both the grilled onion butter and herb gravy will also do something wonderful to winter's storage potatoes.

garlic and bay leaves. (If the peels are thick, peel the potatoes, cradling them in a bit of paper towel to protect your hands.)

Pour the butter and onion mixture over the warm potatoes, and serve right away.

NEW POTATOES *with* HERB GRAVY

As soon as potatoes grow to the size of chicken eggs you can (and should) start stealing them from their beds, because a dish of freshly dug potatoes makes a meal memorable, and the first hot days of summer deserve to be celebrated with properly squandered loot.

Immediately after harvesting them, I wash off the dirt, boil them, and eat them with butter. After that, I make simple sauces to serve alongside the potatoes, and this is the best of them: an herb-rich sauce made with a two-minute egg, milk, and olive oil. It's passed like gravy: in a pitcher, one step behind the potatoes.

SERVES 6

Make the herb gravy (you can do this a few hours before serving): Cover the garlic cloves with 4 inches of water in a small saucepan. Bring to a boil, cook for 3 minutes, and then remove the garlic but save the water. Slip the garlic cloves from their peels. (This step tames their raw-garlic bite.)

Bring the water back to a boil, add the egg, and boil for 2 minutes. Remove the egg with a slotted spoon and chill it under cold water.

Crack the egg into a blender, scraping out the cooked white in the shell as well, and add the garlic cloves, milk, and ¼ teaspoon each of salt and pepper. Blend on high speed until very smooth. Add the herbs and blend again until smooth. Then, with the blender on low speed, drizzle in the olive oil until the sauce is smooth and emulsified. Pour it into a pitcher. Taste for salt and pepper, add a little more if necessary, and stir in the lemon juice.

Put the potatoes in a saucepan and add enough water to cover generously. Salt the water, bring to a slow simmer over medium heat, and cook until the potatoes test tender when poked with a fork, about 15 minutes, depending on size and freshness.

Drain the potatoes, transfer them to a serving bowl, and serve hot, with the herb gravy to pass at the table. On the plate, crush the potatoes with your fork and pour the herb gravy over the top.

3 cloves garlic, unpeeled

1 large egg

¼ cup whole milk

Fine sea salt and freshly ground black pepper

½ cup (packed) mixed fresh herbs (such as parsley, basil, and dill)

½ cup extra-virgin olive oil

Juice of ½ lemon

2½ pounds fresh small potatoes

NOTE: *Any leftovers are easily repurposed as a potato salad. Dice the potatoes, add some scallions or celery or blanched green beans or peas—whatever green thing you have around—and toss with the herb gravy until lightly coated.*

LACE POTATO PANCAKES

2 teaspoons minced fresh
   rosemary

4 scallions, white and green
   parts, minced

4 medium (about 2 pounds)
   Russet or Yukon Gold
   potatoes

1 large egg

2 teaspoons all-purpose flour

½ teaspoon fine sea salt

½ teaspoon freshly ground
   black pepper

Vegetable oil, for frying

Salted butter, for frying

NOTE: *Russets make a crispier
pancake, but Yukon Golds make a
slightly tastier one.*

Many cultures make a variation of a fried potato pancake, and this is the way the Hesches, my Grandma Dion's family, made theirs on the farm in Buckman, Minnesota. They're much thinner than most latkes— more like crisp brown doilies.

My grandmother taught me how to make these during one of our cooking workshop weekends when I was eleven or twelve. She drilled into me the importance of spreading the potatoes really thinly in the hot skillet—sparsely enough that you can actually see lacy holes in the finished potato pancake—and of frying them hard and fast in plenty of fat. On the back of the recipe card my grandmother wrote, "These are excellent the next day cut into squares and fried again until really crisp."

I like to serve these alongside poached eggs or grilled meat, or as a sweet savory with maple syrup or applesauce.

SERVES 6

Combine the rosemary and scallions in a medium bowl.

Just before cooking, peel the potatoes and grate them coarsely into the bowl containing the scallion mixture. Add the egg, flour, and salt and pepper, and quickly stir together.

Heat a large cast-iron skillet over high heat. When it's hot, add enough oil to thinly cover the bottom, and then add 1 teaspoon butter. For each pancake lay down a spoonful of potatoes, enough to make a roughly 4-inch-diameter pancake, spreading them out with the back of the spoon until very thin, in one layer if possible, so sparsely that small lacy holes appear. (I can usually get 3 pancakes in my 12-inch skillet.) Fry until the underside turns very dark brown and the edges are crispy, 2 to 3 minutes. Flip and cook until brown on the other side. Blot quickly on paper towels and serve immediately.

Repeat with the remaining pancakes, adding more oil and butter for each batch as necessary.

CREAMY YELLOW POTATO SALAD

2½ pounds yellow potatoes

Fine sea salt

10 large eggs

½ cup apple cider vinegar

3 tablespoons honey

1 tablespoon ground mustard

1 cup mayonnaise

3 tablespoons cream horseradish

2 teaspoons cracked black pepper

1 bunch scallions, white and green parts, thinly sliced

2 cups diced celery (from about 6 stalks)

¾ cup diced radishes or cucumbers (from about 8 radishes or 1 large cucumber)

¼ cup chopped fresh dill

Sweet paprika, for garnish

As much as I enjoy a basic mayonnaise-slicked potato salad (especially when made with homemade mayo), when summer barbecuing season comes around I really crave the creamier, brighter potato salad I was reared on.

The boiled dressing is key—and also very old-fashioned. (In old books of American cookery a similar cooked dressing was used not only for potato salad, but also to dress chicken salad.) Tangy and bright, it makes a sunny yellow cloak for the potatoes, and I've also noticed that this potato salad holds up better in the refrigerator, and keeps the potatoes tasting fresher, than any other kind.

Doubling this recipe makes enough to fill an empty gallon ice cream bucket, which is really the traditional yield.

SERVES 10 TO 12

Put the potatoes in a saucepan and add enough water to cover generously. Salt the water, bring to a slow simmer over medium heat, and cook until the potatoes are tender when poked with a fork, about 20 minutes.

Meanwhile, put 6 of the eggs in a saucepan and add water to cover. Bring to a simmer, cook for exactly 2 minutes, and then remove from the heat. Let the eggs sit in the hot water for 10 minutes. Then drain and peel the eggs. Reserve the prettiest 3 for garnishing the top of the potato salad, and dice the remaining 3 hard-boiled eggs.

Drain the potatoes, and when they are cool enough to handle, peel and cut them into ½-inch dice.

Make the boiled dressing: Combine the vinegar, ⅓ cup water, the honey, mustard, and 1½ teaspoons salt in a small saucepan over medium heat and bring to a simmer. Whisk the remaining 4 eggs in a bowl, and pour the hot vinegar mixture into them in a drizzle, whisking until smooth and combined. Pour the mixture back into the saucepan and reduce the heat to medium-low. Cook slowly, whisking all the time, until the mixture thickens and turns opaque, 3 to 5 minutes. Remove it from the heat, let it sit for a minute, and then pour the mixture through a sieve into a wide bowl. Let cool a bit, then stir the mayonnaise, horseradish, and pepper into the dressing base, and whisk to combine. Add the diced potatoes, diced eggs, scallions, celery, radishes, and dill, folding carefully to combine. Pour into a pretty serving bowl.

Using an egg slicer, slice the reserved 3 eggs and lay them out decoratively on top of the potato salad. Dust heavily with paprika.

(This is wonderful served shortly after it's made, but also great made ahead and chilled.)

POTATOES AU GRATIN
with Dried Beef

4 tablespoons (½ stick) salted butter

1½ large (about 1 pound) Vidalia onions, halved and thinly sliced

Fine sea salt and freshly ground black pepper

3 pounds Yukon Gold potatoes

4 ounces (about 14 slices) dried beef

2¾ cups heavy cream

1¼ cups whole milk

Unfortunately, somewhere along the line, good-quality dried, smoked beef became "chipped beef," a debased version of itself.

Meat markets across the Midwest produce a more credible dried beef. When made well—for example, as it is at my family's meat market, where I usually buy it—dried beef deserves to be held up as an American response to *bresaola*, the Italian cured eye of beef. In addition to being salted, rubbed with spices, and dried, the best American-style dried beef is also smoked over fruitwood.

Lean and tangy, dried beef makes an excellent snack on its own with crackers, or wrapped around a thin bunch of grilled asparagus, but the flavors really bloom when it hits a cream sauce. It lends irresistible smokiness to this casserole of creamy potatoes and caramelized onions, a version of the classic "o'gratin" potatoes that I now much prefer to those with cheese.

SERVES 8

Preheat oven to 350°F.

In a large skillet over medium heat, combine 3 tablespoons of the butter and the onions. Season with ¼ teaspoon each of salt and pepper and cook, stirring now and then, until amber brown and caramelized, about 30 minutes.

Meanwhile, peel the potatoes, rinse them, and slice them thinly, a little less than ⅛ inch thick. Stack the sliced dried beef and cut the stack into quarters.

Rub remaining 1 tablespoon butter inside the 9 × 13-inch baking dish. Lay down a single layer of potatoes, slightly overlapping, like shingles. Combine ¾ teaspoon each of salt and pepper in a small bowl. Sprinkle the potatoes with a little of the salt and pepper, and spread half of the caramelized onions on top. Layer half of the dried beef over the onions, and then lay down another layer of potatoes, sprinkling with a bit more salt and pepper. Add the rest of the onions and the rest of the dried beef. Lay down one more layer of potatoes, sprinkling with more salt and pepper.

Mix the cream and milk together, adding any remaining salt and pepper. Pour the cream mixture over the potatoes.

Bake until dark golden brown on top, 60 to 70 minutes. Let sit for 5 minutes before serving directly from the dish.

BITTER GREENS
with Potatoes *and* Side Pork

If you want to know how a rural Minnesota farm family circa 1930 prepared their spring dandelion greens, that would be with potatoes, side pork, hard-boiled eggs, and butter.

Shirley Meyer, who brings these sinfully overstuffed smashed potatoes to my aunt's lake cabin every year, remembers her grandmother making them. She fried the side pork, added its liquid fat to the potatoes, stirred in masses of bitter greens—either yard-picked dandelions or garden-grown green endive—garnished the potatoes with planks of pork, and named it after the healthy part: she simply called it "endive."

No doubt the ingredients used to buffer the bitter greens are rich, but the splash of vinegar really does bring everything into balance, and the spring greens are themselves a tonic.

SERVES 8

Preheat the oven to 200°F.

Put the potatoes in a saucepan and add enough water to cover generously. Salt the water and bring to a slow simmer over medium heat. Cook until the potatoes are tender when poked with a fork, about 20 minutes.

Meanwhile, put the eggs in a small saucepan, cover with water, and simmer for 2 minutes. Remove the pan from the heat and let sit for exactly 10 minutes. Crack the eggs and cover them with cold water. Peel the eggs and chop them coarsely.

While the potatoes are cooking, slowly fry the side pork in a large skillet over medium-high heat until the edges turn very crisp, about 10 minutes. Transfer to a plate and keep warm in the oven. Reserve at least ¼ cup fat in the skillet. Let the skillet cool for a minute, and then add the butter, vinegar, pepper, sugar, and 1 teaspoon salt, and bring to a simmer. Set aside.

Drain the potatoes and transfer them to a very large bowl. Add the warm cream, and lightly smash the potatoes with a potato masher. Add the bitter greens, scallions, and chopped eggs, and mix to combine.

Pour the warm vinegar mixture over the potatoes and mix until well combined. Add more warm cream if the mixture is too thick.

Serve immediately, with the warm side pork on the side.

2½ pounds Yukon Gold or new red potatoes, quartered

Fine sea salt

4 large eggs

1 pound thick-cut side pork (preferably skin-on) or thick-cut bacon

3 tablespoons salted butter

2½ tablespoons apple cider vinegar

1 teaspoon freshly ground black pepper

Large pinch of sugar

¾ cup heavy cream, warmed, plus more as needed

4 cups torn bitter greens (dandelion, endive, or radicchio)

⅓ bunch scallions, white and green parts, sliced

NOTES: *The best side pork, sold these days as "fresh belly" comes with the skin on. Seasoned with salt and pepper, sliced thickly and fried until a crisp, hollow deckle forms at the edge, side pork is only as good as the pig it comes from. That from a heritage-breed pastured hog most closely resembles the side pork eaten a few generations ago.*

If you can't find fresh belly, substitute thick-cut bacon. Cook it and fold it right into the potatoes.

POTATO SKINS
with Smoked Cheddar *and* Bacon

8 medium Yukon Gold potatoes

4 slices (4 ounces) thick-cut bacon

2 tablespoons canola oil

Fine sea salt and freshly ground black pepper

¾ cup (3 ounces) grated smoked cheddar cheese

2 scallions, white and green parts, thinly sliced on the diagonal

Sour cream, for serving

NOTE: *With potato skins, the crisp edges are everything, so be sure to coat that part with plenty of oil.*

When I was a kid, many of the resort supper clubs on the lakes surrounding my hometown were still operational and my parents liked to show up for dinner the traditional way: by boat. We'd float our pontoon to the dock, loop the rope around the post, throw on some shoes, and follow the trail uphill to the restaurant.

Most of the supper clubs originally functioned as lodges for large resorts—or as Prohibition-era forest speakeasies, fabled to have been frequented by mobsters from Chicago or Minneapolis-St. Paul looking for a place to cool off. (Although most often they were patronized by fun-time tourists seeking a watering hole.) They usually had large fieldstone fireplaces, and nearly all of the buildings were made from stacked logs of almost comical girth, trees from another time.

My favorite one, Chateau Paulette, was a dance club and restaurant on Little Sand Lake, and while the slide guitar rang out we kids sat at the table eating the most marvelous potato skins. Their edges were thin and crackling and the middles buttery and filled with a boatload of melted cheese, chewy bits of bacon, and thin slivers of scallion. We decorated them with squiggles of sour cream and leaned around the enormous log posts to catch a glimpse of our parents on the dance floor.

SERVES 8

Preheat the oven to 350°F.

Wrap each potato in a layer of aluminum foil. Put the potatoes in a baking dish, and bake until tender when squeezed through the foil, about 1 hour. Unwrap and let cool a bit.

Raise the oven temperature to 400°F.

Slice the bacon crosswise into narrow strips, and fry them in a skillet over medium heat until chewy and slightly shrunken but not crisp, about 5 minutes. Drain and reserve.

When the potatoes are cool enough to handle, cut them in half lengthwise. With a large spoon, scoop out the potato flesh (reserve it for another use), leaving a 3/8-inch-thick shell. Rub the shells evenly, inside and out, with the oil, and sprinkle the insides with a little salt and pepper.

Arrange the potato skins on a large baking sheet and bake until the edges begin to brown, 25 minutes.

Divide the bacon and cheddar among the hollowed-out potato skins, and bake until the cheese has melted and the edges of the potato skins have crisped and turned brown, 20 to 25 minutes.

Garnish each potato skin with a few pieces of sliced scallion and a small dollop of sour cream, and serve immediately.

Potato Skins with Smoked Whitefish Cream

SERVES 8

Prepare the potato skins as directed, baking them until the edges begin to brown.

In a small bowl, whisk together the egg, cream, Parmesan cheese, lemon zest, salt, and pepper. Gently fold in the white-fish. Divide the mixture among the potato skins and bake until the whitefish mixture sets and begins to turn brown, 15 minutes.

1 large egg

1/3 cup heavy cream

1/2 cup freshly grated Parmesan cheese

1 teaspoon grated lemon zest

1/8 teaspoon fine sea salt

1/4 teaspoon freshly ground black pepper

1 cup (lightly packed) flaked smoked whitefish (from approximately 12 ounces)

Projects

I call this section "Projects" because I think of this collection of recipes as summer or fall side work. I rely on these flavoring elements—which include pickles, syrups, ferments, preserved vegetables, cured meats and fish—to give distinction to simple meals all year round. For example, a basic pot roast tastes so much better with a dollop of homemade Creamed Horseradish (page 285) on the side, and a quick after-work bowl of garlicky pasta feels much more planned when it sports chunks of your homemade salt pork. And there's more: quick refrigerator pickles with a touch of curry that boost ham sandwiches all winter long, fermented-in-the-jar dill pickles (excellent heachache-busters for New Year's Day), frozen logs of fresh chive oil to remind you of green grass, chokecherry nectar to lend a mysterious woodland air to your desserts and cocktails.

With the exception of the headcheese, which is a serious undertaking, you won't find large harvest projects here, or too many conserves that require water-bath canning (there are a couple, but they're small-batch and could just as easily be frozen).

In any number or combination, these condiments will extend the lushness of the growing season throughout the year and, in general, add spice to your life.

SWEET-AND-SOUR PLUMS
in Syrup

This is adapted from *Preserving* in Time-Life's Good Cook series, which was edited by Richard Olney, one of the Midwest's earliest professional eaters. Painter, home cook extraordinaire, writer, wine lover, and roaster of small birds, Olney was Iowa-born but lived most of his life in rural southern France, where he cooked and ate and drank in what seemed to be an opulent, enviable fashion.

I was attracted to the recipe because it calls for whole small plums—a perfect use for our tiny northern plums, which are too small to segment and pit. This preparation results in heavy plums with candied skins and spicy flesh as dense as cheese.

MAKES 7 PINTS

4 pounds small local plums, such as Toka, wild plums, or Italian prune plums

4 3-inch cinnamon sticks

1½ tablespoons coarsely chopped crystallized ginger

2 teaspoons black peppercorns

8 cups sugar

2½ cups apple cider vinegar or white vinegar

Stem and rinse the plums, and poke each one in a few places with a heavy needle on a thin skewer.

Lay the cinnamon sticks, ginger, and peppercorns in the center of a square of cheesecloth, and tie up the corners to make a sachet. In a wide-bottomed saucepan that's large enough to hold the plums, combine the sugar, 1 cup water, the vinegar, and the spice sachet. Bring to a boil and then simmer for 5 minutes. Add the plums and slowly bring the liquid to a simmer again. (Stand watch and be sure not to overcook the plums during this first stage.) Skim off any foam from the surface of the syrup and discard it. Immediately after the mixture comes to a boil, remove the plums from the syrup with a skimmer or a wide sieve, and lay them in a wide nonreactive bowl. Boil the syrup for 5 minutes to concentrate it, pour the syrup carefully over the plums, press a round of parchment paper or plastic wrap onto the surface, and refrigerate for 24 hours.

The next day, repeat the process: Return the entire mixture to a boil, immediately remove the plums with a skimmer, and boil the syrup for 5 minutes on its own. Pour the syrup over the plums, cover, and refrigerate again.

On the third day, return the mixture once more to a boil, remove the plums with a skimmer, and this time boil the syrup for just 1 minute. Return the plums to the syrup and remove from the heat. You can keep the finished plums in a covered container in the refrigerator for up to 6 months.

NOTE: *To can them, ladle the plums and syrup into sterilized pint jars, leaving ¼-inch headspace. Wipe the rims with a cloth dipped in boiling water, and top with the sterilized lids and caps, sealing them snugly but not tightly. Process the jars in a boiling water bath, counting from the time the water returns to a boil: 15 minutes at 0 to 1,000 feet altitude, 20 minutes at 1,001 to 6,000 feet, and 25 minutes at an altitude of 6,000 feet or greater.*

WILD PLUM MANHATTANS

Ice

2 ounces (¼ cup) brandy or rye whiskey

½ ounce (1 tablespoon) dry vermouth, such as Noilly Prat or Cinzano

2 small Sweet-and-Sour Plums (page 263)

2 tablespoons Sweet-and-Sour Plum syrup (page 263)

Many people consider Wisconsin to be the home of the famous Depression-era cocktails that your grandparents and their friends drink, the Old-Fashioned and the Manhattan chief among them. It's been my experience that across the upper Midwest most Manhattans are typically made with brandy, along with a pinkie's worth of dry vermouth, a maraschino cherry, and a spoonful or two of the cherry liquid.

I like to add a few sweet-and-sour plums to mine (two or three if they're small), and in place of the maraschino cherry liquid, a few spoonfuls of the pickling liquid, which is like a heavy fruit syrup enlivened with a touch of vinegar. In fact, sweet-and-sour plums taste very similar to candied cherries, but they give the drink a pleasantly tannic edge.

MAKES 1 DRINK

Fill a highball glass two-thirds full of ice, and add the brandy, vermouth, plums, and plum syrup. Stir, and serve.

PLUM BUTTER

In this era of hybridized sweet fruit, I crave the wilder flavors possessed by most of my Zone-3 yard-tree fruits: my small purple Toka plums, Haralson apples, and Nanking cherries. The plums especially have an untamed tannic streak. When cooked into a soft plum butter, the fuzzy taste almost disappears—but not entirely. It remains in the background, giving counterweight to the sweetness.

I add no spices to this butter because the flavor of these plums is multidimensional enough. This plum butter is easy to make (you don't have to pit the plums) and superb spread on toast.

MAKES 2 PINTS

4 pounds small local plums, such as Toka, wild plums, or Italian prune plums

Juice of 2 lemons

About 2 cups sugar, to taste

Stem and rinse the plums, and pour them into a large wide-bottomed pot. Add water to a depth of ½ inch, cover the pot, and set it over medium-high heat. When the water simmers, reduce the heat to low and cook, stirring now and then, until the plums begin to break down, about 20 minutes.

Mash the fruit roughly with a potato masher, and then push the mixture through a strainer or food mill into a bowl to extract the pits and skins.

Transfer the puree to a clean wide-bottomed pot and bring to a simmer. Cook, stirring constantly, until the puree thickens into a mass and darkens, about 20 minutes. Add the lemon juice and sugar, and cook until the sugar dissolves completely, about 5 minutes.

You can keep the plum butter in a covered container in the refrigerator for up to 1 month, or in the freezer for 1 year. (To preserve it in jars, pour the plum butter into sterilized pint jars, leaving ¼ inch headspace. Wipe the rims with a cloth dipped in boiling water and top with sterilized lids and caps, sealing them snugly but not tightly. Process the jars in a boiling water bath, counting from the time the water returns to a boil: 15 minutes at 0 to 1,000 feet altitude, 20 minutes at 1,001 to 6,000 feet, and 25 minutes at an altitude of 6,000 feet or greater.)

HOT GRAPE CIDER

1 quart homemade grape juice (recipe follows), or 2 quarts store-bought grape juice

1 3-inch cinnamon stick

3 whole star anise

1 teaspoon allspice berries

1 3-inch chunk fresh ginger

I was given this idea by a neighbor when I was over at her house picking her grape surplus. The grapes had gone berserk that year, drowning her arbor in low-hanging vines. As I stood in the pitch-black hidey-hole beneath the vines, she said, "I've already canned thirty-some quarts of juice, so have at it."

She then described what she made with all of that grape juice, the most delicious-sounding drink: hot grape cider. On the coldest of winter days she fills a Crock-Pot with grape juice so that her boys (she has five) can have a hot drink when they come inside from snowblowing, snowmobiling, or whatever.

I add some spices—cinnamon and star anise—to give it a holiday mulled flavor. It tastes similar to a mulled wine, but without the acidity and warm buzz from the alcohol, and is a perfect post-sledding drink for kids and adults alike.

My recipe for homemade grape juice follows, but this can also be made perfectly well with good-quality organic grape juice—although in that case you may not want to dilute it.

SERVES 8 TO 10

In a Crock-Pot or a medium stockpot, combine the juice, cinnamon stick, star anise, allspice, ginger, and enough water to dilute the juice to a drinkable strength. (For home-canned juice, it's usually 1:1, so in this case, add 1 quart water.) Bring to a simmer. Turn off the heat and let steep for at least 20 minutes before ladling into mugs.

HOMEMADE GRAPE JUICE

These directions are more of a formula than a recipe and make a concentrated juice that will require dilution before serving.

Pick the grapes from their stems. Wash the grapes in a large bowl of cold water, scoop them from the water with a sieve, and transfer them to a large stockpot. Add water to reach halfway up the volume of grapes, cover the pot, and set it over medium-high heat. When the mixture boils, reduce the heat to maintain a simmer and cook, covered, until the grapes have all split open, 5 to 10 minutes. Mash the grapes with a potato masher until you have a slush. Let this mixture cool off a bit.

Prepare a jelly bag that is large enough to hold the grape slush, and set it over a large bowl. (Or line a large colander with many layers of cheesecloth; it helps to tie some kitchen string around the perimeter of the colander to keep the cloth from falling down inside.)

Run the mashed grapes through a fine food mill into a bowl. Pour the resulting puree into the jelly bag and let it drip, stirring it once in a while but not pressing on it, until all the juice has been extracted, at least 4 hours. (To make grape leather from the remaining grape pulp, see the sidebar at right.)

Pour the clear juice into a stockpot, add sugar to taste, and cook over medium heat, stirring, until the sugar dissolves, about 15 minutes. Let the juice cool; then pour it into jars or a pitcher, and refrigerate.

The juice will keep in the refrigerator for 1 week for fresh drinking. (To preserve it in jars, pour the hot grape juice into sterilized pint jars, leaving ¼ inch headspace. Wipe the rims with a cloth dipped in boiling water and top with sterilized lids and caps, sealing them snugly but not tightly. Process the jars in a boiling water bath, counting from the time the water returns to a boil: 5 minutes at 0 to 1,000 feet altitude, 10 minutes at 1,001 to 6,000 feet, and 15 minutes at an altitude of 6,000 feet or greater.)

Homemade Grape (or Any Fruit) Leather

Preheat the oven to 200°F.

The leftover grape pulp, the by-product of juice-making, should have the density of jam. Put it into a medium bowl and stir in sugar to taste. Then spread the puree to the thickness of a nickel, as evenly as possible, on a parchment–lined baking sheet. Transfer the baking sheet to the oven. Slip a butter knife or other metal object in the door to prevent it from closing all the way, and bake until the surface of the leather is no longer tacky to the touch. Depending on the moisture of your puree, this may take anywhere between 2 and 5 hours.

Let the leather cool. Then cut each sheet, paper and all, into quarters. Roll each quarter, in its paper, into a cylinder. Tie each roll with a piece of string, and store the fruit leather in a covered container in a cool, dry place for as long as 3 months.

HOMEMADE CASSIS

4 cups fresh black currants

3 cups vodka, or more if needed

⅔ cup sugar, or more to taste

NOTE: *For cleaning currants, see Red Currant Jelly note (page 270).*

For a long time, black currants were banned in the United States because they were carriers of a disease called white pine blister rust, which affected the white pine trees. In recent years they've been welcomed back, and gladly, for it seems that currants grow very well in this area.

Their flavor has the tang of grapes mixed with a stone's earthiness—kind of like eating both the grape and a bit of its stem too. Cassis, or black currant liqueur, expresses the fruit's nuances like nothing else, and it couldn't be easier to make. Simply throw the berries into a large jar, top them off with decent vodka, and wait. Three months later, strain them, add sugar and more vodka to the juice, and bottle the resulting liqueur with a cork stopper.

In the French tradition (from whence it comes) this black currant liqueur is called *crème de cassis* and is added to cocktails—to white wine for a *kir*, and to champagne to make a *kir royale*. These pink cocktails are beautiful, but truth be told, the cassis seems to taste best in the dead of winter, sipped straight from a small thimble glass in front of the fire.

MAKES 1 QUART

In a glass container, combine the black currants and 2 cups of the vodka. (If this doesn't cover them, add a little more.) Cover the container and store it in a dark, cool place for at least 3 months.

Pour the currants into a fine-mesh sieve set over a bowl, and drain for at least 30 minutes to extract all of the juice. Stir the currants periodically to help them drain, but don't press on them. You should have roughly 2¼ cups liquid.

Pour the juice into a saucepan and set it over low heat. Add the remaining 1 cup vodka, 1 cup water, and ⅔ cup sugar, stirring, until the sugar has dissolved. Depending on the growing season for the currants, you may or may not want additional sugar. Taste until it hits the sweet spot: no longer tart, but not confectionery-sweet.

Chill the cassis before pouring it into a sterilized glass bottle. Cork, and store in a cool, dark place for up to 6 months.

RASPBERRY SYRUP

Embedded in this recipe—a standard adapted from Oded Schwartz's book *Preserving*—is a simple formula for making any kind of fruit syrup. It works best for soft fruits that make a lot of juice, such as berries and grapes.

MAKES 3 HALF-PINT JARS

4 cups fresh raspberries, preferably wild

1 tablespoon fresh lemon juice

About 1½ cups sugar, depending on volume of juice

Combine the raspberries, lemon juice, and ⅓ cup water in a large metal bowl. Crush the berries and set the bowl over a pot of simmering water, double-boiler-fashion. Cook very gently until the raspberries begin to dissolve, about 20 minutes.

Pour the mixture into a jelly bag (or a large sieve lined with two layers of cheesecloth) set over a deep bowl. Let the mixture drip, gently stirring the pulp now and then but not pressing on it, until it seems that all of the liquid has been expelled, about 2 hours.

Measure the juice, pour it into a wide-bottomed saucepan, and then measure out an equal volume of sugar (for example, for 1½ cups of juice, you'd need 1½ cups of sugar).

Add the sugar to the juice and set the pan over medium-high heat. Bring the syrup to a rolling boil (watch to make sure it doesn't boil over), boil for 30 seconds, and then remove from the heat. Let it settle for a minute, then carefully skim off the foam. Bring to a rolling boil again and then immediately remove from the heat. Let it settle, and skim it again.

Pour the hot syrup into half-pint jelly jars and let it cool before capping the jars. Store in the refrigerator for up to 2 months or in the freezer for 1 year. (If you want to can the syrup, pour it into sterilized half-pint jars, leaving ¼ inch headspace. Wipe the rims with a cloth dipped in boiling water and top with sterilized lids and caps, sealing them snugly but not tightly. Process the jars in a boiling water bath, counting from the time the water returns to a boil: 10 minutes at 0 to 1,000 feet altitude, 15 minutes at 1,001 to 6,000 feet, and 20 minutes at an altitude of 6,000 feet or greater.)

RED CURRANT JELLY

4 pounds red currants

About 5 cups sugar, depending
on volume of juice

3 tablespoons fresh lemon juice

NOTES: *To clean red currants,
rinse the clumps to remove leaves and
dirt, strip them from their stems, and
then rinse again.*

It takes about five minutes of extra simmering to turn syrup into
jelly. When you use pectin-rich fruits—like apples, raspberries, and
currants—the syrup jells so quickly on its own that there's no point
in messing with added pectin. I get the feeling, from talking to my
neighbors and reading old cookbooks, that back in the day, most
people could make jelly with one hand tied behind their back. The
ratio—equal parts juice and sugar—is one that you don't even have to
think about.

Red currants, which were once plentiful across the upper Midwest,
are on the rebound. Their juice makes a naturally tangy, translucent red
jelly with an intense flavor that might be described as a cross between a
warm strawberry and a wild raspberry.

MAKES 4 HALF-PINT JARS

Combine the red currants and 1 cup water in a large saucepan
and bring to a simmer. Mash the berries with a potato masher,
and cook over medium heat until the berries begin to break
down, 20 minutes.

Strain the mixture through a large-mesh sieve into a bowl,
pushing on the solids to extract the juice. Pour the puree into a
jelly bag (or a fine-mesh sieve lined with two layers of cheesecloth) set over a deep bowl. Let it drip, gently stirring the pulp
now and then but not pressing on it, until it seems that all of the
liquid has been expelled, about 2 hours.

Measure the juice, pour it into a wide-bottomed pot, and
then measure out an equal volume of sugar (for example, for
5 cups of juice, you'd need 5 cups of sugar).

Add the sugar and the lemon juice to the pot, set it over
medium-high heat, and if desired, clip a candy thermometer to
the side of the pot. Bring the syrup to a rolling boil (watch to
make sure it doesn't boil over), boil for 30 seconds, and then
remove from the heat. Let it settle for a minute and then carefully skim off the foam. Return the pot to the heat, bring it to a
simmer, and cook, stirring often, until the syrup starts to make
big bubbles and measures 222°F (230°F if above 1,500 feet altitude), about 5 minutes. Skim off any foam from the surface, and
give it the jelly test: Drop some jelly onto a cold plate. When

the droplet doesn't run when you tilt the plate, or when it holds the track of your finger when you swipe it through the middle, the jelly is done.

Pour the hot jelly into half-pint jelly jars, leaving ¼ inch headspace, and wipe the rims with a cloth dipped in boiling water. Let cool to room temperature, and then check the jell: If the surface bounces when poked and holds up when tilted, it's jelled. If it doesn't, pour the syrup back into the pot and boil vigorously for at least 2 minutes; then do another jelly test. Cap the jars with sterilized lids and store in the refrigerator for up to 2 months or in the freezer for 1 year. (If you want to can the jelly, pour the jelly into sterilized jars, leaving ¼ inch headspace. Wipe the rims with a cloth dipped in boiling water and top with sterilized lids and caps, sealing them snugly but not tightly. Process them in a boiling water bath, counting from the time the water returns to a boil: 10 minutes at 0 to 1,000 feet altitude, 15 minutes at 1,001 to 6,000 feet, and 20 minutes at an altitude of 6,000 feet or greater.)

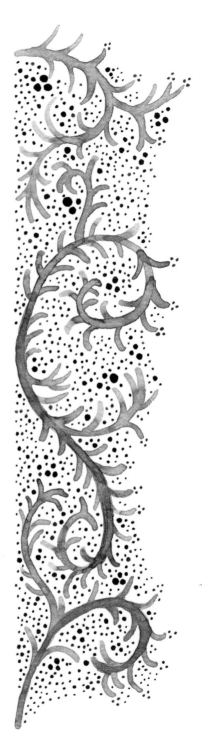

ROASTED PEACH *and* HONEY JAM

2½ pounds fresh peaches,
   pitted and cut into eighths

1 cup sugar

2 teaspoons minced fresh ginger

⅓ cup honey

1 tablespoon fresh lemon juice

Even though this jam requires roasting, I still consider it a good one to make on a hot day; I'd take the heat spurt from twenty minutes of roasting over the blanching and longer, steamy simmering that regular jam requires any time.

I simply slice the peaches, toss them with sugar, and roast them on a heavy baking sheet until they start to break down and their skins start to lift. Then, after a day of macerating during which they absorb the sugar syrup and begin the candying process, they need just minimal cooking to bring them to a jam consistency. What results is a jam that is more like a French compote than a puree. It retains some texture, and the dense, sweet fruit has an intense flavor.

You can do this with any stone fruit—plums work really well—but I love the flavor of fresh summer peaches with honey. You can be creative with jams like these: throw a split vanilla bean or some wide strips of lemon zest or a bouquet of thyme into the fruit before roasting. Your jam will pick up the subtle additions. This recipe doubles easily.

MAKES 3 HALF-PINT JARS

Preheat the oven to 400°F.

On a heavy rimmed baking sheet, combine the peaches, ¼ cup of the sugar, and the ginger. Mix with your hands to combine. Roast, stirring twice, until the peaches are soft and their edges have darkened, 20 to 25 minutes. When they are cool enough to handle, pluck off and discard the loosened peach skins.

Scrape the peach mixture and all of its juice into a 3-quart nonreactive saucepan, and add the remaining ¾ cup sugar, the honey, and the lemon juice. If the peaches were under-ripe and have retained their shape too much, mash them lightly with a potato masher. Bring to a boil and cook for 1 minute. Pour into a nonreactive bowl and cover with a piece of parchment paper cut to fit the surface of the jam mixture. Marinate in the refrigerator for at least 6 hours or overnight.

Pour the jam mixture into a saucepan and bring it to a quick boil. Cook, stirring often, until the bubbles grow bigger, the fruit looks darker, and the jam measures 222°F on a candy thermometer. To test it, drop some jam onto a cold plate and let it cool slightly. If the drop of jam doesn't run when you tilt the plate, or if it holds the track of your finger when you swipe it through the middle, the jam is done. It should feel sticky when pinched between your thumb and forefinger.

You can keep the jam in a covered container in the refrigerator for up to 1 month or in the freezer for up to 1 year. (If you want to can the jam, pour the jam into sterilized half-pint jars, leaving ¼ inch headspace. Wipe the rims with a cloth dipped in boiling water and top with sterilized lids and caps, sealing them snugly but not tightly. Process the jars in a boiling water bath, counting from the time the water returns to a boil: 15 minutes at 0 to 1,000 feet altitude, 20 minutes at 1,001 to 6,000 feet, and 25 minutes at an altitude of 6,000 feet or greater.)

BIRCH WATER *and* BIRCH SYRUP

The birch sap begins to run about a week after the maple sap begins, during that interval when the days are warm and the nights drop below 32°F. Like the hot-and-cold treatment for a sports injury, the alternating freezing and thawing gets the sap flowing.

In the spring, we give the sap a quick run through a fine-mesh strainer, chill it in a pitcher, and drink it straight (an idea borrowed from the Russians). The birch water tastes very clean, with a distant sweetness and a residual woodiness at the end, perhaps how well water would taste if sipped from a cedar dipper.

Like the people who lived in this area long before us, we boil down most of the sap for syrup and keep it all winter to use in cooking, baking, and for pouring over pancakes. Some people still boil down box elder sap (which tastes exactly like sweet potatoes) and of course many process maple sap, but I like the birch. It's what we have here, and it's an underdog. Because it takes 60 gallons (or more) of birch sap to make 1 gallon of birch syrup (compared to the 40 gallons of maple sap to make 1 gallon of maple syrup), the resulting syrup is darker, the woody elements are a touch stronger, and in general its sweetness is harder-won.

Tapping Birch Trees

The procedure for tapping birch trees is identical to that for tapping maples. Silver birches, which grow plentifully around here, are said to have the best sap.

Bore a tap into a birch tree and hang a sap bag or a bucket from the tap. When the bag or bucket fills, strain the sap through a fine-mesh sieve into a clean container.

Move the taps after a while. The first runs taste pure and light; by the third run, a more pronounced woodiness starts to creep in.

You can either keep the sap as birch water, for drinking, or you can reduce it down to birch syrup.

Homemade Birch Syrup

Boil the sap in a large stockpot (preferably outside on a portable burner or over a fire). Keep close watch when the sap turns cinnamon-colored, and when it turns a deeper burnt umber, watch it very closely. When it reaches syrup consistency, the bubbles will grow larger and the boiling become more insistent, and a small drizzle on a plate will hold the trail of your finger. When it is done, strain the syrup and ladle it into sterilized jars. It keeps for months in the refrigerator and freezes very well.

BIRCH WHISKEY SNOW COCKTAIL

Birch syrup can go anywhere maple syrup can go—on pancakes, in custards, and over fruit, among other places—and I've found that in some cases I actually prefer its darker, more feral flavor. I especially like it in cocktails, where its slight bitterness makes the addition of bitters unnecessary.

This cocktail is potent for something so whimsical, and even more so if you want to finish one before the snow melts.

MAKES A PITCHER THAT SERVES 6 TO 8

In a pitcher, mix together the whiskey, syrup, sherry, and bitters if using. Chill thoroughly.

Before serving, fill small highball glasses (or half-pint jelly jars) with snow, packing it down lightly. Drizzle in the cold whiskey mixture, adding as much or as little as desired. Serve with a small spoon.

6 ounces (¾ cup) bourbon or your whiskey of choice

4 ounces (½ cup) birch syrup (see page 274) or maple syrup

2 ounces (¼ cup) dry sherry

2 drops of bitters if using maple syrup

Freshly fallen snow or shaved ice

NOTES: *Birch syrup has an earthiness that naturally tempers the sweetness, so if you substitute maple syrup, add a drop of bitters to replicate it. You can also flavor the snow with homemade cassis (page 268).*

I've read stories that question the safety of eating snow, no matter how far out in the wilderness you live, but I dare to risk it—just once a year, in such a small amount, when it's covered with whiskey.

HOMEMADE BUTTERS

2 pints heavy cream (without additives)

NOTES: *Try to find cream that isn't ultra-pasteurized and doesn't contain added carrageenan (a whipping agent).*

The resulting fresh buttermilk is delicious on its own when cold, but I like to blend it with fresh fruit, syrup, or nuts—raspberries, bananas, maple, pistachios—to make tangy smoothies.

There are beautifully dense sweet butters being made by independent creameries across the Midwest—none of which is close to me. Around here, most of the creamery buildings that once anchored small towns have been turned into antiques stores or restaurants, making an easy source of that thick, lightly salted Midwestern butter more elusive.

Frankly, it make take less energy just to make a small batch of boutique butter at home than it does to go in search of some. There's only one ingredient—cream—and armed with any kind of mixer, the process takes just minutes.

Homemade butter also has the advantage of being much, much fresher than store-bought, and at home you can salt it precisely to your liking or flavor it with any number of aromatic things. When celery is in season, I like to mince the dark green flavorful leaves, mix them in, and spread the butter on bread or, better yet, on a steak hot off the grill. Smoked paprika butter has a natural rapport with grilled shrimp and boiled corn and all kinds of vegetables. But honey Parmesan butter, an unlikely but striking combination, always ends up being the favorite at the table.

MAKES 1½ CUPS

Whip the cream with a mixer (standing or hand mixer), stopping often to scrape down the sides of the bowl, until it is stiffly whipped. Keep on whipping until the butterfat clumps and separates from the buttermilk. Stop the mixer and pour everything through a fine-mesh sieve set over a mixing bowl, pressing on the butter to push out as much liquid as possible. Reserve the liquid to drink (see Notes).

Turn the butter out onto a clean surface and form it into a ball. Knead the butter as you would bread dough, squeezing out droplets of buttermilk. (Use a flat bench scraper to scrape it back together if you have one.) Cover the butter with a clean tea towel to mop up the excess liquid. Remove the towel, knead, and repeat until no more buttermilk surfaces. (The more watery buttermilk you remove, the denser your butter will be.)

Press the butter into a glass or ceramic dish, cover, and chill in the refrigerator for up to 1 week.

LIGHTLY SALTED: Add ⅜ teaspoon fine sea salt while kneading.

HONEY PARMESAN: Before whipping, add 2 tablespoons honey, ½ cup finely grated Parmesan cheese, and 3/8 teaspoon fine sea salt to the cream.

SMOKED PAPRIKA: Before whipping, add 2 teaspoons smoked paprika and ⅜ teaspoon fine sea salt to the cream.

CELERY: Add ½ teaspoon fine sea salt and ¼ cup minced fresh celery leaves while kneading. (Dark green leaves from garden and farmer's market celery give this butter the purest flavor, but those from commercial celery work, too.)

COTTAGE CHEESE

1 quart whole milk, preferably low-heat-pasteurized

½ cup plus ⅓ cup heavy cream

4 teaspoons white vinegar, or more if needed

Fine sea salt

NOTES: *To replicate the consistency of old-fashioned farm-fresh whole milk, which likely wasn't as thoroughly skimmed as it is now, I add a little heavy cream.*

The whey makes an excellent addition to soups—better than vegetable stock, in my opinion.

My great-aunt Irene said that her mother used to hang a bag of fresh cheese curds from a long branch in the front yard until it stopped dripping and would then take it down and stir fresh cream and salt into the curds to make cottage cheese. It was often served as a side dish alongside dinner, though I would add that creamed cheese curds are also perfect for breakfast or dessert, topped with fresh fruit.

MAKES 1½ CUPS

Pour the milk and the ½ cup cream into a heavy-bottomed nonreactive saucepan and set it over medium heat. Clip a candy thermometer to the side of the pan and heat, stirring often to prevent scorching on the bottom of the pan, until the mixture reaches 180°F (the steaming period just before the boil).

Remove from the heat, add the vinegar, and stir gently. You will notice white, fluffy curds separating from the whey, which will turn yellow and look almost transparent. If this doesn't happen, add another teaspoon of vinegar and stir again. Let sit at room temperature for 15 minutes to give the curds time to gather softly together.

To drain the cottage cheese, cut a 4-foot length of cheesecloth, open it up, and fold it into a square three layers thick. Lay the cheesecloth in a fine-mesh strainer, and set the strainer over a bowl. Gently pour the curds and whey into the strainer, and let the cheese drain for 15 to 20 minutes.

Transfer the curds to a bowl and mix with the remaining ⅓ cup cream and salt to taste. The cottage cheese will keep in a covered glass container in the refrigerator for up to 1 week.

CHOKECHERRY NECTAR

Chokecherry bushes are tall and spindly and look like useless brush the majority of the time. Come July, they produce loads of deep purple berries—unfortunately, often set high, in unreachable range. You can jump up and pull the branches down to the ground to reach them, but honestly, the best way to get at these is from the back of a pickup. It helps to have a courteous driver to ferry you from bush to bush, which I do.

The flavor of chokecherries is like rogue black currant—the same deep winy berry flavor but with a punkier nature.

MAKES 3 HALF-PINT JARS

Put the berries in a large stockpot, add 3 cups water, and bring to a simmer. Crush the berries with a potato masher and simmer, covered, until very soft, about 20 minutes. Uncover and let cool.

Push the berries and juice through a food mill into a bowl, and then put the resulting pulpy juice in a very-fine-mesh strainer or a jelly bag set over a bowl. Allow to drip for at least 3 hours.

Measure the juice, pour it into a wide-bottomed pot, and then measure out an equal amount of sugar (for example, for 3 cups juice, you'll need 3 cups sugar).

Add the sugar to the juice and set the pot over medium-high heat. Bring the syrup to a rolling boil (watch to make sure it doesn't boil over) and then remove from the heat. Let it settle for a minute, then carefully skim off the foam. Bring the syrup to a simmer and cook gently for 5 minutes, stirring often. Add the lemon juice and simmer for 1 more minute.

Pour the hot syrup into half-pint jelly jars and let cool completely before capping. Store in the refrigerator for up to 2 months or in the freezer for up to 1 year. (If you want to can the syrup, pour it into sterilized half-pint jars, leaving ¼ inch headspace. Wipe the rims with a cloth dipped in boiling water and top with sterilized lids and caps, sealing them snugly but not tightly. Process the jars in a boiling water bath, counting from the time the water returns to a boil: 10 minutes at 0 to 1,000 feet altitude, 15 minutes at 1,001 to 6,000 feet, and 20 minutes at an altitude of 6,000 feet or greater.)

4 pounds (11 cups) fresh chokecherries

About 3 cups sugar, depending on volume of juice

2 tablespoons fresh lemon juice

NOTES: *This nectar is excellent poured over ice cream or steamed custards (page 331), or simply mixed with sparkling water and lime for a cooling summer drink. From practically any other berry you would extract a higher proportion of juice from the fruit. Depending on the weather, chokecherries can be stingy for liquid, but luckily they're also free, and rampant.*

To clean chokecherries, rinse the clumps to remove leaves and dirt, strip them from their stems, and then rinse again.

FERMENTED DILLS

35 to 40 fresh pickling cucumbers, each no longer than 6 inches

⅔ cup pickling salt

¼ head of fresh green cabbage, cut into 2-inch squares

8 fresh grape or black currant leaves, each the size of a silver dollar

8 cloves garlic

12 dried red chiles (optional)

4 large heads of crown dill, stems trimmed

NOTES: *If you want to grow these ingredients yourself, the only challenge is coordinating crown dill with ripe cucumbers. If it makes it any easier, you can keep crown dill fresh for a few days in a vase of water. (Actually, it makes a beautiful bouquet.) Or you can cut it, put it in a plastic bag, and freeze it, as I remember my grandma did.*

Use young, freshly picked pickling cucumbers. If you need a few days to accumulate the young cucumbers needed to make a batch of pickles, store them in a sealed plastic bag in the refrigerator.

In the Midwest, fermented dill pickles generally come from an Eastern European tradition, where they're often known as "brined" or "open crock" pickles. In my family the recipe comes down through the Bohemian side, and we ferment them right in the jar.

This recipe contains no vinegar, but instead relies on the alchemy of salt brine plus time to transform the cucumbers into firm, tart fermented pickles. Because of the active fermentation, these pickles seem to have a life force: when you spring the lid, carbonation will jump from the surface of the brine, spewing fine pickle dew. The pickles themselves will be sour, and addictive, with bubbles running all the way through.

You will need a source for freshly picked small garden pickles, strong-tasting fresh crown dill (bloomed dill, which sprouts a corona of green seeds), and small grape or black currant leaves, which replace alum as a natural crisping agent.

MAKES 4 QUARTS

Cover the cucumbers with cold water, scrub off their prickly spines, and drop them into a colander.

Combine 13 cups water with the pickling salt in a large saucepan, and bring to a boil, whisking to dissolve the salt.

Into the bottom of each sterilized 1-quart jar drop a layer of cabbage leaves, 1 small grape leaf, 1 garlic clove, 2 red chiles, if using, and a tuft of crown dill. Pack the jar with cucumbers, standing them upright and getting in as many as you can. Top each jar with another garlic clove, red chile, grape leaf, and another tuft of crown dill. Pour hot brine into each jar, leaving ⅛ inch headspace. Wipe the jar rims with a cloth dipped in boiling water. Screw sterilized lids on tight, as tight as you possibly can.

Once they cool, transfer the jars to a warm place (75°F or so) and let the pickles ferment for 1 week. This is the warm jump-start period for the longer ferment; the brine should get cloudy and the lid tops should become tight with pressure. Then transfer the jars to a cooler place (a root cellar would be great, but any place a few degrees cooler than room temperature is fine) and wait at least 6 weeks and up to 6 months before consuming.

Fermenting the Pickles

Fermentation is more intuition than exact science. Making these pickles will require you to case out your house to find the space with the right temperature in which to store them. I will share how the women in my family have told me to do it, and how I do it now, but eventually all fermented-pickle lovers find their own unique storage spots that work for them. (For example, my grandmother used to jump-start the fermentation by storing them for the first twenty-four hours in the trunk of her garaged car, but no one has continued that tradition.)

But it's more forgiving than you might think. When I attended the Better Process course at the University of Minnesota (a.k.a. "canning school") years ago, I remember how precisely we tested the pH of canned jams and vinegar pickles, and the surprising laissez-faire attitude of the instructor when it came to fermentation. The cautions were short and to the point: If the contents of the jar have fermented and taste sour, they're fine.

That said, some jars work out better than others. A cloudy bottom is a good sign, as is an active fizz when you open the jar. If the pickles are soft or slimy, discard them. If they're overwhelmingly salty without any acidity, that means they didn't ferment. They're probably safe to eat, due to the embalming amount of salt in the brine, but they don't taste very good and I always throw them out. In short, trust your taste. If they're good—tart, addictive—go for it.

Pickle Juice

Don't despair when you take the last pickle from the jar—you still have the fermented pickle juice. My mother and her two sisters grew up drinking small glasses of it straight and so did I; my mouth waters at the thought of that tingly, sour juice.

Saving the fermented pickle juice for cooking or drinking is an Eastern European tradition, valuable for adding a final fillip to soups or stews. The Austrian chefs I once worked for always poured a cupful of fermented pickle juice into the goulash at the very end, giving the stew brightness and a final salt correction as well.

In my twenties I would mix cold pickle juice with icy vodka and serve little pickle juice shooters—another kind of lemon drop—to kick off a party. Now I toss the pickle juice into the Bloody Marys at holiday gatherings: a little spicy tomato juice, vodka, pickle juice, celery salt, freshly grated horseradish, and a beef stick for garnish (page 69).

REFRIGERATOR BREAD-AND-BUTTERS
with Curry

Most people who find themselves with an extra basket of cucumbers during the summer season can't resist turning them into a quick batch of these sweet-and-sour refrigerator pickles, which don't require any water-bath canning. A small amount of curry powder adds extra zing but tastes as if it should have been there all along. A little less sweet than some, these pickles never fail to animate a simple ham sandwich.

MAKES 1½ QUARTS

Scrub the cucumbers to remove the spines. With a mandoline or a sharp knife, slice them ⅛ inch thick. Toss them in a large bowl with the pickling salt, and leave to marinate for 30 minutes.

Fill a large bowl with cold water, add the cucumbers, and stir to rinse off the excess salt; then drain well, blotting them dry with a towel. Mix the cucumbers and onion in a dry heatproof bowl.

In a medium saucepan combine 1¼ cups water with the vinegar, sugar, ginger, garlic, chile, mustard seeds, and curry powder. Bring to a boil, whisking to dissolve the sugar. Pour over the cucumbers and onion, and let cool.

Fill sterilized jars with cucumbers and liquid, pushing down on the cucumbers to submerge them in the liquid. Cap, and store in the refrigerator for up to 1 year.

- 4 pounds pickling cucumbers
- 5 tablespoons pickling salt
- ½ small spring onion or Vidalia onion, thinly sliced
- 4 cups white vinegar
- 1¼ cups sugar
- 1 4-inch piece of fresh ginger
- 6 cloves garlic
- 1 fresh spicy red chile, stem removed
- 2 tablespoons yellow mustard seeds
- 2 teaspoons curry powder

PICKLED BEETS

1½ pounds baby beets

1 teaspoon pickling salt

1¼ cups apple cider vinegar

⅔ cup sugar

1 teaspoon cumin seeds

¼ teaspoon caraway seeds

2 whole cloves

6 green cardamom pods, cracked

NOTE: *Lighter on both the vinegar and the sugar than many pickled beet recipes, these beets are perfect for fresh eating—but they're a refrigerator pickle, not something to be canned.*

I love pickled beets, but so many recipes suffer from their overly pushy cloves. As an Austrian chef I once knew said when he tasted some carrots I had dusted with too much of the spice, "Whoa! This tastes like too much Christmas." It's so true: An excess of clove instantly transports you to a Christmas gift shop.

I do add a couple of cloves to this pickled beet brine, but they have assistance from other more interesting bedfellows in the "c" family: cumin, caraway, and cardamom. The earthy caraway and the sweet cloves are bridged with the exotic aroma of cardamom, to stunning effect.

MAKES 1 QUART

Scrub the beets, put them in a large saucepan, and add water to cover generously. Salt the water and bring to a boil over high heat. Skim off any gray froth that surfaces, reduce the heat to maintain a low simmer, and cook, partially covered, until the beets are just tender when poked with a thin fork, 15 to 30 minutes, depending on their size. Drain the beets, and when they're cool enough to handle, hold them in your hand in a paper towel and rub off their skins. Cut into quarters.

Meanwhile, combine 6 cups water, the pickling salt, vinegar, sugar, cumin seeds, caraway seeds, cloves, and cardamom pods in a saucepan. Bring to a simmer, stirring to dissolve the sugar, and then let cool to room temperature.

Drop the beets into a quart-size mason jar (or any airtight container) and cover with the pickling liquid and spices. Refrigerate for at least 24 hours before eating the beets. Pickled beets will keep for months in the refrigerator, although they grow stronger—sweeter and spicier—over time.

CREAMED HORSERADISH

In recent years, chefs have utilized fresh horseradish root as they do aged Parmigiano-Reggiano cheese, finely grating the root at the last minute over fish or meat to dust them with its potent flavor.

This works for a while after I dig up my fresh horseradish in the fall, but my favorite method for preserving the sweet heat of fresh horseradish for any length of time is to cream it. I store it in the refrigerator and try to use it up within a month or two. You can freeze it, but it will turn gray, although with no perceptible loss of flavor.

MAKES 1 CUP

Mix the horseradish, cream, salt, sugar, and vinegar together in a bowl. Pack into clean glass jars and refrigerate for up to 1 month or freeze for as long as a year.

1 cup (lightly packed) freshly grated horseradish root

⅔ cup heavy cream

¼ teaspoon fine sea salt

1½ teaspoons sugar

2 teaspoons rice vinegar

NOTE: *A Microplane grater—or any of those new-style laser-cut graters—reduces the root to a pile of snow within minutes, and because they're so sharp, they create fewer noxious fumes than a standard box grater.*

HOMEMADE SPICY KETCHUP

1 tablespoon coriander seeds

1 3-inch cinnamon stick

1 large sprig fresh rosemary

1 teaspoon black peppercorns

1 teaspoon allspice berries

4 tablespoons (½ stick) salted butter

1 large onion, thinly sliced

1¾ teaspoons fine sea salt

1 jalapeño pepper, split lengthwise

2 tablespoons minced fresh ginger

6 cloves garlic, smashed

5 pounds plum tomatoes, quartered

2 tablespoons (packed) light brown sugar

1½ tablespoons apple cider vinegar

It's truly shocking to experience the lovely rainbow of spices that homemade ketchup once had, in contrast to all that the commercial red has lost. Paired with a meat-market hot dog or a burger made with freshly ground beef, it's really something special.

MAKES 1¾ PINTS

Put the coriander seeds, cinnamon stick, rosemary, peppercorns, and allspice berries in the center of a square of cheesecloth, and tie up the corners to make a sachet.

Heat the butter in a wide-bottomed pot over medium heat, and add the onion and salt. Cook, stirring often, until the onion is wilted and soft, about 10 minutes. Add the jalapeño, ginger, and garlic, and cook for 5 minutes.

Add the tomatoes, stir, and cover the pot. Cook over medium-low heat until the tomatoes release their juices, about 10 minutes. Uncover the pot, raise the heat to medium, and cook until the tomatoes are beginning to break down, about 10 minutes.

Pass the mixture through a food mill into a clean wide-bottomed pot, and add the spice sachet, brown sugar, and cider vinegar. Bring to a bare simmer and cook over low heat, stirring often, until the puree begins to mound on the stirring spoon, 1½ to 2 hours.

Let the ketchup cool slightly, and then pour it into a blender. Puree until smooth. Cool before storing in sterilized glass jars. The ketchup will keep in the refrigerator for up to 1 month or in the freezer for up to 1 year.

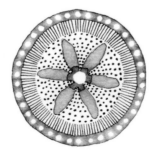

SPRING CHIVE OIL

The chives peak in early spring before they grow purple tips and finally exploding heads. You can shear them off and let the clumps regrow all season long, but they never quite recapture that fresh flavor of the first growth. Early on, I like to make a big batch of chive oil, which I then freeze for use in the winter. It maintains its color and flavor really well—much better than pesto does, in my opinion. An essential component of sauces in my first restaurant kitchen, Danube, I now find it handy for adding a bright summery jolt to sautéed vegetables, dips, sauces, and plain starches, especially mashed potatoes.

MAKES 1½ CUPS

Combine the chives and the oil in a blender, and blend on low, medium, and then high speed, stopping now and then to scrape down the sides, until the oil becomes pureed and bright green, about 3 minutes. Add salt to taste and blend to incorporate. Pour the oil into a shallow dish, and chill immediately in the refrigerator to maintain its bright color and flavor.

Once it's cold, transfer the chive oil to a storage container and refrigerate for 1 week. To freeze it, transfer the oil to small heavy self-seal plastic bags, press on them to remove all the air, seal, and freeze for up to 1 year.

2 cups finely sliced fresh chives
1½ cups canola oil, chilled
Fine sea salt

NOTES: *A few hours before you'd like to make chive oil, chill the canola oil. It helps maintain a bright green color in the finished chive oil.*

This recipe is easily doubled or tripled.

SAUERKRAUT

1 extra-large head cabbage

3 tablespoons pickling salt

Like many of German or Eastern European heritage, I grew up eating fermented sauerkraut, the honest kind. I heard stories of making it on the farm in crocks that couldn't be budged, and watched people cook sausages in its briny juices until the tanginess gave a light pickle to the meat and the fatty round meat juices tamed the bite of the kraut. My grandma Dion made barges of sauerkraut hotdish—flush with creamy sauerkraut, ground beef, and melted cheese—loaded it into Dixie cups impaled with plastic forks, and stood at the kitchen door, handing a steaming cup to each one of us grandkids as we ran by in the late-summer twilight.

The most important part of this recipe is the cabbage, which needs to be freshly plucked from the ground and full of moisture. You can tell when the cabbage is right because it will leak moisture when cut and squeak in the shredder.

This ratio, which I, and so many other kraut-crafters, picked up from fermentation guru Sandor Ellix Katz, has become so popular it's nearly universal. It's reliable and easily scaled up. I can fit approximately twenty pounds of cabbage in my five-gallon crock.

MAKES 3½ QUARTS

Arm yourself with a couple of oversize bowls, a kraut cutter (either the old-fashioned large box kraut cutter or a smaller modern mandoline), a scale, and a 2-gallon or larger crock or bucket. Wash the crock with hot soapy water, rinse it well with boiling water, and let it air-dry.

Cut the cabbage into quarters, and starting at the tips, cut it into shreds the width of a nickel. Shred until you get down to the core. Weigh out 5 pounds of shredded cabbage, put it in the crock, and then add the pickling salt. Mix with your hands until the salt is fully incorporated.

Pack down the surface of the cabbage and wipe the sides of the crock with a clean cloth. Cover the top of the cabbage either with large cabbage leaves (those taken from the out-side of a head are best) or with a clean plate that fits inside the crock. Fill each of three freezer-weight self-seal gallon-size bags halfway with a simple brine—1 tablespoon salt to 1 quart water—and seal the bags. Set them on top of the cabbage leaves or plate. (These bags will fill in the spaces and create a seal, and if for some reason one of them leaks, the brine won't ruin the ferment.)

Cover the crock with a light towel and store it at cool room temperature (65° to 70°F) for a minimum of 7 days and as long as a couple of months. Begin checking your kraut after 7 days. You want to stop it from fermenting further when it tastes good to you. I generally like it best after it has gotten frankly sour, when it is 2 to 3 weeks old.

Some people can and water-bath process their sauerkraut, but that kills its living probiotic juices. I transfer mine into jars, packing the sauerkraut down into its own juice, and store it in the refrigerator. It continues to sour at a snail's pace, and lasts for about 3 months.

Grandma Dion, second from the left

HOG'S HEADCHEESE

*" . . . but then I use all the animal if I care to, and
   what's more, I still do my own stunts."*
                                    —JIM HARRISON,
                                from "Back Home," in
                                The Raw and the Cooked

It's my hunch that making headcheese has always been a crazy adventure in extreme thrift (and that the all-day-simmering pot was the single reason that screened-in summer kitchens were invented). So in the spirit of the thing I wanted to present an authentic recipe—one that calls for a whole head as well as a couple of knuckles and trotters (feet), and takes the traditional few days to complete. In general, I've found that the current craze for buying well-raised (often heritage-breed) whole hogs has left Midwestern chefs with a lot of pigs' heads on their hands, and I've witnessed a surge in headcheese in restaurants across the region.

This recipe comes from Mike Phillips, a chef from Minneapolis, whose latest venture, Red Table Meats, turns out some of the very best cured meats in the upper Midwest. I've been eating Mike's food in various restaurants for a long time, and I know him to be a deeply curious chef, one who tackles each new obsession (pasta, charcuterie) as if on a quest to figure out its origins.

To taste his headcheese, then, is to commune with the original recipe and to experience why it was an essential component of our great-grandparents' tables. It tastes like the most delicious pork roast you've ever had, including its jellied juice in the corner of the roasting pan—only compressed. Some modern recipes add a lot of garlic and herbs to their headcheese, but those are bells and whistles; in this one the brine and its conspiratorial pickling spices do all the work.

The power of a good headcheese lies in the hands of the picker. Those who enjoy standing in the kitchen stripping (and nibbling) the Thanksgiving turkey carcass after the big meal will absolutely love this. Be sure to rope in all the meaty bits, especially the wide strip of woven fat and lean running through the plump cheek, to avoid any overly fatty or soft tissues, and to trim the tongue really well before slicing it into batons. Mike thinly slices the ears and adds them to the mix. They add bright curlicues and a crisp cartilaginous crunch to the finished headcheese, and are considered essential by connoisseurs.

NOTES: *Very important: Even before you purchase the pig's head, find yourself a proper pot in which to brine and cook it. The meat must be entirely submerged in the water, so the pot needs to be taller than the head. If your head is extra-large and requires more brine, here's the formula: 1 gallon water to 1 pound salt to 1 pound sugar.*

I've found that a shelfless garage refrigerator works great for curing the head.

You can replace the individual seasonings—bay leaves through celery seeds—with 1½ cups mixed pickling spice, if you prefer.

Pink salt, or sodium nitrate, gives the headcheese more staying power and a pleasant pinkish hue. You can buy it from your local butcher.

RECIPE CONTINUES

5½ cups kosher salt

5½ cups light brown sugar

10 dried bay leaves

10 dried red chiles

½ cup coriander seeds

½ cup black peppercorns

¼ cup yellow mustard seeds

2 tablespoons allspice berries

1 whole nutmeg

6 whole star anise

1 teaspoon whole cloves

1 teaspoon celery seeds

1½ teaspoons pink salt
    (optional)

1 18- to 25-pound pig's head

2 fresh ham hocks

2 pig's feet, split lengthwise

1 pound carrots, chopped

1 pound onions, chopped

1 pound celery, chopped

1 to 2 teaspoons gelatin, as
    needed

½ bunch fresh parsley, chopped
    (or to taste)

3 sprigs fresh thyme, chopped
    (or to taste)

Freshly ground black pepper

Grated nutmeg

Serve the headcheese in thick slices with crusty bread, Polish or Dijon mustard, and, if you're like my family, a cruet of white wine vinegar on the side.

MAKES 1 9 × 5-INCH LOAF; SERVES 20

Prepare the brine in advance so it will be cool when you add the meat: Combine 1 gallon water, the salt, the brown sugar, bay leaves, chiles, and all of the spices, plus the pink salt, if using, in a large cooking pot over medium-high heat and bring to a simmer, whisking to dissolve the salt and sugar. Add 2 gallons water and allow the brine to cool completely.

Add the pig's head, fresh ham hocks, and pig's feet to the cooled brine and refrigerate for 48 hours.

Drain off the brine, including all the seasonings, but don't rinse the meat. Wash the pot and return the meat to it. Add cold water to cover by 1 inch, and bring to a boil. Skim off any froth that results, and reduce the heat to a simmer. Cook slowly at a lazy simmer for 3½ hours. Add the carrots, onions, and celery to the pot, and cook for another 1 to ½ hours (for a total of 4½ to 5 hours), until the jawbones fall apart.

Remove all the meat from the pot (reserving the liquid and vegetables) and set it aside until it is cool enough to touch. Strain the pot liquid to remove all the vegetables.

Pick all the meat from the head, including the tongue, the cheeks, and behind the skull plate. Avoid all glands and soft fatty parts. Peel the tongue and cut it into long fat strips. Trim the snout and cut it into chunks. Slice the ears in long thin strips from the tips, stopping when their soft crunch grows louder beneath your knife. Put all this meat into a bowl and press a piece of plastic wrap onto its surface.

Pour the strained liquid into a pot and simmer, skimming off as much fat from the surface as you can, until it has reduced by over half, about 1 hour; it should be highly seasoned but not frankly salty. (My yield is usually about 5 quarts.) Pass the stock through a fine-mesh strainer and skim off surface fat with a ladle.

To test the stock's viscosity, ladle ½ cup into a wide container and freeze it for 10 minutes or until it feels cold. You're looking for a good bounce, so if it feels really soft, you'll need to add 2 teaspoons gelatin, and if almost there, 1 teaspoon: Melt 1 quart of the chilled stock until liquid but cool to the touch. Add 1 to 2 teaspoons gelatin and let it bloom for a minute. Add a ladleful of hot stock to melt it, and then pour the melted gelatin into the stock.

Ladle a few cups of hot stock over the meat—just enough to make a moistened mixture, not so much as to set the meat swimming. Add parsley and thyme to your liking, and season the mixture with pepper and nutmeg.

Line a 9 × 5-inch loaf pan with enough plastic wrap to overhang by 3 inches on every side. Pack the meat into the pan, running the tongue pieces lengthwise. Wrap the plastic up over the headcheese and chill it deeply in the refrigerator, at least 8 hours and up to 1 week. (Tightly wrapped, it can be frozen, too.)

To serve, pull the headcheese from its mold by lifting the plastic wrap. Transfer it to a cutting board and cut it into fat slices.

HOME-PICKLED FISH
with Basil *and* Lemon

½ cup pickling salt, plus a pinch

1 pound filleted northern pike
    or lake herring

¾ cup sugar

2½ cups white vinegar

2 teaspoons yellow mustard
    seeds

1 tablespoon black peppercorns

2 teaspoons allspice berries

1 lemon, thinly sliced

1 small Vidalia onion, thinly
    sliced

2 cups (lightly packed) fresh
    basil leaves

No matter what they fish for—walleyes, bluegills, or muskies—good anglers around here also bring in lots of northern pike, a juicy fish whose only negative trait is a haywire curved bone structure that makes filleting difficult. Traditionally this fish has been pickled: cut into chunks, salt-cured, and then dropped into a spicy pickling liquid, whose acids dissolve the fish's tiniest bones. When our friend Chad Eischens brought over a jar of his own pickled northern for me to try, it had rings of fresh lemon floating in it—a perfectly targeted addition to the sweet-and-sour fish.

You can use either Great Lakes herring or fresh northern pike for this recipe, but the fresher the better. This recipe is easily doubled.

MAKES 2 QUARTS

Combine the ½ cup pickling salt with 2 cups water in a medium saucepan and bring to a boil, stirring to dissolve the salt. Remove from the heat, add 5 cups cold water, and chill the brine completely.

Cut the fish into bite-size pieces and drop them into the cold brine. Refrigerate for 48 hours.

For the pickling liquid, combine the sugar, vinegar, mustard seeds, peppercorns, and allspice in a saucepan. Bring to a simmer, stir to dissolve the sugar, and add a pinch of pickling salt to taste. Remove from the heat, let cool completely, and then chill.

Drain the fish from its brine, but don't rinse the fish. Discard the brine.

Fill a 2-quart jar with layers of the fish, lemon slices, onion slices, and basil leaves. Pour in the pickling liquid and spices, and refrigerate for at least 48 hours before tasting the fish. Store for up to 4 weeks, refrigerated.

RULLEPØLSE

2½ tablespoons pickling or
  kosher salt

1 tablespoon sugar

1 teaspoon black peppercorns

3 dried bay leaves

2 sprigs fresh rosemary

12 dried juniper berries

2 whole cloves

1¼ pounds top round steak
  in 1 rectangular piece

1 12-ounce pork tenderloin

⅔ cup finely minced onion, plus
  1 whole large onion

1 teaspoon freshly ground black
  pepper

1½ teaspoons ground ginger

1 teaspoon ground allspice

½ cup chopped fresh parsley

This spiced, brined pork-and-beef terrine is a traditional Scandinavian Christmas specialty, common enough around here to make an appearance in the supermarket meat case during the holiday season. Traditionally, both meats were cured in a heavy brine for days before being rolled together and cooked, but now, thanks to refrigeration, a quicker dip in the cure is all they need, and that's more for flavor than for preservation.

In keeping with the original Scandinavian recipe, there is no garlic but instead a raw onion slush that adds a sharp, orthodox aroma to the air as it cooks but settles down in the finished rullepølse, leaving behind just its peppery wake.

Slice this cold terrine thinly on a serving board, and serve it with spicy mustard and rye toast.

SERVES 12 AS AN APPETIZER

For the brine, combine 2 cups water with the salt, sugar, peppercorns, bay leaves, rosemary, juniper berries, and cloves in a saucepan, and bring to a boil. Cook until the salt and sugar have dissolved. Add 3 cups cold water, and pour the brine into a 9 × 13-inch baking dish to cool. Refrigerate.

Lay the steak on a cutting board and cover it with a sheet of plastic wrap. Pound it first with the tenderizing end of a meat mallet and then with the flat end to an even ½-inch thickness.

Trim the bulky edges and any tough silverskin from the pork tenderloin.

Submerge the steak and the tenderloin in the cold brine, and cover. Refrigerate for at least 12 hours and as long as 36 hours, turning the meats once in the brine.

Drain the meats, rinse well, and pat dry with paper towels. Preheat the oven to 350°F.

In a bowl, combine the minced onion, ground pepper, ginger, allspice, and parsley. Stir well.

Cut a 3-foot length of cheesecloth and open it up in the middle, so that you have a large rectangular piece. Lay the steak on the lower half of the cheesecloth, and spread the onion mixture evenly across the expanse of meat. Set the pork tenderloin on the lower half of the steak. Tightly roll the steak around the pork, tucking in the ends, and then roll the cylinder up in the cheesecloth, twisting one end hard and securing it with a rubber band or a bit of kitchen string. Twist the other end hard in the other direction to tighten the roll, and secure the same way.

Slice the whole onion into thick round slabs, and lay them in the bottom of a covered baking dish, such as a chicken roaster, that will snugly fit the rullepølse. Lay the rullepølse on top of the onions and add 1 cup water to the pan. Bake until an instant-read thermometer inserted in the center of the roll measures 170°F, about 1½ hours.

Let the rullepølse cool to room temperature, and then transfer it to a 9 × 13-inch baking dish. Top it with a wide, flat-bottomed pan that covers the rullepølse, and weight the pan down with heavy cans or a bag of rice. Chill in the refrigerator for at least 12 hours and up to 2 days.

To serve, unwrap the rullepølse and slice it thinly. It will keep, refrigerated, for 10 days.

HOMEMADE SALT PORK

¾ cup fine sea salt

½ cup (lightly packed) light
 brown sugar

½ whole fresh pork belly
 (6 to 7 pounds), preferably
 the meaty end

3 cloves garlic, finely grated

2 teaspoons freshly ground
 black pepper

1 tablespoon minced fresh
 rosemary

NOTE: *Any salt pork you don't use
right away can be tightly wrapped
and frozen.*

In the history of Midwestern cooking, salt pork has been one of the major building blocks; it was especially crucial in the nonrefrigerated era. At that time, after the fall slaughter, home cooks would salt the pork bellies, pack them in crocks, and cover them with a preserving brine. During the winter, chunks of salt pork were pulled out to flavor pots of sauerkraut or baked beans or soup.

To make salt pork, you simply rub a fresh pork belly with salt—enough to cure the meat plus some sugar to temper the salinity—and let it cure for forty-eight hours in a cold, dark place.

This recipe is the one that my family has used at Thielen Meats of Pierz since 1922. It's pretty universal and simple to pull off at home. They generally make it plain at the meat market, but my cousin Matt and I came up with this garlic-and-rosemary version; the seasonings subtly penetrate the meat.

MAKES 6 TO 7 POUNDS

Combine the salt and brown sugar in a bowl. Put the pork belly in a large, high-sided 9 × 13-inch baking pan, and rub both sides thickly with the salt and sugar cure—as much as will adhere to the meat. Then rub with the garlic, pepper, and rosemary.

Cover the pan with heavy foil to block out any light, and refrigerate for 24 hours. Flip the pork over, return it to the refrigerator, and continue to cure for another 24 hours.

Fill a huge basin or a clean sink with cold water. Add the pork belly and soak it for 10 minutes to remove the excess salt. Blot the belly dry with paper towels.

Cut the salt pork into 6 equal pieces. Tightly wrap each one in plastic wrap and refrigerate for up to 1 week or freeze for up to 6 months.

CHICKEN STOCK MAKES 2 QUARTS

Rinse the chicken and put it into a tall stockpot. Add 3 quarts water and the salt and bring to a boil over high heat. When a cloud of gray foam rises, skim it off and discard. Add the bay leaves and peppercorns, reduce the heat until the liquid bubbles calmly, and cook for 30 minutes, uncovered.

Add the onion, carrots, celery, garlic, and herbs to the stock, and stir to incorporate. Continue cooking at a slow simmer for 1 hour, or until the stock tastes concentrated. Strain the stock through a colander, and discard the solids, and then strain the stock through a fine-mesh sieve. Skim the fat from the surface of the stock with a ladle, and let cool to room temperature before storing in a covered container in the refrigerator. The stock will keep in the refrigerator for up to 1 week or in the freezer for up to 6 months.

3 pounds mixed bony chicken parts (such as backs, breastbones, and wings)

1 teaspoon fine sea salt

2 dried bay leaves

1 teaspoon black peppercorns

1 onion, halved

2 carrots, cut into thirds

2 stalks celery, halved

6 cloves garlic, sliced crosswise

Small handful of fresh parsley stems or fresh thyme

BEEF STOCK MAKES 2 QUARTS

Heat a wide-bottomed pot over medium-high heat. Add enough oil to thinly coat the bottom. Add the bones to the hot pan, season with the salt, and brown lightly. Pour off the excess fat, add water to cover by 1 inch (about 11 cups), and bring to a boil over high heat. Skim off the foam, add the bay leaves and peppercorns, and reduce the heat until the liquid bubbles calmly; simmer for 30 minutes.

Add the onion, carrots, celery, garlic, rosemary, and parsley stems, and simmer until the stock tastes concentrated, about 1½ hours. Strain the stock through a colander to discard the solids, and then strain the stock through a fine-mesh sieve. Skim the fat from the surface of the stock with a ladle, and let cool. Store in the refrigerator for up to 1 week or in the freezer for up to 6 months.

Canola oil

5 pounds mixed meaty beef bones, such as crosscut shin bones and ribs

1 teaspoon fine sea salt

2 dried bay leaves

1 teaspoon black peppercorns

1 large onion, halved

2 large carrots, halved

3 celery stalks, halved

1 head garlic, halved crosswise

1 sprig fresh rosemary

Small handful of fresh parsley stems

Open any spiral-bound community, church, or league compilation cookbook from any area of the Midwest and you will find that the sweet recipes outnumber the savories by about two to one. Is this because we need so many formulas for cakes, pies, and other baked goods? Partly. I also think that people in this region like to skip to the end of the story, if you know what I mean.

The farming tradition has something to do with the desire for sweets, because the traditional farm day was padded with them: plain sheet cakes, cookies, or bars accompanied both the morning and afternoon coffee breaks. Generations after a family has left their farming roots you will find evidence of a latent sweet tooth that, with or without the manual labor, continues to throb at the end of a meal.

To that end, this chapter offers a few of the most iconic pies, cakes, custards, and baked desserts. I merely dipped my toes into the water of the pie heritage we have in the Midwest, perhaps our most defining sweet category. But as I also believe that pie is a very personal thing, I'm offering up a bunch of crusts and fillings and declaring them all interchangeable, although some crusts support a certain filling better than others. For example, I think the leaf lard crusts go well with tart fruit fillings, and the butter-nut crusts work well for the refrigerator pies. Outsiders may assume there's only one standard crust recipe, but like the Italian diversity of recipes for pasta dough, in reality there are hundreds. (For my go-to savory dough, see page 159.)

As my grandma taught me at the dawn of my cooking vocation, baking recipes, especially those involving a dough, are necessary at first, but at some point you should surrender their authority to your own intuition; for a pie to be successful the dough needs to feel correct to your hands, and that comes with practice. With that in mind, I tried to write all of the recipes in this section—and especially the ones for pie—in a way that allows the senses to lead.

ADDIE'S MACERATED APPLE PIE

8 cups sliced peeled apples
   (from 6 to 8 medium or
   large apples)

1 cup sugar, plus more for
   dusting the pie

Grated zest and juice of
   1 lemon

2 tablespoons dark rum
   (optional)

1 teaspoon vanilla extract

5 tablespoons cornstarch

½ teaspoon grated nutmeg

All-purpose flour, for rolling
   the dough

Leaf Lard Crust (recipe follows)

2 tablespoons unsalted butter,
   cold, cut into thin pats

Heavy cream, for the pie wash

NOTES: *The way that I was
taught to finish my pies—with
a cream wash and a dusting of
sugar—gives them what* Farm
Journal's Complete Pie Cookbook *from 1965 calls the "sugar-
sparkle crust."*

*The best apple pies are made from
sweet-tart apples, but it's always a
safe bet to use a combination of sweet
ones (such as Honeycrisp) and tart
ones (such as Haralson or Granny
Smith).*

This pie is what you might call a relic. It's as close as I'll come to making an apple pie that tastes like those my Grandma Dion and her sisters—and most rural women, I'm guessing—made before the dawn of industrial food.

Back in the day, many people canned fall apples in large quart jars, just enough for a single pie, pressing down on them until the juice flowed up over the top. When my grandma ran out of canned apples, she macerated sliced fresh apples with a little sugar, lemon, and spices—and now sometimes I add rum—giving the apples time to lose and then reabsorb their juices, resulting in a filling that was soft, slippery, and full of devastating apple flavor.

MAKES ONE 9- OR 10-INCH DOUBLE-CRUST PIE

In a large bowl, toss the apples with the sugar, lemon zest and juice, rum (if using), vanilla, cornstarch, and nutmeg. Macerate at room temperature for about 2 hours or, refrigerated, overnight.

Preheat the oven to 375°F.

Dust a worktop and rolling pin with flour. Roll out one dough disk a little less than ¼-inch thick, about 14 inches in diameter. Fold the dough in half and transfer it to a 9- or 10-inch pie plate. Unfold. Press the dough into the corners, leaving the overhang. Refrigerate the first crust while you roll out the second disk of dough.

Remove the bottom crust from the fridge and fill it with the macerated apples. Tuck the pats of cold butter beneath the top layer of fruit. Top with the second piece of dough, and trim both to a ½-inch overhang. Tuck the overhang into a roll and crimp the edge, pressing down to hook some of the dough over the edge of the dish. Cut a hole in the center of the pie, as well as some decorative vents.

Brush the top of the pie with cream, dust it with sugar, and bake for 20 minutes. Then reduce the temperature to 350°F and bake for another 20 minutes.

Cover the edges of the pie with foil and continue to bake until the center juices bubble and thicken, 25 to 35 minutes, for a total of about 1 hour and 10 minutes. Let the pie cool until it is just warm to the touch before slicing and serving.

LEAF LARD CRUST

My grandmother said that a crust was best when made with rendered leaf lard—the cleanest, densest, and most pristine fat on the hog, always specially reserved for pastries.

Leaf lard dough feels more delicate than butter dough. It has a tensile strength to it, like silk, and rolls like a dream. When baked and cut into, the leaf lard crust sends crumbs flying across the plate.

MAKES DOUGH FOR ONE 9- OR 10-INCH DOUBLE-CRUST PIE

Mix the flour, sugar, and salt in a large bowl. Add the lard and the butter, and cut them in with a pastry blender until the largest pieces are the size of peas and the mixture begins to clump on the pastry blender. Shuffle through the mixture with your hands, pinching chunks of lard to flatten them.

Add 4 tablespoons of the ice water and mix with a fork. Pinch a clump of dough in your hands: If it feels moist and clumps together easily, it's probably hydrated enough. If it feels really crumbly, add another tablespoon or two of ice water until you can form a baseball-size clump of dough, packing it on as if you were making a snowball.

Divide the dough in half and form each half into a flat disk. Wrap both disks in plastic wrap and refrigerate for at least 1 hour and up to 2 days.

Thirty minutes before you're ready to roll out the dough, remove it from the refrigerator and let it sit at room temperature to soften.

- 2½ cups all-purpose flour
- 2 tablespoons sugar
- ¾ teaspoon fine sea salt
- 6 ounces rendered leaf lard, cold, cut into cubes
- 2 tablespoons unsalted butter, cold, cut into cubes
- 4 to 6 tablespoons ice water

Leaf Lard

For those who don't know what leaf lard is—and trust me, you are not alone—it's the pure white fat that hangs around a pig's kidneys. Homesteaders used to single it out for its density and pristine flavor and rendered it for use in making pies and pastries, anything on the sweet side of the kitchen. The backfat lard was rendered and used for preserving sausage patties and salt pork and for frying.

When you open up an entire hog for fabricating, you can see where the leaf lard comes from. It's right there, the first thing you see after you remove the long, rosy tenderloins: a nimbus cloud of fat—opaque, hard, and flaky—clinging to the kidneys. It separates easily from the rest, and when you hold it in your hands you can feel its higher purpose. Unlike the backfat, it has no oily sheen, but instead, a snowy butter-like density. After being rendered and chilled, it transforms into an even thicker block, without any kind of meaty aroma. It almost goes without saying, but leaf lard makes an exquisite pie crust, with a flakiness just short of honeycombed.

BLUEBERRY PIE
with a Butter Crust

6 cups blueberries

¾ cup sugar, plus more for dusting the pie

Grated zest and juice of 1 lemon

5 tablespoons cornstarch

All-purpose flour, for rolling the dough

Flaky Butter Pie Crust (recipe follows)

2 tablespoons unsalted butter, cold, cut into thin pats

Heavy cream, for the pie wash

Ice cream, for serving

I like blueberry pie best when the filling is tart enough to lash dramatically against the buttery, crumbling crust, when ice cream isn't just a lump accessory but actually needed to call a truce between the pastry and the fruit.

Unfortunately, grocery store blueberries seem to have gone the way of most grocery store pork—largely diminished of natural flavor and acidity. To coax commercial blueberries into tasting more like tart wild blueberries, I mix them with lemon juice and zest.

MAKES ONE 9- OR 10-INCH DOUBLE-CRUST PIE

Preheat the oven to 375°F.

In a bowl, toss the blueberries with the sugar, lemon zest and juice, and cornstarch, and mix until combined.

Dust a worktop and rolling pin with flour. Roll out one dough disk a little less than ¼ inch thick, about 14 inches in diameter. Fold the dough in half and transfer it to a 9- or 10-inch pie plate. Unfold. Press the dough into the corners, leaving the overhang for now. Refrigerate the first crust while you roll out the second disk of dough.

Remove the bottom crust from the refrigerator and fill it with the berry mixture. Tuck the pats of cold butter beneath the top layer of berries. Top with the second piece of dough, and trim both to a ½-inch overhang around the pie. Tuck the overhang into a roll and crimp the edge, pressing down to hook some of the dough over the edge of the dish, holding the pie. Cut a hole in the center of the pie, as well as some decorative vents.

Brush the top of the pie with cream, dust it with sugar, and place it in the oven. Bake for 20 minutes. Then reduce the temperature to 350°F and bake for another 20 minutes.

Cover the edges of the pie with foil and continue to bake until the center juices bubble and thicken, 25 to 35 minutes more, or about 1 hour and 10 minutes total.

Let the pie cool until it is just warm to the touch before slicing and serving.

FLAKY BUTTER PIE CRUST

In recent years I've raised my ratio of butter to flour. I've found that if you're using normal commercial butter (as I do: Land O'Lakes), you need the extra butter to make an extraordinarily flaky crust. If you make your pie crust with high-butterfat butter (such as Plugrá or my local Hope Butter), you can get away with just eight ounces for 2½ cups of flour.

MAKES ENOUGH FOR ONE 9- TO 10-INCH DOUBLE-CRUST PIE

Mix the flour and salt in a large bowl. Add the butter and cut it in with a pastry blender until the largest pieces are the size of small peas and the mixture begins to clump on the pastry blender. Shuffle through the mixture with your hands, pinching chunks of fat to flatten them.

Stir the vinegar and 5 tablespoons of the ice water together in a bowl, and add the liquid to the flour; mix with a fork. Pinch a clump of dough in your hands: If it feels moist and clumps together easily, it's probably hydrated enough. If it feels really crumbly, add another tablespoon or two of ice water until you can form a baseball-size clump of dough, packing it on as if you were making a snowball.

Divide the dough in half and form each half into a flat disk. Wrap both disks in plastic wrap and refrigerate for at least 1 hour and up to 2 days.

Thirty minutes before you're ready to roll out the dough, remove it from the refrigerator and let it sit at room temperature to soften.

- 2½ cups all-purpose flour
- ¾ teaspoon fine sea salt
- 9 ounces (2 sticks plus 2 tablespoons) unsalted butter, cold, cut into cubes
- 1 teaspoon apple cider vinegar
- 5 to 7 tablespoons ice water

NOTE: *If you prefer an old-fashioned lard crust for this pie, see page 305.*

MAPLE TARTE AU SUCRE

Single-Crust Butter Dough
(recipe follows)

2 large eggs

1 large egg yolk

½ cup (lightly packed) light
brown sugar

1 tablespoon all-purpose flour,
plus more for rolling the
dough

Pinch of fine sea salt

1 cup heavy cream

¾ cup maple syrup

1 tablespoon bourbon

This recipe is here in memory of my Grandma Thielen's father's family, who had a maple-sugaring operation in a small town outside of Montreal. Two generations later, my grandmother possessed no interest in any kind of food production. Tall and slim, she ran the family business, played a mean game of bridge, read books in her downtime, and rarely took to the kitchen—except to cook the Sunday prime rib roasts, in heels and a tight-waisted apron.

Not a single family recipe came down to me through her, but I have no doubt that her Quebecois relatives, the Le Blancs, made plenty of powerful maple *tartes au sucre*, because such a pie is a sugar shack tradition.

The maple custard is flavored with whiskey instead of vanilla so as not to overpower the maple flavor. For balance, top each slice with a dollop of lightly sweetened whipped cream or Yogurt Whip (page 321).

MAKES ONE 9-INCH PIE

Preheat the oven to 350°F.

Dust a work surface and rolling pin with plenty of flour. Roll out the dough, giving it a half-turn after every few rolls to keep it from sticking to the work surface. Fold one half of the crust over your pin, brush the excess flour from the bottom, and transfer the crust to a 9-inch pie plate. Unfold the crust and press it gently into the corners. Trim the crust to within ½ inch of the lip of the pie plate, and then fold the overhang under, all the way around. Crimp the edge decoratively and pinch it to the edge of the lip, so that it stays put while cooking. Chill the crust for 15 minutes.

Press a square of aluminum foil against the bottom and sides of the pie shell, fill it with dried beans, and bake until the crust has turned a darker shade of ivory, about 30 minutes. Remove the foil and let the crust cool a bit.

Reduce the oven temperature to 325°F.

In a mixing bowl, whisk together the eggs, egg yolk, brown sugar, the 1 tablespoon flour, and the salt until smooth, with no pockets of flour remaining. Add the cream, maple syrup, and whiskey, and whisk until smooth. Pour most of the filling into the crust and carefully transfer the pie plate to the oven.

Then pour the rest of the filling into the crust in the oven. Bake the pie until the filling no longer jiggles loosely in the center, 50 minutes.

Let the pie cool completely before serving. Store any leftover pie in the refrigerator (not because it necessarily needs it, but because it might be even better cold).

SINGLE-CRUST BUTTER DOUGH

This crust is almost dark with caramelized butter, yet still delicate enough to cradle a candy-like filling. It holds up well even after a night or two in the refrigerator—a must because the maple is a whittling pie, one you take down sliver by sliver.

MAKES ENOUGH FOR ONE 9-INCH SINGLE-CRUST PIE

- 1¼ cups all-purpose flour
- 1 tablespoon sugar
- ¼ teaspoon plus a pinch of fine sea salt
- 9 tablespoons (1 stick plus 1 tablespoon) unsalted butter, cold, cut into cubes
- 4 to 6 tablespoons ice water
- ½ teaspoon apple cider vinegar

Mix the flour, sugar, and salt in a large bowl. Add the butter and cut it in with a pastry blender until the largest pieces are the size of small peas and the mixture begins to clump on the pastry blender. Shuffle through the mixture with your hands, pinching chunks of butter to flatten them.

Mix 4 tablespoons of the ice water with the vinegar in a small bowl, and add this to the flour mixture. Mix quickly with a fork to combine. Pinch a clump of dough in your hands: If it feels moist and clumps together easily, it's probably hydrated enough. If it feels really crumbly, add another tablespoon or two of ice water. Squeeze the dough into one mass, packing it on as if you were making a snowball.

Form the dough into a wide, flat disk, wrap it in plastic wrap, and refrigerate it for at least 30 minutes and as long as 2 days.

Thirty minutes before you're ready to roll out the dough, remove it from the refrigerator and let it sit at room temperature to soften.

BLACK BOTTOM OATMEAL PIE

All-purpose flour, for rolling the dough

Emily and Melissa's Butter Pie Crust (recipe follows)

1½ cups old-fashioned rolled oats

6 tablespoons heavy cream

4 ounces semisweet chocolate, finely chopped

6 tablespoons (¾ stick) unsalted butter, melted

¾ cup (packed) light brown sugar

½ teaspoon fine sea salt

¼ teaspoon ground ginger

1 cup dark corn syrup

2 teaspoons apple cider vinegar

1 teaspoon vanilla extract

4 large eggs, lightly beaten

This recipe (including the impossibly buttery crust) comes from the wildly popular pie shop in the Gowanus area of Brooklyn called Four & Twenty Blackbirds—a place that can be credited with bringing the Midwestern pie-and-coffee break to Brooklyn. Emily and Melissa Elsen, sisters, co-owners, and chief pie-makers, come from Hecla, South Dakota, a town with a population of 210. Descended from a long line of skilled bakers and raised on a continuous flux of pies—berry, orchard fruit, custard, refrigerated cream—they bake just like their Grandma Liz did, according to seasonal windfall.

This one definitely belongs to the cold season. And do not believe the health promise from the oats; this pie is luscious candy. With its chocolate bottom, honeyed custard middle, and glassy caramelized top, Emily says it tastes "like a big warm oatmeal chocolate chip cookie."

MAKES ONE 9-INCH SINGLE-CRUST PIE

Preheat the oven to 350°F.

Dust a work surface and rolling pin with plenty of flour. Roll out the dough, giving it a half-turn after every few rolls to keep it from sticking to the surface. Fold one half of the crust over your pin, brush the excess flour from the bottom, and transfer the crust to a 9-inch pie plate. Unfold the crust and press it gently into the corners of the pie plate. Trim the crust to within ½ inch of the lip of the pie plate, and fold the overhang under, all the way around. Crimp the edge decoratively and pinch it to the edge of the lip, so that it stays put while cooking.

Line the crust with a square of parchment or foil, and fill it with dried beans. Parbake the crust for 20 minutes. Remove it from the oven, remove the foil, and let it cool a bit.

Meanwhile, spread the oats on a rimmed baking sheet and bake, stirring once or twice midway through toasting, until lightly toasted and fragrant, 10 to 12 minutes. Allow to cool.

Reduce the oven temperature to 325°F.

To make the black bottom, or chocolate ganache, bring the cream to a boil in a small saucepan and pour it over the chocolate in a small bowl. Cover and let sit for 5 minutes. Then whisk gently until smooth. Pour the ganache into the pie shell and spread it evenly over the bottom and up the sides. Refrigerate until set, for at least 10 minutes and as long as a few hours.

To make the custard filling, combine the butter, brown sugar, salt, and ginger in a large bowl. Whisk in the corn syrup, vinegar, and vanilla. Whisk in the eggs, mixing until thoroughly combined. Pour in the oats and mix well. Pour the filling into the chilled ganache-coated pie shell.

Bake the pie in the lower third of the oven until the filling is evenly puffed and bounces back slightly when pressed with a fingertip, 1 hour. Transfer the pie to a rack and allow it to cool to lukewarm before slicing.

EMILY AND MELISSA'S BUTTER PIE CRUST

MAKES DOUGH FOR ONE 9-INCH SINGLE-CRUST PIE

1¼ cups all-purpose flour

1 tablespoon sugar

½ teaspoon fine sea salt

8 tablespoons (1 stick) unsalted butter, cold, cut into cubes

4 to 5 tablespoons ice water

2 teaspoons apple cider vinegar

Mix the flour, sugar, and salt in a large bowl. Add the butter and cut it in with a pastry blender until the largest pieces are the size of small peas and the mixture begins to clump on the pastry blender. Shuffle through the mixture with your hands, pinching chunks of butter to flatten them.

Mix together 4 tablespoons of the ice water and the vinegar in a small bowl, and add to the flour mixture. Rake the flour mixture quickly with a fork to combine. Pinch a clump of dough in your hands: If it feels moist and clumps together easily, it's probably hydrated enough. If it feels really crumbly, add another tablespoon of ice water. Squeeze the dough into one mass, packing it as if you were making a snowball.

Form the dough into a wide, flat disk, wrap it in plastic wrap, and refrigerate it for at least 30 minutes and up to 2 days.

Thirty minutes before you're ready to roll out the dough, remove it from the refrigerator and let it sit at room temperature to soften.

RHUBARB-LIME ICEBOX PIE

Sweet Shortbread Crust (recipe follows)

2½ cups (10 ounces) diced rhubarb

½ cup plus 2 tablespoons sugar

⅓ cup fresh lime juice (from about 4 limes)

1 14-ounce can sweetened condensed milk

4 large egg yolks

1½ cups heavy cream

½ teaspoon vanilla extract

So many people in this area grow rhubarb in their yards that the local grocery stores don't even bother to sell it in the spring. Come May, everywhere you turn there's rhubarb crisp, or rhubarb pie, or stewed rhubarb over ice cream. Following the local tradition of adding rhubarb to every reasonable thing during the season, here's a pie that looks and tastes like a pink Key lime pie.

The creamy filling gets its requisite tartness from a quickly stewed pot of fuchsia rhubarb, to which you add the elements of a classic Key lime custard: egg yolks and condensed milk. The color depends on the rhubarb you use—the redder the stalk, the pinker the pie. (If you like, add a drop of red food coloring to a filling made with greenish rhubarb, although I happen to love the natural blushing mauve color.)

And take a cue from those retro diners famous for their icebox pies: Whip the cream just until soft and billowy and sculpt it into a dramatic pompadour on top.

MAKES ONE 9-INCH PIE

Preheat the oven to 325°F.

Combine the rhubarb, ½ cup of the sugar, and the lime juice in a saucepan over medium-low heat and bring to a simmer. Cook, uncovered, until the rhubarb is broken-down, 10 minutes. Let cool for a few minutes. Then blend the stewed rhubarb with a stick blender (or, alternatively, transfer it to a food processor and process) until smooth. Add the condensed milk, blend to combine, and add the egg yolks. Blend until smooth.

Pour the filling into the baked pie shell and bake until it is completely set in the middle, 30 minutes. Let the pie cool to room temperature, and then chill it in the refrigerator until completely cold, at least 3 hours.

Combine the cream, the remaining 2 tablespoons sugar, and the vanilla in a mixing bowl and whip until lofty and forming peaks. Top the pie with the whipped cream and serve. Keep any leftover pie in the refrigerator.

SWEET SHORTBREAD CRUST

MAKES ENOUGH FOR ONE 9-INCH SINGLE-CRUST PIE

Preheat the oven to 350°F. Spray a 9-inch pie plate with non-stick spray (or rub it with a little canola oil).

    Combine the shortbread crumbs, sugar, ginger, and melted butter in a bowl, and mix with a fork to combine. Press the crumb mixture into the prepared pie plate, making sure to push it all the way up the sides and to pinch a little lip above the rim of the pie plate. Bake until fragrant and light brown, 10 minutes. Remove the crust from the oven and reduce the oven temperature to 325°F if making Rhubarb-Lime Icebox Pie.

Nonstick spray or canola oil

1½ cups finely ground shortbread crumbs (from plain Sandies cookies or other shortbread)

5 tablespoons sugar

½ teaspoon ground ginger

3 tablespoons salted butter, melted

SOUR CREAM RAISIN PIE

Sweet Pecan Pie Crust
   (recipe follows)

1 cup raisins

⅓ cup Madeira wine

5 large egg yolks

2 cups sour cream

¼ cup honey

¼ cup plus 3 tablespoons sugar

¼ cup all-purpose flour

1 teaspoon vanilla extract

1 teaspoon ground cinnamon

½ teaspoon ground ginger

¼ teaspoon ground cloves

1¼ cups heavy cream

In pirouetting glass pie cases across the upper Midwest you will find sour cream raisin pie in regular rotation. For the filling, chopped raisins, warm holiday spices, egg yolks, and sour cream cook slowly into thick decadence, with a resulting texture that falls somewhere between pudding and cheesecake. Some versions flaunt high meringue tops, but I've always thought the saccharine cloud looming over an already sweet filling to be overkill. I prefer mine the way they make it at Third Street Market on my hometown's main street: with a whipped cream top (into which I can fold even more sour cream). I also like to incorporate ground pecans into the crust to tenderize it, and a splash of Madeira in the raisins to deepen their flavor.

MAKES ONE 9-INCH PIE

Preheat the oven to 375°F.

Put the dough disk between two large pieces of plastic wrap, and roll out the dough to a 13-inch diameter, a shy ¼-inch thickness. Remove the top sheet of plastic, and flip the dough over into a 9-inch pie plate. Press it gently into the corners. Trim the dough to a ½-inch overhang, and fold the edge over into a roll. Crimp the crust decoratively and pinch it to the edge of the pie plate, so that it stays put while cooking. If there's time, chill the crust for 20 minutes.

Line the crust with aluminum foil and fill it with dried beans. Bake for 15 minutes. Then remove the foil and beans, and bake until the crust is golden brown, another 20 to 25 minutes. Set it aside to cool.

With a large knife, roughly chop the raisins. Combine the raisins, Madeira, and ⅔ cup water in a small saucepan and bring to a boil. Simmer uncovered over medium-low heat until the liquid has nearly all evaporated, about 10 minutes. Set aside to cool.

In a large heatproof bowl, whisk together the egg yolks, 1½ cups of the sour cream, the honey, ¼ cup of the sugar, and the flour, vanilla, cinnamon, ginger, and cloves. Stir in the raisins.

Fill a medium saucepan halfway with water and place it over high heat. When the water simmers, set the bowl of raisin custard on top, to make a double boiler. Reduce the heat, and alternating between a whisk and a rubber spatula, slowly stir the raisin mixture until it thickens (it will start to look like cake batter), 5 to 8 minutes. Remove it from the heat.

Stir the filling mixture often as it cools. When it feels just warm to the touch, transfer the mixture to the refrigerator. Stir it every once in a while until it chills completely, about 1 hour—it will become thicker still. When it is cold, pour the filling into the cooled pie crust.

Whip the cream with the remaining 3 tablespoons sugar until firm peaks form. Add the remaining ½ cup sour cream and whip, slowly, until soft crinkles form again. Pile the cream onto the center of the pie and spread it to the edges. Chill the pie for at least 2 hours before slicing.

SWEET PECAN PIE CRUST

Because this crust, with its nuts and sugar, is a little richer than normal pie dough, I like to roll it out between two pieces of plastic wrap.

MAKES ENOUGH FOR ONE 9-INCH SINGLE CRUST PIE

- 1¼ cups all-purpose flour
- ⅓ cup finely ground pecans
- ¼ cup sugar
- ⅛ teaspoon salt
- 8 tablespoons (1 stick) unsalted butter, cold, cut into ½-inch cubes
- 4 tablespoons ice water
- 1 teaspoon apple cider vinegar

Mix the flour, pecans, sugar, and salt in a large bowl. Add the butter and cut it in with a pastry blender a little more than you normally do for pie crust: until the butter bits are the size of lentils and the mixture begins to clump on the pastry blender.

Mix the ice water and vinegar together in a small bowl, and add 2 tablespoons of this to the flour mixture. Rake the flour mixture quickly with a fork to combine. Pinch a clump of dough in your hands: If it feels moist and clumps together easily, it's probably hydrated enough. If it feels really crumbly, add more of the ice water–vinegar mixture until it clumps.

Form the dough into a wide, flat disk, wrap it in plastic wrap, and refrigerate it for at least 30 minutes and as long as 2 days.

Thirty minutes before you're ready to roll out the dough, remove it from the refrigerator and let it sit at room temperature to soften.

RØMMEGRØT

3 cups whole milk, plus ½ cup
more if needed

2 cups heavy cream

1¼ cups all-purpose flour

1 tablespoon sugar, plus more
for garnish

¼ teaspoon fine sea salt

Ground cinnamon, for garnish

NOTES: *If you use high-quality
cream, preferably something from
a local dairy or farmer's market,
the subtle nuances come barreling
through; the slow cooking develops
all the flavors already present in the
cream, and there's nothing added to
distract from them.*

*My in-laws serve this with the
main course at holiday meals, but
I tend to bump it to an after-dinner
dessert slot.*

The first Christmas I spent cooking with my husband's Norwegian-
American side of the family (many of them dairy farmers) I saw cream
in a brand-new light. The most intriguing dish on the table was
rømmegrøt (ROO-me-gret), a traditional Norwegian cream pudding,
pure white but for a few freckles of cinnamon dusted across the top.

The method for making rømmegrøt may seem odd to modern cooks,
as it did to me: You reduce the cream until beads of butter pool at the
edges, which you then skim off and use to garnish the final pudding.

It's a genius way to highlight the purity of good dairy, creating a
pudding that tastes as clean as snow—but much richer, of course.

Pour the 3 cups of milk into a large saucepan, place it over
medium heat, and heat the milk to just below the boiling point.
Remove the pan from the heat and set it aside.

Bring the cream to a simmer in a medium saucepan. Cook
over medium-high heat, stirring often, until it has large bubbles
and coats the back of a spoon, 10 minutes.

Sift ½ cup of the flour over the top of the cream and whisk
to incorporate. Reduce the heat to medium and simmer lightly,
stirring now and then to make sure the bottom doesn't scorch,
until the butter bubbles out of the mixture, about 5 minutes. It
will pool at the sides and in pockets in the center. Tilt the pan
and carefully skim off the butter with a small ladle; deposit it in
a small bowl. Continue cooking and skimming the butter until
you have 2 to 3 tablespoons butter in the bowl. This will take
about 10 minutes.

Whisk the remaining ¾ cup flour into the cream mixture
(the mixture will be very thick), and then gradually add the
reserved scalded milk, whisking until the mixture reaches a thick
pudding-like consistency. (If it's too thick, drizzle in up to ½ cup
additional milk.) Add the sugar and salt, and cook over low
heat, stirring often, to remove any flour taste from the pudding,
10 minutes.

Pour the pudding into a shallow, wide heatproof bowl,
sprinkle it heavily with sugar and cinnamon, and pour the
reserved butter on top. Keep warm in a low oven for up to
1 hour before serving.

Kalvdans: First Milk Pudding

After hanging out with Aaron's cousins in the milking barn, we folded ourselves into the tight-as-a-hook entryway and knocked off our muddy boots by wedging one against the other. Aaron's grandma had sent us to their farm to fetch the protein- and nutrient-rich colostrum so that she could make *kalvdans,* or first-milk pudding, a delicacy straight from the old Norwegian farmhouse kitchen playlist—one that's still popular among the Norwegian-American farmers in my husband's family. They told me that *kalvdans* means "calves dance," so named for the happy wiggle that calves give when they first get the rich colostrum from their mothers.

In the sunny checkered kitchen, Grandma Annexstad was already straining the bucketful of rich cream, which looked to me exactly like nature's version of sweetened condensed milk. Shiny and yellow, it flowed slowly in a broad cable, linking one vessel to the other.

It seemed as if we were stealing something pretty important from a poor baby calf, but everyone in the room, three generations of Norwegian-American dairy farmers, reassured me that the calf would get its fill—the mother had a surplus of colostrum, and we were taking from her second batch. I figured they should know.

With typical Scandinavian restraint, Grandma Annexstad whisked some fresh milk into the first milk and poured it into a buttered pan. Within an hour in the oven it developed a lovely brown skin and the solid texture of a ricotta cheesecake. She scooped it out with a wide spoon and served each trembling hill with a pour of fresh cream over the top and a thick dusting of sugar and cinnamon. The pudding was moist and tender but almost flaky, as if you were digging into a square of warm, buttery, old-fashioned cake yeast.

This is dairy-love, compounded and condensed. And not only is it delicious—and rare—but they say it's very good for you.

RHUBARB BAKED
in Wild Raspberry Syrup

1½ pounds (7 to 8 large) stalks rhubarb

½ cup wild raspberry syrup, homemade (see page 269) or store-bought

¼ cup sugar

½ vanilla bean, or 1 teaspoon vanilla extract

NOTE: *In place of the homemade wild raspberry syrup, any fruit syrup, either purchased or home-made, can be used for this recipe.*

Midwestern recipes for baked rhubarb are as old as the hills. But when you bake the rows of ruby spears in a shallow bath of wild raspberry syrup, the dish feels fresh and new. The rhubarb glows a wild pink, tastes like warm fruit of the forest, and is always heavenly laid next to a cool custard or spooned over ice cream or yogurt.

I dodge rhubarb's habit of quickly elapsing from raw to overcooked by boosting the small amount of raspberry syrup with some extra sugar; the higher sugar density of the syrup helps the rhubarb to keep its shape, but the fruit still tastes quite tart.

Preheat the oven to 325°F.

Trim and discard the ends of the rhubarb, and rinse the stalks. Cut the stalks into ¾-inch-thick slices on a deep diagonal, keeping them neatly stacked together. Transfer the sliced rhubarb to a 9 × 13-inch baking pan, making rows of cut rhubarb until you have filled the pan.

Warm the raspberry syrup in a microwave oven until hot. Add the sugar to the warm syrup and stir to dissolve. If using the vanilla bean, slice it lengthwise, scrape out the pulp, and throw the pulp into the syrup and the pods in with the rhubarb. If using vanilla extract, add it to the syrup.

Pour the raspberry syrup evenly over the rhubarb, and bake, uncovered, until the rhubarb is soft but not mushy, 15 to 18 minutes.

Midway through baking, remove the pan from the oven, and gently tilt the pan and spoon the syrup over the rhubarb to glaze it.

Allow the baked rhubarb to cool, glazing it once more with the syrup as it cools. Refrigerate the rhubarb in the pan. (To transfer it to another container and keep its shape, just tip and slide.) The rhubarb will keep in the refrigerator for up to 1 week, and gets firmer and brighter as it sits.

BAKED APPLES
with Sour Cherries, Rosemary, *and* Yogurt Whip

For baked apples, you want to use a tart variety that can take the heat, such as a Cortland or a Northern Spy. But even my favorite Haralsons, which tend to blow out in the pan, are uncommonly delicious when cooked with vanilla, sour cherries, and rosemary, dropped with a soft thud into a bowl, and garnished with Yogurt Whip.

I rarely cook with vanilla beans because they're so expensive and hard to find here, but I crave them the most when making rustic baked or sautéed fruit desserts—anything with a golden juice into which the fine black grains of vanilla can flow. Using just half a bean adds serious fragrance, especially when entwined with a couple sprigs of fresh rosemary, an herb that keeps excellent company with apples.

Preheat the oven to 375°F.

Slice the top ½ inch from all of the apples and discard. With a large melon baller or a thin spoon, scoop out the cores, making sure to leave ½ inch at the bottom.

Cut the vanilla bean in half lengthwise, scrape out the pulp, and mash it into the butter on a cutting board. In a small bowl, combine the vanilla butter (or vanilla extract and butter), brown sugar, maple syrup, and cherries.

Arrange the apples in a 9 × 13-inch baking dish and divide the brown sugar mixture among the cavities. Surround the apples with the rosemary, lemon juice, and ⅓ cup water.

Bake the apples in the oven for 30 minutes. Then tip the apples over to disgorge their fillings into the pan, tilt the pan, and spoon the juice and cherries back over the apples to glaze them. Bake for another 20 to 30 minutes, repeating the process of glazing them once more, until the apples are tender and the pan juices have thickened. If at any point the pan juices evaporate, add a few tablespoons of water.

For the yogurt whip, combine the heavy cream and granulated sugar in a mixing bowl. Whip the cream just until stiff and crinkled. Stir in the yogurt and whip again until soft peaks form. (Oddly enough, this yogurt-enhanced whipped cream stays more billowy, and for longer, than regular whipped cream.)

Serve the baked apples in individual bowls, topped with the yogurt whip.

BAKED APPLES

6 large tart baking apples

½ vanilla bean, or 2 teaspoons vanilla extract

3 tablespoons salted butter, at cool room temperature

3 tablespoons (packed) light brown sugar

3 tablespoons maple syrup

½ cup dried sour cherries

2 sprigs fresh rosemary

1½ tablespoons fresh lemon juice, preferably from Meyer lemons

YOGURT WHIP

1 cup heavy cream

1½ tablespoons granulated sugar

¾ cup whole-milk yogurt

NOTE: *Be sure to rinse off the spent vanilla pod after cooking; let it dry it on a towel and then add it to a jar of white sugar. When the jar has accumulated a few pods, you'll have a nice vanilla-scented sugar, great for dusting doughnuts or just making a sugar toast treat.*

RED BERRY MOLDED DESSERT

2 pounds mixed fresh berries,
   such as hulled strawberries,
   raspberries, and red currants,
   heavy on the strawberries

1 cup sugar

1 teaspoon freshly ground
   cardamom seeds

¼ cup fresh lemon juice

3 envelopes (6 teaspoons)
   unflavored powdered gelatin

Lightly sweetened whipped
   cream, for serving

NOTES: *If you can find red currants for this, definitely use them;
they pop exquisitely in the finished
dessert. If not, use just strawberries
and raspberries.*

*For years before I found that I could
buy cardamom seeds (otherwise
known as decorticated cardamom)
from Penzeys, I smashed the green
pods and picked out the seeds by
hand. The decorticated cardamom
saves a lot of time, of course, and
it's tons better than preground
cardamom. Adding this spice to
sweet desserts always seems to me a
Scandinavian thing—like Finnish
cardamom bread, for instance—and
I've found it to be a good mimic of
the floral, citric side of any berry's
personality.*

If we're lucky, the strawberry harvest carries on long enough to
coincide with the raspberry and red currant harvests. When this
triumvirate occurs, I am always reminded of the particularly Northern
European appreciation for mixed red berries, and if they're transformed
into quivery jelled towers, how well they go with whipped cream.

Red Jell-O and white cream. For a native Midwesterner, especially
those of us raised on small-town potlucks and buffets, it's a pairing that
reaches deep, one probably first experienced when we were still teething.

Combine half of the mixed berries, ¾ cup of the sugar, the
cardamom, and the lemon juice in a saucepan. Mash the berries
thoroughly with a potato masher, add 2 cups water, and bring to
a simmer. Cook gently until the sugar and some of the berries
have dissolved, about 5 minutes. Remove from the heat and let
cool until warm to the touch.

Meanwhile, combine the gelatin and ⅓ cup water in a small
dish, and mix together.

Add the gelatin to the lukewarm berry juice (scraping the
dish to get all of it), and stir until the gelatin has dissolved. Pour
the mixture through a fine-mesh sieve into a bowl, pressing on
the pulp with a rubber spatula to extract the juice. Discard the
pulp. Stir the juice until it cools.

Meanwhile, mash the remaining strawberries with the
remaining ¼ cup sugar in a bowl. Add the remaining raspberries
and currants, leaving them whole, and set aside.

Chill the berry juice in the refrigerator, stirring it now and
then, until it just begins to thicken. Then fold in the fresh
berries. Pour the mixture into a 9- or 10-cup Bundt pan, or a
large Jell-O mold. Chill thoroughly until set, at least 4 hours or
as long as overnight.

To unmold the dessert, run a thin knife around the perimeter
of the mold, and around the center post if it has one, and then
dip the bottom of the mold into a deep bowl of hot water until
you can feel it loosen a bit. Turn a platter upside down on top of
the mold and invert it. If the mold doesn't release, dip the bottom again in hot water. To serve, cut in slices.

CRANBERRY *and* Port Tart

SPICED COOKIE CRUST

7 tablespoons unsalted butter, at room temperature, plus more for the foil

⅓ cup confectioners' sugar

⅓ cup finely ground walnuts or almonds

¾ cup all-purpose flour

1 teaspoon ground cinnamon

½ teaspoon ground ginger

¼ teaspoon ground cloves

¼ teaspoon fine sea salt

FILLING

2 tablespoons unsalted butter

3 cups (1 12-ounce bag) domestic or wild highbush cranberries, rinsed

1 cup plus 1 tablespoon ruby port wine

1¼ cups (lightly packed) light brown sugar

1 tablespoon all-purpose flour

2 large eggs

NOTES: *Wild highbush cranberries aren't technically cranberries at all, but* Viburnum trilobum *grow wild across this area, taste a lot like them, and can be used in this tart.*

Should the cranberry puree yield less than 1 cup, just return the cranberry pulp to the saucepan, add 4 table-spoons water, cook for 5 minutes and add to your puree.

This one's an ode to my great-aunt Helen, whose Cranberry, Walnut, and Port Jell-O—a deep ruby bowl thickly frosted with cream cheese and decorated with twelve perfect walnut halves like the face of a clock—was always the highlight of our holiday.

To my generation, a tart is more festive than Jell-O, even if it's in a crystal bowl, so that's how I have reimagined it. The softly set jammy filling is of the fiercest magenta color, with an undercurrent of port flavor and an acidity that hangs on the safe side of sour. Set into a crumbly crust flush with warm spices, the whole thing tastes something like a linzer torte. Serve it with lightly sweetened whipped cream.

MAKES ONE 9-INCH TART

Preheat the oven to 350°F.

For the crust, combine the butter and confectioners' sugar in a medium bowl and mix with a wooden spoon until smooth. Mix in the finely ground nuts. Sift the flour, cinnamon, ginger, cloves, and salt into a bowl, and add to the dough. Mix until combined. Press the dough evenly into a 9-inch tart pan, making sure to reach the top and using all of the dough. Chill the dough in the pan for at least 15 minutes.

Bake the crust until fully amber brown, 25 to 30 minutes.

For the filling, melt the butter in a small skillet over medium-high heat. Cook, stirring, until the butter turns nut brown, about 2 minutes. Set it aside to cool.

Combine the cranberries with 1 cup of the port in a small saucepan, and bring to a simmer. Cover tightly, and cook over medium-low heat until the cranberries look ruby red and the liquid has begun to thicken slightly, about 20 minutes. Uncover, and smash the cranberries with a rubber spatula. Cook, stirring, for 5 minutes, until thick. Push the cranberry mixture through a food mill or a sieve into a bowl. Measure out a scant cup cranberry puree for the tart filling and let cool.

Whisk the brown sugar, flour, eggs, brown butter, and remaining 1 tablespoon port in to the cranberry puree until smooth.

Set the still-warm tart crust on a baking sheet and pour the filling into it. Bake the tart until the filling is set, 25 minutes.

Serve at room temperature.

CHOCOLATE LAZY-DAISY
SHEET CAKE

Lazy is right. This is a classic moist, midnight-black cocoa cake baked in a regulation 9 × 13-inch baking pan and topped with a broiled coconut lazy-daisy topping. It shares a family resemblance with German chocolate cake but is much easier to make, and possibly even more luscious: the coconut caramel saturates the top inch beneath the crispy topping, as if it were a chocolate *tres leches* cake.

Sheet cakes are very popular in the Midwest, and for good reason. For a large party, they're more practical, and even though they contain the same volume of batter as a layer cake, sheet cakes enforce the illusion of feeding more people. Best of all, they can be cut into squares right in the dish and left at the top of the buffet line for self-service.

SERVES 20

Preheat the oven to 350°F. Butter and flour a 9 × 13-inch baking pan.

Sift the flour, cocoa powder, and salt together into a medium bowl. In a small dish, pour the boiling water over the baking soda; stir to combine.

Melt 10 tablespoons (1 stick plus 2 tablespoons) of the butter. Pour into a large bowl, and whisk in the granulated sugar, buttermilk, eggs, coffee, and vanilla. Add the flour mixture, whisk until smooth, and then stir in the baking soda mixture, scraping the dish to get all of it.

Pour the batter into the prepared baking pan and bake until a thin cake tester inserted into the center of the cake comes out clean, about 35 minutes. Let the cake cool.

Turn on the broiler and position an oven rack 6 inches below it.

For the topping, combine the remaining 8 tablespoons (1 stick) butter, the brown sugar, and the coconut milk in a saucepan over medium-high heat. Bring to a simmer, stirring, and cook until the grains of brown sugar melt, about 1 minute. Stir in the flaked coconut and remove from the heat.

When the broiler is ready, spread the coconut topping gently and evenly over the top of the cake. Broil the cake, keeping watch and rotating as necessary, until the entire surface has browned, about 3 minutes. Cool before cutting the cake into squares.

- 2¼ cups cake flour, plus more for the baking dish
- ½ cup unsweetened cocoa powder
- ¾ teaspoon fine sea salt
- ¼ cup boiling water
- 1 tablespoon baking soda
- 9 ounces (2 sticks plus 2 tablespoons) salted butter, plus more for the baking dish
- 2 cups granulated sugar
- 1 cup buttermilk
- 2 large eggs
- ¾ cup brewed coffee, cold
- 2 teaspoons vanilla extract
- 1½ cups (lightly packed) light brown sugar
- ½ cup coconut milk
- 2 cups flaked or shredded coconut (sweetened or unsweetened)

PEAR *and* HONEY CAKE

Unsalted butter, melted, for the pan

4 firm-ripe pears, such as yellow or red Anjou

9 ounces (2 sticks plus 2 tablespoons) unsalted butter, at room temperature

¼ cup plus 2 tablespoons light honey

2 tablespoons Kirsch, rum, or cider

2¾ cups all-purpose flour, plus more for the pan

1 teaspoon baking powder

¼ teaspoon fine sea salt

2⅓ cups sugar

6 large eggs

1½ teaspoons vanilla extract

2 tablespoons fresh lemon juice

NOTE: *To ensure that the cake leaves its mold perfectly—even the sharpest and most intricate of the Nordic Ware bundt pans (which are made in Minnesota, by the way)— try this trick: Coat the inside of the pan with a thin layer of melted butter, and when it cools, go over it once more with the butter to even it out before shaking an even dusting of flour around the inside of the pan.*

This cake, the pear-stuffed love child of French butter cake and American bundt, is the perfect thing to bake in my finest, craziest-looking bundt pan. The finished cake requires no thick glaze or frosting, decorations that tend to mar the delicate impressions.

I've made it so many times, but the loveliness of the cake dropping out of its mold never fails to take my breath away. I brush it with the reduced pear cooking liquid to give it some sheen and to give the edges an addictive caramel chewiness, but really, this cake needs no accompaniment—except maybe a shimmering cup of black coffee.

SERVES 8 TO 10

Preheat the oven to 400°F. Prepare a 10-cup Bundt pan by brushing it with melted butter, sifting a little flour over it, tilting the pan, and knocking out the excess flour (see Note).

Peel, quarter, and core the pears. Heat a large skillet over high heat, and add 2 tablespoons of the butter. When it melts, add the pears. Cook, stirring once or twice, until browned in spots, about 3 minutes. Off the heat, add 2 tablespoons of the honey and the Kirsch, and stir to combine. Cook for another minute to let the flavors blend. Pour the pears into a colander set over a bowl. Reserve the drained pears and the liquid separately.

In a mixing bowl, sift the flour, baking powder, and salt together twice.

Put the remaining 8 ounces (2 sticks) butter in another mixing bowl and whip with an electric mixer. Gradually add 2 cups of the sugar and then continue whipping until creamed, light, and fluffy. Add the eggs one at a time, whipping after each addition and scraping down the sides of the bowl. Add the vanilla and remaining ¼ cup honey, and mix to combine. Add the flour mixture in three additions, mixing just enough to combine, no more. (Overmixing the cake at this point will make it tough.) Gently mix the pears into the batter with a rubber spatula.

Pour the batter into the prepared Bundt pan, and bake for 10 minutes. Reduce the oven temperature to 325°F and bake until a toothpick inserted into the center of the cake comes out clean, 50 to 60 minutes. Let the cake cool for 20 minutes. Then carefully cut around the center post to loosen the cake, and unmold it onto a platter. Let the cake cool completely.

For the glaze, heat the reserved pear cooking liquid with the remaining ⅓ cup sugar and the lemon juice in a small skillet over medium-high heat. Boil until the glaze bubbles thickly and a droplet feels sticky when pinched between your thumb and forefinger. (How long this takes will depend on how much liquid your pears released during cooking.) Cool slightly before brushing on the cake in three applications.

MEYER LEMON ANGEL FOOD CAKE
with Honeyed Strawberries

2¼ cups sugar

1¼ cups cake flour

½ teaspoon fine sea salt

3 teaspoons (lightly packed) grated lemon zest, preferably from Meyer lemons

⅓ cup freshly squeezed lemon juice, preferably from Meyer lemons

1 teaspoon vanilla extract

⅛ teaspoon almond extract

⅛ teaspoon lemon extract

1½ cups egg whites (from 11 to 12 eggs), at room temperature

½ teaspoon cream of tartar

1 pound fresh strawberries, quartered

2 tablespoons honey

¼ teaspoon ground fennel seeds

Confectioners' sugar, for serving

2 cups heavy cream

NOTES: *Thankfully my local grocery store stocks Meyer lemons, which have a more fragrant, sweeter juice than standard lemons. They're slightly more expensive but they also yield more juice, so it's kind of a wash.*

Super-fine sugar, whether purchased or made in a food processor, gives the cake a finer texture.

An all-American classic, angel food cake becomes part of a very important trilogy when combined with shiny honey-glazed strawberries and a floating cloud of thick, rich whipped cream. This cake's subtle boost of Meyer lemon juice, as well as a triple shot of extracts—almond, vanilla, and lemon—balances out the cotton-candy sweetness of the pillowy cake.

MAKES ONE 10-INCH CAKE; SERVES 8 TO 12

Preheat the oven to 350°F.

Pulse 2 cups of the sugar in a food processor until super-fine.

In a large bowl, sift the cake flour and salt together three times. In a small bowl, combine the lemon zest and juice with the vanilla, almond, and lemon extracts.

Using an electric mixer, beat the egg whites and cream of tartar in a large, very clean bowl at medium-high speed until foamy and opaque. Gradually add the superfine sugar, ½ cup at a time, adding the last of it at the end when the egg whites stand upright and softly hold their shape.

Next, take off the beaters and with a large whisk incorporate half of the flour by hand, to keep from overmixing. Add the lemon-juice mixture and stir to combine. Finally, add the rest of the flour and whisk gently until smooth.

Pour the batter into an ungreased 10-inch tube pan, and using a spatula, smooth the top. Bake the cake until a cake tester inserted in the center comes out clean, 40 to 45 minutes.

While the cake is baking, mix together the berries, honey, and fennel in a bowl and set aside to macerate.

Turn the cake upside down onto a cake rack and leave it to cool completely. To unmold the cake, run a knife around the perimeter of the pan and around the center post, and turn the pan over gently to release the cake onto a platter. Put the confectioners' sugar in a fine-mesh strainer and dust the top of the cake heavily.

Before serving, whip the cream with the remaining ¼ cup sugar. Cut the cake into slices with a serrated knife, and serve with the marinated berries and whipped cream.

Lacquered Day-Old Angel Food Cake with Pears

One day when our neighbors Dick and Jane popped by, I put on the coffee and pulled the cloth from the angel food cake, which was at that point two days old. To freshen it up, I decided to fry the cake in caramelized sugar and butter, giving it a crackling sugar armor—a little save-the-coffee-break measure that has turned into a good habit. (Or maybe a bad one.)

Go ahead and fry it until the outside turns the color of your favorite pot's dark bottom: the small blackened spots have the savor of fancy bitters. I like to add a diced pear to the caramelized pan, toss it in the caramel, and serve it with the cake, but it's also fine served solo, with whipped cream.

A warning, though: Don't touch the caramelizing cake with your fingers and don't taste it until it has cooled down—the lacquer is molten caramel and it will stick and burn. Maneuver the cake in the pan with a wide butter knife and always wait until the outside has solidified into a hard glass crust before cracking into it.

SERVES 2

Pour the cream and ½ tablespoon of the sugar into a mixing bowl, and whip with an electric mixer until soft peaks form.

Heat a medium skillet over medium-high heat, and when it's hot, sprinkle the 3 tablespoons sugar evenly across the bottom of the skillet. Stand by as it melts, tilting the pan to shake the white sugar into the melting caramel. When the sugar has half melted and the liquid has begun to turn amber, stir with a wooden spoon to completely dissolve every lump of sugar.

Add the butter and stir to combine. Add the cake slices and reduce the heat to medium-low. Cook, turning each slice over and over with a butter knife and the wooden spoon, until the cake is fully coated with glaze, about 2 minutes.

Transfer the slices to individual plates, and add the pear to the skillet. Cook quickly over medium-high heat so that the pears pick up a little of the sticky amber pan bottom. Serve immediately with the cake and the whipped cream.

½ cup heavy cream, cold

3½ tablespoons sugar

1 tablespoon unsalted butter

2 large slices angel food cake

1 pear, ripe but firm, peeled, cored, and cut into 1-inch dice

PERSIMMON PUDDING

1⅓ cups all-purpose flour

2 teaspoons baking soda

½ teaspoon fine sea salt

1 teaspoon ground cinnamon

1 teaspoon ground ginger

1 large egg

1¼ cups persimmon puree

¾ cup sugar

10 tablespoons (1 stick plus
2 tablespoons) butter,
melted, plus more soft butter
for preparing the mold

⅔ cup orange juice

1 teaspoon vanilla extract

½ cup dried currants

Boiling water

NOTES: *To make this with fresh store-bought persimmons, simply push the soft ripe persimmons through a food mill, measure out 1¼ cups, and proceed with the recipe from there.*

This cake should be eaten warm, with lots of whipped cream.

If using a bowl instead of a mold, cover it with plastic wrap and then with a layer of foil.

Persimmons grow wild on the eastern edge of the Midwest, and quite densely in southern Indiana, where my sister-in-law, Sarah, lives. Some people gather them and make their own persimmon puree (not without difficulty, because the process involves milling out the large beetle-shaped seeds), but in places of high persimmon concentration you can buy the packaged pureed pulp nearly everywhere.

Unripe persimmons have a chalky, powerful amount of tannins—the same puckering acid present in rough red wines and unripe bananas—which dissipates completely when they're dead-ripe. The puree from ripe persimmons is sweet and mild, and I think it can go basically everywhere that pumpkin goes.

Persimmon pudding is a pudding in the English tradition, meaning that it's really a moist steamed cake. Brown and softly fruity, this one gets an acidic bump from the addition of orange juice, a persimmon cake trick that I picked up from Amanda Rockman, pastry chef of the Bristol in Chicago. Because of its brown color, Sarah's young kids often mistake the persimmon pudding for chocolate cake—and for now, she doesn't correct them.

SERVES 8

Butter a 9-cup English pudding mold or a 2-quart bowl. Set out a large stockpot into which the mold or bowl will fit comfortably.

Whisk the flour, baking soda, salt, cinnamon, and ginger together in a bowl. In another bowl whisk together the egg, persimmon puree, sugar, butter, orange juice, and vanilla.

Add the dry ingredients to the wet ingredients, and whisk until smooth. Add the currants and stir to incorporate.

Pour the batter into the prepared mold and clamp on the lid. Put the stockpot on a burner, set the mold in the stockpot, and pour in boiling water to reach two-thirds of the way up the sides of the mold. Bring the water to a simmer again over medium heat, and cover the stockpot tightly. Steam the pudding (adding more boiling water if necessary to maintain the level) over low heat until a thin skewer inserted in the center of the pudding comes out clean, 1½ to 2 hours.

Remove the mold from the hot water and let the pudding cool a bit before unmolding it.

STEAMED CUSTARDS
with Chokecherry Nectar

A pastry chef I once worked with told me that the secret to a really soft and delicate custard was replacing some of the cream with a more watery liquid—something he'd learned from making *chawanmushi*, the impossibly soft steamed Japanese custards made with eggs and brothy dashi.

For my rendition of the cold custard that my mother often kept on hand in our refrigerator, I now make a light and wobbly steamed custard and then top it with either homemade chokecherry nectar or homemade cassis.

To echo the woodland mood of the wild chokecherries, I like to infuse the cream with a few crushed juniper berries and a sprig of fresh rosemary. It sounds unlikely, but when mixed with sugar and milk, the scrubby herbal notes of these two piney aromatics naturally complement the chokecherries.

SERVES 8

Combine the cream, 1 cup water, the juniper berries, rosemary, and sugar in a medium saucepan set it over medium heat. Stand by the mixture as it heats. When a ring of bubbles forms at the edge, remove the pan from the heat, cover it, and let the mixture steep until it is just warm to touch.

In a medium bowl whisk together the eggs and egg yolks.

Prepare a large steamer with a lid, such as a double-decker bamboo steamer basket, over a wok or a pot of simmering water.

Pour the warm cream mixture slowly into the eggs, whisking constantly. Pour the entire custard through a fine-mesh strainer into a bowl or a pitcher.

Divide the custard among 8 half-pint glass jars and wrap the top of each one tightly with plastic wrap. Set the jars in the steamer, cover tightly with the lid, and steam gently until the custard jiggles tightly and evenly from edge to edge, 17 to 20 minutes.

Remove the steamer baskets and let the custards cool to room temperature. (You can also serve them chilled, but I think they're more properly trembly when just cool to the touch.)

To serve, top each custard with a thin layer of chokecherry nectar.

1½ cups heavy cream

10 dried juniper berries, smashed with the side of a knife

1 sprig fresh rosemary

½ cup sugar

2 large eggs

4 egg yolks

Chokecherry Nectar (page 279), for serving

NOTES: *You can make these in half-pint canning jars, which fit inside a bamboo steamer basket, but ceramic ramekins or shallow teacups are fine too.*

In place of the nectar you can use any purchased berry syrup or top the custards with a spoonful of barrel-aged maple syrup (see page 380).

GLORIFIED RICE PUDDING
with Candied Pineapple *and* Rum Cherries

¾ cup dried cherries

⅓ cup dark rum

2½ cups finely diced fresh pineapple (from ½ large pineapple)

⅓ cup (lightly packed) light brown sugar

1 tablespoon fresh lime juice

1 teaspoon vanilla extract

1 cup white rice, such as sushi or jasmine

2 tablespoons salted butter

1¾ cups whole milk

½ cup granulated sugar

Pinch of fine sea salt

1 3-inch cinnamon stick

1¾ cups whole-milk yogurt

1½ cups heavy cream

¾ cup slivered almonds, toasted, for serving

NOTES: *This is deliciously rummy, but if you want to avoid the rum, cook the dried cherries in apple juice.*

More than any other fruit, pineapple seems to pick up odors from the cutting board or the knife, so make sure to give your board and knife a good scrub before you begin, and immediately swoop the fruit to a bowl after cutting it.

Glorified Rice—or rice pudding mixed with canned fruit cocktail and Cool Whip topping—has a specific geographical place in the Midwestern buffet landscape. At fund-raiser dinners in my hometown it is always placed toward the end of the line—after the hotdishes and ham, after the cold macaroni salads and the savory Jell-O, but decidedly before the floodplain of sweet bars and coffee. Glorified Rice inhabits this hazy no-man's-land between salad and dessert, which makes me wonder if it has a proper home in either one. Perhaps it has always just belonged to the second pass, the return trip made for more meat, a hill of Glorified Rice, and another lemonade.

At my house, though, I make it for dessert. And while this version shares the name and spirit of the original, I have given it a massive overhaul.

Caramelized pineapple (a recipe I learned from pastry chef Pichet Ong when we worked at the restaurant 66 together) stands in for the canned tidbits, along with some rum-soaked sour cherries. Tangy whole-milk yogurt and a thick stream of liquid cream take the place of the commercial topping. And yet every kernel of rice is just like the classic: inflated, lovingly saturated with milk, almost buoyant.

SERVES 8 TO 10

Combine the cherries, rum, and 3 tablespoons water in a small saucepan and cook over medium heat until the cherries have absorbed the liquid, 3 minutes. Set aside to cool.

Combine the pineapple and brown sugar in a large skillet, and cook over medium heat until the pineapple caramelizes to a golden brown and the liquid in the pan clings to it, about 20 minutes. Stir in the lime juice and vanilla, and scrape the pineapple into a wide bowl to cool. (Both the pineapple and the cherries can be prepared a day or two ahead and stored in the refrigerator.)

Bring 8 cups of water to a boil in a saucepan, and add the rice. Boil for 4 minutes, just long enough to strip the starch from the rice. Drain.

Dry out the pan and add the butter. Melt it over medium heat, and then stir in the rice to coat it with the butter. Add the milk, sugar, salt, and cinnamon stick, and bring to a simmer.

Cover the pan tightly and reduce the heat to low. Steam until the rice is tender and has absorbed most of the milk, 30 to 35 minutes.

Turn the rice out onto a baking sheet to cool. Discard the cinnamon stick.

Put the cooled rice in a large bowl. Add the pineapple and cherries, and mix gently with a rubber spatula. Stir in the yogurt. Press a piece of plastic wrap directly on the surface of the pudding, and chill it thoroughly in the refrigerator, at least 2 hours or as long as overnight.

Before serving, paddle the rice well to loosen and add the cream, mixing until just combined. Turn the rice into a serving dish and garnish with the toasted almonds.

EARLY-

There are sweets, and then there is baking.

Growing up here, I have always felt a distinct but fuzzy difference between the two, and now I think it comes down to this: You make sweets with the intention of serving them as an after-dinner dessert. Baking, though, is generally a bit less sugar-forward, and it's what you do early in the day to take the chill out of the house, or just to get your hands in the dough, and it's more often served as a snack or offered to others as a gift.

A decision to bake also includes a desire for the process itself: time spent kneading, rolling, frosting, or sifting sugar over a pan of finished bars. I've found that many people who bake in quantity do it out of a benevolent impulse. As such, many of the recipes in this section are perfect for giving away: Peanut Maple Fudge Bars for the work potluck, a pan of Finger Rolls to bring to your aunt's house for soup night, a fragrant loaf of Curried Shaker Squash Bread for a friend who needs some comfort.

And if there is no occasion at all but you still can't shake the impulse to dust sugar and pat dough, you can always do as a retired woman in my cousins' hometown does: make a batch of Old-Fashioned Potato Doughnuts with Coffee Glaze (page 350) in time for midmorning coffee break and ferry them quickly to a local business whose employees might appreciate them, dropping them off while they're warm and still dripping.

LEMON BARS

This lemon bar is pretty canonical, with a pale, fragile bottom and a bright, bracing lemon curd. Like many lemon-bar aficionados, I like mine on the tart side, but not skewering. I've found that adding a teacup of sour cream rounds off the razor-sharp edge of lemon and brings the bar into balance, while still keeping it tart enough to effectively transport a midwinter Midwesterner someplace else. After all, isn't there a bit of fantasy in the sandy bottom and the searing tropical citrus beneath the topping of blinding white sugar? I think so.

MAKES 30 BARS

Preheat the oven to 350°F. Line a 9 × 13-inch baking pan with a piece of parchment paper, leaving at least 3 inches overhanging on two sides.

For the base, mix together 1½ cups of the flour, the confectioners' sugar, and the salt in a large bowl. Cut the butter into the flour with a pastry blender until it clumps together and only very small bits of butter remain. Distribute the mixture in the prepared baking pan, raking it with your fingertips to spread it out evenly and about ½ inch up the sides of the pan, and then patting it down. Bake the base until it is very light golden brown, 13 to 15 minutes.

Meanwhile, in a medium bowl, whisk together the sour cream, sugar, eggs, lemon juice, and remaining ⅔ cup flour until very smooth.

Pour the lemon filling onto the base and bake until set, 25 to 30 minutes. Let cool completely.

To serve, run a knife around the perimeter of the pan. Using the overhanging parchment as a handle, lift out the pastry and transfer it to a cutting board. Cut it into bars and dust thickly with confectioners' sugar shaken from a fine-mesh sieve.

1½ cups plus ⅔ cup all-purpose flour

½ cup confectioners' sugar, plus more for serving

½ teaspoon fine sea salt

10 tablespoons (1 stick plus 2 tablespoons) unsalted butter, cold, cut into cubes

¾ cup sour cream

2 cups sugar

4 large eggs

1 cup fresh lemon juice

TOFFEE BARS

12 tablespoons (1½ sticks)
  unsalted butter, plus more
  for the pan

1¾ cups all-purpose flour

1 teaspoon baking powder

½ teaspoon grated nutmeg

½ teaspoon fine sea salt

2 cups (lightly packed) light
  brown sugar

3 large eggs

1 teaspoon vanilla extract

½ cup whole hazelnuts

NOTE: *To dress them up, you can
drizzle melted milk chocolate over
these bars and stud the top with
large flakes of salt . . . but they're
perfect plain.*

Sometimes known as butterscotch bars, these buttery plain-Jane brown sugar bars are the most popular kind to tote to potlucks, school functions, and family emergencies. With no bold flavors to distract from their perfect chewiness, they're the chess pie of the Midwest, and they rate number one among children—and probably among most adults as well, if they'd admit it.

I like to scent this dough with nutmeg and to press hazelnuts into the batter before baking (the baking time allows for them to toast perfectly), although walnuts also work well.

MAKES 24 BARS

Preheat the oven to 350°F. Lightly butter a 9 × 13-inch baking pan, preferably a light-colored aluminum or steel pan. (Dark pans cause over-browning.)

Heat a large skillet over medium heat, add the butter, and cook until the butter foams and turns amber brown, about 3 minutes. Pour the butter into a large bowl and set aside until it's cool enough to touch.

Meanwhile, sift the flour, baking powder, nutmeg, and salt together into a bowl.

In the bowl of a stand mixer, or using a hand mixer, combine the brown sugar with the butter and mix until combined. Add the eggs and vanilla, and mix until smooth, thick, and light, about 3 minutes. Stir in the flour mixture and mix until incorporated.

Pour the batter into the prepared baking pan and spread it into an even layer, smoothing the top. Scatter the hazelnuts, pressing them lightly to submerge them about halfway in the batter.

Bake until the surface wrinkles evenly and turns nut brown, about 35 minutes. Let cool completely, at least 2 hours, before cutting the pastry into 2-inch bars.

Savor Wisconsin, *1984*

Savor Wisconsin

PEANUT MAPLE FUDGE BARS

Desserts made to resemble candy bars are very popular here in the rural Midwest, and when the candy bars being emulated come from the Pearson Candy Company in St. Paul, Minnesota, that's when I join in.

Pearson is a company that built its reputation on high-quality nuts and winning, no-nonsense combinations. The Nut Goodie bar, for example, which debuted in 1912, is still a marvel: a thick peanut butter–infused layer of chocolate enrobing a maple fudge filling dotted with fresh peanuts.

The only thing I added was a chocolate shortbread base, to facilitate lifting and handling. I stuck with a simple maple fudge made with sweetened condensed milk (the candy-maker's friend), softened with a lump of cream cheese. The base is the only thing that requires baking; the rest is just a matter of chilling and layering.

I cut these smaller than other bars because they're so rich.

MAKES 25 SMALL BARS

Preheat the oven to 350°F. Line an 8-inch-square baking pan with two pieces of parchment paper, leaving at least 3 inches overhanging on all sides.

For the base, mix together the flour, confectioners' sugar, cocoa powder, and salt in a medium bowl. Add the melted butter and mix thoroughly until you have a soft dough. Break the dough into small pebbles and spread it evenly in the bottom of the lined baking pan, then gently press the dough into the pan in an even layer. Bake until it turns a shake darker, 15 minutes. Let base cool a bit.

Meanwhile, make the chocolate layer: Put the chocolate in the top of a double boiler, or in a metal bowl set over a pan of simmering water. Add the peanut butter and heat gently until melted and combined, stirring occasionally.

Pour ½ cup of the warm melted chocolate mixture over the baked base, and spread it out evenly. Refrigerate until set. Reserve the remaining chocolate mixture on top of the stove while you prepare the maple filling.

RECIPE CONTINUES

BASE

¾ cup flour

¼ cup confectioners' sugar

2 tablespoons unsweetened cocoa powder

Pinch of fine sea salt

4 tablespoons (½ stick) melted salted butter plus 6 tablespoons (¾ stick)

CHOCOLATE LAYER

10 ounces semisweet chocolate, chopped

½ cup smooth peanut butter

MAPLE FUDGE

8 tablespoons (1 stick) salted butter

⅔ cup sweetened condensed milk

¾ cup maple syrup

1 cup (lightly packed) light brown sugar

⅛ teaspoon salt

3 tablespoons cream cheese

◻ ◻

¾ cup lightly salted roasted peanuts

For the maple filling, melt the butter in a 2-quart saucepan over medium heat. Add the sweetened condensed milk, maple syrup, brown sugar, and salt and bring to a simmer. Boil softly, stirring often, for 10 minutes, or until the mixture reaches the firm ball stage, or 245°F on a candy thermometer. (Gauge the doneness using the cold-water test: Fill a bowl with very cold water and drop about ½ teaspoon of the mixture into it. If it forms a soft ball that you can easily pick up, it's ready.)

Fill a sink with at least 6 inches of cold water, and set the saucepan into it (making sure not to slosh water into the fudge). Stir constantly with a sharp-edged wooden spoon, scraping down the sides of the pot, until the mixture starts to turn granular, about 5 minutes. When it starts to look like beach sand and becomes increasingly hard to stir, remove the pan from the water and add the cream cheese. Stir, scraping the sides, until the mixture is smooth and light.

Immediately spread the maple filling in an even layer over the cooled chocolate layer. Scatter the peanuts on top and press them very lightly into the maple filling.

Gently heat the remaining chocolate mixture to return it to a liquid state. Drop the chocolate from the side of a rubber spatula onto the maple layer, making wide swipes across the peanuts, taking care to cover them completely.

Return the baking pan to the refrigerator and chill until completely set, about 4 hours. Cut into small bars.

POPPY-SEED STREUSEL BARS

When I was growing up, my family ate poppy-seed coffeecake at every occasion, momentous or minor, all year long. Made following a family recipe from my great-grandmother's Bohemian side, the cake was composed of a rich bread dough swirled with a jammy poppy-seed filling and topped with a rubble of pale sugary streusel. My grandma cut it into long rectangles and set it in the middle of her kitchen table next to the other ever-presents: the plate of butter, the paper napkins, and the dish of dill pickles. "Mudding" the cut sides with a heavy coat of butter was the only acceptable way to eat it.

The rich poppy-seed filling was the clue to the family origins (pointing east of Germany, certainly), but the pale buttery streusel on top was my favorite part. One day when I didn't have time to wait for the yeast dough to rise, I decided to keep the filling and lose the cake, and just make everything out of the streusel.

The resulting bar is more delicate than the cake, as crisp as a sugar cookie at the edges with a buttery, chewy bottom and a midnight-colored slash of tangy poppy seed–raisin filling. Most bar cookie recipes use brown sugar or oats to make a soft pat-in-the-pan crust, but this one sticks with the earlier era's white ingredients: just soft butter, white sugar, white flour. The tenderness of this dough reminds us why those refinements were made in the first place.

This recipe will have you up to your wrists in damp sugar sand. It's totally farmhouse luxurious.

MAKES 30 BARS

¾ cup poppy seeds

¾ cup whole milk

1 cup raisins

3 cups sugar

½ cup heavy cream

2 teaspoons apple cider vinegar

3 cups all-purpose flour

½ teaspoon fine sea salt

1½ cups (3 sticks) salted butter, at room temperature, cut into chunks, plus more for the pan

Combine the poppy seeds and milk in a blender and process on high speed, stopping a few times to scrape down the sides, until the poppy seeds look bruised and broken. Add the raisins, 1 cup of the sugar, the cream, and the vinegar. Process until smooth and no bumps of raisin remain.

Pour the mixture into a medium skillet and bring to a simmer over medium heat. Stirring often to prevent it from sticking to the bottom of the skillet, cook at a slow bubble (reducing the heat as the mixture reduces and thickens) until the poppy-seed mixture shows a wide trail when you swipe the bottom of the skillet with a spoon and it has the texture of applesauce or warm jam, about 30 minutes. (You can make this filling ahead of time and refrigerate it.)

RECIPE CONTINUES

Preheat the oven to 375°F. Lightly butter a 9 × 13-inch baking pan.

In a large bowl, combine the flour, remaining 2 cups sugar, the salt, and the butter. With your hands, work the butter into the flour until it feels damp and holds its shape when squeezed in your palm. Scoop 5 loose cups of the streusel mixture into the prepared baking pan. Rake the streusel with your hands, as you would sand, until it feels evenly spread out; then gently press the crust into the pan. Bake the bottom crust until just set, 12 to 15 minutes. Let the crust cool for 10 minutes.

Pour the poppy-seed mixture over the crust and smooth it to within ½ inch of the edge with a flat knife or offset spatula. Squeeze the remaining streusel mixture into nuggets and drop them decoratively on top, leaving a few places for the filling to show through.

Bake until the peaks of the streusel turn light golden brown, 35 to 40 minutes. Cool in the pan before cutting into 2-inch squares.

Grinding Poppy Seeds

To expose the real flavor of poppy seeds, they need to be cracked or ground flat.

You can use a hand-cranked grinder, which is how many modern-day Eastern Europeans do it. Years ago most American kitchens were equipped with a hand grinder mounted on the counter, which was used to grind ham for ham salad, or to grind poppy seeds or nuts. Now you can find these hand grinders in junk shops, but in my experience they're usually rusty.

You can also grind poppy seeds in a clean coffee grinder or, as my grandma did later in life, you can mix them with liquid and grind them in a blender. The only point is to grind them finely—on the recipe card my grandma has "finely" underlined three times for emphasis. The final result should look like an espresso grind.

And whatever you do, do not open the blender top while you're blending. Poppy seeds will fly all over your kitchen, and they are insidiously tiny and resistant to wiping up, worse than glitter.

NOTE: *New grinders can be purchased at Lehman Hardware & Appliances, www.lehmans.com.*

Mom's BUTTER CARAMELS

2 cups heavy cream

2 cups sugar

1 cup (2 sticks) unsalted butter, plus more for the pan

2 cups light corn syrup

Large pinch of fine sea salt

2 teaspoons vanilla extract, or 1 vanilla bean, slit and pulp scraped

2 cups whole walnuts or pecans, toasted (optional)

NOTE: *Light corn syrup is what keeps these caramels soft. You can also use Lyle's Golden Syrup, although it will give the flavor of the caramels another dimension.*

Small caramels wrapped individually in waxed paper are holiday currency here, and you see them everywhere: next to the cash register, in the bowl at the salon, and at Christmas parties. Usually they're made with brown sugar. My mother makes her caramels with white sugar cooked to the same lucid amber color, and in hers you can really taste the butter. Her caramels are softer than any others—just firm enough to hold in your hand—and much more prone to melt in your mouth.

As a child, I remember legions of women in this town asking my mother for this recipe (and she gave it away to only a few), so I thank her for letting me print it.

MAKES ABOUT 100 CARAMELS

Butter an 8-inch-square baking pan, preferably one with sloped easy-release corners, such as a Pyrex baking dish.

In a heavy wide-bottomed stockpot (enameled cast-iron or thick stainless steel would work well), combine 1 cup of the cream with the sugar, butter, corn syrup, and salt. Bring very slowly to a simmer. After the mixture has boiled for a few minutes, add the remaining 1 cup cream. Cook steadily over medium-high heat, keeping the bubbles coming, stirring intermittently with a wooden spoon, and scraping down the sides of the pot now and then.

Cook the caramel until it reaches the low end of the soft ball stage, or 238°F on a candy thermometer. (To test it by hand, prepare a bowl of ice-cold water. Drop about a teaspoon of hot caramel from your spoon into the water and immediately gather the caramel into a ball and pull it out of the water. At the correct consistency, the ball should hold together but sort of droop in your hand.)

When the caramel can form a soft ball, add the vanilla extract (or vanilla pulp and pod), and the nuts, if using. Stir to combine, and pour the mixture into the prepared pan, scraping the pot to get it all. Let the caramel cool at room temperature overnight before slicing.

To portion the caramels, cut a large stack of 6-inch squares of waxed paper. Cut around the perimeter of the baking pan to loosen the caramel, and running a spatula beneath it, flip the entire block of caramel onto a cutting board in one piece. Cut 10 long strips, and then cut the strips crosswise into 10 pieces each so that you have 100 two-bite rectangles of caramel.

Roll each caramel in a piece of waxed paper, twisting the ends to secure them. These last for months at room temperature, and leftovers can be melted down for making caramel apples or for using as the base for caramel rolls.

CHOCOLATE CHIP COOKIES

1½ cups (3 sticks) unsalted butter, at room temperature

2 cups granulated sugar

2 cups (lightly packed) light brown sugar

1 scant cup peanut butter

3 large eggs

2 tablespoons brewed coffee, cool

1½ teaspoons vanilla extract

4⅔ cups all-purpose flour

2 teaspoons baking soda

1½ teaspoons fine sea salt

2 12-ounce bags semisweet chocolate chips, or 24 ounces semisweet chocolate, chopped

NOTE: *For best results, chill the dough thoroughly before baking.*

I now think of chocolate chip cookies as wintry fare, but in childhood, I vividly remember them belonging to summer: They were stored in a clean gallon ice cream bucket with a vicious plastic snap top, into which we kids dug repeatedly, blindly, fishing around until we felt the melting eye of a chip before tearing off outside with a few in hand. I now understand the logic: cookies are good portable summer food. Like sandwiches, stone fruits, and corn on the cob, cookies give energy without requiring utensils. (And they are lake food par excellence: I will never forget that sensation of eating a chocolate chip cookie with a wet hand, pacing in the shallows, my bottom half submerged in the lake.)

In the spirit of summer and entertaining, this recipe makes a large batch. (Freeze half of the dough in a long cylinder if you don't want to bake it all at once.) Plush and chewy, these are new-style, with some added peanut butter for flavor and plenty of half-melted chocolate. For best results, chill the dough overnight and make the cookies big so that the centers stay moist and just ever-so-underbaked. They're best within two days of baking, but I must weakly confess that older cookies bounce back perfectly when microwaved for exactly 20 seconds each.

MAKES 48 COOKIES

Preheat the oven to 375°F.

In the bowl of a stand mixer fitted with the paddle attachment, beat the butter until it's soft and light. Add the granulated and brown sugars, and beat until well incorporated and slightly fluffier, about 3 minutes. Add the peanut butter and mix until combined. Add the eggs one at a time, beating until each is incorporated before adding the next, and then mix in the coffee and vanilla.

Measure the flour, baking soda, and salt into a bowl and whisk to combine. Add the flour to the butter mixture in four additions, beating slowly. Stir in the chocolate chips by hand. If you have time, chill the dough.

Drop large (3-tablespoon) cookies onto light-colored cookie sheets, leaving room for them to spread. Bake until golden brown on top, 12 to 14 minutes. For a chewy texture, don't overbake.

Curried SHAKER SQUASH BREAD

Come fall, any rural kitchen hooked to a garden will be overrun with winter squash and pumpkins. You see them overflowing wagons, sitting on newsprint pads in garages and basements, and piled next to front doors in a state that is half decoration and half short-term storage.

If you have plans to keep them for the winter in any kind of quantity, stewing them down into a puree and canning or freezing it is your best bet. Some things never change, and the Midwest is flush with recipes that call for that squash or pumpkin puree: pies, breads, and savory bakes.

This bread is based on one I found in a book of Shaker recipes that I picked up while visiting the Amana Colonies in Amana, Iowa. I added a bit of curry. Composed of mostly sweet spices, the flavor is about 95 percent perfectly expected, but just off-center enough to keep things interesting.

MAKES 1 LOAF

Preheat the oven to 350°F. Rub a 9 × 5-inch loaf pan with a little butter and coat it with a thin layer of flour; tap out the excess flour.

Sift the flour, curry powder, baking soda, baking powder, salt, cinnamon, and cloves together into a medium bowl.

Whisk the sugar and butter together in a large bowl. With a hand mixer, beat in one egg and whip until lightened. Add the second egg and whip until thickened, pale yellow, creamy, and fluffy. Add the squash puree and beat until combined. Then add the milk. Add the flour mixture to the batter and mix with a wooden spoon until just combined.

Pour the batter into the prepared loaf pan, and bake until a tester comes out clean, 60 to 65 minutes.

Unmold the bread while it is still warm, but let it cool completely on a wire rack before slicing.

Unsalted butter, at room temperature, for the pan

1½ cups all-purpose flour, plus more for the pan

1¾ teaspoons curry powder

1 teaspoon baking soda

¼ teaspoon baking powder

½ teaspoon fine sea salt

½ teaspoon ground cinnamon

¼ teaspoon ground cloves

1 cup sugar

8 tablespoons (1 stick) salted butter, melted

2 large eggs

1 cup buttercup squash puree or canned pumpkin

¼ cup whole milk

Old-Fashioned
POTATO DOUGHNUTS *with* COFFEE GLAZE

DOUGHNUTS

1 large (about 1 pound) russet potato, cubed

¾ cup granulated sugar

3 tablespoons salted butter, melted

3 large eggs

¾ cup buttermilk

3 to 4 cups canola oil

3 cups all-purpose flour, plus more for shaping

5 teaspoons baking powder

1 teaspoon salt

1 teaspoon grated nutmeg

COFFEE GLAZE

⅓ cup strong brewed coffee or espresso, cold

2 teaspoons vanilla extract

3 cups confectioners' sugar, plus more for dusting (optional)

This is an old family recipe, but I found a nearly identical version in the *Greatest Chefs of the Midwest*, a cookbook from the 1920s, so it's a recipe that must have been in heavy circulation at some point. I can see how it would have been very popular because of the addition of mashed potatoes, which most farm families usually had left over from the noonday meal.

Here mashed potatoes effect their usual magic on the dough, adding an almost surreal lightness as well as extra staying power—although these craggy nutmeg-scented doughnuts rarely last long.

The coffee glaze can conveniently be made out of the morning's leftover cold coffee. My grandmother always rolled the doughnuts twice in confectioners' sugar instead; first when hot and a second time once cool.

MAKES 12 DOUGHNUTS AND 12 DOUGHNUT HOLES PLUS SCRAPS

Put the potato cubes in a saucepan and cover generously with water. Bring to a boil, cover, and simmer over medium heat until the potatoes are very tender when poked with a thin fork, 20 minutes. Drain the potatoes and push them through a potato ricer or a sieve into a bowl.

Measure 1 lightly packed cup of potato into a large bowl, add the sugar and butter, and whisk to combine. Whisk in the eggs and buttermilk.

Pour at least 4 inches of oil into a large, deep pot, and heat it to 380°F. (The oil will rise up another 4 inches with the addition of the doughnuts, so make sure your pot is large enough to contain it.)

Sift the flour, baking powder, salt, and nutmeg together into a bowl. Sift half of the flour mixture into the potato mixture, mixing with a wooden spoon until combined. Add the rest of the flour and mix until just combined. The dough will be a little sticky. Turn the dough out onto a well-floured surface and pat it out with floured hands until it is about ½ inch thick.

Using a doughnut cutter, cut out 12 doughnuts. Gently transfer each circle to a floured plate to await frying, reserving all the holes for a single fry batch.

Add 3 or 4 doughnuts to the hot oil, as many as will fit in a single layer. (Don't worry if they droop or twist. Craggy, crunchy, messy doughnuts are possibly more delicious than perfect doughnuts.) Fry them to a deep brown on one side and then gently flip them with chopsticks or a pair of tongs, and fry the other side to a deep brown. Remove with a slotted spoon or a skimmer to a wire rack to drain.

Bring the oil back to 380°F each time before frying the remaining doughnuts, holes, and the scraps, too. (Cook's treats.)

For the coffee glaze, combine the coffee and vanilla in a large bowl. Add the confectioners' sugar, cup by cup, whisking until combined and smooth.

To glaze the doughnuts, plant them face-down in the glaze, turn them up, and set them on a rack to drain and set. Alternatively, dunk them in confectioners' sugar.

PEANUT BUTTER GRANOLA

½ cup light honey

¼ cup smooth peanut butter

1 teaspoon ground cinnamon

Pinch of fine sea salt

8 tablespoons (1 stick) salted butter

4 cups old-fashioned rolled oats

1 cup unsweetened shredded coconut

1 cup roasted salted peanuts

1 cup dried currants or raisins

In the 1970s, back-to-the-landers, both the dabblers and the truly committed, moved to areas of the rural Midwest where land was affordable. At that time around here, land was going for a dollar an acre, which is about as cheap as it gets. Years later, I am appreciative of the gifts that generation brought with them, including elaborate rainwater storage, a solid campfire tradition, solar panels, good music, and granola.

Adding a lump of peanut butter to my basic granola recipe has an oddly tenderizing effect, giving the granola streusel-like qualities. It's quite savory, and stands up well to sweet milk.

MAKES 6 CUPS

Preheat the oven to 325°F.

Heat the butter in a medium skillet over medium heat until the foam turns amber.

Whisk the honey, peanut butter, 2 tablespoons water, cinnamon, and salt together in a large bowl until smooth. Whisk in the browned butter in a stream until the mixture is emulsified and smooth. With a wooden spoon or a rubber spatula, mix in the oats, coconut, and peanuts.

Divide the granola evenly between two heavy baking sheets, spreading it out evenly. (I line mine with either a silicone sheet or parchment paper for easier cleanup.) Bake for 20 minutes.

Pull the baking sheets from the oven and spoon the darkening edges of the granola into the center, and then spread it out evenly again. Sprinkle with the currants. Bake until the granola is dark amber brown, 5 to 10 minutes.

If you like your granola clumpy (as I do), don't stir it again when it comes out of the oven; let it cool completely on the baking sheets before transferring it to an airtight container. The granola will keep for about 2 weeks.

CARDAMOM CARAMEL ROLLS

Early in my freshman year of college, I received a heavy box from my mom in the mail. I was surprised to find that it contained a dozen sweet rolls, each one fully impregnated with homemade butter caramel. I brought them back to the quad, where the girls and I polished them off. Later that night, my mom called and said, "Did you get the caramel rolls? You should really share those." I responded that I had. "Oh good," she said, relieved. "Because when I went to mail that box I couldn't believe that it weighed twelve pounds. That's a pound a piece!"

I've come to think of those rolls as "the freshman twelve" in a box. And now I know: when it comes to sweets, it's best not to weigh them.

Instead of the customary cinnamon, I take a cue from the Finnish bakery in nearby Menahga and add a hefty pinch of cardamom to the caramel, which casts the rolls in a more floral, romantic light.

MAKES 12 ROLLS

To make the dough, combine the water and pinch of sugar in a small bowl, sprinkle the yeast on top, and jostle the bowl gently to submerge the yeast. Within 5 minutes the yeast should activate and look foamy; if not, begin again with fresh yeast.

In a large mixing bowl, combine the milk, eggs, remaining 2 tablespoons sugar, the salt, and 1 cup of the flour. Whisk until smooth. Add the proofed yeast mixture and the remaining 3¼ cups flour, and switching to a broad wooden spoon, mix until the dough comes together. Turn the dough out onto a lightly floured surface and knead it, with the assistance of a dough scraper, adding the butter in chunks, stretching the corners of dough to the center, turning, stretching again, and repeating, until all of the butter has been incorporated.

Put the dough into a lightly oiled large bowl, flipping the dough to coat the top with oil. Cover with a clean kitchen towel and leave to rise in a warm room until doubled in size, a little over 1 hour. Then punch down the dough and refrigerate until cold, at least 2 hours and as long as overnight.

Meanwhile, prepare the caramel: In a medium bowl, mix together the butter, brown sugar, honey, heavy cream, rum,

SWEET DOUGH

¼ cup lukewarm water

2 tablespoons plus a pinch of granulated sugar

2¼ teaspoons active dry yeast

1 cup whole milk

2 large eggs

1 teaspoon fine sea salt

4¼ cups white bread (high-gluten) flour, plus more if necessary

12 tablespoons (1½ sticks) unsalted butter, at cool room temperature

Canola oil, for the bowl

CARAMEL

6 tablespoons (¾ stick) unsalted butter, at room temperature

1¼ cups (lightly packed) light brown sugar

¾ cup light honey

½ cup heavy cream

1 tablespoon rum

¾ teaspoon ground cardamom seeds (preferably freshly ground)

¼ teaspoon fine sea salt

SUGAR LAYER

½ cup granulated sugar

4 tablespoons (½ stick) unsalted butter, at room temperature

RECIPE CONTINUES

NOTE: *It's always a conundrum: How do you have freshly baked caramel rolls ready in time for brunch? Instead of refrigerating the raw filled buns overnight and then taking them out early in the morning to thaw and rise—which takes hours, because the dough and the pan are both stone-cold—I've started rolling out the chilled dough in the morning. If you set the buns in a room-temperature pan, it takes only about an hour for them to rise, because the rolling takes a lot of the chill out of the dough.*

cardamom, and salt; beat until combined. Spread this mixture evenly over the bottom of a 9 × 13-inch baking pan.

Roll the chilled dough on a lightly floured surface to form a rectangle a little larger than the baking pan, about 10 × 14 inches.

For the sugar layer, combine the granulated sugar and butter in a small bowl. Spread this mixture in a thin layer over the rolled-out dough.

Starting at one of the long sides, roll the dough into a tight cylinder. With a serrated knife, cut the dough into 12 equal rolls. Arrange the rolls in 3 rows of 4 rolls each in the baking pan. Set the pan, covered with a thin towel, in a warm place and leave the rolls to double in size, about 1 hour.

Meanwhile, preheat the oven to 350°F.

Bake the rolls until the tops turn dark brown, 45 minutes.

Let the rolls cool for 5 to 10 minutes. Then carefully upend them: Invert a baking sheet over the baking pan, and using two pot holders, grip the pan and sheet together and quickly flip them over.

Serve the rolls warm or at room temperature. Tightly wrap any leftover caramel rolls and reheat them slightly before serving.

MORNING BUNS

You can find morning buns everywhere in Madison, Wisconsin (but curiously not in nearby Door County, Wisconsin, or in Minneapolis . . .). They're sort of a mash-up of the caramel roll and a sugar-heavy cinnamon bun. Unlike caramel rolls, which are generally baked in a pan, morning buns are always baked in jumbo muffin tins so that all of the sweet buns' edges take on a crunchy coat of sparkly sugar.

Combine the ¾ cup maple sugar, ¾ cup granulated sugar, cinnamon, and nutmeg in a dish. Mix well.

Generously butter and sugar a 12-cup jumbo muffin pan.

Roll out the chilled dough to form a large rectangle, about 10 × 14 inches, on a lightly floured surface.

Spread the butter in a thin layer over the dough. Sprinkle the maple sugar mixture evenly over the butter, and press it down gently.

Starting at one of the long sides, roll the dough into a tight cylinder. With a serrated knife, cut the dough into 12 equal rolls. Place a roll in each of the muffin cups, and let them rise in a warm place until doubled in size, 45 minutes to 1 hour.

Meanwhile, preheat the oven to 350°F.

Combine the remaining ¼ cup maple sugar and ¼ cup granulated sugar in a shallow bowl, and stir together well.

Bake the buns until the tops turn dark brown, 30 to 35 minutes.

Let the rolls cool for 10 minutes. Then carefully upend them: Invert a baking sheet over the muffin pan, and using two pot holders, grip the pan and sheet together and quickly flip them over. Immediately roll the hot buns in the sugar mixture to coat.

Serve the buns warm or at room temperature. Tightly wrap any leftover buns in foil and reheat them slightly before serving.

- ¾ cup (lightly packed) maple sugar or light brown sugar, plus ¼ cup for rolling the finished buns

- ¾ cup granulated sugar, plus ¼ cup for the pans and rolling the finished buns

- 1 teaspoon ground cinnamon

- ½ teaspoon grated nutmeg

- Sweet dough (see page 353), prepared through the first rise and refrigerated until cold

- 6 tablespoons (¾ stick) unsalted butter, at room temperature, plus more for the pan

FINGER ROLLS

1 russet potato, cubed

2 teaspoons (scant 1 packet) active dry yeast

Pinch plus 3 tablespoons sugar

1¾ teaspoons fine sea salt

¾ cup whole milk

1 large egg

5 cups white bread (high-gluten) flour, plus more for shaping

Canola oil, for the bowl

4 tablespoons (½ stick) unsalted butter, at room temperature, plus more for the pans

They're called "finger rolls" after the width of the puffy folded buns all stacked in a loaf pan, and they are exactly the kind of bun you hope you'll find when you head down to the church basement for the lunch following a family event. Passed the length of a banquet table, these soothing, buttery white pull-aparts are very community-building.

You can make the dough in a standing mixer if you prefer, but it's pretty quick to whip it together by hand. And don't worry about the uneven line of your folded buns in the pan: When the bread rises it fills in all gaping holes, and I say, the more irregular the better.

Kids love to make sandwiches from these rolls because they can pull two pieces from the loaf without using a knife.

MAKES 24 ROLLS

Put the potato cubes in a saucepan, cover with plenty of cold, lightly salted water, and bring to a simmer. Cover and cook until they are very tender, about 20 minutes. Strain, reserving the cooking water separately. Put the cooked potato in a small bowl, cover with about 1 cup of the potato water, and mash with a potato masher until smooth, making a cloudy potato-water pulp.

Measure out ¼ cup of the remaining plain potato water, and let it cool in a small bowl. When it reaches bathwater temperature (about 110°F), add the yeast and the pinch of sugar and shake the bowl to submerge them. Within 5 minutes the yeast should activate and look foamy; if not, begin again with fresh yeast.

In a large mixing bowl, combine the mashed potato pulp with the remaining 3 tablespoons sugar, the salt, proofed yeast mixture, milk, egg, and 2 cups of the flour, whisking until smooth. Switching to a wooden spoon, vigorously beat the batter until strings of gluten form, 2 to 3 minutes. Add the remaining 3 cups flour cup by cup, beating as you go, until the dough begins to clean the bowl. Turn the dough out onto a lightly floured surface and begin to knead, stretching the corners of the dough to the center, turning, and adding more flour as needed to keep it from sticking terribly to your hands. Knead for 8 to 10 minutes, until the dough is bouncy and perfectly smooth.

Oil a large bowl and add the dough ball, turning to coat the dough with oil. Cover it with a clean kitchen towel and leave it in a warm room to rise until doubled in size, 1½ to 2 hours.

Punch down the dough and leave it to rise again until doubled in size, about 1 hour.

Preheat the oven to 375°F. Brush two 8½ × 4½-inch loaf pans with soft butter.

Divide the dough into two equal pieces. Roll each ball of dough into an 18 × 12-inch rectangle, a little bigger than a legal pad. Brush the rectangles with the butter. With a large knife, cut each rectangle of dough into 3 long strips and then cut it crosswise into 4 pieces, making 12 pieces per dough ball. Fold down the top half of each square to make a rectangle. Stack the rectangles, edges facing down, in the prepared loaf pans.

Set the pans in a warm place, covered with light towels, and leave the rolls to double in size, 1 to 1½ hours.

Meanwhile, preheat the oven to 350°F.

Bake the rolls until dark golden brown, 30 to 35 minutes. Invert the pans to remove the loaves, and serve each loaf in a towel-lined rectangular basket.

CREAM POTATO LEFSE

4 large (2½ pounds) russet potatoes, unpeeled

1 cup heavy cream

⅔ cup vegetable oil

6 tablespoons sugar

3 teaspoons fine sea salt

1¾ cups all-purpose flour, plus more for rolling

Lefse is a thin Norwegian potato flatbread traditionally made for the Christmas table. Not unlike a flour tortilla, it is cooked on a hot griddle until lightly browned on both sides. The delicate dough requires some finesse to work with, but it's easy once you get the hang of it.

Sometimes I assist my mother-in-law, Carolyn, in making a giant batch for the holidays, a process that goes quickly when you have the right setup, which includes a cloth-covered rolling pin, a cloth-covered rolling board, and a wide electric griddle. In areas with a Scandinavian-heritage population, you can find these items at any hardware store.

In Norwegian-American families, the buttering and rolling of the *lefse* for the holiday dinner table is a task that always falls to one of the kids, and even now my husband, Aaron, continues to take his duty seriously. A strict butter-only advocate, he vocalizes when someone (usually me) sprinkles a piece with sugar. If his grandfather, Ingvald Annexstad, were still around, he'd vehemently agree with his grandson and, I'm certain, roll that buttered *lefse* around a bat of cold leftover *lutefisk*.

MAKES ABOUT 36 *LEFSE*

Put the potatoes in a saucepan, add enough water to cover generously, and salt the water. Cover and cook at a slow simmer over medium heat until the potatoes are tender when poked with a fork, about 40 minutes. Drain, and push through a ricer into a bowl, discarding the skin. Measure 7 cups very lightly packed riced potatoes into a large bowl (save the rest for another purpose).

Immediately add the cream, oil, sugar, and salt to the potatoes and mix until smooth. Let cool to room temperature, and then store in the refrigerator, uncovered, until very cold, at least 3 hours and preferably overnight.

Preheat an electric griddle to 450°F.

Add the flour to the potato dough and mix with a wooden spoon to combine. Scoop up a golf-ball-size ball of dough and pat it into a 3-inch-diameter round on a heavily floured surface. Roll out the *lefse*, letting the roller sit lightly in your hands so that its weight flattens the dough into a 6-inch-diameter round.

Run your flat *lefse* stick (or thin spatula) underneath the dough and flip it onto the hot griddle. Cook until brown spots form on both sides, about 1 minute; you want it cooked through but still pliant enough to roll. Stack the *lefse* on a plate, and when they are cool, store the pile in a plastic bag at room temperature.

NOTES: Lefse *need not be reserved for the holiday season. It's handy to have around as a snack, goes well with soup, and can be put to use as a sandwich wrap for ham, cheese, or pickles.*

To get the traditional setup for rolling lefse, *gather together a long wooden lefse stick, a cloth-covered board for rolling (this prevents the soft dough from sticking), and a heavy rolling pin, covered with a sleeve. Traditional lefse pins are as thick as softball bats and deeply ridged.*

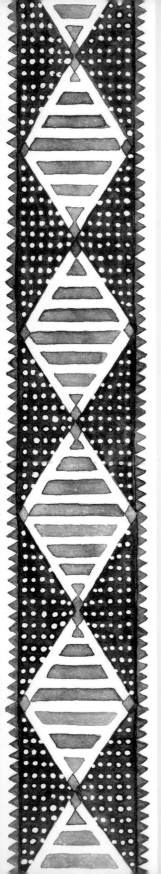

Cookstove Bread

When we first lived in the cabin, we didn't have any power or running water, and there were two groups of people—the older descendants of the original homesteading Two Inlets families and the crew of back-to-the-landers who settled here in the 1970s—whose expertise was invaluable to us. (And still is.)

Most of our elderly neighbors around Two Inlets didn't get electricity until the 1950s, and so their back sheds were still filled with things that could be of use to us. It seemed that every time we visited they gave us something new—which was usually something old. We brought home parts for our discontinued machines, kerosene lanterns, water kettles, four-sided stovetop toasters, pressure cookers . . . and a lot of advice. (Because of this time I am the proud owner of at least three old pressure cookers, the oversize aluminum ones that look like bombs with their many clamp locks and gauges; they continue to terrify me and to take up valuable storage space.) As our unannounced visits became more regular, and our place became more organized, they lent us their stories in increasingly large measure.

By the time we met Mike Schultz, he was in his eighties. When he wasn't out in his large garden he was sitting in his chair across from a big black woodstove that filled an awkwardly large footprint in the modern kitchen. The air in the house still held the scent of old creosote, the smoke having long ago soaked into the drywall. The place was homey, but the kitchen had one of the telltale signs of having been vacated by a woman: a John Deere calendar hung too centrally, the first thing you saw.

We had come to get large rocks to line the dirt walls of our well pit, and he was amused to be parting with them. "Buy them?" He laughed at my overly polite offer, and then raised me. "What would you say to twenty dollars a load? That's a deal. I spent so many years picking those rocks, they're probably worth triple that."

He told us how he personally grubbed out the stumps in his fields, which now comprise one of the most epic, pastoral landscapes in Two Inlets. Like many people of his generation, he never gained any faith in the practice of spreading pesticides and herbicides on his crops, preferring to stick to the old-fashioned fertilizer: manure. This made his fields organic, but he never mentioned it.

He ran pigs in the fields behind the house to let them dig up the last of the stumps and leave their droppings, and later he planted potatoes there. One particularly good year in the late 1980s, when he had more potatoes than he could eat, he trucked them to the restaurants and grocery stores in town to sell them—and came back home with every one of them. Even offered dirt-cheap, the proprietors all preferred to buy potatoes from their distributors, which came from who knows where. He couldn't understand it.

And then there was the time we stopped by to drop off a loaf of white bread I'd made from my grandma's recipe. It reminded him of his wife, who at this time was living in the nursing home. Pointing at the big black wood-fired cookstove sitting in the middle of the room, he said, "She wouldn't give it up. She made the best bread you've ever tasted in that thing. She baked a few times a week, in the winter or in the middle of a heatwave. Her bread had a shiny top. Like cherry wood." In their move from their original house to the newer one, his wife refused to do her baking in the new modern stove, which explains why the cookstove sat where it did, bulging halfway into the living room. Our neighbors confirmed the reason that she refused to make the shift: Her bread had really been something to be proud of, high and light with a burnished brown crust.

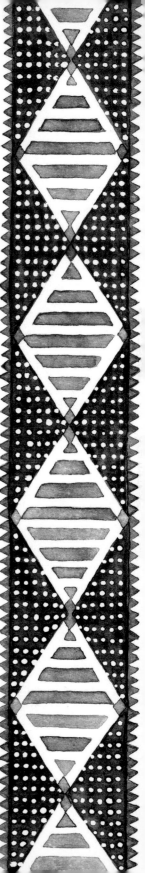

Addie's Farmhouse
WHITE BREAD

1 large (12 ounces) russet
    potato, cubed

2½ teaspoons active dry yeast

Pinch plus 3 tablespoons sugar

¼ cup solid vegetable
    shortening, melted, plus
    more for forming the loaves

2 teaspoons salt

7 cups bread flour, plus more
    for kneading

Canola oil, for the bowl

NOTE: *To make properly springy
white bread, you need fresh, high-
protein bread flour. If you can find
fine, white flour with the germ added
back in, all the better.*

My grandmother Adeline Hesch won a purple Grand Champion ribbon with this recipe for farmhouse white bread at the Minnesota State Fair in 1938. She was just a teenager, and often described the mouths of all the old ladies falling agape as she walked up to claim her prize.

My grandma always whaled on her bread, her arms spinning as if connected to a steam wheel, and it came out beautifully. She taught me to pause at a certain point in the process, when you have added about half of the flour but the dough is still wet and sticky, and spend a few minutes in an isolated spell of heavy beating to "work the gluten." If you do it right, the dough begins to stiffen and roll in its bowl, air bubbles rise to the surface, and strings of dough cling to the sides of the bowl before snapping off.

Then she added the rest of the flour and began to knead it. With the right amount of flour, the bread would squeak—*tweek! tweek!*—as if there were birds inside taking the brunt of each fresh punch.

Her finished loaves would pass a crucial test: When she pinched off a clump from a slice and pulled downward, it would unravel in a long, looping strip, like a piece of string cheese—which she took as evidence that she had properly beat the duff out of it.

In recent trips across the Midwest I've seen similar towering loaves of farmhouse white bread sitting alongside the ryes and *miches* and sourdoughs in artisanal bakeries, all of them just as lofty as my grandmother's, but none I've met yet have passed the string cheese test.

MAKES 2 LARGE LOAVES

Put the potato cubes in a saucepan, cover with 4 cups water, and salt the water. Bring to a boil, cover, and simmer over medium heat until the potatoes are very tender when poked with a thin fork, 20 minutes. Drain, reserving 3 cups of the cooking water, and save the potatoes for another use.

Measure out ¼ cup of the potato cooking water and pour it into a small bowl. Add the yeast and the pinch of sugar and shake the bowl to submerge them. Within 5 minutes the yeast should activate and look foamy; if not, begin again with fresh yeast.

In a large mixing bowl, combine the remaining 2¾ cups lukewarm potato cooking water, the melted shortening, remaining 3 tablespoons sugar, the salt, and 1 cup of the flour. Whisk until smooth. Add the proofed yeast mixture and 2½ cups of the flour, and whisk again until smooth. Switch to a broad wooden spoon (or a stand mixer fitted with a dough hook) and beat the dough until it begins to roll and snap and you see long strings of gluten forming, about 8 minutes. Add the remaining 3½ cups flour, cup by cup, beating as you go; the dough will begin to pull away from the sides of the bowl. Turn out the dough onto a lightly floured surface and begin to knead, stretching the corners of dough to the center, turning, and adding more flour as needed to keep it from sticking to your hands. Knead for a good 10 minutes until the dough is bouncy and smooth.

Oil a large bowl and add the dough, turning to coat it with the oil. Cover with a clean kitchen towel and leave to rise in a warm plate until doubled in size, about 1 hour.

Punch down the dough and leave it to rise again until doubled in size, about 45 minutes.

Divide the dough into two equal pieces. Grease two 10 × 5 × 3-inch metal bread pans with melted shortening. Shape the dough into cylinders to fit the length of the pans, and put each loaf in, fold-side down. Rub the top of the dough with more shortening and leave to rise until they tower at least 3 inches over the lip of the bread pans, about 1 hour.

Preheat the oven to 375°F.

Bake the bread until the loaves are dark golden brown and sound hollow when tapped, 45 to 50 minutes.

Let the bread cool slightly, remove from the bread pans, and let cool completely before slicing.

Potato Water

A large pot of boiled russet potatoes, the accompaniment to the daily roast, was the backbone of my great-grandmother's kitchen on the farm in Buckman, and in many others across the region. The leftover mashed potatoes were added to doughnuts, noodle doughs, and other baked goods to give the doughs pliancy, moisture, and natural staying power. And when she drained the boiled potatoes, she always saved the cloudy "potato water," which went into bread, gravy, soup, anything that could use a flavorful, mild liquid.

Originally, the potato water was a kind of natural leavening. When cake yeast was hard to come by, farm families made a sourdough slurry from the leftover potato water. After days of absorbing microbes and a few fresh flour feedings, it reacted kind of like yeast. Somewhere along the line they found that the milky potato water had a softening effect on the bread as well. So even after yeast arrived in cakes and packets, the potato water stayed in the bread. Its presence gives what seems like a rather plain loaf some distinction, and helps us to understand what made this kind of white bread so popular.

The Pickle Sandwich

Pickle sandwiches are born out of the farmhouse kitchen table. The ever-present stack of sliced homemade white bread, the butter, the fermented dill pickles . . . it doesn't take a scientific mind to put them together into a sandwich. I imagine it was always the thing that you took away from the table if you hadn't quite gotten your fill, and at my grandma Dion's house the pickle sandwich functioned similarly, usually as the afternoon snack. She assigned the pickle sandwich a lot of extra drama, as was her way, and I grew up thinking it was the food of royals. And when made with her soft, chewy white bread, plenty of thick salted butter, and paper-thin overlapping slices of fermented dill pickle, it sort of is.

One-Day BUTTERMILK RYE

This bread, with its mixture of wheat, white, and rye flours and molasses, is based loosely on the delicious buttermilk rye that Jorg Toll makes at the German diner on main street in Park Rapids. The finished loaf has the deep substance of good Berliner bread and that elusive smoky rye crust that I crave, a mysterious, honeyed, Black Forest edge.

MAKES 1 EXTRA-LARGE LOAF

In the bowl of a stand mixer, combine the buttermilk, boiling water, molasses, and yeast. Stir to combine and leave until the yeast is foamy, about 10 minutes.

Mix the buttermilk mixture with the whisk attachment, and then add the butter, whole wheat flour, and 1 cup of the white flour. Mix for about 3 minutes to develop the gluten. Switch to the dough hook and gradually add the rye flour and the remaining 1½ cups white flour, adding another ¼ cup white flour if needed to make a stiff dough that begins to clean the bowl. Add the cocoa powder and salt. Mix for a full 6 minutes. (If you're mixing by hand, knead it for about 10 minutes.) The dough will be slightly tacky to the touch but will clean the bowl. Turn off the mixer and let the dough rest, covered with a towel, for 10 minutes.

Shape the dough into a ball, put it in an oiled bowl, and turn to coat it with oil. Cover the bowl with plastic wrap and let rise the dough rise in a warm place until doubled in size, about 2 hours.

Punch down the dough and let it rise again until doubled, about 2 hours.

Shape the dough into a ball, put it on a cornmeal-dusted baking sheet, and let it rise until almost doubled again, about 1½ hours.

Preheat the oven to 425°F.

With a sharp or serrated knife held at a 45-degree angle to the dough, make a shallow slice across. Bake for 45 minutes. Turn off the oven but don't open the door, and bake for 15 minutes longer. The crust will be dark and caramelized. Let the bread cool completely on a wire rack before slicing thinly.

1½ cups buttermilk

1 cup boiling water

¼ cup molasses

2 teaspoons (scant 1 packet) active dry yeast

6 tablespoons (¾ stick) salted butter, melted

1 cup whole wheat bread flour

2½ cups white bread flour, plus additional ¼ cup if needed

2 cups medium rye flour

2 tablespoons unsweetened cocoa powder

2 teaspoons fine sea salt

Canola oil, for the bowl

Cornmeal or wheat germ, for dusting

NOTE: *I must say the inspiration to make bread most often strikes me in the early morning, usually on days when I'm up to watch the sun rise. So in finding a way to integrate bread-baking into my life on a more regular basis, I came up with this one-day rye. Because proficiency eludes me until I've had my second cup of coffee, I had to find a way to make it klutz-proof: When you combine boiling water with cold-from-the-fridge buttermilk, the resulting liquid is the perfect temperature in which to proof the yeast.*

BRUNCH

In my experience, people from most regions of the country will say, "People around here are really into brunch." Because it's pretty much common everywhere, maybe embracing the tradition of brunch—that leisurely weekend late breakfast/early lunch—simply means loving where you live. In other words, stretching the morning meal into the afternoon encourages you to better appreciate the view, both the place and the people, around you.

It's true here, too: people in the Midwest are really into brunch. No matter where you take it, at home or out, this meal is definitely all about breaking your general ration. So if you're a habitual oatmeal person, go for the hash, and if you're on a diet of morning boiled eggs, bring out the waffle maker.

A word on eggs, because whether savory or sweet, most of the recipes in this chapter are based on them: You want to buy the freshest eggs you can find, preferably eggs from a farm or a small-time chicken keeper. Shell color doesn't matter, but usually these eggs have brown or light pastel shells. More important, they come from truly free-ranging chickens who eat bugs, scraps, and vegetation in addition to their allotted feed. The yolks show it: they're yellower, much tastier, and also more nutritious than mass-market eggs. In the height of summer, the yolks will be orange and have such a deep flavor that it almost seems as if someone added curry powder to the chicken feed.

In urban areas, farm eggs can be found at co-ops, natural food stores, and farmer's markets. In the country, they're simultaneously more common and trickier to find. For example, I buy my farm eggs at the independent bookstore in Park Rapids, next to the post office, and when they're out, from the natural healing/hair salon just past the grocery store, and if they're out, from the feed and seed store. They all stock farm-fresh eggs raised by local people, and not one of them charges more than $3 a dozen for them.

BACON SOUFFLÉ EGGS
with Garlic Greens

Years can go by without these bacon soufflé eggs in your life, and when you return to them they reward you just as you remembered, like a meeting with a childhood friend that requires no catch-up. A minute in the hot bacon fat, a little shake of the pan, and you have perfectly inflated eggs with delectable brown edges and a soft custard interior.

A pound of bacon should yield sufficient fat to fry six to eight eggs, but it really depends on the lean-to-fat ratio of the bacon. Remind yourself that this is not an everyday sort of breakfast, so err on the generous side. (And thinking ahead, you can save up bacon fat before you plan to make these.)

If it helps, think of the infamous quote from my aunt Renee, she of the meat market side of the family where bacon, and grandkids to eat it, are both plentiful. "You would actually fry a measly quarter pound?" she scoffed. "I wouldn't dirty a pan for less than a pound and a half."

SERVES 4

1 bunch (1 pound) Swiss chard or kale

1 pound thick-cut bacon

1 tablespoon salted butter

3 cloves garlic, sliced

Fine sea salt and freshly ground black pepper

8 large eggs

Toast, for serving

Preheat the oven to 200°F.

Strip the leaves from the tough main center stems of the Swiss chard and cut or rip the greens into bite-size pieces.

In an extra-large heavy (preferably cast-iron) skillet, fry the bacon over medium heat until crisp on the edges but still malleable, about 10 minutes. Transfer the bacon to an ovenproof plate, and place in the oven to keep warm. Keep the fat in the skillet.

For the greens, heat another large skillet over medium heat. Add the butter and 1 tablespoon of the bacon fat to that skillet, and when it sizzles, add the garlic and fry for 1 minute. Add the Swiss chard, stirring and turning it over to wilt. Season with a little salt and pepper, and fry until the greens are tender, about 4 minutes.

Heat the skillet of bacon fat over medium-high heat, and when a drop of water sizzles in the fat, crack the eggs into the skillet, as many as will fit comfortably at once. Begin gently shaking the skillet (cover your hand with an oven mitt if you like), sending the fat in waves over the eggs. As the eggs puff and brown on the edges, keep shaking the skillet, dislodging the eggs from the bottom with a large serving spoon if necessary.

RECIPE CONTINUES

Tilt the skillet away from you and spoon the hot fat over the tops of the eggs to cook the yolks. When the eggs have inflated but the yolks are still soft, they are done. (It will take about 3 minutes.) Remove them from the skillet with a slotted spoon or a metal spatula, blot their bottoms to remove excess fat, and serve on top of the garlic greens, with the reserved bacon and the toast alongside.

Grease Eggs

On certain childhood Sundays in January in northern Minnesota, during the high season of NFL football, I felt as if the entire world were wrapped in high-R insulation: the four-foot snowdrifts hugging the side of the house were matched on the inside with high-cut plush carpet and kids walking around in afghan capes. To further insulate us, my mom stood in the kitchen making Great-Grandma Hesch's "grease eggs," a once-in-a-while treat straight from the farmhouse in Buckman.

First she fried up a couple of pounds of tangy thick-cut bacon, and after she had transferred the dripping pink cords to a platter, she cracked eggs into the hot bacon fat left in the pan. What happened next was a performance I never wanted to miss: As soon as the eggs began to sputter in the grease, my mom jerked the pan in a rolling motion, basting the eggs in waves of fat, her wrist keeping the steady beat of a drummer. The whites puffed up and blistered and within seconds formed lacy shells topped with crisp, coppery balloons—bits that were, without a doubt, the best part.

I twisted my fork along the egg's edge to remove the dark spine of crust, to savor it in once piece, and I remember this as the first time in my life that I tolerated the yolk spilling out all over my plate. I learned to mop it up with toast and counter it with bacon. These days I find that I like these eggs best over a pile of sautéed greens for balance—still with the necessary bacon garnish, of course.

Even as a kid I thought that the given name for these eggs was a little coarse, because they're really quite delicate and actually not that greasy. Recently this matter somehow came up in a conversation with my friend Ross (a New York friend, but originally from the Midwest), who remembered his grandmother frying eggs in bacon fat. "Did she shake the pan so that the fat rolled over them and turned the whites crispy-crunchy?" I asked. "Yes, exactly!" he said. My hope hung in the air that she had a better name for them. "What did she call them?" I gushed. He paused a second before shrugging. "She called them eggs."

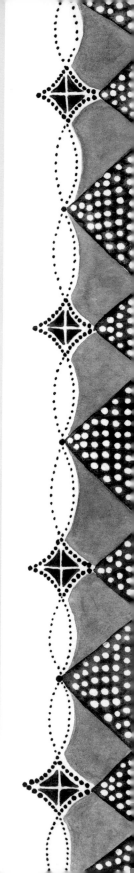

HONEY DUTCH BABY

4 large eggs

3 tablespoons plus 2 teaspoons honey

¾ cup half-and-half

¾ cup all-purpose flour

¼ teaspoon fine sea salt

5 tablespoons salted butter

There's some question whether the puffed oven pancake should be attributed to the Dutch or the Germans. As a child I ate at local *Pannekoeken* restaurants and observed the servers in Dutch country-girl costumes carrying a simple puffed pancake high above their heads, shouting, *"Pannekoeken! Pannekoeken!"* at top volume. The same recipe in some Midwestern cookbooks is referred to as a "German Oven Pancake." And then I've also heard a few people who live in communities largely settled by Germans refer to themselves as "Dutch," when I'm pretty sure that they're German and what they mean is that they're "Deutsch." (Case in point: the German "Pennsylvania Dutch.") If such confusion exists over personal heritage, how will we ever sort out the pancake provenance?

No matter where it comes from, the Dutch baby and its flour-egg-dairy ratio is a miracle of suspension and a weekend breakfast standard. It swells to dramatic heights in the oven but shrinks slightly after coming out. Stand close by to catch all the action, and be ready with the melted butter and honey once you cut into it.

SERVES 4 TO 6

Preheat the oven to 425°F.

In a blender or a large bowl, blend together the eggs, 3 tablespoons of the honey, and the half-and-half until smooth and light. Add the flour and salt, and blend until very smooth. (You can make this batter the night before and keep it refrigerated.)

Heat a 12-inch cast-iron or otherwise ovenproof pan in the oven. When you are ready to cook the pancake, add 3 tablespoons of the butter to the pan, and when it melts, add the batter. Bake the pancake in the oven until it is dark golden brown and puffed, 20 to 25 minutes.

As the pancake bakes, melt the remaining 2 tablespoons butter and 2 teaspoons honey together for serving with it. When the pancake comes out of the oven, cut it into wedges and serve immediately with the honey butter.

GRAHAM GEMS

For this recipe, the pan came first. Junk stores in this area have hawked cast-iron gem pans (a muffin pan with shallow wells) for as long as I can remember, and for years I passed them by. I wanted one to hang decoratively on my pantry wall, but as for baking in it, I thought, "Who wants to make a thin muffin?"

It turns out that I do.

I began with a cryptic recipe for graham gems found in an old farmhouse cookbook, and tweaked quantities and ingredients from there. With just a smidgen of sugar and lots of whole wheat graham flour, they're more corn pone than muffin; by a stretch I'd call them a northern graham cornbread.

I tend to make them in the winter, when the arctic air blows sweetly in around the perimeter of the old windows over the sink, and when the quick jolt of heat from the oven substantially evens out the heat in that part of the house. Whereas sweet muffins in the morning have always left me confused about how, when, and where I should insert the necessary savory-something, with lightly sweetened gems I have no such problem. Split and buttered, gems go perfectly with eggs.

MAKES 12 GEMS

Set a cast-iron gem pan (or regular muffin pan) on a baking sheet and put the baking sheet in the oven. Preheat the oven to 400°F.

When the oven is nearly preheated, make the batter: In a bowl, whisk together the egg, egg whites, cream, and vinegar until smooth. Set a fine-mesh sieve over the bowl and pour the graham flour, all-purpose flour, baking powder, baking soda, salt, sugar, and nutmeg into it.

Sift the dry ingredients into the wet ingredients, and whisk briskly to combine, taking care not to overmix.

Pull the preheated gem pan from the oven and brush the wells with the butter. Divide the batter as evenly as you can among the 12 hollows.

Bake until golden brown, 12 to 14 minutes. Serve immediately, or keep warm in a towel-lined basket, as you would biscuits.

1 large egg

2 large egg whites

⅔ cup heavy cream or half-and-half

1 teaspoon cider vinegar or white wine vinegar

⅓ cup graham flour

⅓ cup all-purpose flour

1 teaspoon baking powder

½ teaspoon baking soda

½ teaspoon fine sea salt

3 tablespoons sugar

½ teaspoon grated nutmeg

2 tablespoons salted butter, at room temperature

NOTE: *Graham flour, a coarser wheat flour, can be found in large supermarkets and in health food stores.*

GINGER AEBLESKIVERS
with Apple Butter

½ cup apple butter

2 cups all-purpose flour

1 teaspoon baking powder

½ teaspoon baking soda

½ teaspoon fine sea salt

1 teaspoon ground ginger

½ teaspoon ground cinnamon

¼ teaspoon ground cloves

3 large eggs

1 cup buttermilk

¼ cup sugar

¼ cup molasses

1 teaspoon vanilla extract

⅓ cup canola oil

8 tablespoons (1 stick) salted butter, melted, plus more for the pan

½ cup confectioners' sugar, sifted

Aebleskivers are Danish pancake balls made in a cast-iron *aebleskiver* pan, which you can find in kitchen supply stores, in small-town hardware stores in places with a Scandinavian population, and in Indian and Thai markets. The batter resembles waffle batter (this one has a light gingerbread spicing), and the apple filling is a traditional addition. Stand by the pan as you make these, and flip each one either with a special *aebleskiver* turner or two toothpicks. Polish the finished *aebleskivers* with some melted butter, shake some confectioners' sugar over the top, and serve immediately.

MAKES ABOUT 40 *AEBLESKIVERS*

Spoon the apple butter into a small plastic bag, push it into one corner, twist the excess bag behind it, and snip the tip to make an opening about ¼ inch wide. Set the bag, snipped corner pointing up, into a teacup.

Sift the flour, baking powder, baking soda, salt, ginger, cinnamon, and cloves together into a bowl. Separate the eggs, putting the yolks into one large bowl and the whites into a mixing bowl.

Add the buttermilk, sugar, molasses, and vanilla to the egg yolks, and whisk until combined. Drizzle in the canola oil, whisking, until the mixture is smooth and emulsified.

Start to preheat your *aebleskiver* pan over medium heat.

With a stand mixer fitted with the whisk attachment or a hand mixer, beat the egg whites to soft peaks. Add the flour mixture to the egg yolk mixture, and whisk until just smooth. Add the egg whites and use a rubber spatula to gently fold them into the batter until it's smooth and no large streaks of white remain.

The *aebleskiver* pan should be hot enough to sizzle on contact with a droplet of water. Quickly brush the wells of the *aebleskiver* pan with melted butter. Spoon in batter to fill the wells three-quarters full. Push the tip of the apple butter bag into the center of each batter-filled well and give it a little squeeze, injecting about ½ teaspoon or so of apple butter into each *aebleskiver*.

Cook over medium heat until the underside of each *aebleskiver* is dark golden, about 2 minutes. Using two toothpicks or a

RECIPE CONTINUES

special *aebleskiver* fork, flip them over in their wells. Cook until the batter is set inside, another minute or two.

Transfer the *aebleskivers* to a plate and repeat with the rest of the batter. (You can keep the finished *aebleskivers* warm in a low oven or serve them as you make them.) Before serving, drizzle them with the melted butter and dust thickly with the confectioners' sugar.

Brinkmann Apple Butter

According to Marie (Brinkmann) Fogleman of St. Louis, the home-made apple butter she grew up making in Washington, Missouri, was nothing like the molasses-colored jam of the same name that you now find in stores. The Brinkmann apple butter was light and coppery, and fragrant with the natural perfume from the tart Jonathan apples they used.

For years, the large extended family got together on the family farm—and later in Marie and her husband Dennis's backyard in St. Louis—to make apple butter, gathering for two days to pare apples and to take turns swishing the long, flat paddle over the bottom of the old copper pot, keeping the spitting, thickening butter from burning. As they took turns stirring they fortified themselves with apple wine ("a dead giveaway—that wine always turned our cheeks pink") and slow-baked a ham or smoked a turkey to feed the crew.

The first day, they pared the apples; on the second they cooked the apple butter. Toward the end of that second day, just when the apple butter began to sputter and grow dense, Marie's sister would put a few loaves of homemade white bread into the oven. When the apple butter was thick enough to sit upright in a spoon and when it showed a faintly bluish cast when held up to the sun, it was done, and ready to pot up in sterilized jars—although they always saved some for spreading on the fresh warm bread and more for ladling warm over vanilla ice cream.

Johnson Family
SWEDISH PANCAKES

These are nothing at all like flapjacks. Thicker than a crêpe and more elastic than a cottony flannel cake, these thin, coaster-size Swedish pancakes were common when I was growing up in northern Minnesota, and were just as likely to be found on a restaurant brunch buffet as at a friend's house, especially those of Scandinavian ancestry.

On many an adolescent morning at my friend Chelsey Johnson's house, we awoke to the sight of her dad frying these pancakes on an electric griddle, and a table set with an entourage of fitting garnishes: lingonberry jam, whipped cream, maple syrup, black coffee in a tight-waisted Chemex pot. As always in high winter, the searing arctic light bounced off the snow dunes outside and shot blinding glare across the table. Even now, the sight of a properly rolled Swedish pancake—soaked with syrup and bleeding jam from the inside—reminds me of those white, cold mornings, and the enviable way that Chelsey rolled her pancakes: knuckles flashing, with the dexterity of a good metal guitarist.

SERVES 4 TO 6

In a large bowl, whisk the eggs and milk together until smooth. In another bowl, sift the flour, sugar, and salt together. Sift the flour mixture into the egg mixture, whisking to combine. Whisk in the butter until smooth. Let the batter sit at room temperature for at least 30 minutes.

Heat an electric skillet or a large cast-iron griddle over medium-high heat. Brush the surface with butter. Pour 5-inch-diameter pancakes, using about 3 tablespoons batter for each. Cook until dark golden brown on the underside, 1 to 2 minutes. Flip, and cook for another minute. Stack the pancakes as they come off the skillet, and repeat, buttering the skillet every third batch.

4 large eggs

2¼ cups whole milk

1½ cups all-purpose flour

¼ cup sugar

½ teaspoon fine sea salt

2 tablespoons salted butter, melted, plus more for the skillet

¼ cup sugar

PAPER-THIN DOUBLE-SMOKED HAM
over Watercress

1 teaspoon ground mustard

1 teaspoon (lightly packed) light brown sugar

1 tablespoon red wine vinegar

1 teaspoon Dijon mustard

3 tablespoons olive oil, plus more for the eggs

Fine sea salt and freshly ground black pepper

8 eggs

5 ounces (2 small bunches) fresh watercress

6 ounces thinly sliced double-smoked ham

NOTE: *If you can't cajole your butcher into slicing a double-smoked ham thinly on the slicer, just get out your sharpest knife and shave off thin slices as best you can.*

A very elegant friend once taught me how to make a typical Italian dish of prosciutto draped over a pile of lightly dressed arugula—a sort of salad on a platter. Since moving to a rural area where buying prosciutto involves mail-order, I've recalibrated the idea and now regularly make a watercress salad tossed with a sweet-hot mustard dressing and draped with fine slices of locally found double-smoked ham.

For brunch this plate acquires half a dozen soft-boiled eggs, split, salted, peppered, and arranged artfully around the cress. I like to serve this with toast made from nice bread, well buttered, and Bloody Marys spiked with sour pickle juice (page 69).

SERVES 4 AS A MAIN DISH OR 6 AS A STARTER

In a small bowl, whisk together the ground mustard, 1 teaspoon water, the brown sugar, and the vinegar, Dijon mustard, olive oil, and ¼ teaspoon each of salt and pepper.

Put the eggs in a saucepan, cover with water, and bring to a simmer. Cook the eggs at a simmer for exactly 4 minutes. Drain the water from the eggs and cover them with cold water. When they are cool enough to handle, gently roll each egg against the side of the pot to crack the shell, and then peel it under the water. Blot the peeled eggs, slice them in half lengthwise, and season with salt, pepper, and a drizzle of olive oil.

In a large bowl, lightly coat the watercress with some of the mustard dressing, and pile it onto a wide platter. Drape the cress with thin slices of double-smoked ham and drizzle with the remaining dressing. Position the soft-boiled eggs around the perimeter of the salad, and serve.

Double-Smoked Ham

Chefs across the region are making mind-blowing European-style cured hams from our great heartland pastured hogs, but in the countryside, at large supermarkets and rural meat markets, cooked hams still predominate. And the best of the cooked hams are double-smoked. They dodge excessive brining and take up extra residence in the smokehouse, and they aren't exactly shy.

The ham I grew up with, for example, is a titan: a giant bone-in crosshatched joint that gets a double-dip in my family's fruitwood-fired smoker in Pierz. Such hams are cured (but not overly water-added; avoid those dripping with saline) and smoked until the meat fibers shrink and tighten, leaving the distilled essence of pork, smoke, and salt— heavy on the smoke. Across the Midwest meat markets and specialty stores stock them year-round, but before Easter and Christmas there is a double-smoked ham blitz and they seem to be everywhere.

This type of ham is mild enough to eat in slab form alongside creamed potatoes and spears of asparagus for Easter; but it's also bold enough, when shaved or cut into cubes, to flavor a whole batch of beans or pasta or whatever you like.

MAPLE-LACQUERED BACON
with Crushed Peanuts

¼ cup roasted salted peanuts

¼ cup maple syrup

12 slices good-quality thick-cut
bacon, cut in half

Coarsely ground black pepper

Barrel-Aged Maple Syrup

Maple syrup is commonly made
across much of the Midwest, and
in recent years a few outfits have
begun aging it in used charred
whiskey and brandy barrels, a
highly flavorful practice.

Tim Burton at Burton's Maple-
wood Farm in Medora, Indiana,
hot-packs his maple syrup in
three different distillery seconds—old rum, Kentucky bourbon, and brandy barrels—and
then submits the barrels to a fire
infusion by charring the outside,
the pressure forcing the maple
syrup into contact with the oak
stays. My favorite, his brandy-
infused maple syrup aged in oak
barrels from the nearby Starlight
Distillery has a strong barrel
influence. It's deep and brash; a
little bit country, if you will.

Barrel-aged maple syrup
complements custards and
does wonders for this Maple-
Lacquered Bacon. While I
personally consider it too dear
to pour into the Maple Tarte au
Sucre (page 308), it certainly
could be done.

In recent years many variations of sugar-lacquered bacon have become
popular, but mixing maple and meat is an old idea in this area, one that
can be traced back to the stewpots of the Anishinabe (Ojibwe) people
of the upper Midwest. The original native diet from around here didn't
include much salt, and they seasoned with touches of sweetness, such
as maple sugar or dried wild berries. Unadulterated maple syrup, the
very best sweetener of all, has a surprisingly multidimensional flavor,
adding earthiness and a touch of acidity to everything it hits.

The lacquered edges of the bacon, where the maple pools and
caramelizes, push this snack into sweet territory, but I think the
crushed peanuts help to steer it back into the land of the savory. I
like to serve this addictive little tidbit as part of a special weekend
breakfast, or with drinks before dinner.

SERVES 6

Preheat the oven to 375°F. Line a baking sheet with a silicone
mat or parchment paper.

Put the peanuts in a plastic bag and pound it with a rolling
pin until they are finely crushed.

Pour the maple syrup into a shallow bowl and give each
bacon slice (both sides) a generous dip in the syrup. Lay the
bacon on the prepared baking sheet, and sprinkle it with black
pepper. Bake for 20 minutes. Flip the bacon over and bake until
it is crisp at the edges and caramelized on the bottom, another
10 to 15 minutes.

Remove the baking sheet from the oven, flip the bacon
again (it should look shiny and feel like it's starting to stiffen),
and sprinkle the chopped peanuts evenly over the bacon slices.
Nudge the bacon slices to unmoor them from the baking sheet,
and let cool for a minute to firm up. Transfer to a long platter to
serve.

Breakfast WILD RICE

This is hardly a recipe, but it's a very habitual breakfast in my house. A pile of warm smoky wild rice tastes best with a small wedge of butter shoved into its center, garnished with toasted pecans and maple syrup and a moat of cold milk poured around the perimeter. Tender and light, wild rice is high in protein and keeps me operating in high gear well into the lunch hour.

SERVES 6

1 cup natural wild rice

Pinch of fine sea salt

6 teaspoons salted butter

Maple syrup

Toasted pecans or hazelnuts

Whole milk

Put the wild rice in a fine-mesh sieve and rinse it under cold running water, swishing the rice with your hand until the water runs clear. Dump it into a small saucepan and add water to cover. Pour off any black bits or floating kernels, and pour the rice back into the sieve to drain.

Combine the wild rice, salt, and 2 cups water in the saucepan. Bring to a simmer, cover tightly, reduce the heat to low, and steam until the rice is tender and curls into a lowercase "c" shape, 20 minutes. (If there's any excess liquid in the pot, simply strain it off.)

Spoon the rice into bowls, add a small teaspoon of butter to the center of each pile, and garnish with maple syrup, nuts, and milk, as desired.

POTATO *and* THREE-ONION HASH
with Smoked Lake Trout

There are a few things that actually turn out better when made by Sunday cooks than by the weeknight regulars: a properly pan-fried hamburger, rice and beans, and hash.

I enter my own husband, Aaron, as Exhibit A. He'd be the first to say that he's a very occasional cook in our kitchen, and that he has always made much better hash than I have.

But I'm learning. To master the hash I had to learn to release the dogma of the professional kitchen and all its attendant tics. Here are a couple of the things he taught me:

Add raw onions and garlic, not cooked. As the raw onions and garlic cook, they give off steam, which gives moisture to the hash. The professional cook in me initially wanted to avoid the steam—because steam prevents browning—but in this case that should be ignored. You fry the hash so long, it doesn't matter.

Fry it hard, in plenty of fat. The unattended pan should steam and hiss and in general alarm those waiting for it. As they sit about sipping coffee, fretting about an imaginary burned bottom, their faith in the cook becomes restored when it turns out perfectly—and it will, if there's enough fat.

Use cast iron. Only. Here's a family favorite, with yellow potatoes, leeks, and smoked Lake Superior lake trout.

SERVES 6

Put the potatoes in a saucepan, add water to cover generously, and salt the water. Bring to a slow simmer and cook until the potatoes are about half-cooked when poked with a fork, 15 to 20 minutes. (You can proceed to the hash immediately or cool the potatoes and store them in the refrigerator for making hash the next day.)

Chop the potatoes into bite-size pieces. Heat a heavy, wide-bottomed pan (preferably cast-iron) over medium-high heat and add the oil. Add the potatoes, onion, and ½ teaspoon of the salt, and fry until dark golden brown on the bottom, 5 to 10 minutes. Flip and add the leek, scallions, garlic, and butter. Season with the remaining ½ teaspoon salt and the pepper. Fry, flipping when the underside turns dark brown, for another 10 minutes or so. Add the smoked fish and fry and flip until it has warmed through. Serve immediately.

1½ pounds (about 5 small) Yukon Gold potatoes

3 tablespoons canola oil

1 medium onion, diced

1 teaspoon fine sea salt

1 medium leek, white and green parts, chopped

1 bunch scallions, white and green parts, thinly sliced

6 cloves garlic, sliced

4 tablespoons (½ stick) salted butter, cut into chunks

½ teaspoon freshly ground black pepper

1 cup flaked boneless, skinless smoked lake or rainbow trout

NOTE: *Truth be told, if I want hash in a hurry I will poke the potatoes with a fork, wrap them in paper towels, and microwave them for 4 to 5 minutes to parcook them before frying. They come out a touch dryer than the parboiled potatoes, but that can be remedied with extra butter, and it's a whole lot faster.*

CRISPY LENGUA HASH

1 bunch scallions, white and green parts

1 cup chopped fresh cilantro

8 cloves garlic: 5 finely grated, 3 sliced

Fine sea salt

2 tablespoons plus 2 teaspoons canola oil

1 (about 2½ pounds) beef tongue

1¼ pounds (4 medium) potatoes, such as Yukon Gold

½ sweet onion, chopped (1 cup)

1 poblano pepper, diced

1 jalapeño pepper, minced

3 tablespoons salted butter

4 to 6 poached eggs, for serving

NOTES: *First-time tongue eaters are always surprised by how mild-tasting it is, with none of the liverish qualities of the other semi-strange cuts. With a flavor nearly indistinguishable from roasted beef chuck, if there's anything disarming at all about tongue, it would be its hyper-tenderness.*

Sometimes, because cooking tongue takes so long, I will double the recipe and make two at once: I use the first for sandwiches and the second for hash.

Tongue, once popular among farm families in the Midwest, is now commonly found at the bottom of a local ranch's deep freeze, wrapped in white butcher's paper, and sold for a song. In fact, the people around here who are keeping the taste for tongue alive, and who make something more ambitious from it than cold-tongue-and-mayo sandwiches, are recent immigrants from Mexico and Central America.

Driving through small towns across Iowa and Nebraska, I always keep my eyes peeled for an authentic-looking Mexican or Central American restaurant or grocery store—and it doesn't take me long to find one. (In some parts of Nebraska I've had an easier time finding a good corn tamale than an honest bowl of soup.) And I thank these newcomers for spreading the gospel because it is tongue that is responsible for the best taco I've ever had.

We were driving from Lincoln, Nebraska, back to Minnesota, and the tiny pink-painted Mexican restaurant glowed like a beacon. I ordered the *lengua* (tongue) tacos. It took some time, but when they arrived the tortillas were properly slack and each cube of tongue was perfectly caramelized to midnight blackness, crisp on the outside and as tender as all-day stewed beef on the inside, like a cross between pork belly and pot roast.

At home, I lose the tortillas and serve the tongue as a hash so that I can channel my energy into putting an honorable brown edge on the *lengua*. When served with poached eggs, it's a serious brunch offering—although it also makes a great dinner.

SERVES 4 TO 6

Make a green salt cure for the tongue: Mince the scallions finely, add ½ cup of the chopped cilantro, and run your knife through the mixture until it is very finely minced. Transfer it to a bowl, add the grated garlic, 2 tablespoons kosher salt, and 2 teaspoons of the oil, and mix until you have a thick paste.

Put the tongue in a large covered baking pan (a chicken roaster or a large enameled cast-iron pot) and smear the green cure under and on top of the tongue. Refrigerate for at least 4 hours and as long as 2 days.

Preheat the oven to 300°F.

Add 2 cups water to the baking pan, cover it tightly, and bake in the oven until the tongue very tender when poked with a thin fork, about 4½ hours. When it is cool enough to handle, pull off the skin and trim off any membranes. (You can prepare the tongue the day before. Store it, tightly wrapped, in the refrigerator.) Dice the tongue into bite-size pieces, discarding any soft tissue (most of that at the back of the tongue).

Put the potatoes in a saucepan, add water to cover generously, and lightly salt the water. Bring to a boil and cook until the potatoes are tender, 20 minutes. Drain, peel if desired, and dice into small bite-size pieces.

Heat a heavy (preferably cast-iron) 12-inch skillet over medium-high heat. Add the remaining 2 tablespoons oil and the potatoes, and fry for a minute. Add the onion, diced tongue, poblano, jalapeño, and butter, and season with ½ teaspoon each of salt and pepper. Fry, flipping the hash infrequently and only when the bottom has browned deeply, for about 10 minutes. Add the garlic slices and continue to fry until all surfaces have turned brown and crusty, 15 to 20 minutes total. Add the remaining ½ cup cilantro, and serve immediately, topped with poached eggs.

SPICY BRUNCH SALAD
with Smoked Ham Hocks

2 (1¾ pounds) meaty smoked
   ham hocks

1 pickled habanero (see page
   387), stemmed, seeded if
   you like, plus 3 tablespoons
   pickling liquid

1 small clove garlic

3 tablespoons Dijon mustard

1 teaspoon honey

Fine sea salt

½ cup canola oil

6 slices whole-grain bread

Salted butter, at room
   temperature, for the toast
   and eggs

6 large eggs

Freshly ground black pepper

10 cups frisée or mixed light
   greens

NOTE: *This salad calls for frisée,
a crisp, light green, twiggy French
lettuce, one of the hardest-to-find
greens out there. Here in the rural
heart of the country, I've come up
with a grocery store substitution that
mimics frisée's dense, crisp texture:
buy two heads of Bibb lettuce and
reduce them to the lime-green hearts
(save the outer leaves for tomorrow's
salad), and mix the Bibb hearts with
sliced celery hearts and a handful of
watercress.*

This gutsy concoction from chef Howard Hanna at The Rieger in
Kansas City contains almost too much voltage to be called a salad. The
ham-egg-greens thing is pretty comforting, but the pickled habanero
vinaigrette propels it into bold new territory. It's the sort of thing you
want to eat *late*—either late at night or late in the morning.

Howard's original version includes succulent nuggets of cured
and smoked pigs' cheeks (made in-house, of course), but at home I
swap in some slow-cooked smoked ham hocks, which makes for easier
shopping.

SERVES 6

Cover the ham hocks with water in a small saucepan and bring
to a simmer. Cover the pan and cook slowly until the meat is
very tender when poked with a fork, about 2 hours. Keep warm
in the water until you're ready to serve the salad. (Alternatively,
you can cook the hocks overnight in water to cover in a Crock-
Pot on the low setting.)

For the vinaigrette, combine the pickled habanero, pickling
liquid, 2 tablespoons water, and the garlic, mustard, honey, and
¼ teaspoon salt in a blender. Process until smooth. Add the
canola oil in a stream, processing until the dressing is thick and
smooth.

To serve, drain the warm ham hocks. Pick out the chunks of
meat and cut them into bite-size pieces if they're large. Toast the
bread until crisp and then butter it lightly. Fry the eggs in butter
to your liking, seasoning them with salt and pepper. Toss the
greens with enough of the dressing to lightly coat.

Divide the greens among six plates and scatter the ham over
them. Set a fried egg in the middle of each, and garnish with a
side of toast.

PICKLED HABANEROS

Combine the vinegar, 1 tablespoon water, sugar, honey, and habaneros in a saucepan. Bring to a simmer, remove from the heat, and let steep until cool. Cover and refrigerate for up to 1 month.

MAKES ½ PINT

½ cup apple cider vinegar

¼ cup sugar

2 tablespoons honey

6 habanero chiles

Pickled Habanero Egg Salad

Plain egg salad profits greatly from being mixed with a little leftover pickled habanero dressing.

MAKES 2 CUPS

Mix 6 chopped hard-boiled eggs, 2½ tablespoons pickled habanero vinaigrette, 2 tablespoons mayonnaise, and 1 tablespoon minced fresh cilantro or scallion greens in a small bowl, and season with salt and pepper to taste.

EGG DISH
with Bacon *and* Spinach

12 large eggs

12 slices (12 ounces) thick-cut bacon, cut into ½-inch-wide pieces

1 leek, white and green parts, halved and cut into 1-inch pieces

1 bunch (10 ounces) spinach, stemmed and chopped

Fine sea salt

10 tablespoons (1 stick plus 2 tablespoons) salted butter, plus more for the dish

5 tablespoons all-purpose flour

3 cups whole milk, cold

3 cups (10 ounces) shredded aged cheddar or Gouda cheese

2 teaspoons chopped fresh thyme, or 1 teaspoon dried

2 teaspoons garlic powder

Freshly ground black pepper

⅛ teaspoon grated nutmeg

5 cups (12 ounces) diced ciabatta bread

NOTE: *To get this in the oven in the morning in time for brunch, you can boil the eggs, cook the bacon and vegetables, and make the cheese sauce the day before. Keep them all in the refrigerator overnight.*

This traditional Midwestern egg dish—a layered casserole of eggs, cheese sauce, bacon, and spinach, topped with a crunchy mess of garlicky, buttery croutons—is an Easter brunch favorite. It's all the more luxurious for using hard-boiled eggs instead of raw eggs, which crumble into the velvety sauce. It's also the only egg casserole I've ever known to reheat well, which makes it a good candidate for potlucks.

SERVES 8

Put the eggs in a saucepan and cover generously with water. Bring the water to a boil, reduce the heat to a simmer, and cook for 2 minutes. Remove the pan from the heat and let the eggs sit in the water for exactly 10 minutes.

Pour off the hot water and cover the eggs with fresh cold water. Crack the eggs gently, and return them to the cold water. Peel the eggs underwater.

Heat a large skillet over medium heat, and when it's hot, add the bacon and cook, stirring, until it is crisp at the edges, about 8 minutes. Remove the bacon and leave a thin layer of fat in the skillet. Add the leeks and cook, stirring, until they start to wilt, about 3 minutes. Add the spinach and ¼ teaspoon salt, and cook until the greens are wilted, 2 to 3 minutes more. Transfer the vegetables to a bowl.

Heat a medium saucepan over medium heat and add 4 table-spoons of the butter. When it foams, add the flour, whisk to combine, and cook until the mixture bubbles in the center. Add the cold milk all at once, and when it comes to a boil, cook gently, whisking, until the mixture thickens and no flour taste remains, about 3 minutes. Add the cheese and whisk until smooth. Remove the pan from the heat and whisk in the thyme, 1 teaspoon of the garlic powder, ¼ teaspoon pepper, and the nutmeg.

Melt the remaining 6 tablespoons butter. Put the bread cubes in a medium bowl and add the melted butter, the remaining 1 teaspoon garlic powder, and a large pinch each of salt and pepper, and toss to combine.

Preheat the oven to 350°F.

Rub a 9 × 13-inch baking dish with a little butter. Slice 6 of the eggs and layer them in the dish. Dot the egg layer evenly with half of the vegetables and half of the bacon. Add 1 heaping cup of croutons. Cover with 6 more sliced eggs, the rest of the vegetables, and the rest of the bacon. Evenly distribute the remaining croutons on top.

Bake until the sauce bubbles and the croutons turn golden brown and crisp throughout, 40 to 45 minutes. Let the egg dish sit for 5 to 10 minutes before serving.

GERMAN LEMON WAFFLES

3 large eggs

1 large egg white

¼ cup sugar

¼ cup fresh lemon juice

⅓ cup canola oil

1 cup buttermilk

½ cup heavy cream or
half-and-half

Grated zest of ½ lemon

1 teaspoon vanilla extract

2 cups all-purpose flour

1 teaspoon baking powder

½ teaspoon baking soda

¾ teaspoon fine sea salt

2 tablespoons salted butter,
at room temperature, for
preparing the waffle iron,
plus more for serving

Maple syrup, for serving

The idea for these light, lemony waffles came from a book called *Pancakes Aplenty*, written in the 1950s by the *Chicago Tribune*'s resident food editor, Ruth Ellen Church. With more than 150 recipes for pancakes, crêpes, and waffles—sweet and savory—she makes the case for what I've long thought of as "pancake infinity," or the incredible diversity that can spring from the same small handful of ingredients: eggs, flour, milk, and butter. I gave these lemon waffles a subtle update: an extra egg white for added crispness, and some lemon zest.

MAKES 7 OR 8 LARGE BELGIAN-STYLE WAFFLES

Preheat a waffle iron.

Separate the 3 eggs, putting the yolks in a large mixing bowl and the whites, plus the extra white, in another large mixing bowl.

Whisk the yolks with the sugar and lemon juice until smooth. Add the oil in a thin stream, whisking until smooth, and then add the buttermilk, cream, lemon zest, and vanilla, whisking until combined.

Sift the flour, baking powder, baking soda, and salt together into a bowl. Add the dry ingredients to the egg yolk mixture, whisking until fairly smooth, though a few lumps are fine.

With a stand mixer fitted with a whisk attachment or a hand mixer, whip the egg whites until they hold soft peaks. Gently whisk one-third of the whites into the batter, and then carefully fold in the rest of the whites with a rubber spatula.

Brush a little butter on the waffle grates, and add about ¾ cup batter (or whatever will fill your waffle iron). Cook as directed. When done, spread the waffles with soft butter and serve with maple syrup.

Acknowledgments

This book had a long incubation period, so the thanks I owe to the people who contributed to it reach quite a long way back.

First, to my husband, Aaron Spangler: Thanks for all you do to make our life work, including the essential dreaming. I'm so grateful for your perspective, as well as your wanderlust, which propels us out into the field.

To my family—I owe a big debt to your discriminating (picky!) tastes; may food always be the family glue. Thanks to my relatives at Thielen Meats of Pierz, as well as my aunt Joan Dion, and especially to my aunt Renee Thielen and my mom, Karen, for cooking for the photo shoot and crew, and introducing everyone to the joys of hot ring bologna.

Thanks to Maurice and Carolyn Spangler for taste-testing and taking care of Hank, and to Maurice for letting me steal all the shell beans from your garden that year. Thanks to my sister-in-law, Sarah Fogleman, for joining me in Chicago.

So many people have taught me to cook, but for top mentors, I want to thank (in addition to my mom, and her mom) chefs Jean-François Bruel, David Bouley, Gregory Brainin, Shea Gallante, Thomas Kahl (T1), Gray Kunz, Mario Lohninger, Thomas Mayr (T2), and Jean-Georges Vongerichten, as well as the countless fellow line cooks who shared their days with me.

Thanks to all of my friends who lent their time or resources to this book, and to those who either fed us or gave us all shelter on road trips across the Midwest: Matt Bakkom, Jon Billings, Todd Bruce, Bob Bruers, Bruce Brummitt and Cheryl Valois, Bette, Richard, Dora, and the well-missed Lewy DeWandeler, Kate and Bill Drehkoff, Michael Dagen, Josie Davidow; Merle Doehling, Chris Hand, Tracy Thew and kids, Alice and Ken Haug, all the Kuebers (but especially Katie Kueber), Paul and Quinn Kulik, Willi Lehner, Vera and Mark Mercer, Hesse McGraw and Kobi Newton, Natalie Moore-Goodrich and Bard Goodrich, Todd Nelson, Keri Pickett and Michal Daniel, Vern and Michelle Schultz, Stella Shymanski and son Ron and his wife, Tom and Winnie Thelen, Tresa Undem, Jim Wallace, Jim and Penny Woster, and Kevin Woster and Mary Garrigan. Special thanks to Ted Lee and E. V. Day for great conversations about regional home-cookery and crucial early encouragement, and to Rob Fischer and Sara Woster for lending their extra bedrooms and plates, wineglasses, and tablecloths to the photo shoot.

Lee Dean, my amazing editor at the Minneapolis *Star Tribune,* I owe you big for giving me the opportunity to dig deep into the Midwestern culinary consciousness. Thanks also to Rory Palm at the *Park Rapids Enterprise,* for the column that allowed me to write to my hometown audience. Thanks to Julie Caniglia, Chelsey Johnson, and Brad Zellar for their insightful readings of early excerpts.

Thanks to all the Midwestern chefs who lent me their recipes, including Steven Brown, Jonny Hunter and Garin Fons, Koren Grieveson, Howard Hanna, Paul Kulik,

Mike Phillips, Michael Symon, Paul Virant, Jared Wentworth, and Midwestern expats living in New York City: Alex Raij, Gavin Kaysen, and Emily and Melissa Elsen.

To my agent, Janis Donnaud, thank you for so gracefully shepherding this project to fruition. I am grateful for your perceptive, honest advice, and for your fierce advocacy.

At Clarkson Potter, thanks to my editor, Rica Allannic, for your crucial shaping and eagle-eye editing. Thanks to Marysarah Quinn, a fellow Minnesotan whose vision and design of this book evoked everything I hoped for—and then some. Thanks also to Pam Krauss, Doris Cooper, Ashley Phillips, Tricia Wygal, Kim Tyner, Kate Tyler, Erica Gelbard, Donna Passannante, and Carly Gorga.

Amber Fletschock, thank you for all the work you've put into the illustrations. Our meetings at the Menagha bakery, where you rolled out your beautiful drawings amid half-eaten doughnuts and elderly Finnish onlookers, are memories I treasure. Jennifer May, thank you for following me into enclosed spaces, through farm fields and across long, flat states. I'm indebted to you for making this place look as epic as I know it to be. Thanks to Kendra McKnight for your beautiful food styling, your life-saving testing, and for being so extremely capable. Thank you to Kate Hays, Sandy Perez, and Kay Yamaguchi for careful recipe testing. Alison Hoekstra, thanks a million times over for going the distance and finding the perfect props to make these photos feel like home. Thanks to Luisa Fernanda Garcia Gomez for being tireless, and especially for that vinegar shot when you knew we needed it. Thanks to Nick Torres and Angelina Momanyi, my hardworking interns.

Last, to Hank, a very patient boy of singular tastes . . . thank you for eating Wisconsin cheese with me. I know it is not quite the same as American.

INDEX